Convergences
Inventories of the Present

EDWARD W. SAID, GENERAL EDITOR

On Human Diversity

Nationalism, Racism, and Exoticism in French Thought

Tzvetan Todorov

Translated by Catherine Porter

Harvard University Press

Cambridge, Massachusetts
London, England

Copyright © 1993 by the President and Fellows of Harvard College
All rights reserved
Printed in the United States of America
Second printing, 1994

This book was originally published as *Nous et les autres: La Réflexion française sur la diversité humaine*, by Editions du Seuil, copyright © 1989 by Editions du Seuil.

Harvard University Press gratefully acknowledges the assistance of the French Ministry of Culture in preparing this translation.

First Harvard University Press paperback edition, 1994

Library of Congress Cataloging-in-Publication Data

Todorov, Tzvetan, 1939–
     [Nous et les autres. English]
     On human diversity: nationalism, racism, and exoticism in French
thought / Tzvetan Todorov; translated by Catherine Porter.
         p. cm.—(Convergences: inventories of the present)
     Translation of: Nous et les autres.
     Includes bibliographical references and index.
     ISBN 0-674-63438-1 (cloth)
     ISBN 0-674-63439-X (pbk.)
     1. Ethnology—Philosophy. 2. Ethnology—France—History.
3. Philosophy, French. 4. Nationalism. 5. Racism. I. Series:
Convergences (Cambridge, Mass.)
GN345.T6313   1993
305.8—dc20   92–24568
                          CIP

Contents

Preface

I came to know evil during the first part of my life, when I lived in a country under Stalinist rule. I became acquainted with it gradually: for the first few years after the war I was too young fully to grasp the news that a relative or family friend had suddenly disappeared, or had been forced to move to some out-of-the-way town, or had abruptly lost his assets. Then, too, my immediate family approved of the new regime and benefited from it, in the beginning. Things got more complicated toward the end of 1948, when other friends of my parents, people from our own circles, landed in prison or were maligned in the newspapers (which I was then old enough to read), or when my father began to have trouble at work. Still, I remained a fervent pioneer until 1952. Then came Stalin's death and the gradual discovery, which for me coincided with the passage through adolescence, of the vacuity of the official discourse that I encountered daily.

I was never a direct victim of the regime, since my reaction—like that of many of my compatriots—was not to protest or challenge it, but to take on two distinct personalities: one public and submissive, the other private and independent. And yet in another sense I was a victim after all, like all my countrymen; and my private personality was not, as I thought then, a pure production of my own will, for it was forged in reaction to my environment. It was then that I became acquainted with evil. It lay in the glaring disparity between what people in power said and the lives they led and allowed us to lead, which seemed to devolve from quite different principles. It lay in the obligation to make a public display of one's adherence to the official doctrines, and in the way these declarations robbed the noblest terms of their meaning: "liberty," "equality," and "justice" became words that served to mask repression and favoritism, the flagrant disparities in the way individuals were treated. It lay in the assertion that there was a correct approach to every subject, and one only, and in our awareness that this position was determined by and for those in positions of authority at the time, since "truth" was now merely an effect of force. It lay in the unlimited and arbitrary power that resided, we felt, with the police and the national security forces, with party members and other officials who could at any moment deprive you of your job, your house, your friends, or your freedom. It lay in the encouragement of submissiveness and mediocrity; it lay in the system of informing on others that had become the quickest way to get ahead; it lay in the fear of being afraid. The material discomforts, the lack of consumer goods, and the long lines were not evils in themselves (they could better be called misfortunes), but they became evils to the extent that they unquestionably proceeded from the other features of the regime; they were its emblems, as it were. Of course this evil was not homogeneous—had it been, life would have been impossible. I continued to meet wonderful people, or to benefit from splendid gestures made by people who were not always wonderful in themselves. And in the absence of a decent public life, private life was lived to the fullest (although I was not really aware of this at the time): loves, friendships, intellectual and artistic passions were intense.

When I came to France and the second part of my life began, my experience of evil was extended in two ways. On the one hand (as might have been expected), although this experience became less direct, it took on much greater breadth. Through books and personal encounters I became better acquainted with the genocide perpetrated by the Nazis and with the effects of the atomic bombs on Japan. Other readings taught me the horrors of conventional warfare as well as those, in the less recent past, of colonial wars and regimes. These are not evils I have seen with my own eyes, yet I sense their relationship with the ones I have experienced personally, and I do not hesitate to recognize evil as evil. (I am more inclined to hesitate where good is concerned.) I sense that I have come upon a sort of absolute that will never loosen its hold. My attachment to the democratic ideal is not merely rational: I become passionate when it is called into question, and I am aware that I bristle in responding to my interlocutor.

The second way in which my experience of evil was extended is of an entirely different nature. I gradually discovered that with very few exceptions the people I was getting to know lacked an ethical sense comparable to the one with which I found myself encumbered. Of course I knew people with very decided convictions, but these convictions were political, not ethical, and they consisted of projects for the future rather than reactions to present situations in all their diversity. To make matters worse, the goals that inspired them were most often variants of the very principles I had learned to mistrust so deeply in my homeland.

"But why is he telling me all this?" my reader is asking, perplexed. I shall come to that; but first I need to evoke one further aspect of my experience.

Just as I was beginning to notice the absence of reactions of an ethical nature in most of my new companions, I was also observing another characteristic that may have been the result—or the cause—of the first one: namely, the fact that their professed convictions had no perceptible influence on their behavior, or vice versa. By and large, these people led "petit-bourgeois" lives while laying claim to a revolutionary ideal— which, had it been achieved, would have made certain aspects of their existence impossible; and yet these were aspects to which they seemed quite attached. I did not expect their lives to be perfect illustrations of their faith: no saint myself, I could hardly require sainthood of my companions. (Besides, who wants to live with saints?) Still, I was shocked to observe the complete discontinuity between the way people lived and the way they talked, the confrontation—of which these people themselves were unaware—between two autonomous if not opposing tendencies. This was something very different from the tension be- tween a desire and its necessarily imperfect realization. Once again, it was undoubtedly my prior experience, my aversion to words unsup- ported by actions, that led me to react as I did. I recognized that I wanted both to let my own experience nourish my thinking, insofar as possible, and to be prepared to live by the conclusions to which rea- soning might lead me.

Now, one aspect of my own life at the time did not correspond very closely to this ideal: the relation between professional activity and everything else, or rather the absence of any such relation. Intrigued by the problems of literature and language, I had gone on to study what are called the human (and social) sciences. But nothing I had come to think about language or literature bore any relation to my convictions or my affinities as I experienced them in the time that was not devoted to work. What is more, the logic of these sciences seemed to exclude any interference of this sort *a priori*, since the quality of my work was considered good to the extent that it was "objective"—that is, to the extent it allowed me to hide any traces of my identity, or the value judgments I might make. In one part of my existence, then, albeit a limited one, I was reproducing the inconsistency, or at least the compartmentalization, that I was prepared to criticize in people around me.

When I became conscious of that separation, I began to feel a growing dissatisfaction with the aforementioned human and social sciences (a category that, to my mind, includes history) as they are practiced today. The separation between one's life and one's words, between facts and values, seems to me deleterious, especially for these disciplines (the separation, that is, and not the distinction: it is also possible to distinguish and connect). Here in fact is the locus, in my mind, of the most interesting difference between the human sciences and the rest (the natural sciences). The two are often contrasted on other grounds: the degree of precision of their results, or the nature of the mental operations they entail, or the conditions of observation that come into play. For me, the difference in subject matter (human versus non-human) implies a second and crucial difference in the relation that is established between the scholar and the object of his or her study. Many things separate geologists from the minerals they work with; in contrast, there is very little to separate historians or psychologists from their object of study, that is, other human beings. This does not imply that scholars in the latter group aspire to less precision, or that they reject the principle of reason, but that they refuse to eliminate the distinguishing feature of such studies—that is, the community of subject and object, and the inseparability of facts and values. In this area, thinking that is not nourished by personal experience quickly degenerates into scholasticism, and can satisfy only the scholars themselves— or bureaucratic institutions, which adore quantitative data. How can one deal with what is human without taking a position? I subscribe fully to the words of Simone Weil: "The acquisition of knowledge causes us to approach truth when it is a question of knowledge about something we love, and not in any other case" (*L'Enracinement*, in English *The Need for Roots*, p. 242). Thus it is that I have come to prefer the moral and political essay to the human and social sciences.

It is true that the relationship in question is not always obvious: certain aspects of human beings that can be studied have more to do with human subjectivity and values than others. How are we to know where good and evil reside when a philosopher tells us he prefers being to nothingness, or thought to reason? How am I to relate linguistic hypotheses about the syntactic structure of sentences to my own personal subjectivity? It is undeniable that the observation of forms can go a long way without values and subjectivity. But to get at the problem from the other direction, philosophical abstractions can become more accessible to us with the help of the mediating agency of political and moral thought, for this thought is related to the most abstract meta- physics as well as to everyday life. It may be difficult to be sure whether one is for or against rationality; things become a little clearer when one understands that the decision is also a choice for or against democracy. As Tocqueville pointed out, philosophical doctrines have practical con- sequences; and it is through these consequences that they affect me as well.

It will be clearer now that, if the subject of this book is the relation between "us" (my own cultural and social group) and "them" (those who do not belong to it), the relation between the diversity of human populations and the unity of the human race, this choice of topic is not divorced either from the current situation of the country in which I live, France, or from my own personal situation. And no one will be surprised to see me attempting to find out not only how things have been but also how they ought to be. Not one *or* the other, but one *and* the other.

The evolution that I have just described had already led me to publish *La Conquête de l'Amérique* (*The Conquest of America*, 1982), a book dealing with the same theme and in which I adopted the same attitude. It is a book to which I am still attached, and yet after finishing it I did not feel unalloyed satisfaction. I liked the narratives that I had brought back to life, those of Columbus and Cortés, Montezuma and Las Casas, but I had the impression that my own conceptual analysis of those narratives did not get to the heart of the matter. Thus, I did not want to abandon the topic, and yet I saw no point in repeating the exercise with new material, for I would have kept running into the same difficulties. That is when I decided to turn for help to the thinkers of the past. After all, had not authors surely more intelligent than I, philosophers and politicians, scholars and writers, been debating the same question from time immemorial? And if I were to analyze their thinking, might I not be able to profit from their insight? This is how I moved from the level of events to the level of reflection.

But by the same token, as my field was no longer limited by a specific narrative, it grew much too large. Was I to read all the thinkers of all time? However vast my ambitions, they could not take me that far! My first restriction was territorial: I chose to limit myself to France. Several factors seemed to justify that decision. First of all the fact that, a foreigner by origin myself, I had been living in France for quite some time; getting to know the country better struck me almost as an obligation. Furthermore, French thinking on the question that interests me is part of a long and rich tradition: occupying a central position in European history, it has absorbed the contributions of other traditions and has influenced them in turn. If one were to come to grips with the French tradition alone—a task that is after all a manageable one on the human scale—one would possess a significant sampling of European history (ours, mine) taken as a whole.

Then I set myself a limit in time. The central question that I wanted to grapple with had to do with the present; my historical investigation thus became, inevitably, research into the origins of our own times. For this reason, one particular historical period received special attention: a period lasting roughly two hundred years, from the beginning of the eighteenth century to the beginning of the twentieth (but I have not hesitated to violate that rule on occasion, for I refer both to Montaigne and to Lévi-Strauss). Finally, within that period, I chose my authors in terms of a two-fold criterion, subjective and objective: my capacity to engage with their thinking, thus a certain affinity; and the authors' own notoriety, in their times or ours. After much groping, I found myself finally with about fifteen authors that I was able to study in detail, some more closely than others: Montesquieu, Rousseau, Chateaubriand, Renan, Lévi-Strauss.

The genre I have chosen is not history but reflection on history, which explains why what follows does not offer an exhaustive (or even sustained) description of a given period, but an analysis of a few representative thinkers; this choice of genre also explains why the overall outline is thematic rather than chronological. However, history is not far away: even though I began with some very general categories (ourselves and others, unity and diversity, beings and values, the positive and the negative), the themes I ended up choosing stood out because of the role they have played in the recent past. I observed that, in France, during the two centuries in question, the reflection on human diversity had focused on a few major questions, and these are the ones I chose to study. Namely: the opposition between universal and relative judgments; races; the nation-state; and nostalgic exoticism. These concepts provide the themes for the various sections of the book;

within each section I return to an approximately chronological order. The fifth and last section is different: there, before coming to my own conclusions, I examine two works by the author whose thinking has impressed me as the most instructive of the entire tradition: Montesquieu.

Ideologies are thus the object of this book, and perhaps this choice warrants a word of explanation. I shall not discuss races as such, or racist behaviors, but rather doctrines that deal with the subject of race; my topic will not be colonial conquests, but rather the justifications that were produced for them; and so forth. Is there not a sort of scholastic complacency here, since discourse is easier to deal with than events? I hope not. Two convictions lie behind my decision. The first is that I do not take the doctrines of the past purely as an expression of their authors' *interests:* I recognize in them, in addition, a certain dimension of truth. To take the route of discourse to gain access to the world is perhaps to take an indirect route, but it gets us there nevertheless (and it has other advantages). My second conviction is that discourses are also events, driving forces of history, and not merely representations. Here we need to avoid the all-or-nothing alternative. Ideas do not make history on their own: social and economic forces also intervene; but ideas are not purely a passive effect, either. They make acts possible, in the first instance; and then they make it possible for these acts to be accepted. We are dealing, after all, with decisive acts. If I did not believe that, why would I have written this very text, which also seeks to influence behaviors?

The book I have written thus presents itself as a hybrid, half history of thought, half essay in political and moral philosophy—which may of course disappoint uncompromising devotees of both genres. But from the point of view of the tradition, are not all genres hybrids? I cannot write a pure opinion piece, but I do not wish to content myself, either, with a mere reconstruction of history. At the risk of incurring the disadvantages of both—of being as pretentious as an essayist and as boring as a historian (in the worst case!)—I have committed myself, as others have done, to follow this intermediate path. I am not comfortable with generalizations or with details: only their encounter satisfies me. But I can spell out a little more clearly how I see each of these two aspects of my work.

The history of thought: to my mind, this is to be distinguished both from the history of ideas and the history (or the study) of works. The distinctive feature of thought is that it emanates from an individual subject. The history of ideas, for its part, examines anonymous ideas by situating them not in the synchronic context in which someone conceived them, but in the diachronic series composed of other formulations of the same idea. The history of works, in turn, focuses on the description and interpretation of particular texts, not on the integral thought of a single author. These distinctions indicate a tendency, however, rather than an exclusive choice. In order to be able to analyze an author, I have chosen to evoke the general intellectual context in which he functioned. Thus, the introductory chapter of each part deals with the history of ideas rather than the history of thought. Similarly, certain works that are particularly important from my perspective (*L'Esprit des lois*, "Supplément au voyage de Bougainville," *Les Natchez*, *L'Essai sur l'inégalité des races humaines*) raised questions for me about their very structure. The history of thought is the dominant, but not the only, form my analysis takes.

This choice entailed a further consequence. Confronted with a text, one can seek above all to explain it (on the basis of social causes or psychic configurations, for example) or else one can try to understand it: I opted for the second approach. As a result, I do not spend much time on the "prehistory" of texts, on what brought them into being. I pay a great deal more attention to their "aftermath," since I raise questions not only about the meaning of texts but also about their political, ethical, and philosophical implications. In brief, I postulate that if someone said something, it is (also) because he or she intended to do so; whatever forces may have been acting through that person, I hold him or her responsible for the words written. In this respect, my way of reading is only the illustration of one of the theses I am defending.

As for the other aspect of this work, the word that best characterizes my project (if not its execution), I find, is "dialogue." This implies, above all, that I am not interested solely in the meaning of my authors' texts (my analysis is not a "metalanguage," radically different from an "object-language," the former referring to the text and the latter to the world), but that I am also interested in their truth value. It is not enough for me to have identified their arguments (this is the first—and obligatory—step in the process); I also attempt to find out whether I can accept those arguments: I also speak about the world. To the extent possible, I situate these dialogues within history, or I project them onto it. First of all, I attempt to juxtapose the various ideas of a given author; then I reconstruct dialogues among the authors. At the beginning, in particular, it is Rousseau who responds to my other characters—Montaigne, La Bruyère, or Diderot. Later, it is Tocqueville who responds to Gobineau, and John Stuart Mill to Tocqueville. At the end, Montesquieu is challenged by his critics—Helvétius, Condorcet, or Bonald; Montesquieu and Rousseau also criticize each other. At other points, not finding such a dialogue in history, or not in a form that satisfies me, I put myself forward—brashly—in the role of interlocutor, and I practice interpellative criticism on my own behalf.

To choose dialogue also means avoiding the two extremes of monologue and warfare. Whether the monologue is the critic's or the author's hardly matters: in either case, there is a prediscovered truth that needs only to be exposed; whereas, faithful in this respect to Lessing, I prefer to seek truth rather than to dispose of it. There is such a thing as textual warfare as well, and I have not always avoided it: when one has nothing in common with the author one is confronting, when one feels only hostility for his ideas, dialogue becomes impossible and is replaced by satire or irony; the understanding of texts suffers as a result (this may have happened in my own case with the authors representing what I call "popular racialism").

Finally, I also see the practice of dialogue as opposed to the discourse of seduction and suggestion, in that it appeals to the reader's rational faculties rather than seeking to capture the imagination or to plunge one into a state of admiring stupor. The other side of this coin is that my arguments will sometimes appear a bit too down to earth; but that is again a consequence of my desire not to separate life from speech, not to declare what I cannot assume. It is for the same reason that I have larded my text with so many quotations: I want my readers to be able to judge everything on their own, and so I try insofar as possible to place in their hands the whole dossier (for I do not suppose that readers will have in hand all the books I mention).

It is finally my concern for the reader that has led me to adopt the simplest possible reference system: a title and a page number in the text refer to the bibliography at the end, where some additional information also appears (dates, further references). I have profited very considerably, it goes without saying, from the information presented in the editions of the texts I was analyzing, and from commentaries on those texts. Among the historians of thought on whom I have relied I should like to mention in particular Victor Goldschmidt (for the eighteenth century) and Paul Bénichou (for the nineteenth). As for the authors whose work I do not examine here but whose thought has influenced me, I do not mention them in the text: if I assert something in the text, it is because I am prepared to take responsibility for it myself. I shall thus limit myself to listing here the possible—and often contradictory—influences of dead and living authors such as Max Weber and Jürgen Habermas, Leo Strauss and Hannah Arendt, Karl Popper and Isaiah Berlin, Raymond Aron and Louis Dumont, without omitting my friend Luc Ferry.

And now our serious work can begin.

On Human Diversity

1

The Universal and the Relative

Ethnocentrism

The Classical Spirit

Human diversity is infinite. If we want to study it, how are we to proceed? As a way of getting started, let us say that we need to distinguish between two interrelated perspectives. From the first of these perspectives, the diversity in question is that of human beings themselves. Thus, we are trying to discover whether we form a single species or several (in the eighteenth century, the debate was couched in terms of "monogenesis" and "polygenesis"); and, if we assume there is just one species, we want to know the significance of the differences that exist between human groups. In other words, this is the problem of human unity and human diversity. The second perspective displaces our focus onto the question of values. Are there universal values and thus the possibility of making judgments across frontiers, or are all values relative (to a place, to a historical moment, or even to the identity of the individuals concerned)? And, if we recognize the existence of a universal scale of values, how far does that scale extend? What does it encompass? What does it exclude? The problem of unity and diversity in this case becomes the problem of the universal and the relative: this is the issue with which I shall begin my inquiry.

The universalist option may take various forms. *Ethnocentrism* deserves to head the list, since it is the most common among them. As I shall use the term here, ethnocentrism consists in the unwarranted establishing of the specific values of one's own society as universal values. The ethnocentrist is thus a kind of caricature of the universalist.

The latter, in his aspiration to universality, starts with a particular phenomenon that he then undertakes to generalize, and this particular phenomenon is of necessity a familiar one: that is, in practice it must be found in his own culture. The only difference—but it is obviously a crucial difference—is that the ethnocentrist takes the path of least resistance and proceeds uncritically: he believes that his values are the only values there are, and he is satisfied with this belief; he never really attempts to prove it. On the other hand, the nonethnocentric universalist (we might at least try to imagine such a creature) would try to find a rational basis for the fact that she prefers certain values to others; she would even be particularly vigilant with respect to those aspects of her own tradition that struck her as universal, and she would be prepared to abandon what was familiar to her in favor of a solution observed in a foreign country or arrived at by deduction.

Ethnocentrism thus has two facets: the claim to universality on the one hand, and a particular content (most often national) on the other. Examples of ethnocentrism abound in the history of thought in France and elsewhere; nevertheless, if one is seeking the most appropriate illustration—and for the moment I am simply looking for an illustration that will enable me to set forth ideas—the choice seems predetermined: it would be what Hippolyte Taine, in *Les Origines de la France contemporaine* (in English, *The Origins of Contemporary France*), called "the classical spirit," that of the seventeenth and eighteenth centuries, and which is sometimes identified (outside France) with the spirit of France itself. To begin with, we need to note that mainstream thinking in those centuries was fond of representing man "in general," above and beyond all his variants. The French language itself was viewed as universal, since it was considered the language of reason; and indeed French was used beyond the borders of France. When Pascal states the goal of his work, he writes: "*First part:* Wretchedness of man without God. *Second part:* Happiness of man with God" (*The Origins of Contemporary France*, p. 118). The word "man" is in the singular, accompanied in the French text by the definite article ("Misère de l'homme sans Dieu. Félicité de l'homme avec Dieu"). What Pascal says is understood to be applicable to all human beings, to man in general. At the beginning of the "Avis au lecteur" (Notice to the Reader) that introduces his maxims, La Rochefoucauld uses similar language: "Here I am offering to the public a portrait of man's heart." The question whether this heart always remains the same, in all times and places, does not even arise.

As for La Bruyère, he would be prepared to raise the question, but only so as to dismiss it. In his "Prefatory Discourse" to the *Characters* of the Greek author Theophrastus, a text that in turn precedes his own *Caractères*, La Bruyère justifies his project as follows: "In short, Mens souls and Passions change not, they are yet the same still as they were, and as they are described by *Theophrastus*" (n.p.). He returns to the topic in the very first part of his text: nothing has changed in the world, and the ancient authors remain completely contemporary. His own work aspires less to originality than to timelessness and universality: "If I may be allowed to speak without modesty about my own work, I am almost tempted to believe that my portraits must be accurate expressions of man in general, since they resemble so many individuals" ("Préface," *Discours prononcé à l'Académie française*, [Speech Delivered at the French Academy], p. 488).

La Bruyère is not unaware of the changes wrought by time. As he himself wrote: "We who are now Modern shall be Ancient in a few days" ("Prefatory Discourse," n.p.); and also: "No Uses or Customs continue in all ages, but vary with the times" (ibid.). But these changes affect only the surfaces of things: "The world will be the same a hundred years hence as it is now; there will be the same stage and the same decorations, though not the same actors" ("Of the Court," *Characters*, 99, p. 219)—a seemingly unimportant difference. La Bruyère can thus observe his own times and draw conclusions about the entire span of history, just as he can declare outright that he knows only France, and within France only court life, while continuing to expect his remarks to be of universal import: "Though I frequently take them from the court of France and from men of my own nation, yet they cannot be confined to any one court or country, without greatly impairing the compass and utility of my book, and departing from the design of the work, which is to paint mankind in general" ("Preface," *Characters*, pp. ii–iii).

The goal is to depict mankind in general, and the means is to describe the men one knows best; for La Bruyère, as it happens, these are representatives of the court. The arrangement already contains a potential for ethnocentrism (and "sociocentrism," the identification of an entire society with just one of its social groups). The universalist aim is definitely present among the representatives of the "classical spirit" in France; we have no fault to find with them on that account. It is not clear, however, that the means deployed are adequate to the task at hand.

The Origin of Values

In theory, the seventeenth-century moralists were not unaware of human diversity; in certain respects they were even relativists after Montaigne's fashion. They were quite prepared to recognize that custom has us in its grip; but custom is of course most often national. Pascal's well-known formulations come to mind: "We are creatures of habit [*la coutume est notre nature*]" (*Pascal's Pensées*, p. 156). "What are our natural principles if not our normal principles?" (p. 166). "Each should conform to the customs of his own country" (p. 139). But if customs are at once powerful and varied, how can we know man without taking his customs into account? Pascal does not raise that question. To be sure, describing the diversity of human lifestyles does not really fall within the scope of his project. Still, he runs into this difficulty at one point when he refers to the various religions found throughout the world. He is not unaware that he is taking on a risky subject. "We have to admit that there is something astonishing about the Christian religion. 'It is because you were born in it,' someone will say. Far from it; I set my face against it for this very reason, because I was afraid that prejudice would influence me; but though I was born in it, I soon found that it was astonishing" (p. 231). Oddly enough, the one time he has to face up to the concrete diversity of customs, Pascal immediately adopts an absolutist position. It may be that, for others, nature is just a first custom, but not for him; if he defends a religion, it is because that religion satisfies certain absolute criteria, not because it is the religion of his own country. But of course religion is not a custom for Pascal. And he continues to make the same case: others are slaves of custom because they are ignorant of the true faith: people who know the true faith live in the absolute, beyond custom.

Pascal's practice thus does not conform to the relativist principles he formulates. Yet it could be defended as such: Just because my own country possesses certain values, I do not necessarily have to condemn them; that would be reverse ethnocentrism, which is no more convincing than the standard sort. I can indeed subscribe to a particular religion, compare it to others, and find it the best of all. But the coincidence between the ideal and the personal obviously has to make me especially cautious in my choice of arguments, for fear "that prejudice would influence me."

What are Pascal's arguments? He says: "There are three ways of acquiring faith: reason, habit, grace. The Christian religion . . . alone has reason [for its ally]" (p. 222); but that is no more than a way of begging the question. And in other passages: "*Falseness of the other religions.* They have no witnesses" (p. 223). "Mahomet was not foretold; Jesus Christ was" (p. 224). The Christian religion is "the only one that has always existed" (p. 268). But Pascal's arguments depend very heavily on the historical data he chooses to consider, and his choice seems highly subjective. In order to maintain the proposition that the Chris-tian religion is a religion for all time, Pascal finds that he needs to be "against the history of China" (p. 228). However, rejecting facts is no way to escape from custom. Pascal's reasoning is circular, and as such it exemplifies the ethnocentric spirit: one begins by defining absolute values on the basis of one's personal values, and one then pretends to judge one's own world in the light of this false absolute. "No religion except ours has taught that man is born in sin; none of the philosophical sects has admitted it; none therefore has spoken the truth" (p. 195). What is "ours" defines what is "true," which does not prevent this "truth" from coming back to enhance the prestige of what is "ours," draping "ours" in its own colorful garments! Pascal's universalism is of the most commonplace variety: it consists in identifying uncritically one's *own* values with values in general. In short, it amounts to ethno-centrism.

La Bruyère is also conscious of the diversity of customs, and he follows Montaigne in welcoming difference. All those who do not resemble us we deem barbarians, which is a great error; nothing would be more desirable than to see people "get loose from that prepossession in favor of their own Customs and Manners, which they not only take up on trust without any deliberation, but peremptorily pronounce all others contemptible, which are not conformable to themselves" ("Pref-atory Discourse," n.p.). And he is quick to condemn the narrow eth-nocentrism of others: "Our prepossession in favor of our native country and our national pride makes us forget that common sense is found in all climates, and correctness of thought wherever there are men. We should not like to be so treated by those we call barbarians; and if some barbarity still exists amongst us, it is in being amazed on hearing natives of other countries reason like ourselves" ("Of Opinions," p. 339).

Barbarians are those who believe that the others, those around them, are barbarians. All men are equal, but not all men know it; some believe themselves superior to others, and that is precisely where they are inferior; therefore all men are not equal. This definition clearly cannot fail to raise certain logical questions, since the fact of observing that certain people believe themselves superior and are in reality inferior leads me to pronounce a judgment characteristic of those I am condemning—namely, that the others are inferior. My report of this type of inferiority needs to be explicitly separated from the behaviors on which my judgment is based. From here on, we might find no further fault with La Bruyère's argument, were it not for its concluding formula: "reason like ourselves." Are we to believe that there is only one good way of reasoning, which is our own? Are foreigners praised only because they know how to reason as we do? What if they reasoned differently? For we cannot have it both ways: either reason is truly "of all times and places," a universal and distinctive feature of the human race, in which case the criterion of "reasoning like ourselves" is superfluous; or else it is not, and our own way of reasoning is the only good one.

La Bruyère in fact leans toward the second solution, which is once again the ethnocentric (or egocentric) version of universalism. No sooner has he defined the barbaric with the help of a criterion independent of country of origin than he renounces his definition in favor of a more familiar one: "All strangers are not barbarians, nor are all our countrymen civilized" ("Of Opinions," p. 339). La Bruyère's universalism turns out to be merely tolerance, indeed a very limited tolerance: there are *also* good foreigners, those who are capable of reasoning as we do. And the following fragment, which supposedly proves that La Bruyère knows how to put himself in the place of another, that he is prepared to give each individual viewpoint its due, takes him a step further toward ethnocentrism: "In spite of our pure language, our neatness in dress, our cultivated manners, our good laws and fair complexion, we are considered barbarians by some nations" (ibid.). Not only is La Bruyère convinced that our own laws are good, our manners cultivated, and our language pure (what might that actually mean?), but he also believes that fairness of complexion is evidence of nonbarbarianism. Now there is a truly barbarian idea! Even supposing La Bruyère's statement to be ironic, the way his arguments are linked cannot fail to be disturbing.

La Bruyère is unaware of his own ethnocentrism. He describes France in passing as "a country which is the centre of good taste and politeness" ("Of Society and of Conversation," p. 124), whereas perhaps only the idea that everything has a center is characteristic of the French tradition. And if he has the good grace to imagine the Siamese trying to convert Christians to their own religion, he nonetheless explains the success of the Christian missionaries in Siam by the special quality of the Christian religion—which is, as it happens, his own. "May it not be caused by the force of truth?" ("Of Freethinkers," p. 470). Like Pascal, then, La Bruyère takes as an absolute truth something that is a characteristic of his own culture. From this false universalism, it is only a short step to a true relativism: "When we have cursorily examined all forms of government without partiality to the one of our fatherland, we cannot decide which to choose; they are all a mixture of good and evil; it is, therefore, most reasonable to value that of our native land above all others, and to submit to it" ("Of the Sovereign and the State," p. 245). Here what is in question is the nationalist variant of relativism (since there is no universal, one may as well prefer what one finds at home), although it does have the advantage of being presented as a choice rather than a necessity.

La Bruyère shows only a fleeting interest in other nations, moreover. Unlike Montaigne, he openly condemns travel: "Some men give the finishing-stroke to the spoiling of their judgment by their long travels, and thus lose the little religion which remained to them. They meet daily new forms of worship, different manners and morals, and various ceremonies; . . . the variety puzzles them, and as each thing pleases their fancy more or less, they are unable to come to a decision" ("Of Freethinkers," p. 461). He seems to be more attracted by diversity within a given society, as his chapter titles attest: "Of the Town," "Of the Court," "Of the Great," "Of the Sovereign and the State," "Of Women," and so on. But appearances are misleading: La Bruyère in fact never deviates from his unitary vision. He sees social groups as concentric circles, each of which reflects or tempers the preceding one, contributing nothing radically new: the people imitate the city, which imitates the court, which imitates the prince; there is certainly no escape from centralization here. "The city makes a man take a dislike to the country; the country undeceives him as to the city" ("Of the Court," p. 220); one senses that this series could go on indefinitely. As Rica says in Montesquieu's *Lettres persanes (Persian Letters)*, "the sovereign imposes his attitudes on the court, the court on the town, and the town on the provinces; his mind is the pattern which determines the shape of all the others" (letter 99, p. 184).

Ethnic groups do not interest the seventeenth-century moralists, for they do not really count: there is no indispensable way-station between the individual with his personal psychic configuration and humanity in general; moreover, that is what makes it so easy to deduce the features of the latter on the basis of the former. When La Bruyère wonders "why the whole bulk of mankind does not constitute one nation" ("Of Mankind," p. 284), he notes that living under the same roof with more than one person is not easy either. The only difference that matters is the difference that obtains between individuals; the difference between cultures has no role to play here.

Scientific Ethnocentrism

Another example of the ethnocentrism characteristic of the "classical spirit" can be observed in the work of the Ideologue Joseph-Marie de Gérando. His text, a pamphlet published in 1800 by the Société des Observateurs de l'Homme, to which he belonged, is interesting as a historical document of some importance: it was intended to facilitate future investigations undertaken by travelers in distant lands and to make such investigations more scientific. Although the Société itself was short-lived (1799–1805), de Gérando's text can be viewed as the first properly ethnological document in the French tradition.

Starting with the opening lines of his pamphlet, *L'Observation des peuples sauvages*, de Gérando grapples with the main shortcoming of earlier observations, what Rousseau, as we shall see, called "the yoke of national prejudices." "For example, they [explorers] habitually judge the customs of Savages by analogies drawn from our own customs, when in fact they are so little related to each other . . . They make the Savage reason as we do, when the Savage does not himself explain to them his reasoning" (*The Observation of Savage Peoples*, p. 66). We have to beware our unconscious tendency to project ourselves onto others. And just as we must not make out savages to be exactly like ourselves, we must not assume that all savages are alike. "It is not our intention to speak of the savage in *general*, nor to suggest that savage peoples are all of a common type: this would be absurd" (p. 78, n. 1). So much for intentions; let us now see how they are carried out.

Let us not dwell on the fact that de Gérando seems to know in advance the answer to many of the questions that he nevertheless invites future travelers to pose. He writes casually: "*No doubt* the Savages cannot have a large number of abstract ideas" (p. 73); "the ideas with which the Savages *would be* least occupied are those belonging to reflection" (p. 74); "since the idioms of the Savages are *probably* very scanty . . ." (p. 76); "this variety, though much less apparent, *no doubt,* than that seen in civilized societies . . ." (p. 87; emphasis added throughout); and so on. These expressions are not critical for de Gérando's overall thesis.

More serious is the fact that his concrete method of collecting information turns out to be the speculation of philosophers ("while philosophers spent time in vain disputes . . . about the nature of man" [p. 65]), in this case Condillac. In the context of Condillac's systematic description of the human being, de Gérando's originality lies in the way he transforms the master's assertions into questions. "Does he [the Savage] go back from the knowledge of effects to the supposition of certain causes, and how does he imagine these causes? Does he allow a first cause? Does he attribute to it intelligence, power, wisdom, and goodness? Does he believe it to be immaterial?" and so on (p. 84).

De Gérando's point of departure is a universalist and rationalist framework: he knows what man in general is like, and he is trying to determine where individual men fit in with respect to the ideal type. Once again, we cannot criticize the project as such; it becomes questionable, however, at the point where de Gérando takes categories offered by contemporary philosophy as if they were universal categories, making no attempt to verify them by using available data about the physical and mental life of other peoples. Thus, when he splits his investigation into "two main categories: the state of the individual, and that of society" (p. 78), or when he declares that "society at large . . . is presented to us under four different kinds of relations—political, civil, religious and economic" (p. 91), de Gérando elevates to the level of universal conceptual instruments some ideas that only a hundred years earlier would not have applied very well even to his own society. He may not undertake to judge the mores of savage peoples directly on the basis of his own, but he judges them exclusively on the basis of his own mental categories—which, after all, are not so far removed from his mores.

The warnings de Gérando proffers against the ethnocentrism of others thus do not suffice to keep his own thought from being ethnocentric, any more than they keep La Bruyère from disregarding other peoples: the universalist is all too often an unwitting ethnocentrist. The reason for this blindness can perhaps already be discovered in the preface to de Gérando's pamphlet (probably written by Jauffret rather than de Gérando himself): the sort of study advocated by de Gérando's text was aimed at "any society differing . . . from those of Europe" (p. 60). De Gérando's writing thus illustrates a commonplace truth: anyone who lacks self-knowledge will never succeed in knowing others. Knowing another and knowing oneself are one and the same thing.

The General by Way of the Particular

The critique of ethnocentrism was nevertheless widely practiced in the eighteenth century; Fontenelle and Montesquieu had gotten their readers used to it. If Helvétius is to be believed, ethnocentrism is a failing from which no nation can claim to be exempt. "Were I to run through all the nations, I should every where find a different behaviour: and each people, in particular, would necessarily think themselves in the possession of that which is most polite" (*Traité de l'esprit*, in English *Essays on the Mind and Its Several Faculties*, p. 54). What is called wisdom in each country is nothing but that country's own distinctive folly. As a result, the judgments that one nation brings to bear on another inform us about those who are speaking, not those who are being discussed: among other peoples, the members of a given nation value only what is like themselves: "Every nation convinced, that she is the sole possessor of wisdom, takes all others for fools; and nearly resembles the inhabitants of the Marian islands, who, being persuaded that theirs was the only language in the universe, concluded from thence, that all other men know not how to speak" (p. 106).

But such a critique risks ending up as pure relativism. Rousseau was perhaps the first writer to offer a systematic criticism of the ethnocentrism of classical philosophy—without renouncing its universalism, it is important to note. (This did not keep Taine from including him among the representatives of that same "classical spirit.") Rousseau takes up the debate in earnest in a celebrated long note (note X) in his "Discours sur l'origine de l'inégalité" ("Discourse on the Origin of Inequality"), which is a dissertation devoted to knowledge of other cultures. He begins by criticizing the travelers' descriptions on which that knowledge is based: instead of encountering the other, the traveler generally encounters a distorted image of himself. "Although the inhabitants of Europe have for the past three or four hundred years overrun the other parts of the world, and are constantly publishing new collections of travels and reports, I am convinced that the only men we know are the Europeans" (*The First and Second Discourses*, p. 218). But Rousseau is not much more indulgent with the "philosophers," who allow themselves cheap generalizations: "Hence that fine adage of ethics, so much harped on by the ruck of Philosophasters, that men are everywhere the same, that, since they everywhere have the same passions and the same vices, it is quite useless to seek to characterize different Peoples; which is about as well argued as it would be to say that it is impossible to distinguish between Peter and James because both have a nose, a mouth, and eyes" (p. 219).

In place of debatable knowledge of this sort, Rousseau imagines another kind of knowledge that he outlines as follows: it is necessary to "shake off the yoke of National prejudices, to get to know men by their conformities and their differences, and to acquire that universal knowledge that is not exclusively of one Century or of one country but of all times and of all places, and thus is, so to speak, the common science of the wise" (ibid.).

Thus, Rousseau distinguishes two aspects of the study he is advocating. On the one hand, we need to discover the specific features that characterize a given people, and the features, if any, that make it different from ourselves. To achieve this, one must be educated, one must be impartial (rather than charged with a mission of converting or conquering), and one must be capable of ridding oneself of one's "national prejudices," that is, of ethnocentrism. But this is only half the battle. For on the other hand, after noting the differences, one must return to the universal idea of man, an idea that does not grow out of pure metaphysical speculation but that absorbs the entire body of accumulated empirical knowledge. A formulation from about the same time in *Essai sur l'origine des langues* (*On the Origin of Language*) confirms the necessary character of the relation between ethnology and philosophy, between the particular and the general: "When one wants to study men, one must consider those around one. But to study man, one must extend the range of one's vision. One must first observe the differences in order to discover the properties" (pp. 30–31).

"I hold it to be an incontestable maxim that whoever has seen only one people does not know men; he knows only the people with whom he has lived" (*Emile*, V, p. 451). Rousseau wants knowledge to go beyond appearances, wants it to go far enough to grasp the very nature of things as well as beings. But if we know only our own country, our own countrymen, we view as natural what is only habitual. The first impulse to search authentically for "nature" comes from the discovery that two forms may correspond to the same essence, and that our form is therefore not (necessarily) essence. Rousseau repeatedly advocates the paradoxical enterprise of discovering properties by way of difference. "It is trivial to learn languages for their own sake; their use is not as important as people believe. But the study of languages leads to that of grammar. Latin has to be learned in order to know French. Both must be studied and compared in order to understand the rules of the art of speaking" (IV, p. 342).

It is rather surprising to note that Rousseau, whose approach is always viewed as purely deductive, in fact recommends an entirely different method here. "Good" universalism is thus first of all a universalism that does not deduce human identity from a principle, whatever it may be; rather, it starts by becoming thoroughly familiar with the particular, and then progresses by feeling its way (whether Rousseau himself always followed his own precepts is quite another question). "Good" universalism is based, moreover, on familiarity with at least *two* particulars (as in the case of languages, French and Latin), and thus on the establishment of a dialogue between them; here Rousseau demolishes the false self-evidence that is the ethnocentrist's point of departure, the deduction of the universal on the basis of a *single* particular. The universal is the horizon of understanding between *two* particulars; we shall perhaps never attain it, but we need to postulate it nevertheless in order to make existing particulars intelligible.

Scientism

Nature versus Morality

We shall never be done with ethnocentrism once and for all. But let us set it aside provisionally in order to look at a second figure of universalism that I shall call *scientism*. This is no less perverse a figure and probably a more dangerous one, for people are not usually proud of being ethnocentric, whereas one can take pride in professing a "scientific" philosophy. I shall take the first illustration of this attitude from one of Rousseau's contemporaries, Denis Diderot.

Diderot deals with the question of the universal and the relative in his "Supplément au voyage de Bougainville" ("Supplement to Bougainville's 'Voyage'"). In this text, under the cover of rather playful dialogues on exotic topics, he confronts the serious problem of how to establish ethics given the plurality of civilizations and thus, ultimately, the problem of moral standards. Since different societies do not have common values, how can we appreciate and judge them? We have already seen the ethnocentrist's response, which also seems to have been the response one of Diderot's characters would have made before reading Bougainville's text: "Up to now, I had always thought that a person was never so well off as when at home. Consequently I thought that everyone in the world must feel the same. All this is a natural result of the attraction of the soil, and this is an attraction that is bound up with all the comforts one enjoys at home and is not so sure of finding away from it" (p. 193). At the end of the discussion, the interlocutors revert to this conclusion, although they had previously recognized the existence of more than one possible "center." "B. Let us follow the good chaplain's example—be monks in France and savages in Tahiti. A. Put on the costume of the country you visit, but keep the suit of clothes you will need to go home in" (p. 238).

If the basis for morality were in fact to be found in submission to existing mores and in the self-satisfied admiration with which people regard them, the discussion would end right here. But this is not at all Diderot's view. The following passage offers a better formulation of the problem: "You cannot condemn the morals of Europe for not being those of Tahiti, nor our morals for not being those of Europe. You need a more dependable rule of judgment than that. And what shall it be?" (p. 217). The relativist would forbid us to pass judgment on the mores of a foreign country. We must not accept that restriction, but we must not be satisfied, either, to apply the standards of our own country to another, as the ethnocentrist would have us do; we must find a universal ideal. Furthermore, the terms Diderot uses to describe the two societies, in order to praise "Tahiti" and condemn Europe, all convey judgments and thus imply the existence of values. The discourse of his Tahitian hero Orou clearly demonstrates the absurdity of the relativist position and establishes the necessity of moral transcendence. Orou questions the confidence that one might have in specific individual holders of moral authority, whether magistrate or priest: "Are they really masters of good and evil? Can they transform justice into injustice and contrariwise? Is it within their power to attach the name of 'good' to harmful actions or the name of 'evil' to harmless or useful deeds? One can hardly think so because in that case there would no longer be any difference between true and false, between good and bad, between beautiful and ugly—only such differences as it pleased your great workman, your magistrates or your priests to define as such. You would then have to change your ideas and behavior from one moment to the next" (p. 208).

If only statutory law exists (rooted in custom), it does not deserve the name of law. But where is the absolute standard to be found? Diderot responds: "If morality were to be based on the eternal, universal relations of men with one another . . . the code of morality appropriate to men should rest on no other foundations than [what makes man what he is]" (p. 228). At first glance, such a response seems simply a step backward in time. The ancient philosophers indeed established nature as the ultimate criterion of values (whence the expression "natural law"); morality itself was thought to be grounded in nature and the cosmic order. However, since the Renaissance (at least), confidence in the reference to nature has been shaken: Montaigne's relativism and empiricism, like those of many others, have led us to doubt the existence of a standard that transcends specific customs. The "naturalism" of the ancients has been more or less supplanted by the "artificialism" of the moderns. One might suppose that Diderot's position amounts to reestablishing a link with the traditional approach. In fact, that is not the case at all, for the relations between nature and morality in Diderot's text are quite different from those in his predecessors' work, and the difference arises simply from a drastic change in the meaning of the word "nature."

In reality, Diderot is not at all interested in establishing a basis for morality; it may be that he is even attempting to destroy it. By basing morality on nature—which also means basing law on fact—and thus by basing what must be on what is, he succeeds in eliminating any need for morality. Unlike the relativist's credo (or the empiricist's, or the positivist's), however, Diderot's credo refers to a phenomenon viewed as universal (human nature) rather than to any particular society. Diderot is looking for a basis for human behavior, and he chooses to look to "nature," that is, to what constitutes man as such. Nature and morality have thus become two claimants to the same title, that of guide to behavior, and Diderot prefers the former to the latter. In his view, one must choose between "natural man" and "moral and artificial man," whom he sometimes simply calls "moral man" (p. 235). To say that nature is or is not moral has no meaning: "Nature includes both vices and virtues along with everything else" (p. 230); these notions are grounded precisely in morality and not in nature. This idea is already expressed in the subtitle of the "Supplement," which offers a good summary of Diderot's overall intentions: "[A dialogue between A and B] on the undesirability of attaching moral values to certain physical acts which carry no such implications" (p. 187). If we want to know where to turn for behavioral guidance, we have the following answer: "Pay close attention to the nature of things and actions, to your relations with your fellow creatures, to the effect of your behavior on your own well-being and on the general welfare" (p. 209). The most significant phrase here, paradoxically, is "pay close attention" *(attache-toi)*, which implies acquiring knowledge and then acting in accordance with that knowledge, whether things or actions—thus, human beings—are in question. Every thing has its "nature," and we need only become acquainted with that nature if we want to know how to behave in relation to the thing itself. Like the ancients, Diderot sees himself as a "naturalist"; but like the moderns, he begins by "denaturing" morality. This makes his response much more ambitious than that of the empiricists who were his contemporaries: a universal guide to behavior does exist, and this guide is the truth of our nature, not morality, which is necessarily "artificial."

The principal example in the "Supplement" involves sexual behavior. The "nature" of human sexuality is free exchange: there is no obligation of fidelity beyond a month; there are no constraints. Still, one question inevitably arises: What happens if the two partners do not agree? Let us assume they will not be kept together by force. But what becomes of their relationship? If one partner desires sexual contact and the other refuses, one of the two will not have acted in accordance with "nature." How are we to ascertain which one? Diderot's reply is that it is in the nature of males, thus of half the population, to be violent, and to want to impose their will upon others, that is, upon women. Now since violence is in nature, we have to accept it. "We have consecrated the woman's resistance, we attach blame to the man's violence—violence that would be only a slight injury in Tahiti, but becomes a crime in our cities" (p. 233). Clearly stated, this means that rape is not a crime, and that women have to submit to men. But does this not amount to giving up any basis for behavior except force? Is this not just a way of identifying might with right?

Once the rule has been established, it can be applied outside the realm of sexuality. Diderot thinks, for example (and here he follows Helvétius' doctrine), that it is in the nature of the human being (or in man's?) to act exclusively in his own *interest*. "A man . . . will give you what he has no use for, and he will always ask for something he has need of" (p. 222). Diderot adds the following argument: "Tell me, if there is anywhere on the face of the earth a man who, if he were not held back by shame, would not prefer to lose his child—a husband who would not prefer to lose his wife—rather than lose his fortune and all the amenities of life?" (p. 220). We may think that such generous fathers and husbands do exist, after all; but let us accept Diderot's assertion for a moment. La Rochefoucauld shared this pessimistic view of the nature of men, but he was glad of the existence of what Diderot here calls shame, since, in the name of "honnêteté," shame was elevated to the status of a social ideal and could restrain men's evil inclinations, could lead them toward a gentler and more pleasant life. Diderot, on the contrary, would like to eliminate shame and subject social life directly to self-interest (since in his view that is where the truth or "nature" of social life lies).

More than any particular example, it is the principle that counts. Diderot states that "incest does not offend nature" (p. 218), and perhaps it should not offend morality, either. This example had already been discussed at length by philosophers of the empiricist and artificialist tradition, such as Locke, who shared Diderot's view as to the absence of a natural basis for the prohibition of incest but used this view as an argument in praise of the wisdom of institutions. Diderot takes the artificialist logic to the extreme, and then abruptly reverses it: if something is not natural, it does not deserve to be respected; thus, incest cannot be condemned. But how are we to know where to draw the line? It may be that tomorrow (tomorrow?) a biologist will prove to us that aggression is in the nature of man and that *therefore* we must allow it, or murder, or torture, or the desire to humiliate others; nothing authorizes us to take the opposite stand. This is indeed the conclusion reached in Diderot's own day by the characters of the Marquis de Sade, whose *La Philosophie dans le boudoir (Philosophy in the Bedroom)* is nothing but a reworked and amplified version of the arguments presented in the "Supplement." "Destruction being one of the chief laws of Nature, nothing that destroys can be criminal" (III, pp. 238–239). "Cruelty, very far from being a vice, is the first sentiment Nature injects in us all" (III, p. 253). Sade's favorite argument is justification by reference to nature: "All man-made laws which would contravene Nature's are made for naught but our contempt" (III, p. 226). "For a bridle have nothing but your inclinations, for laws only your desires, for morality Nature's alone" (V, p. 323).

How shall we proceed to discover this "nature"? Diderot replies: "Let's begin at the beginning. Let us put nature resolutely to the question and see, without prejudice, what answers she will give on this question" ("Supplement," p. 229). The way this fine program is carried out is instructive: in order to discover the truth about one human institution, marriage, Diderot turns to the observation—which may be easier, or more revealing—of animals: "The preference you speak of can be observed not only among human beings but also in various other animal species" (p. 229). The way had been prepared by the use of the terms "male" and "female" in the place of "man" and "woman"; the substitutions already implied an interest limited to the animal nature of humans. Does zoology then hold the key to truth about society? Are human societies and their rites reducible to instincts? After putting nature in the place of morality, Diderot calls upon specialists in animal science to inform us about human beings.

Now an assimilation of this sort always involves the danger that one may move from comparing human beings and objects to treating them as objects. In a similar fashion, de Gérando, a faithful disciple of the Encyclopedists, stated: "Weary of its centuries of vain agitations in vain theories, the pursuit of learning has settled at last on the way of observation . . . The Science of Man too is a natural science, a science of observation, the most noble of all" (*The Observation of Savage Peoples*, p. 61). But are the terms "science of observation" and "natural science" truly synonymous? De Gérando pushes his naturalist dream so far as to imagine laboratory conditions for the study of savages: rather than putting up with the discomforts of on-site observation (heat, insects), would it not be wiser to *transplant* the savage to Paris? In order to achieve the best possible conditions, one would also bring along his natural environment, that is, his family. "We should have in miniature the model of that society in which they were reared. So the naturalist is not content to bring back a branch, a flower that is soon withered;

he tries to transplant the whole tree or plant, to give it a second life on our soil" (p. 101). No sooner is it formulated than de Gérando's ethnology slips over into botany. The idea of asking the savages, let alone their families, if that is also what *they* want never comes up; what matters is for the scientist to be able to study them at leisure. The inclusion of the science of man among the natural sciences immediately entails the reduction of the human being to the status of an object.

This knowledge becomes, for Diderot, the minor premise of a syllogism which has the following major premise: one can never successfully resist nature. "You are mad if you believe that there is anything in the universe, high or low, that can add or subtract from the laws of nature . . . You may decree the opposite, but you will not be obeyed" ("Supplement," p. 209). Man is entirely determined by his nature; he disposes of no personal liberty whatsoever; he lacks any ability to escape from his destiny, which has been established once and for all.

Diderot's syllogism concludes with particular rules of behavior that are all in harmony with one aspect or another of our "nature." It follows that it is quite simple to recognize good and bad laws. Science holds their secret: we need only know nature, in order to have access to that secret. A good law is one that follows nature (in other words, what is right is what conforms to the facts): if such is the case, then "the religious law would perhaps become superfluous, and the civil law should become nothing more than an explicit statement of the laws of nature . . . Or else, if it is considered necessary to preserve all three sets of laws, civil and religious law should be strictly patterned on the law of nature, which we carry with us, graven on our hearts, wherever we go, and which will always be the strongest" (p. 228). To make his case, Diderot uses Tahiti to embody his ideal. Another way of putting it would be to say that the best society is the one that has the fewest laws (for in such a society one follows nature in everything). "How concise the legal codes of nations would be if they only conformed strictly to the law of nature!" (p. 234).

A bad law, obviously, is one that is opposed to human nature. Most European laws are of this sort, and to Tahitians they look like shackles. Any law that contradicts nature is tyrannical: there is no difference between a despot and an enlightened prince, between an unjust law and a law that is useful to society: "If you want to become a tyrant, civilize him [man]; poison him as best you can with a system of morality that is contrary to nature. Devise all sorts of hobbles for him" (p. 235).

"Watch out for the fellow who talks about putting things in order!" (ibid.).

What becomes of man when the laws of nature, civil laws, and religious laws do not coincide? He finds himself obliged to serve several masters at once, unable to submit wholly to any one of them. Now nothing is more abject in Diderot's eyes than a hybrid being: "Do you know what will finally happen? You will come to despise all three, and you will be neither man, nor citizen nor pious believer; you will be nothing at all" (p. 208). As soon as one stops being a single thing, one is no longer anything at all. One has the choice among hypocrisy, unhappiness, stupidity, and abnormality, but there is no satisfactory way to experience heterogeneity. Diderot goes so far as to prefer total subjection to the hybrid state. "I can only assure you that you won't find the human condition perfectly happy anywhere but in Tahiti. And in only one little spot on the map of Europe will you find it even tolerable [that is, Venice, which had a reputation at the time for absolute despotism]—there a set of haughty rulers, anxious about their own safety, have found ways and means of reducing man to what you would have to call a state of bestiality" (p. 237). Absolute evil is better than mitigated evil, for Diderot: at least unity is maintained.

In the final analysis, not only is morality unnecessary to society; it is actually harmful. "I find these strange precepts contrary to nature, and contrary to reason. I think they are admirably calculated to increase the number of crimes" (p. 206). What was taken for a cure is in reality a cause of the illness. In this, too, Diderot is going right along with Helvétius, who might have inspired the musings of the "Supplement": "Dissoluteness is then only politically dangerous in a state, when it countervenes the law of the country" (*Essays on the Mind*, II, 14, p. 75). For Diderot attributes extreme importance to the action of the laws; in this he shares the views of both Helvétius and Condorcet: "If the laws are good, morals are good; if the laws are bad, morals are bad" (p. 228). But the resemblance stops here. Helvétius is a relativist: according to him, no law is based on nature; laws may be more or less appropriate, not more or less natural. Condorcet, for his part, wants to make laws better in order to improve society: justice has to be universal (in his case, rational rather than "natural"). As for Diderot, he believes in the universal nature of man, but he recognizes that most laws are pure conventions: they are effective, to be sure, but their effects are bad.

The positions expressed in the "Supplement" are radical ones. But they do not lead Diderot himself to extreme conclusions. He does not have the revolutionary temperament, and he is content to recommend that laws be amended so they will be more in tune with nature. "We should say to ourselves—and shout incessantly too—that shame, dishonor and penalties have been erroneously attached to actions that are in themselves perfectly harmless" (p. 238). But there is no call to rebellion here: "We should speak out against foolish laws until they get reformed, and meanwhile we should obey them as they are" (ibid.). Moreover, we have to ask whether what we encounter in the "Supplement" actually represents Diderot's own opinions, or whether it represents the closely related yet divergent views of his characters—Orou, the chaplain, the old man, A, B? The text ends with an about-face: A and B wonder what their wives would think about the topics they have just been discussing; and A suggests: "Probably the opposite of what they would say" (p. 239). This statement targets social hypocrisy, in the first place, the habit of repressing "nature"; but can we not imagine, too, that Diderot's entire dialogue may be articulated in the same vein? Nonetheless, as Diderot says in another text: "One must be happy in accordance with the inclination of one's own nature, there is my entire morality" (*Tablettes* [Tablets], p. 219).

Freedom

Human nature is the same everywhere; it determines everything that matters in human behavior; science is the best way to know human nature; science must therefore govern ethics and politics. All these ideas come to be associated with the encyclopedist spirit represented here by Diderot. They gain wide acceptance, while Diderot's own potential reservations on the subject go unnoticed. But as we shall discover in examining the position of another illustrious representative of the Enlightenment, Jean-Jacques Rousseau, it would be a mistake to equate the scientistic doctrine present in the *Encyclopedia* with the spirit of Enlightenment as a whole.

Rousseau does criticize relativism, as we shall see. However, that does not mean he will settle for just any universalism, and in no event does he allow his position to be mistaken for Diderot's or that of the "philosophers." He condemns out of hand Diderot's conclusion, "namely, that the sole duty of man is, to follow in everything the inclinations of his heart" (*Les Confessions,* in English *Confessions,* IX, vol. 2, p. 115).

The initial opposition between Rousseau and Diderot is rooted in a scientific disagreement. For Diderot, as we have seen, human nature belongs entirely to the realm of biology, or even zoology. Such an approach is unacceptable to Rousseau, for it implies that one can disregard society, reason, and morality and still preserve human identity, whereas this is not the case. Thus, he writes in the "Lettre à d'Alembert" ("Letter to D'Alembert"): "The argument drawn from the example of the beasts proves nothing and is not true. Man is not a dog or a wolf. It is only necessary in his species to establish the first relations of society to give to his sentiments a morality unknown to beasts" (*Politics and the Arts,* pp. 86–87). It is not the zoologist who holds the key to the truth about the human species but rather, Rousseau would say, the philosopher.

But the most important divergence comes to light later on. For it is not a question, in Rousseau's mind, of substituting a specialist in human cultures for a specialist in nature, of replacing a biologist with a historian. Rousseau is contesting the existence of a rigid determinism that would leave no room for human freedom. What distinguishes human beings from animals, indeed, is that animals are wholly subject to the laws of their own nature, whereas human behavior cannot be entirely predicted by any law, whether biological or historical; freedom, or the possibility of exercising one's will, is the distinguishing feature of the human species. Montesquieu had already declared (and we shall return to this) that the possibility of evading the law is the distinguishing feature of humanity. Rousseau goes further, declaring that animals obey nature, while man can control his own destiny as "a free agent" ("Discourse on the Origin of Inequality," *The First and Second Discourses,* p. 148). The difference between animals and men lies in the absence or presence not of reason but of freedom, thus in the nonintegrality of the determinism that governs human behavior. This is why, according to Rousseau, the principal characteristic of human behavior is *perfectibility*—that is, something that has no positive content but that allows human beings to acquire all contents. This is what gives the concepts of "human nature" and "universality" an unexpected twist: what is common to human beings is not any particular trait (in this sense it is pointless to wonder whether man *is* good or evil, moral or immoral), but their freedom, their capacity to transform themselves (potentially for the better). In this way, Rousseau takes note of a characteristic deficiency in modern thought (the absence of a *natural* basis for the precepts that govern behavior), and he proposes to seek a new sort of basis in freedom and will instead of nature.

Here again, then, the debate on the level of knowledge is extended to the level of ethics. As it happens, Rousseau is particularly eager to shatter the illusion of continuity between the two levels, the illusion that what should be can be deduced from what is, that ethics can be deduced from science. The autonomy of each of these domains must first be affirmed, even if we may ask in a second phase whether ethics and science also have common roots. Diderot sought to establish a code of behavior based solely on the biological nature of man. That is scientifically absurd. But it is also morally unacceptable: Benjamin Constant, who is on Rousseau's side here, makes the following remark: "Power is only too ready to represent its own excesses, its capricious and willful excesses, as a series of natural laws. From the recognized inferiority of one race and the superiority of another to the enslavement of the former, the distance is all too short" ("De M. Dunoyer et de quelques-uns de ses ouvrages" [On M. Dunoyer and Some of His Works], pp. 554–555). Today's readers know even better than Constant's contemporaries how far one can go in seeking to be in conformity with "nature."

But even if Diderot had taken history and anthropology as his starting point, his code would have been no better grounded. That the facts are what they are proves only one thing: that such was the will of the strongest. To "base" justice on fact is necessarily to "base" it on power (it suffices to have been the most powerful to confront others with an accomplished fact)—that is, in reality, to empty it of all substance. This is why Rousseau attacks not the zoologists but his fellow philosophers, when, like Diderot, they go about deducing morality from nature. In *Du Contrat social* (*On the Social Contract*), Rousseau says the following about Grotius: "His most persistent mode of reasoning is always to establish right by fact. One could use a more rational method, but not one more favorable to tyrants" (I, 2, p. 47). The justification of an iniquitous act by the "laws of history" is no more convincing than its justification by the "laws" of racial superiority. Rousseau spells it out: "It is necessary to know what ought to be in order to judge soundly about what is" (*Emile*, in English, V, p. 458). Far from having to submit to science, ethics will be responsible for evaluating the work of the scientist.

We are witnessing the formulation of a decisive opposition here, one that prefigures countless conflicts in the two centuries to follow. Diderot and Rousseau are both resolutely on the side of modernity, in favor of rational knowledge freed from the tutelage of religion. But Diderot believes in wholesale determinism, and he leaves virtually no room at all for human freedom; hence science, which is most apt to reveal to us the way this determinism functions, replaces ethics and is charged with formulating the goals of mankind and society. Rousseau, for his part, without denying the existence of some degree of determinism, whether physical or social, recognizes freedom as its counterpart; what is more, following Montesquieu, he makes freedom the hallmark of humanity. Now if I dispose of a certain freedom, I can act according to my own will, and choose my acts: I assume responsibility for them and by that very token I allow them to be judged good or bad. Thus, ethics is recognized in its autonomy: irreducible to science, it exercises over science not a tutelage in the manner of religion, but the right of an overseer, making it permissible to judge whether the results achieved are useful or dangerous. It follows that—if Diderot and Rousseau both represent the philosophy of Enlightenment—in the broader sense, Rousseau alone is a representative of *humanism*. In the pages that follow, I shall continually rely on this terminological distinction: expressions such as "the philosophy of the Enlightenment" or "the Encyclopedists" will designate the movements of ideas, in their ideological complexity, as they existed in the eighteenth century, while terms such as "scientism" and "humanism" will refer to coherent systems of thought that do not belong to a particular historical period. This is why, even though they contradict each other, humanism and scientism can coexist in Enlightenment philosophy.

The Universal State

Whatever its importance may be for the history of ideologies over the past two centuries, scientistic doctrine interests us here not on its own account but only to the extent that it has implications for our topic, the diversity of peoples and the plurality of judgments. Now in this connection scientism is rapidly enriched by a new conclusion. Condorcet, the last of the Encyclopedists, takes charge of its formulation. This conclusion involves the transformation of the world from an agglomeration of countries into a single State—a transformation that is, as Condorcet sees it, both desirable and inevitable.

Condorcet starts from a two-fold postulate. In the first place, human nature is the same everywhere; since our rational faculty constitutes part of human nature, this faculty is therefore likewise universal. In the second place, only reason is capable of distinguishing what is just from what is unjust; therefore it is incumbent upon universal reason to formulate the principles of justice that are valid everywhere and for everyone. Thus, for Condorcet natural law becomes rational law, while remaining just as universal as its predecessor. From this starting point, Condorcet goes one step further: since the principles of justice are everywhere the same, laws must be the same as well. In other words, laws must not result from natural law *and* from the physical, social, and historical conditions of a nation, as Montesquieu would have it; they must proceed from the principles of justice alone. Thus, it is no accident that Condorcet first formulates his opinions on this topic in a commentary on Montesquieu's *De l'esprit des lois (The Spirit of the Laws)*, which is at the same time his first incursion into the domain of political philosophy. "As truth, reason, justice, the rights of man, the interests of property, of liberty, of security, are in all places the same; we cannot discover why all the provinces of a state, or even all states, should not have the same civil and criminal laws, and the same laws relative to commerce. A good law should be good for all men. A true proposition is true everywhere" ("Observations sur le vingt-neuvième livre de *l'Esprit des lois*," in English "Observations on the Twenty-ninth Book of the Spirit of Laws, by the late M. Condorcet," p. 274). This is how reason and its finest incarnation, science, begin to dictate political decisions.

All men are equal in rights, for they share the same nature; the rights of men are the same everywhere. Laws are the "obvious consequences" of these rights, as Condorcet says elsewhere ("Fragment de justification," p. 575), and they must not be encumbered with considerations of climate, mores, or historical evolution. For one cannot have it both ways: either the laws in question concern rules of etiquette, commercial practices, or perhaps private behaviors, in which case they may be allowed to vary, but then such rules do not deserve to be called laws; or else they address what is essential in man's public behavior, and in this case the fact that they are rooted in custom cannot be used to justify them. Reason must dismantle prejudices without letting itself be influenced by information about the country's climate or its national character.

But once all people are equipped with the same laws, there is no reason to stop along such a promising path. The progressive diffusion of enlightenment will bring peoples closer together. Prejudices are multiple, while truth is unitary; by conforming to truth, peoples will come to be more and more alike. They will intensify exchanges of all sorts—commercial exchanges, but also spiritual ones—either by adopting the language of the most enlightened peoples (English and French), or by creating, on a purely logical basis, a universal language; we know that during the last days of his life, while he was in hiding in a cellar in the rue Servandoni, Condorcet was working on the invention of such a language. Such means as these, he believed, would bring about the realization of his ideal of seeing men "form a single whole, and work toward a single end" (*Esquisse d'un tableau historique des progrès de l'esprit humain*, in English *Sketch for a Historical Picture of the Progress of the Human Mind*, p. 168).

Condorcet died in his prison before he had the time to see his project through. But his legacy was transmitted intact thanks to the Ideologues (Destutt de Tracy was the first to publish Condorcet's commentary on Montesquieu) and it flourished in the work of the man who was to give scientistic doctrine its definitive form, the Utopian Henri de Saint-Simon. In Saint-Simon, indeed, we do not merely find the postulate of a wholesale determinism governing the world, and the conclusion according to which knowledge (science) must orient behavior (ethics). We also find another characteristic feature of scientism to which we shall have occasion to return and which was absent in Condorcet: Saint-Simon turns science into a religion. The dream of a universal State, finally, takes on more precise form in Saint-Simon's writings, in particular in a pamphlet written in 1814 in collaboration with the young Augustin Thierry entitled "De la réorganisation de la société européenne" ("On the Reorganization of the European Community"). To a Europe torn apart by the Napoleonic wars, Saint-Simon offers the solution of unification.

His declared point of departure, of course, is science. From its remote origins right up to 1814, the art of politics has been based on particular interests and prejudices; it is time to bring order into politics, by importing the major principles of the physical sciences, "reason and experience [observation]" (I, 4, p. 39). Equipped with these two powerful tools, Saint-Simon begins to look for what would be "the best possible constitution" (I, 7, p. 45), the one that might, in consequence, be suitable for all peoples on earth. "I wish to enquire if there is a form of government good in itself, founded on certain, absolute, universal principles, independent of time and place" (I, 4, p. 39). This constitution would be universal and eternal, for it would proceed from the nature of things and from the rigor of syllogisms.

Saint-Simon and Thierry unhesitatingly sweep away all the objections that come to mind. Faithful to Condorcet's teachings, they disregard national variations: "It is untrue to say, as Montesquieu believed, that each nation needs its own form of government (for there can be only one form of good government, as there is only one form of right reasoning)" (I, 6, pp. 44–45). Moreover, it would be useless to struggle against the force of facts and the logic of reason. The divergences that exist within or among nations stem only from the fact that each is defending its own interests and refuses to move toward the higher ground of truth; for there is but a single truth.

Thus, all the European states, if they wish to follow Saint-Simon's advice, must adopt the same constitution, based on observation and logic—a constitution that, as it happens, turns out already to exist, as the constitution of England. Indeed, unlike other peoples, the English have had the wisdom to provide themselves with laws guaranteeing "the liberty and happiness of the people" (I, "To the Parliaments of France and England" [dedication], p. 31), that is, the eternal values. Once this constitution is adopted, the peoples of Europe will readily unite in a confederation equipped with common institutions, a uniform educational system, and a single moral code (for there is only one good one). Thus will be achieved the catholic dream of a united Europe, a dream that could not be achieved in the Middle Ages for want of sufficient enlightenment; peace will reign in place of war.

Saint-Simon skips rapidly over the relations between this European State and the rest of the world; but it is clear that ultimate unification does not pose any problems of conscience for him. "To colonize [*peupler*] the world with the European race, superior to every other human race; to make the world accessible and habitable like Europe—such is the sort of enterprise by which the European parliament should continually keep Europe active and healthy" (II, 5, 49). We learn nothing about how the inferior races will "decolonize" *(dépeupler)* the rest of the world; we surmise, however, that this universal State will be modeled on Europe.

The young Auguste Comte, like Augustin Thierry, was a member of Saint-Simon's entourage during the early years of the Restoration. He had very bad memories of this period, however, and toward the end of his life he spoke of "my disastrous connection in my early youth with a depraved juggler" (*Système de politique positive* [System of Positive Politics], III, p. xv). For Comte, the line of succession by way of Saint-Simon is compromising: Saint-Simon claims his work is based on science, but in reality he knows nothing about science; thus, he degrades the scientistic project itself. Skipping over Saint-Simon, Comte sees himself as a successor to Condorcet, who counts as a real scholar; Comte repeatedly calls him "my eminent precursor" or even "my spiritual father." But what he borrows from Condorcet is really no different from the Saint-Simonian legacy (Saint-Simon did not implement the project perfectly, but the ideal remains the same): this is because politics must be "subordinated to history" (ibid.), and consequently morality must be subordinated to science. In other words, Condorcet, Saint-Simon, and Comte all share the same scientistic doctrine.

Like Condorcet and Saint-Simon, Comte believes it is possible to establish—with the help of science—the one and only "correct" constitution, which will rapidly impose itself on all peoples, transcending national differences. "The fundamental laws of human evolution, which establish the philosophical basis of the ultimate regime, are necessarily appropriate to all climates and all races, except for mere differences in speed" ("Discours préliminaire" [Preliminary Discourse], I, p. 390). In the end, humanity will constitute a single society. The task of positivism, the only truly universal doctrine, is to help men progress along this path; that is why Comte devotes lengthy passages to the description of the unification process. Why unification? Not only because it is desirable, but—also and especially—because humanity is already evolving in this direction.

Here it must be said that, unlike Saint-Simon and even Condorcet, Comte takes actual observation as his starting point, and his observations are occasionally so compelling that we are obliged to credit Comte with a prophetic clairvoyance. He uncovers several characteristics of contemporary society that are destined, he believes, to spread throughout the globe. These include, first of all, industrial life and thus a certain organization of labor; second, a homogenization of aesthetic tastes; third, international agreement on the content and methods of science. To these he adds, in fourth place, the preference for a particular political form, the democratic republic, and, fifth, a morality that is based not on any theology but on the "religion of humanity" that Comte advocates. One hundred fifty years after Comte's prophetic formulations, we are in a good position to recognize that he was right: even if the tendencies he identified are not all evolving at the same rate, humanity is unquestionably more homogeneous today, in every respect, than it was in Comte's day.

A second factor in favor of unification, according to Comte, is the role played by the past, or rather by an improved recollection of the past. The presence of memory reduces the possibilities that are open to us at every moment: the past "silently regularizes the future" (II, p. 465). Nevertheless, one must not go too far in trusting to the natural course of history; one must help history proceed straight toward its proper goal. Comte's observations are thus coupled with a program of action designed essentially to facilitate and accelerate the course of history.

This program has several phases. First there is to be a qualitative ripening, then a quantitative extension. The action will begin in France, the "core of humanity," the land of the "central people" (as with many other thinkers, Comte's universalism does not exempt him from chauvinism). First of all, temporal power will be carefully distinguished from spiritual power, and the focus will be entirely on the latter. Only after spiritual unity is established will it be possible to focus on political institutions; the inverse procedure would be likely to have wholly negative consequences. Now the process of spiritual improvement requires patient education, not laws or decrees; Comte places great stress on this point. During the lengthy "transition period," all opinions must be heard. "Didactic monologue" has to give way to "real discussion" (I, p. 122). Education itself will be taken away from the State, which otherwise might orient it too strongly in the direction of its own interests. Hearts and minds have to adhere to the new doctrine not under constraint but freely, because they see its superiority.

However, once these spiritual principles have been agreed upon, it is to be expected that they will influence temporal power: the separation of the two is clear-cut, but it is provisional. Institutions will then bring themselves into harmony with the principles, and social mores themselves will follow the same movement. In the course of this ultimate phase, Comte writes, "without altering liberty, the government will march openly toward the universal ascendancy of the religion of Humanity, which henceforth will tend to win acceptance for its regime as well as for its dogma and its cult" (IV, p. 445). We may wonder whether a government is capable of imposing itself so completely without "altering" individual freedom, if only a little. Once the truth has been established, discussion, it seems, must halt.

The agreement reached in France, the center of the world, is destined to be exported beyond her borders. Here again, Comte identifies several phases. In the course of the first one, the French solution will be extended to what he calls the West—that is, Italy, Spain, England, and Germany. Here the same order of evolution that prevailed in France will be respected, and care will be taken not to put the cart before the horse: unification will be spiritual at first, temporal only later on; education will once again antedate institutions. But the institutions cannot wait forever. Comte thus indicates the precise form they will need to take: the West will be governed by a Positive Committee composed of thirty men representing the five countries, to whom will be added "six elite ladies, two Frenchwomen and one from each of the other Western branches" (I, p. 385). This committee will organize a joint navy, will establish a common currency, and so on.

Comte always takes the precaution of asserting that, unification notwithstanding, distinguishing national characteristics will be respected: his formulas maintain the two terms, unity and variety, in a symmetrical legitimacy. "Local differences have to second the universal destination" (IV, p. 481); "that just diversity" must not "alter in any way the fundamental unity of the great positivist republic" (I, p. 82). But it is hard to see what role the distinguishing national characteristics would play, in practice, since the entire West is to have the education, morality, and customs established in France! One detail illustrates especially well the subordinate role to be played by these distinguishing features: all the member countries of the West will have the same flag, but with "a simple border in the current colors of the corresponding population" (I, p. 388).

During the third and last period, the Western model will spread to the rest of the world. Here again, several phases will be required: first, North America and South America will both be linked to Europe through the intermediaries England and Spain; the collaboration of the Poles and the Greeks will be assured, and they can play the role of intermediaries vis-à-vis the peoples of the East. Then the rest of the white race will be targeted; next the yellow race; finally the blacks. The Positive Committee, enriched by representatives of these new populations, will end up with sixty members. What France is to the West, the West will be to the universe: "The human presidency is irrevocably conferred upon the West" (IV, p. 365); but the objective is nevertheless universal: "Westernness constitutes only a final preparation for true humanity" (I, p. 390). Moreover, this universal State will not be without internal subdivisions. Comte believes that the ideal subdivision is the size of a region like Tuscany or else a state like Belgium; consequently, he is opposed to the unification of Italy, for nothing is to be interposed between the region and the universe. He sees the population of the globe ultimately distributed among seventy republics, each consisting of 300,000 families, each family with seven members . . .

The most appropriate means for this universal expansion of the West is once again the education of elites: this has the double advantage of being rapid and gentle. Comte passes harsh judgment on the military and colonial conquests of the past. History shows "the ineffectiveness of incorporations that are not spontaneous" (II, p. 463). This is illustrated, for France, by the examples of Algeria, Corsica, and even Alsace. Military occupation resolves nothing; there have to be "spontaneous convergences toward the normal state of humanity" (IV, p. 502). Thus, in a first phase one must proceed toward "a dignified restitution of Algeria to the Arabs" (IV, p. 419) and contribute to the "necessary decomposition of the colonial system" (IV, p. 519). It is then permissible to hope that the non-Western peoples will not bear a grudge for too long, and will forget these first forced and disastrous contacts, in order to accept with good grace the new relations that are to lead to progressive unification. We may wonder whether Comte is not offering yet another proof of his clairvoyance here: it is in the wake of the dismantling of the colonial system that the Westernization of the world has been proceeding at an accelerated pace.

Although the diversity of human "races" does not pose special problems for the unifying project, Comte offers two different—and incompatible—solutions. The first falls within the great Enlightenment tradition: the differences between the populations of the earth are only differences in pace, lags or advances along a single common path; thus, they tend to disappear. There may be some backward races, but there are no (definitively) inferior races. That is why Comte thinks that the very notion of race is misleading, since it makes a substantive difference out of what is only a temporary delay. "Mere differences in intensity and speed are mistakenly cast as radical diversities, each with its own laws, in such a way as to rebuff any truly general conception, and thus any sound explanation" (II, p. 405). It is incumbent upon whites to participate in the elevation of the other races to their own level.

But Comte proposes a second solution for the same problem, one that allows him to continue to maintain the idea of a universal State. This solution consists in thinking of human races no longer as (in the long run) identical, but as complementary in their differences. Comte posits the existence of three great human faculties, intelligence, action, and feeling, and he declares that each of the three great "races," white, yellow, and black, has uncontested superiority in terms of one of these faculties. Whites are most intelligent, yellows work hardest, blacks are the champions of feeling. Now all three faculties are equally necessary and precious; without being the same, the races are thus "equivalent." Furthermore, supreme happiness implies their concordance: "The total harmony of the Great-Being thus requires the intimate cooperation of its three races, speculative, active, and affective" (II, p. 462). One can imagine the future universal State with its factories in Hong Kong and Tokyo, its universities in Paris and London, and its festivals in the African bush . . .

Auguste Comte claimed that he never reread his manuscripts before sending them to the printer, for fear life would prove too short to allow him to say everything he had to say. One result of that decision is that his books are wordy and inelegant. His arithmetical imagination and his cult of womanhood also sometimes take forms that may amuse—or bore—the modern reader. The core of his doctrine remains powerful, however: not only is his "religion of humanity" a generous one, but his intuitions about world history have turned out to be profound. Nevertheless, his ethical principles, like his historical observations, are disguised and in the last analysis compromised by the scientistic form in which his thinking was presented. Comte believed in an integral determinism that governed the world, in the need to submit ethics and politics to science, and finally in the need to make science a religion. That is why, instead of contenting himself with a penetrating description of the advent of a universal society, or at least the preparation for such a society, he adopts the posture of a movement leader and gives himself over to childish daydreams. His work demonstrates even more amply than Condorcet's or Saint-Simon's that the idea of the universal State flows naturally from the scientistic project. And it takes a truly acrobatic effort to disengage Comte from his positivism, which is another name for scientism.

Montaigne

Custom

Both ethnocentrism and scientism are figures—perverse figures—of the doctrine of universalism. Turning now to the rival doctrine known as *relativism*, we find that any meditation on relativist doctrines in France ought to begin with Montaigne. We can best approach Montaigne's thinking about the universal and the relative by looking at the way he analyzes the notion of custom.

Montaigne has some trouble determining just how far the power of custom extends. Does everything boil down to custom, including the basis of morality, the laws of reason, and the principles of human behavior? Or is there a universal foundation, a human nature that may be hidden by customs but that does not change? One sentence from the essay "Of Custom, and Not Easily Changing an Accepted Law" illustrates these hesitations particularly well. "Whoever wants to get rid of this violent prejudice of custom will find many things accepted with undoubting resolution, which have no support but in the hoary beard and the wrinkles of the usage that goes with them; but when this mask is torn off, and he refers things to truth and reason, he will feel his judgment as it were all upset, and nevertheless restored to a much surer status" (*Essais*, in English *Essays*, I, 23, pp. 84–85). The first part of the sentence describes the way of the world in apparently neutral terms. Many things that seem to us subject to no doubt are merely grounded in habit; these things are simply prejudices, however powerful or hidden, that it behooves us to eradicate. But there is a "but": when we turn to universal values, to truth and reason, we are shaken rather than reassured. Might reason be so profoundly rooted in customary practice that it is no longer capable of detaching itself without running grave risks? In fact, the answer is no, for an opposition arises within the opposition, and the "but" is followed by a "nevertheless":

the ultimate state (the reference to truth alone) will be preferable to the comfortable old habits all the same.

Despite Montaigne's reservations, then, the sentence seems to indicate that he inclines toward the universalist position. However, this is not the lesson that can be drawn from the bulk of his writings, nor from what is presented as his explicit project. Any interpretation of Montaigne's thought encounters the same difficulty: the *Essays* do not develop a homogeneous philosophical system, and for every affirmation tending in a given direction others can be found to contradict it. There are nevertheless some convergences and significant intersections that make it possible to glimpse a hierarchy among the various theses. In the essay "Of Custom" itself, in fact, we encounter a significant gradation. The starting point, expressed in the sentence we have already examined, serves to illustrate the following idea: "For in truth habit is a violent and treacherous schoolmistress. She establishes in us, little by little, stealthily, the foothold of her authority; but having by this mild and humble beginning settled and planted it with the help of time, she soon uncovers to us a furious and tyrannical face against which we no longer have the liberty of even raising our eyes" (p. 77).

Here the return to truth and reason proves to be more problematical than we had imagined. Where can we get a grip that will let us lift off the yoke, if our eyes present us with truths that are really only prejudices? How can we resist if our mind cannot isolate custom as an object of its reflection, since the very rules by which it operates are dictated to it by custom itself? Under these conditions, reason is merely the servant of the violent schoolmistress we have seen: far from being capable of distinguishing between what is custom and what is not, its role is to find plausible justifications for the widest variety of customs; reason disguises "my" culture as nature. "I think that there falls into man's imagination no fantasy so wild that it does not match the example of some public practice, and for which, consequently, our reason does not find a stay and a foundation" (p. 79). "Whence it comes to pass that what is off the hinges of custom, people believe to be off the hinges of reason: God knows how unreasonably, most of the time" (p. 83). We have taken a further step here: the existence of reason independent of custom is now in doubt.

The appearance of the word "unreasonably" gives us pause, however. If it is possible to qualify acts as reasonable and unreasonable, this is because reason still exists, independently of customs. In short, Montaigne continues to use the instrument he has just declared unusable. It seems difficult to imagine that he is not conscious of this; but then how are we to understand his insistence on the nonexistence of reason? We are supposed to take it quite literally, if we can judge by a neighboring passage: "The laws of conscience, which we say are born of nature, are born of custom. Each man, holding in inward veneration the opinions and the behavior approved and accepted around him, cannot break loose from them without remorse, or apply himself to them without self-satisfaction" (ibid.). Natural reason cannot emerge from customary reason, for nature, in this context, does not exist; one cannot emancipate what is not there. Man is entirely governed by habit and self-interest, and he is incapable of rising above his condition.

The argument on which Montaigne relies is the one all empiricists use: the diversity of human experience. But what this argument refutes is an extreme version of the idea of "human nature," the version according to which this "nature" is directly observable and essences coincide with phenomena. Such a theory—which seems to have few supporters—amounts to a simple rejection of sensory data (the diversity of individuals, mores, objects). It is possible to take the diversity of phenomena into account, however, and nevertheless to posit the existence of common rules, of an abstract identity. By continuing to use reason in his own battle against it, Montaigne himself illustrates this possibility, in spite of himself. In order to develop his arguments and make himself understood, he needs to refer to a standard that transcends the spatio-temporal determinations of the speaking subject; that sort of "reason," at least, is shared by Montaigne and his reader.

The same aporias occur in Pascal, whose position is very close to Montaigne's in this respect. We think we get our ideas from natural reason, he declares, whereas in reality they are the product of custom. "Habit provides us with our most effective and most widely accepted proofs; it bends the machine which carries the mind with it without our thinking about it. Who has ever been able to prove that tomorrow will come, and that we shall die? And what could be more generally believed? It is therefore habit which convinces us of the fact" (*Pensées*, p. 100). There are obviously many reasons besides habit that make us believe that the sun will rise tomorrow and that humans are mortal: to be sure, these are received ideas, but it so happens that they are also true. Now according to Pascal we have no other nature beyond the one we get from custom: "But what is nature? Why is habit not natural? I am very much afraid that nature is only a first habit, as habit is a second nature" (p. 166). And yet, if everything is nature (or custom), what does it mean to say that custom is natural?

Returning to Montaigne, we find that, having given up the search for the nature of things on the level of knowledge, he transposes his quest to the level of ethics and judgment. For him no morality or politics can claim allegiance to principles that are more "natural" (or more absolute) than others. The judgments men proffer may be absolutely dissimilar, but this fact does not worry Montaigne in the slightest. In another essay, he writes: "I should be prone to excuse our people for having no other pattern and rule of perfection than their own manners and customs; for it is a common vice, not of the vulgar only but of almost all men, to fix their aim and limit by the ways to which they were born" ("Of Ancient Customs," I, 49, p. 215). Montaigne is thus in this respect a partisan of integral determinism, a determinism that allows human beings no freedom, no choice; here Montaigne's theses and Diderot's, otherwise contradictory, converge. "Everything is culture"; "everything is nature": both writers refuse to leave room for human will, and thus for morality. As a result, no action, situation, or institution can be judged superior to any other. "Nations brought up to liberty and to ruling themselves consider any other form of government monstrous and contrary to nature. Those who are accustomed to monarchy do the same" ("Of Custom," I, 23, p. 83). Montaigne reports the fact without attempting to judge it: his long experience has taught him that any judgment is the expression of habit alone. Consequently, nothing allows him to assert that liberty is a good thing and its absence a bad one; to insist on this would be to display ethnocentrism and to disguise habit as universal reason. All the dangers of relativism are already present here in embryonic form.

This is even more obvious in the case of judgments about beauty. It would be easy to cite a host of examples illustrating the instability of the human ideal. "It is likely that we know little about what beauty is in nature and in general, since to our own human beauty we give so many different forms" ("Apology for Raymond Sebond," II, 12, p. 355). Granted; but is it legitimate to shift from the aesthetic plane to the ethical?

Also in the "Apology," Montaigne launches a direct attack on those who believe in natural law. For Montaigne, natural law does not exist. He seems to base his reasoning on the following syllogism, which he

draws from the skeptical tradition. *Major premise:* "For what nature had
truly ordered for us we would without doubt follow by common consent" (p. 437). *Minor premise:* "There is nothing in which the world is
so varied as in customs and laws" (ibid.). *Conclusion:* Laws are based not
on nature and truth but on tradition and arbitrariness. "The laws of
our country—that is to say, the undulating sea of the opinions of a
people or a prince" (ibid.). Natural law may have existed once upon a
time, but nothing remains of it today: "It is credible that there are
natural laws, as may be seen in other creatures; but in us they are lost"
(p. 438).

Such a deduction may be less rigorous than it appears. At first
Montaigne seems not to want to recognize the two meanings of the
word "law," law as regularity and law as commandment. "Thou shalt
not kill" is obviously not a law in the first sense of the term, since
murders abound; but it could be in the second sense (stemming from
natural law), and could allow an act to be judged at any time, in any
place. In particular, the skeptic's argument according to which if something is not universally present it cannot be true (or just) is unconvinc-
ing. Injustice also exists; what is universal is not the presence of just
acts (or laws), but our very capacity to distinguish justice from injustice.
Once again, the corollary of this refusal is a radical empiricism that
does not recognize the existence of what it does not see. In the same
text Montaigne declares that the proof that religions are arbitrary (and
in this sense not true) is that there are so many of them. But this proof
proves nothing: not only because diverse ritual forms may mask an
identical religious feeling, but also because the multiplicity of religions
does not prove that all religions are equally valid.

Montaigne writes: "If man knew any rectitude and justice that had
body and real existence, he would not tie it down to the condition of
the customs of this country or that. It would not be from the fancy of
the Persians or the Indians that virtue would take its form" (p. 436).
One has the impression that he is trapped by a radicalism that he
himself has helped institute, an approach that locks him into the alternative of all or nothing: since a nation's traditions visibly influence its
laws, the very notion of an abstract and universal justice has to be
rejected! But why would those two factors, natural law and the spirit
of a nation (to use Montesquieu's vocabulary), be mutually exclusive?
Can we not envisage them interacting with each other rather than as
alternatives to each other? No: for Montaigne, since not everything is

"natural," nothing is. In his blind attachment to "custom," not only does Montaigne give up absolute judgments, he also abandons the unity of the human race. "There is more distance from a given man to a given man than from a given man to a given animal" ("Of the Inequality That Is between Us," I, 42, p. 189). It is easy to imagine all the consequences that can be drawn from such a maxim. Do not certain men deserve to be treated worse than animals?

This radical relativism is the basis for Montaigne's two principal politico-ethical options: conservatism in one's own affairs, tolerance toward others. We might have imagined that the absence of any "natural" basis for laws would have inclined Montaigne to accept change easily. But the absence of "natural" legitimacy is compensated for, in Montaigne's view, by a historical justification: any law that already exists is, *ipso facto*, better than any law to come. "To my mind, in public affairs there is no course so bad, provided it is old and stable, that it is not better than change and commotion . . . The worst thing I find in our state is instability, and the fact that our laws cannot, any more than our clothes, take any settled form" ("Of Presumption," II, 17, p. 497). This is because, on the one hand, change implies violence (witness the religious wars in France), whereas its benefits are uncertain; on the other hand, change necessarily goes against the consensus, and thus privileges individual reason at the expense of the community's, an outcome Montaigne considers undesirable (in this he is not modern): "For it seems to me very iniquitous to want to subject public and immutable institutions and observances to the instability of a private fancy (private reason has only a private jurisdiction)" ("Of Custom," I, 23, p. 88).

The other, external face of this conservatism is tolerance with respect to others: since there is no reason to prefer one law or custom to another, there is no reason to scorn them, either. Montaigne even makes it a personal rule to value diversity in everything: "Variety is the most general fashion that nature has followed," and therefore "I do not at all hate opinions contrary to mine" ("Of the Resemblance of Children to Fathers," II, 37, pp. 598, 597). What is true for relations among individuals becomes all the more true for relations among nations. "The diversity in fashions from one nation to another affects me only with the pleasure of variety. Each custom has its reason" ("Of Vanity," III, 9, p. 753): here we find reason still subject to custom. Thus, Montaigne can easily forgo the pleasures of ethnocentrism: "It seems to me that I have encountered hardly any customs that are not as good as ours" (p. 754)—and he does not hesitate to scoff at people who are too parochial to be able to appreciate anything unfamiliar: "Whatever is not as we are is worth nothing" ("Apology," II, 2, p. 358). He even considers travel to be the best form of education: "Wonderful brilliance may be gained for human judgment by getting to know men" ("Of the Education of Children," I, 26, p. 116). "The mind is continually exercised in observing new and unknown things; and I know no better school, as I have often said, for forming one's life than to set before it constantly the diversity of so many other lives, ideas, and customs, and to make it taste such a perpetual variety of forms of our nature" ("Of Vanity," III, 9, p. 744).

Thus, not being constrained by any negative judgment, Montaigne can aspire to a sort of new universalism: not because men are the same everywhere (they are not), but because their very differences are, as it were, in-different: Montaigne sees himself becoming a citizen of the world precisely because of his tolerance for others. "Not because Socrates said it, but because it is really my feeling, and perhaps excessively so, I consider all men as my compatriots, and embrace a Pole as I do a French man, setting this national bond after the universal and common one. I am scarcely infatuated with the sweetness of my native air" (ibid., p. 743). He would even go further in this direction than his illustrious predecessor: "What Socrates did near the end of his life, in considering a sentence of exile against him worse than a sentence of death, I shall never, I think, be so broken or so strictly attached to my own country as to do" (ibid.). Montaigne considers himself indifferent to his own country's values, or any others. But is his impartiality then really meritorious?

He has no choice but to condemn those who do not act as he does (forgetting that any condemnation implies adherence to certain ethical values) and who persist in clinging to the customs and practices of their homelands. "I am ashamed to see my countrymen besotted with that stupid disposition to shy away from ways contrary to their own; they think they are out of their element when they are out of their village. Wherever they go, they stick to their ways and abominate foreign ones. Do they find a compatriot in Hungary, they celebrate this adventure: see them rally round and join forces, and condemn all the barbarous customs that they see. Why not barbarous, since they are not French?" (p. 754). The word "barbarous" must have a purely relative meaning, or so it seems here: since all mores are equally valid, differences must depend on one's vantage point, which may be close or distant; the barbarian is the "Other," since we ourselves are civilized, and the Other does not resemble us. Montaigne says the same thing in a well-known passage in the essay "Of Cannibals": "There is nothing barbarous and savage in that nation, from what I have been told, except that each man calls barbarism whatever is not his own practice; for indeed it seems we have no other test of truth and reason than the example and pattern of the opinions and customs of the country we live in" (I, 31, p. 152). Reason and truth, brought in casually here, seem to provide a basis for cultural relativism, for the absolute reign of custom—and all this to the detriment of custom! In this passage, Montaigne defends rational relativism against ethnocentrism. But must we believe what he says?

The Barbarian

The essay "Of Cannibals" focuses specifically on American Indians, people with very different mores from "ours." The text can be used to illustrate the way Montaigne exercises his tolerance with respect to others, allowing us to verify the extent to which his practice corresponds to his theories.

The portrait Montaigne paints of these men is not a very detailed one (if we set aside, as we must, all the qualities with which he credits them through a simple inversion of our defects). They respect only two things, he says, "valor against the enemy and love for their wives" (I, 31, p. 154). If we take him at his word, we find many examples of these two virtues among the "cannibals," who are admirable for that reason. But then is Montaigne suggesting that there are some universal virtues exempt from radical relativism? "It is astonishing what firmness they show in their combats" (p. 155). In all climates and in all circumstances, is bravery then a virtue? For something must allow Montaigne to pronounce a positive judgment on their value system itself. As for their "properly matrimonial virtue" (p. 158), he has some difficulty establishing it, confronted as he is by the "cannibals'" polygamy; but he covers for this by recalling Biblical and classical examples. Polygamy is not evil, and the proof is that major figures in our tradition have praised it. But is this a way of judging that all values are relative? Or is it not rather a way of judging the quality of the "cannibals'" society with criteria derived from our own?

The same thing holds true for the practice of cannibalism, from which the essay's title is taken. This practice is only the logical outcome of the Indians' warlike spirit, which is itself thus undeniably a quality. Eating one's neighbor is not a meritorious activity, of course, but it has its excuses nonetheless: far from being a proof of bestiality, it belongs to the Indians' ritual practices. Furthermore, "Chrysippus and Zeno, heads of the Stoic sect, thought there was nothing wrong in using our carcasses for any purpose in case of need, and getting nourishment from them" (p. 155). Again we find our own wise men being drawn in to justify the Indians' practices. If the great Stoics had not found excuses for it, would cannibalism remain excusable nevertheless?

Montaigne's entire essay in fact sings the praises of cannibalism and condemns our own society: if there are savages somewhere, he implies, they may not be where we expect to find them. If push comes to shove, one can excuse cannibalism, but not "treachery, disloyalty, tyranny, and cruelty, which are our ordinary vices" (p. 156). And Montaigne concludes: "I think there is more barbarity in eating a man alive than in eating him dead; and in tearing by tortures and the rack a body still full of feeling, in roasting a man bit by bit, in having him bitten and mangled by dogs and swine (as we have not only read but seen within fresh memory)" (p. 155).

Montaigne indeed does not bother to hide the fact that he is using a single schema both to grasp humanity's overall evolution and to appreciate its various stages. But then perhaps barbarians have an existence other than the one allowed them by their neighbors' prejudiced vision? Looking more closely, we see that such is in fact the case. Montaigne uses the word "barbarian" in a nonrelative sense—and even in two different senses, each one absolute, but bearing contradictory connotations.

The first sense of the term is historical and positive: a barbarian is someone who is close to the origins of mankind. Now the origins are better than what has come after. "These nations, then, seem to me barbarous in this sense, that they have been fashioned very little by the human mind, and are still very close to their original naturalness. The laws of nature still rule them, very little corrupted by ours" (p. 153). The second sense is ethical and negative: a barbarian is someone who is degraded and cruel; that is why we can call our society more barbarian than another. "So we may well call these people barbarians, in respect to the rules of reason, but not in respect to ourselves, who surpass them in every kind of barbarity" (p. 156). Montaigne sometimes plays on these two meanings, historical and ethical, positive and negative, within a single sentence, as for example with the word "wild" *(sauvage):* "These people are wild, just as we call wild the fruits that Nature has produced by herself and in her normal course [first meaning]; whereas really it is those that we have changed artificially and led astray from the common order, that we should rather call wild [second meaning]" (p. 152).

In the judgment Montaigne passes on the "cannibals'" poetry, he uses the world "barbarous" again in this second, ethical and negative sense. "Now I am familiar enough with poetry," he writes, abandoning his customary modesty, "to be a judge of this: not only is there nothing barbarous in this fancy, but it is altogether Anacreontic. Their language, moreover, is a soft language, with an agreeable sound, somewhat like Greek in its endings" (p. 158). Their poetry is not barbarous because it resembles Greek poetry, and the same is true of their language: the criterion of barbarity is no longer the slightest bit relative, but it is not universal either: it is in fact simply ethnocentric. At the very beginning of his essay on cannibals, Montaigne declared that where opinions are concerned, "we should . . . judge things by reason's way, not by popular say" (p. 150), but he has not followed his own precept. If this popular poetry had not been fortunate enough to resemble the Anacreontic style, it would have been . . . barbarous.

Confronted with the Other, Montaigne is unquestionably moved by a generous impulse. He is admiring rather than contemptuous, and he never tires of criticizing his own society. But does the Other get a fair deal in this maneuver? That seems rather dubious. Montaigne's judgment of positive value is based on a misunderstanding, the projection onto the Other of an image of the self—or, more precisely, of an ideal of the self, embodied for Montaigne by classical civilization. The Other is in fact never perceived or known. What Montaigne praises are not "cannibals" but his own values. As he himself says on another occasion, "I do not speak the minds of others except to speak my own mind better" ("Of the Education of Children," I, 26, p. 108). Now for praise to be worth something, the person to whom it is addressed first has to be recognized in and for himself. If Montaigne were to discover tomorrow that the "cannibals" did not resemble the Greeks, he would

logically have to condemn them. He wants to be a relativist; no doubt
he believes he is a relativist. In reality he has never stopped being a
universalist.

He is a universalist, but an unwitting one; this lack of awareness is
crucial. The conscious universalist has to make explicit the criteria for
judgment that he believes to be universal, and has to try to justify them.
He cannot allow himself simply to declare that his own values are
universal: he must at least try to stave off the objection that this is what
he has done. It is different for the unconscious universalist: his attention
is directed toward the defense of relativist principles, and thus there is
every reason to fear that his own prejudices, habits, and practices
occupy the unclaimed place of a universal ethics. Bravery in warfare
and polygamy, cannibalism, or poetry will be excused or offered as
examples, not in terms of the ethics of the Other but simply because
these features are found among the Greeks, who embody Montaigne's
personal ideal.

The relativist does not pass any judgments on others. The conscious
universalist may condemn others, but he does so in the name of an
openly assumed morality, which may therefore be called into question.
The unconscious universalist is unassailable, since he claims to be a
relativist; however, this does not prevent him from passing judgments
on others and imposing his own ideal on them. He has the aggressive-
ness of the latter and the clear conscience of the former: he is an
assimilator in all innocence, because he has not noticed that the others
are different.

The position of generalized tolerance is untenable, and Montaigne's
text offers good illustrations of its pitfalls. First, it is an internally
contradictory position, since it consists in simultaneously declaring that
all attitudes are equivalent and preferring one of them, tolerance itself,
to all the others. No sooner has he stated that every practice has its
reason than Montaigne condemns a particular practice, that of shutting
oneself off among compatriots while abroad and denigrating the natives; but even to formulate this reproach Montaigne is obliged to judge
practices according to a measure taken from a different realm. Next
(and this is more specific to Montaigne), such a position is incompatible
with his other convictions, and in particular with the myth of the noble
savage—a myth of which he is one of the purveyors, as we shall
see—and with the ideal of antiquity that he holds dear. If the savage is
good (not only in his or her own eyes but also in ours), it is because

goodness is a transcultural quality; one cannot be a primitivist and a relativist at the same time. Barbarity thus ceases to be a pure optical illusion: speaking of the same "cannibals" that gave him the pretext for his relativist definition of the term, Montaigne now declares that we surpass them in barbarity; but anyone who says "surpass" is comparing and judging.

Moreover, if Montaigne has never perceived others, what is his tolerance worth? Am I still tolerant if I do not even recognize the Other's existence and if I am satisfied to offer her an image of my own ideal, for which she has no use? Perhaps what we took for tolerance was only indifference. Is it really necessary to travel? "Change of air and climate has no effect on me; all skies are alike to me" ("Of Vanity," III, 9, p. 744), wrote Montaigne in these same pages; and also: "I feel death continually clutching me by the throat or the loins. But I am made differently: death is the same to me anywhere" (ibid., p. 747). This is no longer an acceptance of different values, but an indifference to values, a refusal to enter their world: the others do not bother me because they do not count.

Deducing the Universal

Rousseau often agrees with Montaigne. But on the particular question of the omnipresence of customs (and thus of the total absence of any human "nature"), he distances himself explicitly. Rousseau reproaches Montaigne, in short, for the lack of rigor with which Montaigne arrives at his conclusions: he has only to find a single exception to declare that nature, or law, or essence, does not exist, instead of interrogating himself, on the one hand, about the particular circumstances responsible for this exception, and, on the other hand, about the structural reasons that make a given situation or behavior seem more "natural" than others. Montaigne's generalizations are simple inductions, or rather accumulations of examples; hence their fragility. Rousseau thus classifies his predecessor among the "allegedly wise": "They dare to reject this evident and universal accord of all nations. And in the face of this striking uniformity in men's judgment, they go and look in the shadows for some obscure example known to them alone—as if all the inclinations of nature were annihilated by the depravity of a single people, and the species were no longer anything as soon as there are monsters. But what is the use of the torments to which the skeptic

Montaigne subjects himself in order to unearth in some corner of the
world a custom opposed to the notions of justice?" (*Emile*, IV, p. 289).

The underlying debate here involves the status of the particular fact
in scientific knowledge, a debate to which Rousseau demonstrated his
sensitivity as early as the period during which he wrote his "Discours
sur les sciences et les arts" ("Discourse on the Sciences and the Arts").
"When such very general objects as the morals and the manners of a
people are at issue, one has to be careful not always to focus too
narrowly on particular examples," he writes in his reply to the commentaries of King Stanislas. "To examine all this narrowly and in some
few individual cases is not to Philosophize, it is to waste one's time and
reflections; for one can know Peter or James thoroughly, and yet have
made very little progress in the knowledge of men" (p. 48). And he
adds, in a commentary on the "Discourse on the Origin of Inequality"
("Lettre à Philopolis" [Letter to Philopolis]): "Man, you say, is such as
the place he was to occupy in the universe required. But men differ so
much according to times and places that with this kind of logic, infer-
ences from the particular to the Universal are liable to lead to rather
contradictory and inconclusive conclusions. A single error in Geography is enough to overturn the whole of this supposed doctrine which
deduces what ought to be from what is seen [to be] . . . When it comes
to thinking about human nature, the true Philosopher is neither an
Indian nor a Tartar, neither from Geneva nor from Paris, but is a man"
(p. 235).

Human nature exists, but it is not accessible to induction, and there
is no reason to be astonished by the meager results Montaigne achieved
using this method. It is not by adding up particular bits of knowledge
that one arrives at general truths; it is by formulating hypotheses about
the structure of each phenomenon. Human nature is not given objectively but must be deduced by reason. This is how Rousseau himself
proceeds in the bulk of his philosophical and political writings, and it
is what ensures the interest of his work even today. This is the source
of the celebrated formula, a paradoxical but perfectly justified one
found in the preamble of the "Discourse on the Origin of Inequality":
"Let us therefore begin by setting aside all the facts" (p. 139). This
does not mean, of course, that one must remain ignorant of the facts:
Rousseau is actually more of a "realist" than any of his contemporaries.

Armed with a superior method of inquiry, Rousseau arrives at a
conclusion opposite to the one reached by Montaigne and Pascal.

"Nature, we are told, is only habit. What does that mean? Are there not habits contracted only by force which never do stifle nature?" (*Emile*, I, p. 39). The example Rousseau cites is that of plants whose branches are forced to grow horizontally. It is not because the phenomenon is attested that this manner of growing is as natural as the other! If I believe that plants grow naturally upward, this has nothing to do with the observation of horizontal and vertical branches. Nature is not simply a first custom.

We have watched Montaigne pass without transition from problems of knowledge to problems of morality; Rousseau follows him along the same path, but in order to contradict him once again. This time their divergence lies not in their methods but in the very basis of their doctrines. Unlike Montaigne, Rousseau believes that "moral principles do not depend on the customs of a people" (*Julie, ou La Nouvelle Héloïse*, in English *Eloisa*, letter 81, p. 304), that "the eternal laws of nature and order do exist" (*Emile*, V, p. 473). The argument Rousseau uses to justify this credo is of the introspective sort: by consulting one's own inner self, by undertaking a scrupulous self-examination, each person can observe, as Rousseau has, that he or she is capable of distinguishing between self-interest and justice, between habit and reason; consequently, natural morality exists. "There is in the depths of souls, then, an innate principle of justice and virtue according to which, in spite of our own maxims, we judge our actions and those of others as good or bad" (*Emile*, IV, p. 289). Such are the arguments that allow Rousseau to refute relativism.

Evolution of Relativism

Helvétius

Despite Rousseau's arguments, relativism is not dead; far from it. Another eighteenth-century figure, Claude-Adrien Helvétius, divides the moralist philosophers (who study the nature of good and evil) into two main camps. Those in the first camp, headed by Plato, maintain that "virtue is always one and the same"; those in the second camp, headed by Montaigne, assert on the contrary that "every nation forms a different idea of it" (*Essays*, II, 13, p. 66). Both groups are wrong, and Helvétius presents himself as occupying a third, intermediary position. But he criticizes the two armies of philosophers in very different terms.

The first group is immersed in pure illusion; its members mistake their dreams for realities. The second group, on the contrary, holds the correct view, and Helvétius believes, as its members do, that each century and country constructs a different view of good and evil for itself. He also recalls Pascal's formula according to which "nature . . . is nothing but our first habit" (II, 24, p. 117). The only place these philosophers go wrong, in the end, is that they are unable to account for the facts they have correctly observed, and they see capriciousness where there is actually a rigorous logic at work. What Helvétius presents is thus not, in fact, an intermediate position between universalism and relativism, but a relativism based on reason, as opposed to Montaigne's, which would imply that judgments are simply arbitrary.

Helvétius describes himself as a disciple of Locke, for whom nothing exists beyond matter and the sensations we may experience in contact with matter. Consequently, he is loath to use fictions such as God, but he also resists abstractions such as humanity: according to him, we never encounter anything but particular human beings. At the very core of each being there exist only physical sensations of pleasure and displeasure, on the basis of which we extrapolate the ideas of good and evil. The basis for the morality Helvétius presents in his *Essays on the Mind and Its Several Faculties* is that there is no difference between what is pleasurable and what is good, between what pleases me and what I consider just, for the second term of this relation is merely a construction of the mind, destined to conceal the presence of the first term. Human beings can never transcend themselves, cannot rise above their own self-interest, for the simple reason that in a rigorously materialist perspective transcendence does not exist. This is true for individuals as well as for groups. "Every individual judges of things and persons, by the agreeable or disagreeable impressions he receives from them; and the public is no more than an assemblage of all the individuals; therefore it cannot fail of making its interest the rule of its decisions" (II, 1, p. 24).

Thus, Helvétius subscribes to a utilitarian philosophy: the last word on human behavior is self-interest, understood in the sense of "whatever may procure us pleasure or exempt us from pain" (II, 1, p. 24, note b). And he accumulates examples of actions we declare to be upright and meritorious simply because they have satisfied our self-interest. The only difference in this respect is a difference of extension: we may be dealing with individuals, with small groups ("societies"), or with entire nations. Now from one individual to another, one group to another, one society to another, self-interest does not remain the same, nor, consequently, do judgments as to what is good and bad. It is thus the difference in self-interest that establishes and explains relativism.

How, in practice, do we judge others? Naturally, we always have the highest esteem for ourselves: every individual person is spontaneously egocentric, and every people—as we have seen—is ethnocentric. Our judgments about others, which are embellished with the colors of objectivity or impartiality, in reality only describe the distance that separates us from them: the closer they are to us, the more highly we esteem them. "It is then certain, that every person has necessarily the highest idea of himself; and that he consequently never esteems in another any thing but his own image and resemblance" (II, 4, p. 37). On the contrary, what we judge ridiculous in others is only what is foreign to us: "Understanding is . . . a string that vibrates only with the union" (II, 4, p. 34).

It follows that we cannot but deceive ourselves if we try to judge a society by means of criteria other than its own: what would be crimes in our eyes may actually be actions that contribute to the public good. On the other hand, it is possible to pass judgment on the value of a custom or an action in context. We shall then ask whether its usefulness is indeed real or only apparent, for there are customs that are maintained only by the force of prejudice or habit, and those customs deserve to be condemned. No law can be said to be good apart from of its context; the same law will be good in one place, bad in another, useful today and harmful tomorrow.

Thus, the real difference lies not between the relative and the absolute (since everything is relative), but in the dimension of the entities to which our judgment applies. Individual or private interest is opposed here to public interest, that is, the self-interest of the country we inhabit. This is the meaning that the terms "justice" and "virtue" take on for Helvétius. "A Man is just, when all his actions tend to the public welfare" (II, 6, p. 39). "By the word Virtue can only be understood, a desire of the general happiness" (II, 13, p. 67). In practice, as all individuals risk being in disagreement, public interest is that of the majority, "the greatest number of men, subject to the same form of government" (II, 17, p. 88). What is called selfishness or blindness in the individual becomes virtue, uprightness, and justice as soon as the whole country is involved.

At once all contradictions, and even all separations between justice
and power, disappear; it is not possible for justice to be on one side and
power on the other, since justice is only the interest of the majority,
which is, by definition, what is most powerful within a society. "If force
essentially resides in the greater number, and justice consists in the
practice of actions useful to the greater number, it is evident that justice
is in its own nature always armed with a power sufficient to suppress
vice, and place man under the necessity of being virtuous" (II, 24,
p. 116). And since there can be no transcendence, what ought to be
cannot be distinct from what is: "The person of discernment knows
that men are what they were designed to be" (II, 10, p. 58). The role
of the moralist, from this point on, is not to formulate an illusory ideal,
but to seek to put private interests, which govern and will always govern
individual behavior, at the service of the general interest. In this the
moralist's role converges with that of the politician, and more especially
the legislator: Helvétius does in fact believe in the effectiveness of laws
for the transformation of a society. Moreover, that is why he believes
the inequalities among peoples come not from nature but only from
differences among political constitutions: "Contempt for a whole nation is always unjust . . . the superiority of one country over another
depends on the greater or lesser happiness of their forms of government" (II, 22, p. 109).

There is something frightening about this social project, in which
truth and justice invariably emerge from the mouths of the majority,
and in which crime ceases to be crime if it turns out to be useful to the
State. But we can be reassured, for the portrait Helvétius draws of man
does not correspond to reality. It is not true that I cannot distinguish
between what is useful and what is good, between what I consider
profitable to myself and what I consider just; men and women of all
times have made that distinction, even if they have not hesitated to
represent the defense of their own interests as an attachment to the
common good. Helvétius anticipates this objection, but his way of
defending himself against it is such that it deprives his theses of their
empirical value. If someone offers the counterexample of individuals
who do not act in the name of their personal interest, or who do not
judge others in terms of themselves, he has a ready answer: they are
then acting against their deepest convictions, in order to conform to
public opinion (cf. II, 4, pp. 35–36). But we can see that the argument
is circular: Helvétius detects the insincerity because he knows in ad-

vance that no one *can* think otherwise than his hypothesis dictates. Under these conditions, it is hard to see what sort of fact could ever falsify his assertion: the exceptions are disqualified in advance as lies.

Beyond the moral judgments and the empirical verifications to which Helvétius' doctrine might be subject, we have to ask whether it conforms in its own right, as a particular act, to the general explanatory theory it contains. What interest did Helvétius have in writing this book? In his preface, he declares that he is purely a servant of the public welfare, and he agrees to consider his own theses false if they turn out to be harmful (thus, he constructs an entirely pragmatic conception of truth): "If, contrary to my expectation, some of my principles are not conformable to the general interest, this proceeds from an error of my judgment" (p. iii). But it is not certain that the book itself obeys these requirements of pure relativism. Sometimes, indeed, it is reason that seems to make an exception—but reason brings truth in its own wake ("to ascertain this truth, it must be supported by proofs drawn from just reasoning," II, 3, p. 53); "what our persons of distinction in foreign countries call the usage of the world is as different from the true custom of the world, which is always founded on reason, as civility is from true politeness" (I, 9, p. 55). Sometimes the mind itself is subdivided into two types: one is the mind that depends on changes taking place in the world; "the other, whose utility is eternal, unalterable, independent of the various manners and governments, confined to the very nature of man" (II, 19, p. 97), is illustrated by philosophers like Locke or—why not?—Helvétius himself. This mind occupies itself not with Frenchmen or Englishmen but with "man in general" (ibid.).

Helvétius in fact divides humanity into two unequal parts. The vast majority of the population is concerned only with its own private interests, and it judges all things in terms of their perceived usefulness. The remainder of humanity, consisting of just a few individuals, brings together the friends of truth, who aspire only to virtue and justice (cf. II, 2, pp. 26–27, and II, 3, pp. 28–29). Helvétius counts himself among the latter: his own theory, escaping from general relativism, is universally true; otherwise it would be of little interest. "A philosopher who, in his writings, is always supposed to be speaking to the universe, ought to give virtue a foundation on which all nations may equally build, and consequently erect it on the basis of personal interest" (II, 24, pp. 117–118), that is, on the basis of a universal fact. The relativist is thus inevitably led to support an elitist vision of humanity, since everything is relative except his own theory (and possibly that of his predecessors). Owing to his evaluative vocabulary, in fact, Helvétius' entire book is run through with value judgments that have no meaning unless they are absolute—so true is it that a consistent relativist would soon find himself condemned to silence.

We can nevertheless discover within Helvétius' text itself a solution to the aporia in which he is most often confined. The solution consists in adopting Montesquieu's position and, without relinquishing absolute judgments, nevertheless obliging oneself to consider each action and each custom in context. Taking historical and geographical correlations into account does *not* in fact require us to abandon the idea of universal justice and morality. One has to consider, Helvétius writes, "the different vices of nations as necessarily resulting from the different form of their government" (II, 15, p. 78). Vices do not cease to be vices in passing from one country to another, to be sure, but it is also true that they cannot be understood apart from the configurations to which they belong. Such an approach has a two-fold advantage: first, it does not entail giving up all transcultural judgments, and, second, it allows us to see societies as composed of interdependent elements, and not as simple collections of curiosities. Vices, like virtues, are caught up in a complex system of causes, motives, and effects, in which everything affects everything else. However, unlike Montesquieu, Helvétius believes that mores can be transformed fairly readily, given good laws; his inclinations are reformist rather than conservative.

Renan

Montaigne was a relativist owing to his spirit of tolerance: those who believe in absolute truth are severe toward others; to an unprejudiced mind, there are no certainties. Helvétius was a relativist owing to his empiricism: there exists nothing beyond the senses; good and evil are merely extrapolations on the basis of individual sensations of pleasure and pain. A century later, Renan is a relativist because of his historical sense: since his scientific studies have taught him that human judgments vary in time and space (in other words, depend on the context), he decides to make do with that state of affairs. Science, which deals with the true and the false, has no room for the category of the relative; on the other hand, judgments that emanate from the ethical and aesthetic domains have no room for the absolute.

Renan's starting point is very close to that of Enlightenment philosophy. Like Helvétius, he is inclined to present his position as the rejection of two contrary—and equally unsatisfactory—viewpoints. "The great majority of people are divided . . . into two categories, at equal distance from which the truth seems to lie. 'What you seek has been found long ago,' say the orthodox believers of all sects; 'What you seek cannot be found,' say the practical positivists (the only dangerous ones), the political railers, and the atheists" (*Dialogues et fragments philosophiques*, in English *Philosophical Dialogues and Fragments*, p. xxvii). Orthodox believers are thus contrasted with positivists, dogmatists with skeptics. "Dogmatism which thinks it has the everlasting formula of truth, skepticism which denies the truth" are two equally deceptive guides ("L'Avenir religieux des sociétés modernes," in English "The Future of Religion in Modern Society," p. 391). Renan's criticisms of the dogmatists could have been formulated by Voltaire: in the name of truth, Christianity indulged in the severest persecutions of all dissidents. Renan also rebukes "atheists" in terms a deist would use: one cannot live without ideals.

Renan thus chooses to contest these two extremes, while transcending their antinomy; the question is how he manages this. "We reject in the same way frivolous skepticism and scholastic dogmatism; we are dogmatic critics. We believe in truth, although we do not claim to possess absolute truth," he writes in *L'Avenir de la science* (*The Future of Science*, pp. 417–418). But what does this critical philosophy consist of, and what does nonabsolute truth look like? In reply, Renan offers us the following image: "Without looking for absolute perfection, which closely embraced would be nothingness, we may believe that an immense career is open to reason and to liberty" ("The Future of Religion," p. 392).

But he cannot content himself with this evocation of a truth that is always approximate; he seeks greater precision, and this desire leads him to a new key word, *relative*, understood in the sense of "historical" or "cultural." The truths that science succeeds in establishing are always *relative* to a particular situation (which does not make them any less *absolute*). "The great progress of modern thought has been the substitution . . . of the category of the relative for the conception of the absolute," Renan writes in *The Future of Science* (p. 169); and in his inaugural lesson at the Collège de France, he says: "In everything we shall seek after . . . the relative in place of the absolute. There is the future, as I anticipate it, if the future is to belong to progress" ("De la part des peuples sémitiques dans l'histoire de la civilisation," in English "The Share of the Semitic People in the History of Civilization," p. 165). He has thus adopted as his own the formula of the young Auguste Comte (although Comte meant something different by it): "Everything is relative, that is the only absolute principle" (cf. *Système de politique positive*, IV, "Appendice général" [General appendix], p. 11). By the same token, his statements of principle notwithstanding, we can no longer see any significant difference between Renan's relativism and skepticism, or positivism, from which he sought to distance himself.

We can see an example of this slippage from "criticism" to "relativism" in Renan's justifications of the literary genre he has chosen to expose his philosophical concepts: dialogue, and even drama. "The form of dialogue seemed to me convenient for my purpose, as it is free from dogmatism, and as it admits of the different aspects of a problem being successively presented without one being obliged to arrive at conclusions," he writes in the preface to his *Philosophical Dialogues* (p. xxiii); and in the preface to his *Drames philosophiques* (Philosophical Dramas) he writes: "The form of dialogue is, given the current state of the human spirit, the only one that, in my view, is potentially suited for the exposition of philosophical ideas. Truths of that order must not be directly denied nor directly affirmed; they cannot be the object of demonstrations. What one can do is present them by their various facets, showing their strengths, their weaknesses, their necessity, their equivalences" (III, p. 371).

Dialogue is certainly not dogmatic—unless it is a camouflaged monologue, as are certain of Plato's dialogues. But what Renan is evoking resembles conversation rather than dialogue. It is in conversation, after all, that we are content to listen to the opinions of our interlocutors, while waiting to be able to pronounce our own, without worrying about bringing together the various viewpoints: we hear a series of assertions, and no conclusion is possible; nothing is denied, nothing affirmed, everything is *presented;* the positions are cited, as it were, without any need for the interlocutors to adhere to one or another of them and to argue in favor of that adherence. Dialogue, on the other hand, is animated by the idea of a possible progression in the discussion; it does not consist in the juxtaposition of several voices, but in their interaction. (And the project of my own book is to present dialogues, not conversations.) Now Renan himself says that his work leads to juxtaposition, and to impartiality: "Formerly every one had his own system; he lived by it and died for it; now we in succession traverse all the systems, or, what is better still, we have taken them all in at once" (*Philosophical Dialogues*, p. xxv). "Philosophy, at the point of refinement it has attained, manages excellently with a mode of exposition in which nothing is affirmed, in which everything is induced, merges, enters into contradiction, is nuanced" (*Drames*, p. 552). Our refinement consists, then, in being indifferent to all systems, in seeing the justifications of every viewpoint, and thus in adopting none of them.

During his first trip to Greece, in 1865, Renan discovered what he believed to be the incarnation of beauty as well as truth. Wandering on the Acropolis one day, he formulated a prayer, or rather a profession of faith, in which he said among other things: "A philosophy, perverse no doubt in its teachings, has led me to believe that good and evil, pleasure and pain, the beautiful and the ungainly, reason and folly, fade into one another by shades as impalpable as those in a dove's neck. To feel neither absolute love nor absolute hate becomes therefore wisdom. If any one society, philosophy, or religion, had possessed absolute truth, this society, philosophy, or religion, would have vanquished all the others and would be the only one now extant. All those who have hitherto believed themselves to be right were in error, as we see very clearly. Can we without utter presumption believe that the future will not judge us as we have judged the past?" (*Souvenirs d'enfance et de jeunesse*, in English *Recollections of My Youth*, p. 59). The most consistent relativism is Renan's wisdom; history shows that absolute truth and perfect justice have never existed; *therefore* (and it is this transition that carries the weight of the assertion here), good and evil, reason and madness are no longer anything but relative categories. Which leads him to serene contemplation of the world as he finds it: "To tell the truth, in my present state of mind, I am hostile to nothing and to no one" (*Souvenirs*, p. 877).

The scholarly life has thus convinced Renan that science alone deals with truth, and therefore with the absolute; as for values, they are necessarily relative. "Is the word morality applicable to the form which the idea assumed in the ancient Arab, Hebrew and Chinese civilizations, which it still assumes among savage peoples, etc.?" (*The Future of Science*, p. 164). Certainly not, and Renan does not fail to remind us: "Morality itself has always been understood by this race [the Semites] very differently from the way we have imagined" ("Le Désert et le

Soudan" [The Desert and the Sudan], p. 542). But he would not want anyone to confuse his relativism with that of earlier writers: "I am not making one of those common-place objections here, which have been so often repeated since the days of Montaigne and Bayle, and which attempted to prove by means of a few divergences or a few ambiguous terms that in certain peoples the moral sense was entirely absent" (*The Future of Science*, p. 164). The difference is that Renan does not deny the existence of a moral sense—such a sense is indeed the distinctive feature of humanity. He "contents" himself with observing, in a positive and scientific way, that the various moralities have no common essence; and he is not about to try to find one.

Renan also distinguishes himself from Montaigne by the consequence he draws, for his own conduct, from this observation. "In the same way I conceive that in the future the word morality will not be the proper word and that it will be replaced by another. As far as my personal use goes, I prefer to substitute the word aestheticism for it. Face to face with a given action, I ask myself whether it is ugly or beautiful rather than whether it be good or bad" (ibid.). "'Endeavor to be beautiful, and then do at every moment that with which your heart will inspire you;' that is morality in a nutshell. All the other rules in their absolute form are faulty and mendacious" (pp. 166–167). In a spirit very close to that of Baudelaire, who was attempting to subordinate ethics to aesthetics during the same period, Renan seeks to replace the requirement of the good with the requirement of the beautiful. Can we grant that it is only a matter of changing a name? Not very well, unless the meaning has been modified at the outset: there is such a thing as a beauty of evil, and one may have to choose between the elegance of a gesture and its virtue. Renan is not really unaware of this; however, he prefers the "morality" of the artist to that of the virtuous being. "The transcendent immorality of the artist is in its own way a supreme morality." And as far as he himself is concerned, he has decided to govern his life by that principle: "For my own part, I can declare that when I do right, . . . I accomplish an act as independent and as spontaneous as that of the artist who derives from his inner sense the beauty of which he gives an external realization . . . The virtuous man is as an artist who realizes the beautiful in human life as the sculptor does in marble, or the musician in sound" (*The Future of Science*, p. 333). This is his own personal destiny at present; in the future, Renan is convinced, it will be everyone's.

The artist has become the model for the virtuous man. But is the idea of beauty in turn absolute or relative? Renan, a historian, knows the answer better than anyone: "The beauty of a work should never be considered from an abstract point and independently of the surroundings that gave it birth" (p. 176). The masterworks of the past inspire admiration only if the contributions of history have trained us to see them: otherwise misunderstanding prevails. Aesthetic judgment is not simply "historical," moreover, in this sense of the word; it is also individual, since the artist draws beauty from "his inner sense." But does not what is justifiable for aesthetics—a historical or even an individual relativism—lead to the absurd in the field of ethics? Such is nevertheless the analogy on which Renan relies. Barrès will be grateful to him for it: it is Renan, Barrès will one day declare, "who has done so much to give our nation the sense of the relative" (*Scènes et doctrines du nationalisme* [Scenes and Doctrines of Nationalism], 1, p. 84).

Relativism and Politics

Let us look for a moment at the flowering of relativism in the work of two late nineteenth-century epigones, Gustave Le Bon and Maurice Barrès. The basis of Le Bon's relativism is first of all cognitive. Members of different cultures do not inhabit the same worlds; they have nothing in common. Le Bon can observe only "the depth of the gulf that separates the thought of the various peoples" (p. 36), and he posits the following axiom: "Different races cannot feel, think, or act in the same manner, and . . . in consequence, they cannot comprehend one another" (*Les Lois psychologiques de l'évolution des peuples*, in English *The Psychology of Peoples*, p. 35). Thus, just like Montaigne in his worst moments, Le Bon pushes the relativism of values to the point of establishing a discontinuity among the subspecies of humanity.

This cognitive relativism serves as the basis for a moral relativism. In fact, for Le Bon, morality is nothing but custom. "By morality we mean hereditary respect for the rules on which the existence of a society is based. To possess morality means, for a people, to have certain fixed rules of conduct and not to depart from them. As these rules vary with time and place, morality appears in consequence to be a very variable matter, and it is so in fact" (pp. 31–32).

The relativity of values in turn leads to a politics cut off from any reference to transcultural ideals. "All that can be asked of a government is that it shall be the expression of the sentiments and ideas of the people it is called on to govern . . . There are no governments or constitutions of which it can be said that they are absolutely good or absolutely bad. The government of the King of Dahomey was probably an excellent government for the people he was called on to rule over, and the most ingenious European constitution would have been inferior for his people" (p. 136). That is why Le Bon is strongly opposed to France's colonial politics, based on the idea of the underlying sameness of peoples and thus leading to *assimilation:* this is the idea that "landed all the French colonies in a state of lamentable decadence" (p. xvi). One of his disciples, Léopold de Saussure, wrote an entire work, *Psychologie de la colonisation française* (Psychology of French Colonization), not in favor of decolonization, of course, but in favor of a different colonial politics, one that would be respectful of differences and would lead to a state of *association* (we shall come back to this). Le Bon's reasons for refusing this unity of ideals are still "scientific": "It would be as futile to wish to persuade fish to live in the air, under the pretext that aerial respiration is practised by all the superior animals" (p. 136). But can human "races" really be viewed in the same light as animal species?

The judgment Le Bon brings to bear on the relativity of values is ambiguous. On the one hand, he can only rejoice in what strikes him as a triumph of science, and he admires "a just reflection of a modern writer . . . that 'the sense of the relative dominates contemporary thought'" (p. 216) or the declaration of a Minister of Public Instruction that "'the substitution of relative ideas for abstract notions . . . is the greatest conquest of science'" (pp. 216–217). But on the other hand, a civilization that no longer believes that its own values are absolute (a civilization that has broken with ethnocentrism—the only form of universalism conceivable for Le Bon) is a weakened civilization. "The real danger to modern societies lies precisely in the fact that men have lost confidence in the worth of the principles that serve as their foundations" (p. 217). This leads Le Bon to recognize one strong point in a political doctrine which he otherwise treats with the greatest contempt—namely, socialism. "If the future seems to belong to those socialist doctrines which reason condemns, it is because they are the only doctrines whose upholders speak in the name of truths they declare to be absolute" (p. 217). The drama of relativism is that it represents both a higher degree of civilization, the one to which the flourishing of reason gives us access, and a lower degree, to the extent that such a form of civilization is weaker than those forms that believe in absolutes. Strength itself engenders weakness.

Relativism, finally, provides Le Bon with the basis for his rejection of the egalitarian ideal. Classes, sexes, races are all different; what is the use of imposing a common goal on them, as the socialists would do? "The idea of equality, far from being on the decline, continues to make headway. It is in the name of this idea that socialism, which seems destined to enslave before long the majority of Western peoples, pretends to ensure their welfare. It is in its name that the modern woman, forgetting the deep-lying mental differences that separate her from man, claims the same rights and the same education as man, and will end, if she be triumphant, in making of the European a nomad without a home or a family" (p. xvi).

For Maurice Barrès, finally, no question can be answered in the absolute. "The assertion that a thing is good and true always needs to be backed up by an answer to the following question: With respect to what is that thing good or true? (*Scènes*, I, p. 64). Any consistent nationalist will answer that question, obviously, by saying: "with respect to my country." "Nationalism requires us to judge everything with respect to France" (II, p. 177). Truth, justice, reason do not exist apart from nations. "The entire set of these right and true relations among given objects and a specific individual, the Frenchman, constitutes French truth and justice; finding these relations constitutes French reason" (I, p. 13). To each nation its own truth. "German truth and English truth have nothing to do with French truth, and they can poison us" (I, p. 96). To each nation its own conception of justice. "The relativist attempts to distinguish the conceptions [of justice] proper to each human type" (I, p. 68). This is at once an ethical and a scientific requirement. "Society would not be intelligible if universal relativism were not recognized. We who understand the role of laws in a country expect tribunals not of *absolute truth* but of *judicial truth*" (I, p. 38). Everything then is relative—except relativism itself, which is "universal"!

Barrès makes the most of the relativist reference in his commentaries on the Dreyfus affair. "Never has the necessity of relativism been more strongly felt than in this Dreyfus affair, which is at bottom an orgy of metaphysicians" (I, p. 84). In other words, the affair cannot be judged in the name of an abstract justice; it can be judged only in terms of the interests of France. If Dreyfus is proved guilty, the French army will be the stronger for it: that is good for France. If on the contrary Dreyfus is shown to be innocent, that discredits the army and harms the nation. Conclusion: whatever the "absolute" truth of the matter, *French* justice requires that Dreyfus be condemned. Even if Dreyfus is innocent, the Dreyfusards are necessarily guilty. "Their plot divides and disarms France, and this delights them. Even if their client were innocent, they would remain criminals" (I, p. 138). And Dreyfus' final acquittal is, for Barrès, only a new lesson in relativism: on July 12, 1906, the day after the annulment of the proceedings in Rennes that condemned Dreyfus, Barrès declared to the Assemblée Nationale: "For twelve years, Dreyfus was a traitor according to a juridical truth . . . For the last twenty-four hours, according to a new juridical truth, he is innocent. This is an important lesson, Gentlemen, not of skepticism, in my view, but of relativism, which invites us to modify our passions" (Intervention, "Chambre des Députés" [Speech, Chamber of Deputies], pp. 572–573).

But relativism intervenes in still another way in the Dreyfus affair. According to Barrès, the individual can do nothing; he merely provides an external translation of the instincts of his race. Thus, referring to Dreyfus: "Here are ways of thinking and speaking apt to shock the French, but they are most natural for him; they are sincere, and we may call them innate" (*Scènes*, I, p. 160). Since ethical values themselves are a product of the national character, what is odious for a Frenchman is not odious for a Jew, and vice versa. Barrès ultimately finds more excuses for Dreyfus than a universalist would; he goes so far as to wonder whether it is legitimate to judge someone who cannot be held responsible for his acts, since they are dictated by his race. "We are demanding that that child of Shem possess the fine features of the Indo-European race" (I, p. 153). "If we were disinterested minds, instead of judging Dreyfus according to French morality and according to our justice, like a peer, we would recognize him as a representative of a different species" (I, p. 167). Rather than being an artifact of justice, Dreyfus is an artifact of ethnology or even zoology: he illustrates the behavior of a different human species, the Jewish species, which we do not really have the right to judge. "We would not pillory him on Devil's Island, but as a living witness, as an object lesson, we would set him up near a chair of comparative ethnology" (I, p. 167). Relativism thus becomes the logical outcome of determinism.

The enemies here are the intellectuals imbued with the spirit of the Enlightenment; at stake is their faith in the unity of the human race. The "humanitarian spirit" has to be resisted (I, p. 281), for it has the "senseless ambition of imposing unity and immobility on the world" (II, p. 253). These intellectuals "think they are civilizing us," by using an abstract notion of civilization; in so doing, they are disregarding the national traditions, and they are "contradicting our own civilization" (I, p. 102): for Barrès, the word "civilization" is only meaningful in the plural.

In order to wage war effectively against the advocates of universalism, one must attack their philosophical base, which is the Kantian conception of morality. "The theoreticians of the Academy, drunk with an unhealthy Kantianism . . . repeat: 'I must *always* act in such a way that I can will my action to serve as a *universal rule.*' Not at all, Gentlemen; give up those big words "always" and "universal," and since you are French, concern yourselves with acting in accord with the interest of France at this time" (I, p. 37). All values are spatially and temporally determined; thus, we have to give up universalism, which is illusory, and maintain on the contrary our regional and national traditions. We have to combat "this Kantianism of our classes [which] claims to govern universal man, abstract man, without taking individual differences into account" (I, p. 60).

If Barrès sometimes deigns to support the principle of equality, he does not do so in the name of universalism or the unity of the human race, but quite to the contrary, he does so in the name of difference: races are equal in their incompatibility; each one is entitled to deem itself the best of all, judging itself with the help of instruments derived from its own traditions, and in this—but only in this—each one is like all the others. Such ought to be the consistent relativist position. But of course this egalitarian perspective is only a provisional concession to the adversary, since it is in fact impossible to elevate oneself to a comparative position which would be above all national determinations. After speaking of French values, Barrès concludes: "Excited by such truths, I raise my voice and shout that they are as valid for foreigners as for my compatriots and that thus I scorn no nationality, but that my duty is toward my peers" (I, p. 136). The fact that all peoples are alike in the abstract does not prevent me from choosing my camp. Montaigne's relativism allowed its author to cast a jaundiced eye on his own society. Barrès' relativism—but it must be said that his is a relativism of the nationalist variety—facilitates his rejection of others.

It is thus possible to be opposed to equality between oneself and others in two very different ways. La Bruyère believed in the unity of the human race, and consequently he saw all men in the likeness of the French, except that the others did not approach the (French) ideal as well as the French themselves did: there we had an inequality in fact, which arose from the very way the problem was set forth. Le Bon and Barrès, for their part, think that men differ among themselves: equality is eliminated in theory, as an idea. This does not prevent any of them from remaining ethnocentric, and from preferring the French, or the Europeans, to the Dahomeyans, the Siamese, or the Japanese.

It may be argued that, in our day, we run a greater risk of going astray if we follow Barrès than if we follow La Bruyère. The relativism of values, cultural or historical, has become a commonplace of our society; it is often accompanied by the assertion, if not that we belong to different species or subspecies, then at least that cross-cultural communication is fundamentally impossible. And our contemporary xenophobia accommodates itself perfectly well to the call for the "right to be different": an entirely consistent relativist may demand that all foreigners go home, so they can live surrounded by their own values.

Lévi-Strauss

The Relativist Horizon

Ethnology is a modern discipline whose very object may be identified as cultural difference. Within ethnology, the adoption of an approach to the universal-relative opposition is inevitable—but it may not be a simple matter. To illustrate the difficulties inherent in any undertaking in this area, I shall start with the work of the most influential of the French ethnologists, Claude Lévi-Strauss.

First of all, let us note that in his most general and most programmatic pronouncements, such as his inaugural lesson at the Collège de France, Lévi-Strauss affirms the universalist vocation of the ethnologist. In this connection he recalls the existence of a tradition in French ethnology whose ancestor is Marcel Mauss: it is with reference to Mauss that Lévi-Strauss defines ethnology's "ultimate goal," namely, "to arrive at certain universal forms of thought and morality" (*An-*

thropologie structurale deux, in English *Structural Anthropology*, II, p. 25), and he formulates "a question with which it has always been concerned—that of the universality of the human race" (p. 24). The vocabulary and aspirations of Enlightenment philosophy are recognizable here: there is such a thing as "human nature," constant and universal, which is manifested in forms of thought and knowledge (the establishment of truth and falsity) as well as in forms of judgment (the search for good and evil). In a spirit that remains quite classical, Lévi-Strauss seems to attribute a dominant place to the universal: "The outer differences conceal a basic unity" (p. 59), the base being traditionally deemed more worthy than the surfaces. A description that is only slightly less value laden, but more concrete, presents the relation between the two as follows: "It is as if we were asserting that men have always and everywhere undertaken the same task in striving towards the same objective and that, throughout history, only the means have differed" (*Tristes Tropiques*, English, p. 392). If this formula is combined with the previous one, it becomes clear that the goals correspond to the foundations, the base, while the means correspond to the surface, which is an argument in favor of unity. It could be noted as well that this object and this task, instead of being elements of observable reality, are mental constructions, hypotheses necessary to a comprehension of that reality.

However, no sooner is this hierarchy between the universal and the particular outlined than it seems to be reversed, and the reversal is all the more disconcerting since Lévi-Strauss is the spokesperson not of just any human science but precisely of ethnology—that is, the discipline having as its object individual societies, "a discipline whose main, if not sole, aim is to analyze and interpret differences" (*Anthropologie structurale*, in English *Structural Anthropology*, I, p. 14). It is a matter not of denying the existence of features in common beneath the differences, but of proceeding to a kind of distribution of labor: one set of disciplines is to deal with similarities, another with differences. "Because such general characteristics *are* universal, they pertain to biology and psychology. The ethnographer's task is to describe and analyze the different ways in which they are manifested in various societies; the ethnologist's task is to explain them" (p. 13). The universal is off limits to the ethnologist *by definition*: whenever a feature is universal, it becomes by that very token a psychic or biological feature and no longer a social one. Such a choice has the advantage of simplicity. But does it not indicate that an *a priori* decision has been made as to the nature of what is to be studied?

The ethnologist's ultimate goal, according to Lévi-Strauss, is to reach the universal forms of the human mind; but his initial aim (let us forget the term "sole," otherwise we could go no further) is, here, to study differences. Is this not a rather peculiar way to reach a goal, by heading first in the opposite direction? Rousseau had already recommended this approach, however, and Lévi-Strauss is prepared to comply, just as he seems to adopt as his own a conception of the universal that is Leibnizian in inspiration: from the observation of particular facts, one deduces general properties in such a way that each fact appears to be one combination—among various possible combinations—of these general and elementary features. This is in fact Lévi-Strauss's structural project: he refers to "that general inventory of societies which anthropology attempts to construct," and the observable data are then nothing more than "the equivalents of so many choices, from all the possible ones which each society seems to make" (p. 11). Only the particular is observed, but the particular is understood only by way of a detour through the general.

Here we have gotten somewhat beyond the opposition between ends and means; but, despite some wavering and hesitation, we can say that we are indeed looking at a predominantly universalist project. It is not entirely certain, however, that Lévi-Strauss wants to stick to it. Whatever may be said about ultimate aims and deep structures, what ethnologists have to deal with are the differences among societies; inevitably, this fact inflects their position in the direction of relativism. The first universality Lévi-Strauss abandons is that of moral judgment. If there really were "universal forms of morality," we ought to be able to pass comparative judgments on every culture we encounter; yet even when he preserves the image of the inventory of abstract properties, common to all cultures, Lévi-Strauss denies ethnology any right to judge. "We must accept the fact that each society has made a certain choice, within the range of existing human possibilities, and that the various choices cannot be compared with each other" (*Tristes Tropiques*, p. 385). We are thus confronted with "the impossibility of arriving at any moral or philosophical criterion by which to decide the respective values of the choices which have led each civilization to prefer certain ways of life and thought while rejecting others" (*L'Homme nu*, in English *The Naked Man*, p. 636). Wisdom would dictate that we accept without judging: "No society is fundamentally good, but none . . . is absolutely bad; they all offer their members certain advantages, with the proviso that there is invariably a residue of evil, the amount of which seems to remain more or less constant" (*Tristes Tropiques*, p. 387). Those who do not share this opinion manifest "the absurdity of declaring one culture superior to another" (*Structural Anthropology*, II, p. 354).

So the general universalist program turns out to convey a radical ethical relativism: every society is imperfect, and no society is better than any other; thus, totalitarianism—to take an extreme example—is as valid as democracy. The same thing is suggested by the famous comparison of cultures to moving trains: there exists no fixed point— that is, no point beyond a culture—from which we can judge others. We have the impression that a culture is *developing*, and we think we are making an objective judgment about it; in reality, all we see is that it is going in the same direction as we are. Or else, on the contrary, we think that another culture is *stagnating:* this is another optical illusion, for we are in fact only designating the difference of direction between its movement and ours. It is at this point in the argument that Lévi-Strauss resorts to the image "used to explain the first rudiments of the theory of relativity. In order to demonstrate that the dimension and speed of the displacement of bodies are not absolute values, but functions of the observer's position, we are reminded that, for a passenger sitting by the window of a train, the speed and length of other trains vary according to whether they move in the same direction or the opposite way. And every member of a culture is as closely linked to that culture as the imaginary passenger is to his train" (p. 340). It is all a matter of viewpoint: if we pass judgment, it is because we are all interested parties. "The wealth of a culture or of the unfolding of one of its phases does not exist as an intrinsic feature; it is a function of the observer's situation in regard to that wealth, of the number or diversity of the interests he has invested in it" (*Le Regard éloigné*, in English *The View from Afar*, p. 10). We have come back to Helvétius.

The image of moving trains may be helpful for visualizing certain elements of the theory of relativity in physics; but does it suffice to justify ethical relativism? In a sense, it is actually absurd to establish a hierarchy of cultures, since each one is a model of the world (just as it would be absurd, in a sense, to establish a hierarchy of languages). But we would have to add at once that that in no way prevents us from identifying good and evil and thus, potentially, from observing that a given society is, at a particular moment of its history, subject to global condemnation (as is the case with totalitarian societies). From another standpoint, is the individual really a prisoner of the train of culture in which he was raised, without any possibility of distancing himself from it (or even of jumping off the train)? Lévi-Strauss manifests a cultural determinism here whose rigidity is no less striking than that of Gobineau's cherished racial determinism, which we shall have occasion to examine later on. It is essential to recognize that one can understand cultures other than one's own and thus communicate with their members. Does not this experience of *detachment* with respect to the customs and values of one's own society characterize the ethnologist himself? But let us not get ahead of ourselves.

Let us forget for a moment the "ultimate goal" of ethnology, established earlier by Lévi-Strauss, and ask rather to what extent his practice provides us with proof of the viability of his system. Does he forgo all transcultural judgment, as he suggests we should? The choices made by societies cannot be compared to one another, he said. And yet a generalist ethnologist like Lévi-Strauss cannot prevent himself altogether from making comparisons and establishing typologies. But perhaps, even as he compares, he manages to avoid passing judgment? Perhaps he succeeds in remaining morally neutral? Let us take as an example the opposition he makes between traditional and modern societies. The absence of writing in the former and its presence in the latter lead Lévi-Strauss to note a difference in the very nature of human relations. What he calls "anthropology's most important contribution to social science" is that it introduced "this fundamental distinction between two types of social existence: a way of life recognized at the outset as traditional and archaic and characteristic of 'authentic' societies and a more modern form of existence, from which the first-named type is not absent but where groups that are not completely, or are imperfectly, 'authentic' are organized within a much larger and specifically 'unauthentic' system" (*Structural Anthropology*, I, p. 367). But is contrasting the two forms of society in this way any different from comparing them? And does calling one of them authentic and the other unauthentic still amount to abstaining from judgment?

Another example with respect to which "social anthropology would find its highest justification" (p. 30) is his distinction between "hot" and "cold" societies; the ethnologist's role would now be to identify and to preserve social forms appropriate to each, forms that "correspond to a permanent hope for mankind over which social anthropology would have mission to keep watch, especially in the most troubled times" (*Structural Anthropology*, II, p. 30). But can one say of such a mission that it implies no transcultural judgment, no moral choice? Has Lévi-Strauss really succeeded in escaping the absurdity against which he sought to warn us? We are obliged to note that his ethical relativism is only another statement of principle, one that is not followed by its own enactment: Lévi-Strauss is no more able than anyone else to keep from passing judgments. More precisely, and in this he resembles Montaigne more than any of his great predecessors, his starting point is a relativism that, however radical it may be, does not keep him from praising primitive societies and criticizing our own. He professes relativism but practices primitivism—that is, an absolute hierarchy of values, even if it is not the hierarchy most commonly adopted by our society.

Critique of Humanism

Lévi-Strauss in fact subjects the Western world, as it has been constituted since the Renaissance, to a discreet but decisive critique. The core aspect of the Western tradition he targets for criticism might be labeled "humanism."

It is true that Lévi-Strauss does not always use this word pejoratively. Sometimes he retains only a specific reference to the traditional scholarly "humanities"—that is, the study of Greek and Latin; this sort of "humanism" is then a first form of the study of cultures different from ours, and ethnology is nothing but the universal expansion, the logical outcome of that older humanism. But even in this rather specialized sense of the word, the critical element remains perceptible in Lévi-Strauss. "Anthropology [was] able to affirm itself as an enterprise renewing the Renaissance and atoning for it, in order to extend humanism to the measure of humanity" (*Structural Anthropology*, II, p. 32). Renewing and atoning: curiously, if the first term indicates continuity and presupposes the maintenance of the older project, only extended beyond the limits of "our narrow-minded humanism" (p. 51), the second indicates on the contrary that the project itself was a sin rather than a benediction.

What Lévi-Strauss criticizes in Renaissance humanism, which is nothing but the logical outcome of Christian humanism, is thus not simply the fact that it has restricted its sampling of humanity to European cultures alone, while neglecting or spurning the cultures of the other continents: such a reproach would remain compatible with the project of humanism itself, for it would simply show that humanism's accomplishments have not lived up to its initial ambitions. The humanists of the Renaissance or of the eighteenth century saw themselves as universalists, whereas in reality their horizon ended at the edges of Europe; but these limits can be extended without changing the underlying project. What we have to expiate is not the lack of universal extension, which would require only a quantitative correction, after all; we have to atone for a different type of foreshortening, which is "vertical," as it were, rather than "horizontal": namely, the belief that human beings, to the exclusion of all other living species, are the ones who serve as the standard in all things, as the *raison d'être* and goal for every human activity. Humanism—and in this regard its name is not misused—has sought to organize the world around humankind: that is its sin, or more simply its mistake.

In a spirit close to that of other critiques of modernity (sometimes reminiscent of Heidegger, sometimes of ecological manifestos), Lévi-Strauss in fact criticizes, above all, the separation between man and nature, and the subjection of nature to man. "By isolating man from the rest of creation and defining too narrowly the boundaries separating him from other living beings, the Western humanism inherited from antiquity and the Renaissance has deprived him of a bulwark" (*The View from Afar*, p. 23). Western civilization has favored only the perfecting of purely technical mastery over the forces of nature; it "has been entirely devoted, for the last two or three centuries, to putting more and more powerful mechanical means at the disposition of man" (*Structural Anthropology*, II, pp. 341–342). This is the state of affairs that Lévi-Strauss invites us to question.

It is not overstating the case to say that Lévi-Strauss shows affinities with an antihumanist ideology. He himself does not seem to care for the somewhat aggressive connotations of that label, but he nevertheless confirms the direction of his commitment. "I have often been reproached for being antihumanist," he says in an interview with Jean-Marie Benoist. "I do not believe that is true. What I have struggled against, and what I feel is very harmful, is the sort of unbridled humanism that has grown out of the Judeo-Christian tradition on the one hand, and on the other hand, closer to home, out of the Renaissance and out of Cartesianism, which makes man a master, an absolute lord of creation" ("Entretien" [Interview], p. 4). Unbridled or not, this is the only humanism we have within the Western tradition; to be against this "sort" of humanism is to be against the only doctrine that, in Europe, has ever been accorded—and rightly so—that name.

Lévi-Strauss (and here is the Heideggerian side of his critique) holds Descartes responsible for this anthropocentric revolution. This is not serious; what is more so is that he would put the opposing, antihumanist tradition under Rousseau's banner. "Exposing the flaws of a humanism decidedly unable to establish the exercise of virtue among men, . . . Rousseau's thinking can help us to reject an illusion whose lethal effects we can observe in ourselves and on ourselves" (*Structural Anthropology*, II, p. 41). "It is veritably the end of the Cogito which Rousseau proclaims in putting forward this bold solution" (p. 38). Perhaps the reference to Rousseau (essentially to Rousseau the naturalist and autobiographer) gives Lévi-Strauss a better way to express his thought; but it must be said that he comes close to a misreading in his interpretation of Rousseau's position, which is inseparable from the humanist tradition (what is more, this tradition is inconceivable today without Rousseau's contributions). It is indeed on mankind, on human universality, that the Savoyard Vicar, Rousseau's spokesman, bases the exercise of virtue (and the Vicar, as has been noted, owes a good deal to Descartes); but in fact, in order to make Rousseau out to be the father of antihumanism, one has to disregard not only *Emile* and *On the Social Contract* but also the *Confessions* and the *Dialogues*.

It is this narrow Western humanism, an unfortunate amalgam of Christianity (the unity of the human race) and Cartesianism (man at the pinnacle of nature), which is guilty of all the evils that have befallen the world in the last one hundred fifty years. "All the tragedies we have lived through, first with colonialism, then with fascism, finally the concentration camps, all this has taken shape not in opposition to or in contradiction with so-called humanism in the form in which we have been practicing it for several centuries, but I would say almost as its natural continuation" ("Entretien," p. 4). This hidden continuity can be explained as follows: once one has established a definitive boundary between human beings and the other living species and has admitted that the latter may be sacrificed, in extreme cases, to the former, it is only a short step from here to dividing the human species itself into several categories, and acknowledging that the lowest category may be sacrificed for the benefit of the higher ones. It is in this respect that nineteenth-century colonialism and twentieth-century fascism are the natural offspring of humanism. Communist totalitarianism is not exempt from the same explanation: "The communist and totalitarian Marxist ideology is only a ruse of history to promote the accelerated Westernization of peoples who have remained on the outside until very recent times" (ibid.).

These considerations are undoubtedly marginal in Lévi-Strauss's work, and it is probably no accident that they appear in a newspaper interview rather than in one of his published texts. Nevertheless, they remain perfectly consistent with antihumanist principles, which are also present elsewhere, and they give a concrete meaning to more general propositions. That is why their examination may throw some doubt in turn on the principles themselves.

On the geological time scale, it is legitimate to ignore the opposition between totalitarianism and democracy, in favor of underscoring the common effects of industrialization or urbanization (Heidegger does this as well); it is a different matter if the unit of measure is a human lifetime. Stones and plants suffer perhaps as much under a tyrannical government as under a democracy, and from this viewpoint the one is only the historical ruse of the other; but the same cannot be said from the standpoint of human beings, who are obliged to live either inside or outside a totalitarian state. To say that Hitlerian fascism and the massive extermination of Jews it brought about are "almost natural" consequences of humanism implies not only that the speaker is disregarding or repressing the ideological origins of fascism in nineteenth-century *antihumanism* (in France, the racism of Gobineau, Renan, or Vacher de Lapouge—we shall come back to this point), but also that the speaker is willfully cultivating a logical paradox, since he is complacently deducing the thesis of the *inequality* of man on the basis of human *equality*. Finally, to attribute colonial expansion or the "division of Africa" to the humanist project of exporting the Enlightenment is to take at face value what was only propaganda: an attempt, most often a clumsy one, to replaster the façade of a building constructed for quite a different purpose. The reasons for the colonial conquest were political and economic, rather than humanitarian; if we wanted to look for a single general principle, it would be nationalism—which, as Rousseau understood, is incompatible with humanism (we shall come back to this, too).

The term "antihumanism" designates only the critical side of the doctrine, however; if we were to give it a positive label, we should perhaps speak of "naturalism." Lévi-Strauss in fact wants "man" to get back in line, to find a place—a more modest place than the one he has sought to occupy since the Renaissance—among the other living species, in a general natural order (here we are closer to the ecologists than to Heidegger). In the extreme case we may keep the label "humanism," provided we change its meaning: according to Lévi-Strauss, we must aspire to "a wisely conceived humanism, which does not center on man but gives him a reasonable place within nature, rather than letting him make himself its master and plunderer" (*The View from Afar,* p. 14). Man will then respect all forms of life and not just his own. But we may wonder whether this label—humanism—is still usable. Man has to be defined, writes Lévi-Strauss, "not as a moral but as a living being, since this is his most salient characteristic" (pp. 281–282). However, the term "living" clearly does not suffice to characterize man, since this is a feature man shares with ants; thus, what is in question here is not a new definition of humanity, but the replacement of human beings by living beings. Now one might wonder whether the blurring of the boundary between human and nonhuman does not risk favoring divisions between human groups. "Where shall we stop and draw the line?" Renan asked in the course of a similar meditation. "The animal also has its rights. Is the Australian savage to have the rights of man, or those of the animal?" (*Philosophical Dialogues and Fragments,* p. 54).

Thus, we may be somewhat surprised by Lévi-Strauss's effort to find a new basis for the rights of man, one that would make it possible to dispense with the concept of "man"—namely, the right to life. "These present projects offer France a unique opportunity to place the rights of man on a foundation that, except for a few centuries in the West, has been explicitly or implicitly accepted in all places and in all times" (*The View from Afar,* p. 284). But it is only during these few centuries, and only in the West, that it has been possible to raise the question of the rights of man, in the strict sense, and with good reason: it is of a piece with the humanist ideology. The new "basis" for the rights of man imagined by Lévi-Strauss consists in denying their relevance and in diluting them into a general right that would apply to living beings—

but which would have the singular characteristic of being instituted by a minuscule number of those beings, namely those who speak (ants are not expected to participate in the deliberations that are to lead to the establishment of their rights).

The Effects of Humanism

Having rejected the basis for humanism (man's exceptional status in nature and the unity of the human race), Lévi-Strauss also quite logically criticizes its most obvious political consequences—that is, the modern concepts of freedom and equality. What is wrong with our idea of freedom is precisely its relation with universal humanism. "We cannot adopt a rationalist definition of freedom—thus claiming universality—and simultaneously make a pluralist society the place of its flowering and its exercise. A universalist doctrine evolves ineluctably toward a model equivalent to the one-party state" (*The View from Afar*, p. 285). Similarly, for Lévi-Strauss the affirmation of "the natural equality of all men" is "somewhat disappointing for the mind" (*Structural Anthropology*, II, p. 330). Let us note at once that a false argument is at issue here: humanism requires equality before the law, and leaves open the question of natural equality or inequality. However, it is obvious that equality before the law is no better justified. If society is to improve, we have to maintain "those minute privileges, those possibly ludicrous inequalities that, without infringing upon the general equality, allow individuals to find the nearest anchorage" (*The View from Afar*, p. 287).

It is along the lines of the same rejection of humanist values that Lévi-Strauss seems to locate his condemnation of cultural intermixing. Here it should be stressed that he does not oppose all cross-cultural communication. A moderate level of communication, maintained within certain limits, even constitutes an undeniable advantage, one from which Europeans, and particularly Spaniards, benefited with respect to the populations they encountered on the American continent in the sixteenth century. Cortés and his companions certainly profited from their familiarity with other European cultures, with cultures of the past like those of the Greeks and the Romans, with cultures of Africa and Asia glimpsed in the course of their travels; conversely, the Aztecs' ignorance of cultures quite different from their own was a handicap, at least at first. This state of limited communication is what Lévi-Strauss calls "the coalition of cultures."

But if communication accelerates, then differences are blurred and we advance toward the universalization of culture—that is, of one culture at the expense of the others. Now the disappearance of differences would be fatal for all cultures, and not simply for the most easily influenced among them. "There is not—there cannot be—a world civilization in the absolute sense which is sometimes given this term. For civilization implies the coexistence of cultures offering among themselves the maximum of diversity, and even consists in this very coexistence" (*Structural Anthropology*, II, p. 358). Beyond a certain threshold, communication is therefore harmful, for it leads to homogenization, which in turn is tantamount to a death sentence for humanity; and we have seen that for Lévi-Strauss any sort of universalization raises the specter of a one-party regime. Auguste Comte's utopian dream is for Lévi-Strauss a nightmare.

Gobineau, another enemy of intermixing and homogenization who is mentioned by Lévi-Strauss in the same context, had already faced this paradox. The strength of a culture is expressed through its capacity to influence other cultures; but each occasion for influence is an encounter, and each encounter a weakening. A fatality weighs upon the human race: a society's very strength is its undoing. Lévi-Strauss spells out what was simply a source of internal tension in Gobineau's text: "In order to progress, men must collaborate; and in the course of this collaboration they see the gradual pooling of their contributions whose initial diversity was precisely what made their collaboration fecund and necessary" (p. 360).

Given this "double bind" (if you do not communicate you cannot win, and if you do communicate you are bound to lose), in the text entitled "Race and Culture" that opens his latest collection of essays (*The View from Afar*), Lévi-Strauss chooses the lesser of two evils: he opts against intercultural communication. It is impossible, he says in effect, to desire both cultural diversity and familiarity with cultures other than our own; for familiarity is the first step toward the disappearance of that diversity. It is better to stay home and remain unaware of others than to know them too well; it is better to send foreigners back across our borders than to let them submerge us and deprive us of our cultural identity. Rooting is preferable to uprooting. Lévi-

Strauss thus rejoins the tradition of antihumanist French thinkers, from Bonald through Gobineau to Barrès, who are all strenuously opposed to the intermixing of cultures.

One might wonder about the political opportuneness of this doctrine, in an era when the nations of Western Europe are seeking to protect themselves against human invasions originating in the Third World. One might also question its moral rightness—although, as Lévi-Strauss has abandoned the attempt to provide a basis for the exercise of virtue in man, it is not certain that a "natural morality" would find the doctrine defensible. (But how are we to discover what is good for the entire set of living beings? Is it up to the scientists to tell us?) My purpose here is somewhat different: I propose above all to examine the doctrine's truth value and consistency.

Is it true that communication leads to homogeneity and that homogeneity leads to death? So baldly put, such affirmations will never be verified, or even falsified, so great is the distance between the observable facts and the abstract theorem that claims to account for them. It is certain that, as Comte had already seen, today's world is more homogeneous than yesterday's. Industrial society is gradually spreading; Western science is becoming the only science; the democratic ideal and the rights of man are being invoked in all regions of the globe. But must we see in all this an inexorable, irreversible process, with total indifferentiation at the end? I do not think so. Humanity in possession of universal communication will be more homogeneous than humanity without it; this does not mean that all differences will be suppressed. To suppose so implies that differences are the product of mutual ignorance alone: to believe this is to embrace unwittingly the very scientistic thesis proponents of difference would like to combat. If contemporary communications tend to bring people closer together, the weight of history, which will always be with us, pulls us (whatever Comte may have claimed) in the opposite direction. Moreover, the constitution of a universal state is not going to come about overnight, and human populations *need* to see themselves as different if only so they can conceptualize their own identity (the Canadian example comes readily to mind). The differences are displaced and transformed; they do not disappear.

Let me add one further remark. Familiarity with a foreign culture is not the chief reason for the disappearance of native cultures. Local traditions do not need to be subjected to foreign traditions to be destroyed. "Uprooting" is much greater in the move from a village to a suburban workers' enclave within the same country than it is in the case of exile: one is never as conscious of one's own culture as when one is abroad. If there is danger, it does not lurk behind the bush on which Lévi-Strauss has opened fire.

His reasoning runs into yet another difficulty. What he fears is the establishment of a single universal order. What he does, nevertheless, is issue recommendations about how a universal society ought to function. Human migrations and contacts among different ethnic groups are not determined by governments, still less by the society of nations. If Lévi-Strauss's ideas were put into practice, if humanity were to combat the acceleration of contacts, would that not imply a concerted international effort, a first step toward that unwanted universal state? Is not interventionism, which Lévi-Strauss prefers to the liberal attitude of laissez-faire, the best illustration of precisely the universal decision making he dreads?

We cannot help wondering, finally, whether Lévi-Strauss is right to think that universal uniformity is an inevitable consequence of humanism (the term "universalist doctrine" would thus imply "one-party system"). We find two different types of universalism in Lévi-Strauss. One, which he accepts without hesitation, is the biopsychological identity of the species: this is, in a way, a "starting-point" universalism, unchallengeable, but involving no choices at all. "What heredity determines in human beings is the general aptitude to acquire any culture whatsoever; the specific culture, however, will depend on random factors of birth and on the society in which one is raised" (*The View from Afar*, p. 18). That is what Lévi-Strauss also calls (at least in certain texts) the unconscious—atemporal and universal structural laws—or else the symbolic function, "which is carried out according to the same laws among all men" (p. 203); however, these are pure forms without content. "The unconscious . . . is always empty—or, more accurately, it is as alien to mental images as is the stomach to the foods which pass through it" (*Structural Anthropology*, I, p. 203). On the other side, we find the bad universalism, or rather the false universalism, the one that is unwilling to recognize differences, the one that consists in a voluntarist—and, inevitably, unifying—project.

Yet if we look more closely, we find that there are not two universalisms but three (at least!). Alongside the first, which we have already mentioned, there is a universalism that could be called "end-point"

universalism: this is the project of a universal State, with a homogeneous population, that we have encountered in certain texts of the
Encyclopedists (for example, Condorcet) and their scientistic posterity.
But in addition to these two types of universalism there is a third, which
might be called a universalism of "itinerary," with the focus not on
starting points or destinations but on the approach adopted (on
method). If I succeed in communicating successfully with others, I have
to imagine a frame of reference that encompasses their universe *and*
my own. Aspiring to establish dialogue with "others" who are increasingly remote, we must indeed postulate a universal horizon for our
search for understanding, even if it is clear that in practice I shall never
encounter universal categories—but only categories that are *more universal* than others.

Lévi-Strauss never bothers to distinguish explicitly between "end-
point" universalism and universalism of "itinerary." For this reason, his
sometimes justified criticism of "end-point" universalism might seem
to apply just as well to the intermediate variety, whereas this is not at
all the case—as indeed the entire corpus of his own work attests. The
image of trains traveling in various directions over which their passen-
gers have no control does not provide a good description of the human
condition. Man should be compared not with an island (*pace* John
Donne) but with a fragment of a continent. Cultures are not trains
thrust into chaos by a mad switchman. Interactions and even
confluences are possible, if not inevitable.

The Elimination of the Subject

Structural anthropology, as Lévi-Strauss likes to maintain, is at the
other extreme from humanist philosophy. Focusing on the differences
among societies, the ethnologist instinctively rejects the universal
framework that emerged from the Enlightenment. For ethnology to
come into being, "the concept of civilization—connoting a set of general, universal, and transmissible abilities—had to give way to the
concept of culture in its new meaning: it now signified particular life
styles that are not transmissible" (*The View from Afar,* p. 26). A culture
does not transmit itself, any more than it tolerates being blended with
other cultures. The two intellectual sources of ethnology are, if Lévi-
Strauss is to be believed, equally hostile to humanism: these are the
nationalist philosophy elaborated in Germany by Herder and Fichte

on the one hand, and the conservative empiricism of Burke and Bonald on the other; all these doctrines are attuned to the differences (of nation, class, rank) that prevail among men, rather than to the unity of mankind.

A further opposition with humanism involves not the discipline as such but its structuralist version, with which Lévi-Strauss identifies. Humanism glorifies man, and, in man, his distinctive feature, which is his subjectivity. Conversely, "structuralism reintegrates man into nature and . . . [makes] it possible to disregard the subject—that unbearably spoilt child who has occupied the philosophical scene for too long now, and prevented serious research through demanding exclusive attention" (*The Naked Man*, p. 687). If we want mankind to take its place in the line-up of species, we must indeed begin by depriving men and women of their specificity—in other words, their subjectivity. What Lévi-Strauss is seeking to eliminate here is not the subjectivity of the scholar (otherwise he would not speak of "reintegrating into nature") but the subjectivity of the creatures the scholar studies. Structuralism, in its Lévi-Straussian sense, is a method for studying human beings that refuses to take their subjectivity into account.

Lévi-Strauss is obviously not unaware of the fact that subjectivity is a constitutive feature of human beings. "The situation particular to the social sciences is different in nature; the difference is to do with the intrinsic character of the object of study, which is that it is object and subject both at once" ("Introduction à l'oeuvre de Marcel Mauss," in English *Introduction to the Work of Marcel Mauss*, p. 29). In other words, human beings are subjects on the ontological level, but in the social sciences they become objects of knowledge (thus, they are objects on the epistemological level). Now there is no reason to confuse these two levels: the epistemological subject and object are purely relative concepts, synonymous with the observer and the observed, while the ontological subject and object are different substances, either human beings or things. Lévi-Strauss also knows perfectly well that this specific feature of the social sciences (the fact that their object is formed of "subjects") entails a moral precept that does not apply to specialists in the natural sciences: "Our science reached its maturity the day that Western man began to understand that he would never understand himself as long as there would be on the surface on the earth a single race or a single people whom he would treat as an object" (*Structural Anthropology*, II, p. 32).

If one is attempting to break with humanism, however, one must remove all traces of subjectivity from the object studied; this is the conclusion to which Lévi-Strauss is led. When Sartre uses the label "aesthetes" for those who attempt to "study men as if they were ants," Lévi-Strauss replies: "So I accept the characterization of aesthete in so far as I believe the ultimate goal of the human sciences to be not to constitute, but to dissolve man" (*The Savage Mind*, p. 247). We have to choose between two meanings of this somewhat enigmatic formula. Either Lévi-Strauss means that science has to analyze rather than accept indivisible entities (but beyond the fact that this is self-evident, it is hard to see how it would oblige us to treat men as if they were ants), or else (and this is more likely) he is suggesting that the practice of the human sciences implies that human beings are to be pulverized, dissolved like chemical substances. Confirmation of this second interpretation of Lévi-Strauss's sentence is provided by his definition of the task of the human sciences: "the reintegration of culture in nature and finally of life within the whole of its physico-chemical conditions" (ibid.).

In his study of myths, Lévi-Strauss puts us constantly on guard against any attempt to introduce the notion of the subject. "The elimination of the subject represents what might be called a methodological need" (*The Naked Man*, p. 628): myths have to be explained on their own terms, without reference to the will of the subjects who transmit them. Even psychoanalysis is not sufficiently vigilant with respect to myths, for psychoanalysis would allow the subject to be reconstructed on the basis of the concept of the "Other" and a metaphysics of desire; now "there can be no question . . . of smuggling the subject in again, under this new guise" (p. 630). But it is not necessary to see in this exclusion a question of method, and thus of principle. The study of myths has nothing to do with the notion of the discourse-producing individual subject, for the good reason that myths are precisely discourses assumed by the collectivity: what is individual is by definition not a myth. Lévi-Strauss is perfectly aware of this, for he says in the same text: "In order to achieve the status of myth, the created work must cease precisely to be individual" (p. 626). This perspective allows him to maintain the formula according to which men do not think in myths; instead, "myths operate in men's minds without their being aware of the fact" or even "as if the thinking process were taking place in the myths" (*Le Cru et le Cuit*, in English *The Raw and the Cooked*,

p. 12). Yet when we are dealing with an individual author, the contrary is true: we cannot account for Rousseau's thought without questioning his intentions as a subject (and it is perhaps because he neglected this in his study of Rousseau that Lévi-Strauss produced an image bearing so little resemblance to the original). The exclusion of the subject does not follow from the method, nor does it impose a particular philosophical choice; it is the effect of the matter studied. Myths have no subject, whereas works do.

Sometimes Lévi-Strauss is even more radical, claiming that the need to eliminate the human is a consequence not of the structural method but of the scientific project itself. "Insofar as the human sciences succeed in producing truly scientific work, the distinction between the human and the natural must decrease for them. If ever they become sciences in their own right, they will cease to differ from the others" (*Structural Anthropology*, II, p. 294). Let us first eliminate a possible misunderstanding: the "human" is clearly opposed not to the "material" but only to the nonhuman. One may be a materialist and nevertheless recognize the difference between human and nonhuman—not in the physico-chemical composition of bodies, but in behaviors and structures. With this understanding, it is hard to sympathize with a "truly scientific" work that will result in neglecting the distinctive feature of its object. The task of the human sciences, whatever the particular orientation of the scientist may be, can only be the explanation of what is specifically human; proving that there is no such thing may make the human sciences look more like the "hard" sciences, but it will not give us much insight into human beings, who for their part insist on behaving differently from minerals.

Illogical as it may appear, the elimination of human subjectivity is, in Lévi-Strauss's eyes, a necessity imposed by the very fact that one is practicing a science. But as we have seen, Lévi-Strauss is conscious of the moral and political dangers involved in treating others as objects, and he sees this necessity as something like a tragic contradiction. "Its [anthropology's] capacity to assess more objectively the facts pertaining to the human condition appropriately reflects, on the epistemological level, a state of affairs in which one part of mankind treated the other as an object" (p. 55). His discipline owes its existence to the fact that "exotic cultures, treated by us as mere things, could be studied, accordingly, as things" (ibid.). From this viewpoint ethnology would be an evil, and ought to disappear.

It seems to me that we can reassure Lévi-Strauss and those who share his apprehensions: the evil in question is illusory. It is not because the human being becomes an object of knowledge that he becomes an object pure and simple: no internal necessity of the social and human sciences requires this. If the project of structural anthropology consists in reducing subjects to objects, thus in eliminating the human (but I find this hard to believe), it is the "structural" that is to blame, not the "anthropology." It is true that this discipline got a significant boost from nineteenth-century European colonial politics, and we cannot deny that "anthropology is daughter to this era of violence" (p. 55). However, parents' flaws do not necessarily afflict their offspring; genesis is not synonymous with structure. There is nothing immoral in the attempt to understand human beings. What may be immoral is the use made of this understanding—for example, the reduction of persons to the status of things.

The scientist aspires, as he works, to bracket his own subjectivity; in his research, he calls upon "the subject's capacity for indefinite self-objectification, that is to say (without ever quite abolishing itself as subject) for projecting outside itself ever-diminishing fractions of itself" (*Introduction to the Work of Marcel Mauss*, p. 32). But the individual does not thereby stop being a subject; and once he has observed how things *are*, it is the same individual who expresses his opinion as to how they *should be* (Lévi-Strauss, as we have seen, does not hesitate to do this). It is the same with the ethnologist: "Using all societies—without adopting features from any one of them," he will be able "to elucidate principles of social life that we can apply in reforming our own customs and not those of foreign societies" (*Tristes Tropiques*, p. 392). Let us set aside this last restriction. (It is clearly admirable to require ethnologists to manifest a certain discretion in the field; but must they really, on principle, deprive their adopted country of the insights they have acquired in the course of their professional life?) Lévi-Strauss's purpose here seems to be to assert the indispensable connection between knowledge and judgment, between structures and subject. But how can this project be reconciled with the antihumanist program set forth elsewhere?

Distancing or Detachment?

Considering the specific place of ethnology among the social sciences, Lévi-Strauss seems tempted by the following definition: ethnology is the study of a society, undertaken by someone who is not a member of that society. Ethnological specificity would then lie neither in the object ("primitive" societies, even supposing that they are qualitatively different from the others, are not the only ones ethnology can study) nor in the techniques ethnology uses (which are those of all the other social and human sciences), but in the special relationship established between the observer and the object being observed. In numerous passages, this is indeed the way Lévi-Strauss defines what is proper to ethnology. "Anthropology is the science of culture as seen from the outside," he says in one lapidary formulation (*Structural Anthropology*, II, p. 55); but later on he takes pains to be more explicit. The distinguishing feature of the ethnological undertaking, as he sees it, is less the fact of difference between observer and observed than the *distance* between them. Hence the title of his collection of essays, *The View from Afar*, "a title expressing what I consider the essence and originality of the anthropological approach" (*The View from Afar*, p. xi). Hence, too, the frequent comparisons with astronomy: "mission as astronomer of the human constellations" (*Introduction to the Work of Marcel Mauss*, p. 66); "the anthropologist is the astronomer of the social sciences" (*Tristes Tropiques*, p. 378); "a position rather comparable to that of the astronomer" (*Structural Anthropology*, II, p. 63).

The ethnologist's position, which is also characterized by words like "distantiation" (*Structural Anthropology*, I, p. 378) and "estrangement" (*Structural Anthropology*, II, p. 272), is in Lévi-Strauss's view a privilege: "this observation, which has the privilege of being distant" (p. 28); "this privileged status" (p. 63). The advantage arises from the great distance between the two societies involved. "This prerogative of ethnographic knowledge . . . is . . . explained by the relative simplification of a mode of knowledge when it is applied to a very distant object" (p. 47).

Lévi-Strauss's eloquence endows his assertions with the allure of self-evidence. But if we attempt to overcome this effect, we cannot fail to be somewhat perplexed. In what precisely does the privilege of the view from afar consist? The foreigner does not necessarily share the prejudices of those he is observing, but that does not mean he has shed his own, which are often as powerful as the others. Will I learn more about a distant country by listening to the stories of an occasional visitor who has only been there during her paid vacations (but in whose case there will be a considerable gap, a maximal distance), or by questioning an inhabitant of that country who knows it inside out? The narratives of early European travelers are certainly entertaining, but

aren't their accounts generally based on misunderstandings? In privileging "relative simplification," doesn't one risk overlooking complexities, getting bogged down in superficialities? Unlike Lévi-Strauss,
someone like Leo Strauss has always insisted that one must begin by
understanding a culture as it has understood itself (that is what Strauss
calls "interpretation," in the strict sense); ordinary common sense
seems to support this view.

Alongside this first objection (knowledge from a distance is
superficial, if not erroneous) a second one arises. If what defines ethnological knowledge is the observer's status as outsider, there will be
as many descriptions of a given society as there are different observers.
We can thus imagine an Australian tribe getting a Chinese description,
an Indian description, and a European description, each entirely different from the others. And there is no reason to stop here: there will
be the North Chinese description and the South Chinese one, the
French description and the German one, and even—why not?—a description by one of Dumont's disciples and another by one of by
Lévi-Strauss's, and so on *ad infinitum*. The ethical relativism observed
earlier is coupled here with cognitive relativism. Such a splintering,
taken to the extreme, is obviously rather absurd, and yet it is not absent
from a definition of ethnology based only on the difference in viewpoint of the observer, as Lévi-Strauss himself has noted: "In choosing
a subject and an object radically distant from one another, anthropology
runs the risk that the knowledge of the object does not reach intrinsic
properties but is limited to expressing the relative and ever-shifting
position of the subject in relation to it" (*Structural Anthropology*, II,
p. 27).

And yet anthropology has not only run the "risk" constituted by
cognitive relativism; it has proudly claimed this relativism as an asset.
Lévi-Strauss himself has done so, writing virtually the same sentence
in two different contexts: "The ultimate goal is not to know what the
societies under study 'are'—each on its own account—but to discover
how they differ from one another. As in linguistics, the study of *con-
trastive features* constitutes the object of anthropology" (p. 63; cf. *Structural Anthropology*, I, p. 328). Here, then, Lévi-Strauss is embracing a
modern dogma with a paradoxically antidogmatic inspiration. There is
no truth (of identity, of essence, of "intrinsic properties"), but only
interpretations: everything is interpretation, everything depends upon
"viewpoint." This is still another variant of relativism. The reference

to linguistics is significant: it was Saussure who sought to define the sign as pure differential gap. But, in the first place, Saussure's formula does not necessarily give a good account of the way language actually works (no doubt that is why Saussure changed his mind on the very next page of the *Cours de linguistique générale* [*Course in General Linguistics*]): although the formula corresponds clearly enough on the one hand to the relation of a given sign to other signs, it does not serve, on the other hand, to describe the relation linking the sign to the referent. And the extrapolation itself is especially problematic: if we assume that in language there are only differences, it is hard to see why scholarly descriptions, which do not constitute a system the way a language does and which do not have any of the same goals, ought to conform to this specific model. "It suffices to recognize," says Lévi-Strauss (*Structural Anthropology*, II, p. 63): but such an attitude undermines ethnology's claim to scientific status and leads to absurdity.

A third objection can be raised, finally, to the identification of ethnology with a "view from afar": this objection is inescapable as soon as we reflect on the actual practices of the members of the profession. If the sole privilege of the ethnologist were to reside in her "view from afar," she might be expected to cultivate that privilege carefully, to do everything in her power to maintain as great a distance as possible: she would be expected to keep herself from all prolonged contact with the society she is studying, both in person and through reading, for contact might well reduce her distance. Of course the professional rule is just the opposite: before producing a description of a foreign society, the ethnologist is expected to immerse herself in that society completely, during a relatively long period of time, sharing the lives of the indigenous people (this is known as "field work"); and she is not asked to ignore the existing literature on the subject at all costs. Rather than cultivating distance, the ethnologist tends to do just the opposite: she attempts to *identify* with the others. Lévi-Strauss does not deny this; quite the contrary: he sees in the identification with another "the real principle of the human sciences" (*Structural Anthropology*, II, p. 43), and he speaks readily of "the identification of the ethnologist with the group whose existence he shares" (p. 273). "What every anthropologist tries to do in the case of different cultures: to put himself in the place of the men living there, to understand the principle and pattern of their intentions" (*La Pensée sauvage*, in English *The Savage Mind*, p. 250). Rather than a view from afar, ethnology would thus be a view from very close up: "Anthropology . . . [endeavors] to reproduce, in its description of strange and remote societies, the standpoint of the natives themselves" (*Structural Anthropology*, I, p. 363). Here we have come back to Leo Strauss.

We might conclude from this that Lévi-Strauss contradicts himself. The antinomic terms "identification" and "distancing" are maintained simultaneously: cognitive relativism is at once assumed and condemned; the ethnologist must be at once superficial and profound. We might add that this impression cannot be explained away by some evolution in Lévi-Strauss's thinking, for it is produced within the confines of individual texts. But such a demonstration risks remaining purely a rhetorical exercise, a way of sidestepping the real question. That is why I have opted here, as before, for a somewhat different explanation: the problem at issue—distinguishing what is universal from what is relative—is complex in itself and requires a nuanced solution. In his many reflections on the subject, Lévi-Strauss takes into consideration different facets of the phenomenon; thus, each of his assertions may be true in context. His discordant utterances draw our attention, indirectly to be sure, to the complexity of the phenomena he describes. We may reproach him not for the lack of truth in any one of these utterances, but for the absence of any attempt at explicit articulations among them (and thus of an effort to eliminate the impression of contradiction), an absence that can perhaps be attributed to a taste for trenchant formulas.

To get around this difficulty, we might start with the portrait of the typical ethnologist as it is found in *Tristes Tropiques*. What Lévi-Strauss insists on in this text is neither distantiation nor identification (attitudes with respect to the society observed), but detachment—with respect to the society of the observer himself. To experience the ethnological vocation, one must already have experienced "an initial state of detachment" (p. 383); and familiarity with a different society, which is acquired in the course of the ethnologist's work, in turn enables us "to detach ourselves from our own society" (p. 392). The ethnologist's detachment thus intervenes at two different points: it is at once innate and acquired. But his relation to the foreign society is not a simple one either. Lévi-Strauss writes elsewhere that "to attain acceptance of oneself in others (the goal assigned to human knowledge by the ethnologist), one must first deny the self in oneself" (*Structural Anthropology*, II, p. 36); or one must recognize that "'I is another'" before one can discover that the other is an "I" (ibid.). In other words, the goal of ethnological description is to find the universally human, even in the representatives of humanity furthest removed from ourselves, but we can achieve this goal only by undergoing a certain detachment with respect to our own culture. The ethnologist is thus the very same mediator between cultures that Lévi-Strauss seems to attack elsewhere; and what he now praises is no longer fidelity to traditional values but rather detachment from them. A detachment that requires, as we have seen, an initial familiarity with the other . . .

The difficulty here does not take the form of an infinite regression or a vicious circle. We might be able to clarify the above by saying that each of the two movements, distancing oneself from one's own society and approaching the foreign society more closely, has to be a two-fold movement. *Distancing, step one:* In order to feel attracted to others (and without such an attraction there is no happy ethnologist), one must already feel a slight gap between one's own society and oneself; this is what impels me to leave. But it does not yet mean that I am lucid about my own society, for I lack an essential element: an external point of comparison. *Approaching, step one:* I plunge into a foreign society with the desire to understand it from within, as its own members do, and I aspire to identify with those members. But I can never succeed (if I were to do so I would have abandoned the ethnological project). Even living among them, having adopted their language and their mores, I remain different (I still have an accent), for I cannot do away with what I have been, and I continue to think *also* according to the categories I brought with me. *Distancing, step two:* I go back home (literally or mentally), but this "home" is even less close to me than it was before. I can now see it through the eyes of a foreigner, just as I could do in the foreign society. Does this mean I have become a divided being, half Persian in Paris, half Parisian in Persia? No, unless I succumb to schizophrenia. My two halves communicate with each other; they look for common ground; they translate for each other until they reach an understanding. The ethnologist does not lapse into schizoid delirium because he continues searching for a *common* meaning that in the last analysis would be universal.

Then comes the last phase, *approaching, step two:* No longer identifying the universal categories of the mind either with my own mental categories or with those I observe in the others, but not losing sight of the horizon of universality, either, I can study the foreign society—and my own society as well, since for me, as Hugues de Saint-Victor put it so aptly, the whole world has become a place of exile. The experience acquired in the course of ethnological work, according to Lévi-Strauss, "removes from our own customs that air of inherent rightness which they so easily have for anyone unacquainted with other customs, or whose knowledge is partial and biased" (*Tristes Tropiques*, p. 389). Knowledge of others is not simply one possible path toward self-knowledge: it is the only path. "No civilization can define itself if it does not have at its disposal some other civilizations for comparison" (*Structural Anthropology*, II, p. 272); neither can any individual.

The crucial moment of this ethnological education is thus not the moment of distancing (with respect to the others) but the moment of detachment (with respect to oneself). Close contact with others, extensive familiarity with their mores—these are good ways to get there; once that point has been reached (but of course we are talking about a movement that must be begun over and over again), it is not so important to know whether one's gaze is directed toward the others, in which case the distance is a given that one seeks to reduce, or on one's own society, in which case the requisite distance becomes synonymous with detachment. Here is the apparent paradox behind Lévi-Strauss's contradictory formulas: being an outsider is only an advantage if one is at the same time a perfect insider . . .

The Horizon of Universality

But if such, according to Lévi-Strauss, is the truth of the ethnological experience, we are no longer far removed from that universalism "of itinerary" whose absence we regretted earlier. For the horizon of this dialogue between cultures, of this back-and-forth movement between others and oneself, is understanding, which is bounded in turn by universality: a universality achieved not by deduction on the basis of a principle set forth as dogma, but by comparison and compromise, with the help of successive approximations—in other words, a universal that remains as close to the concrete as possible. Contrary to what Lévi-Strauss's relativist declarations might have led us to believe, the description of a society must not be a servile reflection of its own culture or ours. Or, as he himself says elsewhere, "We hope to introduce an additional exigency into our disciplines: to discover, beyond men's idea of their society, the hinges of the 'true' system" (*Structural Anthropology*, II, p. 67); the ultimate rule of knowledge remains "the scrupulous search for truth" (*The Naked Man*, p. 642). One might express this ambition negatively, by saying that the system produced will coincide neither with the one nor with the other; or, positively, by saying that it has to entail the adherence not only of the individual observer but of "all possible observers" (*Structural Anthropology*, I, p. 364)—not only all observers but also "the most distant native population" (p. 363). When he criticizes ethnologists because their descriptions threaten to reduce the specificity of the Other, Lévi-Strauss falls back into an indignant tone that would be the envy of any universalist "of itinerary": "Those who claim that the experience of the other—individual or collective—is essentially incommunicable, and that it is forever impossible, even condemnable, to seek to elaborate a language in which human experiences that are the most remote in time and space would become, at least in part, mutually intelligible—such people are doing nothing but taking refuge in a new obscurantism" (*L'Identité* [Identity], p. 10). And it must be said that, whatever declarations of principle the author may make elsewhere, these words express the only possible basis for ethnological work—and thus for that of Lévi-Strauss himself. Or perhaps especially that of Lévi-Strauss himself, who is customarily reproached by other ethnologists for being interested only in the universal structures of the human mind, and for neglecting the differences!

The universalist horizon of ethnological research has an important consequence, one that some might judge undesirable: among the countless existing societies, one of them has already secured a place for such a discourse aspiring to universality, and that is Western society, which has harbored the development of *science*. This is not to say, of course, that in other societies all thinking of the scientific type is absent or forbidden; it simply has not been institutionalized in the same way. Moreover, we must not think that the categories of Western science, as they may appear to us at any particular moment, are truly universal in their applicability; the contrary is probably most often true. This simply means that the form of scientific thought as it has been established in the Western tradition allows for the improvement of its own contents, because it is subject to the rules of critical discussion. Its criteria—logical coherence and empirical verification—are the same for all. There is thus not only a difference between the two societies, that of the observer and that of the observed, but also an asymmetry: the description that seeks to "discover the hinges of the 'true' system" necessarily takes on a form similar to that of modern science.

Lévi-Strauss is perfectly aware of this asymmetry, even if he does not expose it fully. "The insider's grasp," he writes, "(that of the indigenous person, or at least that of the observer reliving the indigenous person's experience) needs to be transposed into the language of the outsider's grasp," and he specifies: "providing certain elements of a whole which, to be valid, has to be presented in a systematic and coordinated way" (*Introduction to the Work of Marcel Mauss*, p. 31). Do the terms "systematic" and "coordinated" signify anything other than the need to bow to the requirements of scientific discourse as they have been established by Western culture? Science, or what Lévi-Strauss calls "structural interpretation," has one property that by any reckoning distinguishes it from other discourses: "Only structural interpretation can account both for itself and for the other kinds . . . it consists in making explicit a system of relationships that the other variants merely embodied" (*The Naked Man*, p. 628). Lévi-Strauss thus feels justified in defending "scientific knowledge which, however harmful it may have been, and further threatens to be, in its applications, is nevertheless a mode of knowledge whose absolute superiority cannot be denied" (p. 636). Affirming this superiority does not mean locking oneself up in categories derived from a particular culture while excluding the others, for the categories of science are never definitive, and they can be modified through contact with categories derived from other cultures.

But Lévi-Strauss usually refrains from taking such a clear stand, and for good reason: it would risk calling into question his whole anti-humanist position. In the opening passages of *The Raw and the Cooked*, in particular, he asserts several times that there are no qualitative differences between his analysis of myths and the myths themselves, thus between *logos* and *mythos*. "In seeking to imitate the spontaneous movement of mythological thought, this essay . . . has had to conform to the requirements of that thought and to respect its rhythm. It follows that this book on myths is itself a kind of myth" (p. 6). Has the object influenced the discourse that is describing it to the point of being confused with that discourse? Yes, if we are to believe Lévi-Strauss: "If the final aim of anthropology is to contribute to a better knowledge of objectified thought and its mechanisms, it is in the last resort immaterial whether in this book the thought processes of the South American

Indians take shape through the medium of my thought, or whether mine take place through the medium of theirs. What matters is that the human mind, regardless of the identity of those who happen to be giving it expression, should display an increasingly intelligible structure as a result of the doubly reflexive forward movement of two thought processes acting one upon the other, either of which can in turn provide the spark or tinder whose conjunction will shed light on both" (p. 13). If we disregard the Wagnerian style of this passage, we are left with the idea that ethnology has no special privilege with respect to its object, which is a way of denying the specificity, and *a fortiori* the superiority, of scientific discourse, both of which are asserted elsewhere.

The association of thought processes envisaged by Lévi-Strauss seems to be both perilous and suggestive. Perilous, first of all, because it dismisses obvious differences. Lévi-Strauss's discourse deals with Indian myths; these myths deal, as we might expect, not with Lévi-Strauss's analyses, but with the world in which the Indians live and with the categories that enable them to apprehend that world. Lévi-Strauss's analyses imply certain rules—logical coherence, deductions and inductions, implications and analogies—that characterize the discourse of the human sciences and make it possible to falsify that discourse (hence its cognitive superiority); the Indian narratives, for their part, obey other narrative and figurative rules; everyone knows intuitively that there is a difference between the two *genres*. Both method and object of these discourses therefore differ. And yet there is also something sound in Lévi-Strauss's formulation. Over and above the immediate difference of object, both discourses aim at the same unique reality—namely, the mental universe of the Indians. Although they are governed by different constraints, the two discourses also have a common feature: they aspire to make the world more intelligible; and we do not know in advance which one does a better job. Reading Balzac is always preferable to reading his exegetes; similarly, perhaps, reading the Indian myths may be more enriching in the long run than reading analyses of them. What is asserted here, ultimately, is the oneness of the arts and the sciences, in the name of their common search for the truth of the world.

A final example of Lévi-Strauss's hesitations can be found in the pages in which he examines the attitude of recently decolonized peoples toward ethnographic investigations. He notes with some bitterness that "the mere fact of being subjected to ethnographical investigation seems more and more distasteful to these peoples" (*Structural Anthropology,*

II, p. 53), before offering a lucid analysis of the reasons for this rejection. What these peoples are rejecting is not ethnology as such, but the relativist ideology that has frequently accompanied it (whereas, paradoxically, that ideology was nurtured, among ethnologists, by their concern for respecting the specificity of other cultures, and has undeniably contributed to increasing their knowledge of these cultures; but it is not uncommon that an effect should turn back this way against its own causes). "The dogma of cultural relativism was challenged by the very people for whose moral benefit the anthropologists had established it in the first place" (*The View from Afar*, p. 28). Furthermore, "those ethnologists who favor unilinear evolutionism find unexpected support from peoples who desire nothing more than to share in the benefits of industrialization; peoples who prefer to look at themselves as temporarily backward rather than permanently different" (*Structural Anthropology*, II, p. 53).

What Lévi-Strauss does not say is that, all things considered—and if it were absolutely necessary to choose the lesser of two evils, cultural relativism or unilinear evolutionism—the second would still be preferable, on the ethical as well as the cognitive level. We cannot be unaware, in the twentieth century, of the extremes—called "apartheid" and "final solution," among other things—to which giving up the ideal of the unity of the human race can lead. But what has to be rejected in particular is the idea that we are condemned to the sterile choice between relativism and evolutionism. Apart from the domain of technology in the narrow sense, to present evolution as an irreversible process common to all of humanity is obviously a trap, even if "faith in progress" has not been extinguished everywhere. There does exist, however, an idea of the universal that does not lead to the aporias of evolutionism any more than it leads to one-party rule.

Ethnological knowledge itself is inconceivable without a reference to universality, of the sort practiced in modern science. Evoking the possibility of "reverse ethnology" practiced by members of traditional societies on Western societies, Lévi-Strauss is content to say that this idea is "difficult to practice in a systematic manner" (p. 54). But the initial difficulty is of the theoretical order: there are not as many ethnologies as there are types of observers. The former "indigenous peoples" may, of course, "ethnographize" the Europeans, but the result will not be very different from the result that the Europeans themselves could achieve, after *detaching* themselves from their own society. Ethnology is not a separate discipline, opposed to all the other human and social sciences the way the view from afar is opposed to the view from up close, and that is why the argument over ethnological methods inevitably turns into a description of ethnologists' experience. Knowledge of cultures other than our own appears, then, along with historical research, as one of the two major modalities of comparison. As such, in turn, it is not simply one method among others but the only path leading to the requisite detachment from self and to accurate knowledge of social phenomena, whatever their nature may be.

2

Races

Race and Racism

Racism, Racialism

At this point I should like to set aside temporarily the issue of relative and universal judgments in order to look at the second series of problems I mentioned at the beginning of this study, problems of human unity and diversity. Human beings are at once alike and different; anyone can make this trivial observation, since ways of life vary throughout the world while the (biological) species remains the same. The essential problem is to determine just how far the realm of identity extends and where the realm of difference begins; we must try to discover just what relationship obtains between these two realms. Over the past several centuries, reflection on these questions has taken shape as a doctrine of *race*.

Here I must begin by introducing a terminological distinction. The word "racism," in its usual sense, actually designates two very different things. On the one hand, it is a matter of *behavior,* usually a manifestation of hatred or contempt for individuals who have well-defined physical characteristics different from our own; on the other hand, it is a matter of *ideology,* a doctrine concerning human races. The two are not necessarily linked. The ordinary racist is not a theoretician; he is incapable of justifying his behavior with "scientific" arguments. Conversely, the ideologue of race is not necessarily a "racist," in the usual sense: his theoretical views may have no influence whatsoever on his acts, or his theory may not imply that certain races are intrinsically evil.

In order to keep these two meanings separate, I shall adopt the distinction that sometimes obtains between "racism," a term designating behavior, and "racialism," a term reserved for doctrines. I must add that the form of racism that is rooted in racialism produces particularly catastrophic results: this is precisely the case of Nazism. Racism is an ancient form of behavior that is probably found worldwide; racialism is a movement of ideas born in Western Europe whose period of flowering extends from the mid-eighteenth century to the mid-twentieth.

Racialist doctrine, which will be our chief concern here, can be presented as a coherent set of propositions. They are all found in the "ideal type," or classical version of the doctrine, but some of them may be absent from a given marginal or "revisionist" version. These propositions may be reduced to five.

1. *The existence of races.* The first thesis obviously consists in affirming that there are such things as races, that is, human groupings whose members possess common physical characteristics; or rather (for the differences themselves are self-evident) it consists in affirming the relevance and the significance of that notion. From this perspective, races are equated with animal species, and it is postulated that there is the same distance between two human races as between horses and donkeys: not enough to prevent reproduction, but enough to establish a boundary readily apparent to all. Racialists are not generally content to observe this state of affairs; they also want to see it maintained: they are thus opposed to racial mixing.

The adversaries of racialist theory have often attacked the doctrine on this point. First, they draw attention to the fact that human groups have intermingled from time immemorial; consequently, their physical characteristics cannot be as different as racialists claim. Next, these theorists add a two-pronged biological observation to their historical argument. In the first place, human beings indeed differ from one another in their physical characteristics; but in order for these variations to give rise to clearly delimited groups, the differences and the groups would have to coincide. However, this is not the case. We can produce a first map of the "races" if we measure genetic characteristics, a second if we analyze blood composition, a third if we use the skeletal system, a fourth if we look at the epidermis. In the second place, within each of the groups thus constituted, we find greater distances between one individual and another than between one group and another. For these reasons, contemporary biology, while it has not stopped studying variations among human beings across the planet, no longer uses the concept of race.

But this scientific argument is not really relevant to the argument against racialist doctrines: it is a way of responding with biological data to what is actually a question of social psychology. Scientists may or may not believe in "races," but their position has no influence on the perception of the man in the street, who can see perfectly well that the differences exist. From this individual's viewpoint, the only properties that count are the immediately visible ones: skin color, body hair, facial configuration. Furthermore, the fact that there are individuals or even whole populations that are the product of racial mixing does not invalidate the notion of race but actually confirms it. The person of mixed race is identified precisely because the observer is capable of recognizing typical representatives of each race.

2. *Continuity between physical type and character.* But races are not simply groups of individuals who look alike (if this had been the case, the stakes would have been trivial). The racialist postulates, in the second place, that physical and moral characteristics are interdependent; in other words, the segmentation of the world along racial lines has as its corollary an equally definitive segmentation along cultural lines. To be sure, a single race may possess more than one culture; but as soon as there is racial variation there is cultural change. The solidarity between race and culture is evoked to explain why the races tend to go to war with one another.

Not only do the two segmentations coexist, it is alleged, but most often a causal relation is posited between them: physical differences *determine* cultural differences. We can all observe these two series of variables, physical and mental, around us; each one can be explained independently, and the two explanations do not have to be related after the fact; or else the two series can be observed without requiring any explanation at all. Yet the racialist acts as if the two series were nothing but the causes and effects of a single series. This first assertion in turn implies the hereditary transmission of mental properties and the impossibility of modifying those properties by education. The quest for unity and order in the variety of lived experience clearly relates the racialist attitude to that of the scholar in general, who tries to introduce order into chaos and whose constructions affirm the kinship of things that remain separate in the phenomenal world. It must be added that up to now, no proof has been provided for the relation of determinism or even for the interdependence of race and culture. This does not mean, of course, that proof might not one day be found, or that the search for proof is in itself harmful. We must simply note that, for the time being, the hypothesis has turned out to be unproductive.

Here I should like to mention a recent proposal to maintain the causal relation while overturning it. This view no longer holds that physical characteristics determine mental ones; rather, it holds that culture acts on nature. If, within a given population, tall people are preferred to short people, or blonds are preferred to brunettes, the population as a whole will evolve toward the desired end: its value system will serve as a genetic filter. We can also imagine a population that would prefer physical strength to intelligence, or vice versa; once again, conditions will be favorable for an extension of the qualities valued. Such an inversion of perspective opens up new possibilities for the study of mind-body interactions.

3. *The action of the group on the individual.* The same determinist principle comes into play in another sense: the behavior of the individual depends, to a very large extent, on the racio-cultural (or "ethnic") group to which he or she belongs. This proposition is not always explicit, since it is self-evident: what is the use of distinguishing races and cultures, if one believes at the same time that individuals are morally nondetermined, that they act in function of their own will freely exercised, and not by virtue of their group membership—over which they have no control? Racialism is thus a doctrine of collective psychology, and it is inherently hostile to the individualist ideology.

4. *Unique hierarchy of values.* The racialist is not content to assert that races differ; he also believes that some are superior to others, which implies that he possesses a unitary hierarchy of values, an evaluative framework with respect to which he can make universal judgments. This is somewhat astonishing, for the racialist who has such a framework at his disposal is the same person who has rejected the unity of the human race. The scale of values in question is generally ethnocentric in origin: it is very rare that the ethnic group to which a racialist author belongs does not appear at the top of his own hierarchy. On the level of physical qualities, the judgment of preference usually takes the form of aesthetic appreciation: my race is beautiful, the others are more or less ugly. On the level of the mind, the judgment concerns both

intellectual and moral qualities (people are stupid or intelligent, bestial or noble).

5. *Knowledge-based politics.* The four propositions listed so far take the form of descriptions of the world, factual observations. They lead to a conclusion that constitutes the fifth and last doctrinal proposition—namely, the need to embark upon a political course that brings the world into harmony with the description provided. Having established the "facts," the racialist draws from them a moral judgment and a political ideal. Thus, the subordination of inferior races or even their elimination can be justified by accumulated knowledge on the subject of race. Here is where racialism rejoins racism: the theory is put into practice.

The refutation of this last inference is a task not for the scientist but rather for the philosopher. Science can refute propositions like the first three listed, but it may also turn out that what appears self-evident to biologists today may be considered an error tomorrow. Even if this were to happen, however, it would not justify behavior that could be properly condemned on other grounds. Geneticists are not particularly well qualified to combat racism. Subjecting politics to science, and thus subjecting what is right to what is, makes for bad philosophy, not bad science; the humanist ideal can be defended against the racist ideal not because it is more true (an ideal cannot be more or less true) but because it is ethically superior, based as it is on the universality of the human race.

The whole set of features described constitutes racialist doctrine; each of them taken alone can also be found independently of racialism. They are all necessary to racialism; the absence of any one of them produces a related but nevertheless distinct doctrine. We shall discover that the first proposition was rejected as early as the nineteenth century, leading to a "culturalism" that is in other respects very similar to racialism. In the twentieth century, the fourth proposition has also been frequently rejected, in situations where relativist neutrality has been favored over the obligation to judge (whereas this proposition was the only common feature of racialism and universalist humanism). There are also racialists who have no interest whatsoever in any possible political implications of their doctrines (this is the case with the most famous racialist of them all, Gobineau). Still, the conjunction of the five features must be considered the classical model of racialism. On the other hand, the supplementary elements of the doctrine mentioned here are optional—for example, the fear of racial mixing, or the belief that mental faculties are inherited, or the explanation of racial warfare.

Several common features indicate that racialism belongs to the spiritual family of scientism. Indeed, we have seen how the latter is characterized by its affirmation of an integral determinism (which includes the relation of the moral realm to the physical as well as the relation of the individual to the group). Scientism is also characterized by its demand that science formulate society's goals and indicate legitimate means for attaining them. One might call racialism the tip of the scientistic iceberg. Racialist theories are no longer in fashion today, but the scientistic doctrine continues to flourish. This is why I am inclined to conduct parallel analyses of racialist ideas as such and their general scientistic context.

There can be no question of retracing the history of human race relations here, even schematically. Let it suffice to say that the most popular classification works with three races: white, yellow, and black. However, the ordinary racialist simplifies this already-impoverished schema still further: for this sort of racialist there are only two real races, or rather two poles, white and black, between which all the races are arrayed (yellow is an intermediate form). This opposition may have captured attention for reasons that have to do with universal symbolism: white-black, light-dark, day-night pairings seem to exist and function in all cultures, with the first term of each pair generally preferred. The history of humanity being what it is, the exemplary racism, racism par excellence, is thus that of whites toward blacks.

Since I shall be devoting the pages that follow to the study of racialism, perhaps I should say a further word here about racism itself. Is it bound to disappear in the coming years—as everyone, or almost everyone, appears to hope? We may be allowed our doubts. Every society has its stratifications; every society is composed of heterogeneous groups that occupy places valued differently in the social hierarchy. But these places, in modern societies, are not immutable: the peanut salesman can become president. The only differences that cannot be eradicated, in practical terms, are physical differences, those attributed to "race" and those of gender. If social differences are superposed for a long enough time on physical differences, then racist and sexist attitudes rooted in the syncretism of the social and the physical can thrive. The parallel between racism and sexism goes only so far, however, for the situation of women with respect to men is vastly

more complex. So far as "races" are concerned—that is, human groupings whose physical differences are apparent to the naked eye—we are
obliged to observe that the cohabitation of majority and minority
populations possessing distinctive physical characteristics poses serious
problems: the otherwise so dissimilar examples of the United States
and South Africa attest to this, and they are only the best-known from
a much longer list. While cultural plurality within a state does not
necessarily lead to conflict, contrary to what is sometimes alleged (what
state is not already multicultural?), the plurality of races does pose a
serious problem, as soon as it is superposed—and this is usually the
case—on a very real social stratification. The solution involves racial
mixing, that is, the disappearance of physical differences.

Anti-Semitism is a special problem. On the one hand, "Semites,"
unlike blacks, possess no strikingly obvious common characteristics
(hence the Nazis' need to require them to wear the yellow star: how
could they have been recognized otherwise?); thus, the discrimination
is purely cultural (a question of religion, mores, and so on), and cannot
be included within classical racism. On the other hand, racists have
established the category of the "Semitic race"; they have chosen to be
anti-Semites (rather than Judeophobes, for example); and the "Semitic"
case is the most serious one in the history of racialism. We are thus
obliged to take it into account in our investigation of racial theories.

The Establishment of Racialism

Thanks to the work of modern historians, the history of racialism is
well known today. François Bernier first used the word "race" in its
modern sense in 1684, but he did not dwell on it. Outside France,
Linnaeus speculated at length on the human species. In France, there
were arguments over the racial differences between the Franks and the
Gauls, ancestors of the aristocrats and of "the people," respectively
(Augustin Thierry took up these theories again early in the nineteenth
century). But for us, the most appropriate point of departure turns out
to be the beginning of Buffon's *Histoire naturelle* (*Natural History*), the
volume devoted to man, both because it is a synthesis of many travel
narratives of the seventeenth and eighteenth centuries and because the
work is in turn highly influential for later literature; its influence can
be attributed as much to its stylistic qualities as to its scientific authority.

The unity of mankind is at the base of the construction. Buffon is not unaware of mankind's variety, and his conclusion has all the more weight: "Every circumstance concurs in proving that mankind are not composed of species essentially different from each other; that, on the contrary, there was originally but one species" *(Natural History, General and Particular)*. It is not for theological reasons that Buffon takes a stand in support of monogenesis, but precisely because, in his position as a naturalist who relies upon facts, he knows that whites and blacks can procreate together: this fact already proves that they belong to one and the same species.

The unity of mankind has as a corollary the radical difference between men and animals. Buffon, whose entire natural history is written in praise of man, never tires of emphasizing mankind's difference from—and superiority to—the animal kingdom: "Between the faculties of man and the most minute animal, the distance is infinite. This is a clear proof, that the nature of man is different from that of the brute creation; that he himself constitutes a separate class, from which there are numberless degrees of descent, before we arrive at the state of the mere animal" (p. 107). If the difference had to be summed up in a word, it would be the presence or absence of reason: "Man is a reasoning being; the animal is totally deprived of that noble faculty: and as there is no intermediate point between a positive and a negative, between a rational and an irrational animal, it is evident that man's nature is entirely different from that of the animal" (ibid.). In turn, the presence or absence of reason makes itself known by the use of intentional signs: "Man exhibits, by external signs, what passes within him. He communicates his sentiments by words; and this sign is universal. The savage and the civilized man have the same powers of utterance; both speak naturally, and are equally understood . . . Animals are denied the faculty of speech . . . [They lack] the power of reflecting, even in the slightest degree" (pp. 104–105).

It is clear that this declaration of unity is accompanied by a keen sense of hierarchy, and this does not fail to create tension within the text. As it happens, Buffon is occasionally prepared to allow an exception to his categorical distinction, specifically for those representatives of mankind who are ignorant of the hierarchy in question: "[Man's nature is] so superior to that of the brutes, that nothing but the most brutal ignorance could ever dream of confounding them" (p. 102). In fact, the absence of hierarchy is, along with the absence of reason and speech, a distinctive feature of the animal world. "The strongest and most sagacious animals have not the capacity of commanding the inferior tribes, or of reducing them to a state of servitude . . . Among animals, there is no mark of subordination, nor the least trace of any of them being able to recognise or feel a superiority in his nature above that of other species" (p. 103).

Thus, we shall not be surprised to see that, along with the unity of mankind, Buffon also declares that its internal organization is hierarchical—and recognition of the hierarchy itself is a first index of one's place in it. Since men belong to a single species, they can all be judged by the same criteria, and thus they may be found to differ, some being superior to others: for Buffon, unity of the species and absolutism of value judgments go hand in hand. The unity is proved by mutual procreation; as for the hierarchy, it requires the observation of an additional human characteristic. For in fact, besides rationality, men have another common feature that they possess in greater or lesser degree, a feature of which the recognition of hierarchies is only a consequence—namely, their sociability. "[Man] augmented his own power and his knowledge by uniting them with those of his fellow creatures . . . Man commands the universe solely because he has learned to govern himself, and to submit to the laws of society" (*Natural History* [1817], I, "Dissertation on the Nature of Animals," p. 306). "A people who live without the restraint of fixed laws, or of a regular government, can only be considered as a tumultuous assemblage of barbarous and independent individuals, who obey no laws but those of passion and caprice" (*The History of Man*, p. 412). It is clear that for Buffon the term "barbarous" is correlated with "independent"—that is, asocial.

Sociability thus implies the capacity for submission, just as it presupposes the existence of laws, an established order, consistent social practices, and fixed mores. At the same time, sociability (or in any event one of its forms) is the indispensable condition for the propagation of the species, and from the number of inhabitants of a community alone one can conclude that they were highly sociable, and thus superior: quantity implies quantity. "Thus, man in every situation and under every climate, tends equally toward society. It is the uniform effect of a necessary cause; for without this natural tendency, the propagation of the species, and of course, the existence of mankind, would soon cease" (*Natural History* [1817], I, "Of Carnivorous Animals," p. 398). But man also owes to the presence of society the progress of his techniques and his tools, including those intellectual instruments we know as language and writing (practices that bring the criterion of rationality back into play).

Rationality and sociability, interdependent and common to all men, are thus present to a greater or lesser degree, which allows Buffon to contrast "civilization" or the "polis" with "barbarity" and "savagery." More precisely, a whole series of intermediate states leads from the summit to the base. "Mankind descends, by imperceptible degrees, from the most enlightened and polished nations, to people of less genius and industry; from the latter, to others more gross, but still subject to kings and to laws; from these, again, to savages" (p. 397). Buffon's entire discussion "of the varieties of the human species" (this is one of his chapter titles) is articulated in terms of this hierarchical ordering. The nations of Western Europe are at the summit, the other Europeans just below; the populations of Asia and Africa come next, and the American savages are at the very bottom.

Every social difference (of mores, of technology), like every difference in the use of reason, impels Buffon to pass value judgments on the peoples concerned. For example, the small size of a population indicates inadequate social development: that is Buffon's great argument against the Americans. "We may, therefore, presume, that the want of civilization in America is owing to the paucity of its inhabitants" (*The History of Man*, p. 411). Let us note here that Buffon takes the lack of civilization (for us a problematic notion) as his starting point, as if it were a self-evident phenomenon that allows him to deduce the small population size, whereas this is a fact to be determined by observation rather than by deduction.

Buffon holds similar views concerning the existence of "stable social practices": "The Persians, the Turks, and the Moors, have acquired a degree of civilization: but the Arabs . . . like the Tartars, . . . live without government, without law, and almost without society" (p. 351). Or technological progress: "Their houses are low and ill built. In the culture of their lands they are extremely negligent" (p. 376). Or language: "As they have but few ideas, their expressions are limited to the most common objects" (p. 413). Or religious ideas: "They are all equally gross, superstitious, and stupid" (p. 305). And once again Buffon reveals that he is giving us deductions rather than observations:

"All these savages, though they never think, have a pensive melancholy aspect" (p. 416).

By degrees, every element of a civilization turns out to be subject to a value judgment: relativism plays virtually no role for Buffon. Let us read his description of a people living in northern Japan (p. 321): "They live like savages, and their food consists of the fat and oil of whales, and other fishes." (The first "and" suggests a correlation between the two assertions; but does the flesh of marine animals make those who consume it more savage than those who eat meat?) "The women have invented no other ornament but that of painting their eyebrows and lips of a blue colour." (We note the pejorative phrasing once again; are we to believe that black coloring on eyebrows and red on lips is intrinsically superior to blue?) "The sole pleasure and occupation of the men is hunting bears and rein-deer, and fishing whales." (If pleasure is at issue, is it really much more noble to hunt pheasants and partridges?) "Though they have some Japanese customs, as that of singing with a quavering voice." (Even the timbre of the voice becomes an index of civilization—p. 321.) At the very lowest degree of civilization, according to Buffon—his own statements of principle notwithstanding—men come close to living like animals. The Australians "are perhaps the most miserable of the human species, and approach nearest to the brutes" (p. 338), a position for which the American Indian sometimes competes, for he "held only the first rank among animated beings" (*Natural History* [1817], I, "Of Animals Common to Both Continents," p. 464). Asians have little "pig eyes" (*The History of Man*, p. 361), whereas the Hottentots' eyes are simply like those of animals, and their absence of social organization likens them to brutes. Thus, by dint of accentuating the hierarchy, Buffon ends up attenuating the initial gulf he posited between men and animals, and thereby calls into question the unity of the human species with which he began. If only "the Negro and the White could not procreate together . . . , they would be two distinct species; the Negro would be to man what the ass is to the horse; or rather, if the White was man, the Negro would be a distinct animal, like monkeys" (*Buffon's Natural History*, V, "The Ass," p. 191). But Buffon yields to the biological evidence.

It may be interesting to compare Buffon and Voltaire on this point. The latter shares Buffon's convictions as to the near-animal nature of the inferior races. Speaking of Negroes, he never fails to mention that their heads are covered with wool (like sheep) rather than hair, and he betrays no discomfiture in writing that "Negroes and Negresses, when transported to the coldest climates, always continue to produce animals of the same kind" ("Essay on the Customs and the Spirit of Nations," pp. 243–244). Moreover, he has a ready explanation for the Africans' animal nature: "It is not improbable that in warm climates apes have ravished girls" (p. 245). But, unlike Buffon, Voltaire believes in polygenesis, even though he recognizes that rationality and sociability are characteristics common to all mankind: since the differences between the races are so profound, is it not more logical to suppose that humanity arose spontaneously in several different places around the globe and thus that, in the extreme case, humans do not belong to the same species? Freed from religious "prejudices," Voltaire is not afraid to draw this conclusion. "Only a blind man could doubt that the whites, Negroes, albinos, Hottentots, Laplanders, Chinese and Americans are entirely different races" (p. 243). Only a blind man could doubt that the sun *rises* and *sets*, and yet the sun does no such thing; might the same be true of races? But for Voltaire the human races are as dissimilar as animal or vegetable species; more simply put, the races *are* species. "I am quite justified in believing that what is true of trees is true of men: that pears, firs, oaks, and apricots do not come from the same tree, and that bearded white men, woolly headed Negroes, Asiatics with their manes, and beardless men do not come from the same man" (*Traité de métaphysique* [Treatise on Metaphysics], I, pp. 192–193). Voltaire keeps the unitary scale of human values intact, but he gives up the unity of mankind. And it turns out that his polygenesis squares well with the description of the races he and Buffon share; for this reason, perhaps, it is adopted by the nineteenth-century racialists.

Faith in a rigid hierarchy of values, at the top of which sits European civilization, is common to many Encyclopedists. However, there is as yet no reason to speak of racialism: we are still operating within a classification of cultures, not bodies. It is true that Buffon also manifests a characteristic skepticism about the effects of education: human beings are capable of modification, to be sure, but the process takes years and years. The consequences of this doctrine are already apparent in Buffon's views on slavery. For him, blacks are inferior beings, so it is normal after all for them to be subjugated and reduced to slavery. Buffon begins his exposé on the subject by categorizing slaves according to their capacity for work, as well as the strength of the odor they give off when they perspire; no value judgment accompanies this presentation. Then, as he says himself, he takes pity on their fate: not because they are slaves, but because their masters treat them badly, deprive them of food or beat them; such excesses could be avoided. It is never a question of doing away with slavery itself.

Racialist doctrine, properly speaking, receives an indispensable complement at this point, owing to the influence of Buffon's "scientific" attitude. When he inquires about the factors contributing to variety within the human species, Buffon lists three parameters: skin color, body size and shape, and what he calls "the dispositions of different people" (*The History of Man*, p. 302)—that is, their mores. Then he decides to unify the explanation of these three variables. Let us note here a striking feature of Buffon's scientific discourse: before *telling* us that there is continuity between the physical and moral realms, Buffon *suggests* this indirectly. The major figure of monist determinism, as practiced by Buffon, is precisely this type of *coordination:* on the strength of a comma, a conjunction, or an enumeration, the author insinuates without asserting; the reader absorbs what is "presupposed" much less skeptically than what is "posited." By setting out to deal with both physical *and* cultural differences in a single passage, Buffon behaves as if the correlation between the two were already established; when he reaches the point of stating this correlation in the form of a thesis, his reader can do little but acquiesce. We have in fact been prepared for such an assimilation by the frequent use of "coordination" in Buffon's earlier descriptions: "A race of men . . . [whose] countenances are equally savage as their manners," he writes in passing (p. 302). Or, elsewhere: "The natives of this country are very black, savage, and brutal" (p. 336). Who would notice that the main assertion here is conveyed by a comma? And in another passage by a "likewise": "[They] are easily distinguished from the others by their colour, which is much blacker; they are likewise more barbarous and stupid" (p. 346). Conversely, in another country, "the men are likewise very handsome. They are naturally ingenious" (p. 361). Here the relation between mind and matter has become natural.

But Buffon is not content to suggest: he explicitly declares that skin color and ways of life, thus levels of civilization, are related. He writes that "the differences in colour depend much, though not entirely, upon the climates. There are many other causes . . . The nature of the food is one of the principal causes . . . Manners, or the mode of living, may also have considerable effects" (p. 373). What does the relation between skin color and manners consist in? A civilized person avoids wretchedness, while a member of a savage nation is subject to famine and natural upheavals; consequently, Buffon concludes, he is led "to act . . . more frequently like a brute than a man" (p. 373): here again we find the hierarchy that puts unity to the test. Manners and mores thus function through the intermediary of climate and food, heightening or diminishing their effects; but the relation, however indirect, is no less clear-cut: lack of civilization produces blackness of skin. "[They have a] rough and savage manner of living. These circumstances are sufficient to render the Tartars more swarthy than the Europeans, who want nothing to make life easy and comfortable" (p. 443). Blackness of countenance, rigor of climate and absence of civilization are completely fused here.

But if differences in mores are explained by climate and food, these differences nevertheless function autonomously. Buffon imagines two peoples, one civilized, the other barbarian, artificially placed in identical conditions: the differences do not disappear, at least not at once. "Supposing two nations, thus differently circumstanced, to live under the same climate, it is reasonable to think, that the savage people would be more ugly, more tawny, more diminutive, and more wrinkled, than the nation that enjoyed the advantages of society and civilization" (p. 373). The physical and the moral realms are thus irrevocably linked. Now if the relation between skin color on the one hand and climate or food on the other is an uncertain but plausible relation, to the extent that it brings together two physical phenomena, the relation between color and mores is not at all of the same type: these phenomena present themselves from the outset as heterogeneous, and it is the scientist who brings them together. We are now in a position to note that the racialist theory in its entirety is found in Buffon's writings. He considers the existence of the races self-evident, he asserts the interdependence of the physical and the moral realms, he implies the determination of the individual by the group, he proclaims straightforwardly a unitary value system, and finally he draws political and practical consequences from his doctrine (slavery is not illegitimate).

If the interdependence of the physical and moral realms is established, aesthetics can no longer remain separate from ethics; what is more, aesthetic judgments have to play a crucial role. We might have thought that the domain of aesthetic judgment would not fall within the scope of Buffon's unifying and hierarchizing mind. Like everyone else in his day, he knows that tastes vary according to time and place; he says so himself in his book: "The ideas of beauty are so different, so capricious, and even contradictory, that the women, it is probable, have gained more by the art of making themselves amiable, than by beauty itself, of which men form such opposite judgments . . . The taste of beauty, among the ancients, differed widely from ours . . . Every nation has ideas of beauty peculiar to itself; and every individual has his own notions and taste concerning that quality" (pp. 202–203).

Here is a self-evident and sensible position, or so we might suppose. But in fact Buffon is unable to acknowledge that such a large component of human judgment stems from cultural relativism or even from the vagaries of the individual. We can watch him shift over, in practice, from his relativist knowledge to his universalist convictions when he describes an African population: "They have the same ideas of beauty with the Europeans" (up to this point beauty is only an idea, similar to ours or different, for the various populations); "for they are fond of fine eyes, a small mouth, thin lips, and a well proportioned nose" (p. 383): but can we put "small" and "fine" on the same level? Our idea of beauty is characterized by the fact that it *is* beauty . . .

In reality, the word "ugly," a word whose content varies from one people to another, as Buffon ought to know, is one of the words he uses most frequently in these pages. And ugliness, like beauty, is defined by skin color more than by the shape of the face: "less deformed, and whiter" (p. 314); "the fairest and most handsome" (p. 360); "exceedingly fair and beautiful" (p. 362); "the women . . . are fair, beautiful" (p. 367); "a little fairer, well made, and tolerably beautiful" (p. 375); "more tawny and more ugly" (p. 322); "black and deformed" (p. 345); "worse shaped and more ugly" (p. 343); "brown or yellow, and not at all agreeable" (pp. 347–348); "the women, though black, . . . are comely and handsome" (p. 341); "these men, though of an olive colour, are comely and handsome" (p. 342); "the men, in general, are brown and tawny, but, at the same time, pretty comely and handsome" (p. 360); "their features are regular . . . but their complexion is yellow and swarthy" (p. 369) . . .

Buffon's aesthetic ideal is thus as narrowly ethnocentric as his ethical and cultural ideals, but with even less supporting argument. The Europeans serve as his fixed point of comparison to establish the distance that separates other peoples from perfection. Primitive man was white, and any change of color is a form of degeneration; unlike civilization, which is acquired, physical beauty is given at the outset. "The most temperate climate lies between the fortieth and fiftieth degree of latitude, and it produces the most handsome and beautiful men" (p. 444). "Nature, in her most perfect exertions, made men white" (p. 422).

If Buffon's discourse, despite its absurdity, proved to be highly influential, it is because it reached its readers adorned with the prestige of science. On the one hand, through a new effect of contiguity, Buffon's renown as a naturalist served to underwrite the assertions of Buffon the anthropologist; and he himself did not hesitate to use arguments from one area of expertise to give more credence to his ideas in another. "If an example be demanded, I shall produce one from the brute creation [the flesh of the hares]" (p. 404); "an example taken from the other animals will still farther confirm what has been advanced" (p. 438); and so on. Recognizing his authority in one area, the reader is ready to follow him in another; but does an observation about animals really confirm a statement about human beings? Furthermore, Buffon reinforces his authority by subjecting other authors to critical examination; he thus underlines his own probity as a scientist, his own concern for truth, and his text becomes all the more credible. In reality, every time a traveler's narrative contradicts him, he dismisses it as unworthy of confidence, not in the name of other facts but in the name of the doctrine itself. The Americans must be very few in number; travelers report to the contrary, but "it is easy to perceive that these facts are exaggerated" (p. 429). Buffon maintains that the Americans have neither laws nor customs; writers claim they do, but "most authors have mistaken the particular actions of individuals . . . for the general and established manners of a nation" (pp. 411–412), and then "all this is problematical" (p. 416), and so on. This is how Buffon, with an authority well grounded in his prestige as a naturalist and critical thinker, can pass off his racist views, based on "coordination" alone, as a tested scientific theory.

It is important to note here that Buffon's major principles are, in themselves, responsible not for the aberrations of racialism but only for their unwarranted extension. One may well aspire to a unitary and thus universal scale of values, and one may distinguish between civilization and barbarity without at the same time extending the notion of civilization so it will encompass practices involving food, dress, or hygiene: not every difference requires a value judgment. One may want to render the phenomenal world more intelligible and seek order behind chaos, without at the same time believing that all variations have a common origin, and, in particular, that physical differences are responsible for moral and cultural differences (or vice versa). It is legitimate to observe differences between cultures separated in time and space; but it is unacceptable to conclude from these differences that there is discontinuity within the human race (whereas Buffon came to this conclusion implicitly and Voltaire explicitly): this is so both because the conclusion contradicts the results of impartial research, and because it contains the potential for a transgression of the highest ethical values of humanity, those whose establishment is involved in the very definition of what is human.

Popular Racialism

The racialist doctrine set forth by Buffon was destined to be modified in many ways over the next two centuries by a number of more or less original thinkers. But before examining some of their contributions, it would be useful to become acquainted with popular opinion in the second half of the nineteenth century, one hundred to one hundred fifty years after Buffon. I shall focus here on Renan and Le Bon, for their representativeness: the former because he was one of the most influential thinkers of the nineteenth century, the latter because he was a talented popularizer whose works, translated into some ten languages, sold hundreds of thousands of copies (this is the case in particular with *The Psychology of Peoples*). Renan and Le Bon also have their own more original ideas on the subject of race, but I shall set these aside for a time so as to concentrate on the sedimentations, in their work, of the ordinary anonymous racialist ideology of the period, a sort of racial common sense that could have appeared in a "Dictionary of received ideas" of the time.

The original aspect of Renan's contribution, as we shall see, involves the opposition between the Aryan and Semitic "races." What is not original, what he does not ponder at length, what he is content merely to transmit, is the division of humanity into several major races—white, yellow, and black—and the hierarchization of this division. The three races have separate origins: in this respect Renan is in Voltaire's camp rather than Buffon's. Philology, he believed, had managed to establish the common origin of all whites ("in Imaüs or Belourtag"); but the other varieties of the human species are not included: philology "recoils at doing the same for the Chinese race, even more so for the inferior races"—that is, black (*Histoire générale et système comparé des langues sémitiques* [General History and Comparative System of the Semitic Languages], p. 587).

Like Renan, Gobineau, and Taine, whose work he most often simply summarizes and systematizes, Le Bon is a partisan of polygenesis, and he equates the human races with animal species (something Buffon rightly refused to do). "By the aid of clearly defined anatomical characteristics, such as the colour of the skin, and the shape and volume of the skull, it has been possible to establish that the human race comprises several species which are quite distinct and probably of very different origin" (*The Psychology of Peoples*, p. 4). If the term "race" is used in preference to "species," Le Bon suggests, it is in order to avoid offending Christian sensitivities, for Christians maintain that all men belong to the same species: here science is opposed to religious prejudice!

Let us quickly survey the characteristics attributed to the three races.

For Renan, the inferior race includes black Africans, Australian aborigines, and American Indians (these groups are thus linked by virtue of their cultural inferiority rather than on the basis of common physical features). Renan assumes that in the beginning the whole earth was overrun with members of these races; they have been progressively eliminated by members of other races. "Wherever the Aryans and the Semites went—in fact, in every country where they settled—they encountered half-savage races which they exterminated" (*Histoire générale*, p. 585). Let us note that no value judgment accompanies the report of exterminations. The inferior races are defined not only by their primitive or uncivilized status but by their inability to become civilized, their lack of susceptibility to progress: this is what makes it possible to defend the thesis of polygenesis. "An absolute lack of capacity for organization and progress" (p. 586). "Furthermore, we do not have a single example of a savage population that has moved up to civilization" (p. 581). Elsewhere, Renan speaks of "the everlasting infancy of those non-perfectible races" (*The Future of Science*, p. 153), of "peoples doomed to remain stationary" (p. 155). The break with the humanist ideal is quite clear: what Rousseau had presented as the distinctive feature of the human species—that is, its perfectibility—is denied to part of humanity. We no longer find unity in the species, or faith in the capacity of the human will to achieve continually renewed goals; in the place of Enlightenment voluntarism (artificialism) we find a kind of submission to Providence ("doomed").

The classification of the major races proposed by Le Bon (for the moment I shall leave aside his innovative views on the "historical races") is, like Renan's, an adaptation of Buffon's approach. Le Bon distinguishes four (not just three) degrees. At the very bottom of the scale, we find the "primitive races" of which "the aboriginal Australians are cases in point"; "no trace of culture" is found in the primitive races, which "have remained in [a] state bordering on animality" (*The Psychology of Peoples*, p. 27). Their fate is the one Renan had already evoked: "Experience proves that every inferior people which is confronted with a superior people is inevitably condemned to disappear at an early date" (p. 51). We are apparently dealing with a natural process that may be justifiably accelerated to some extent: Le Bon does not spell out the means by which the "disappearance" comes about.

On the next rung of the ladder, we find "the inferior races," of which blacks are the chief example. As Renan had already declared, these races are not perfectible. They are "capable of attaining to the rudiments of civilisation, but to the rudiments only" (p. 27); their members are "barbarians, condemned by their mental inferiority never to shake off their barbarism" (p. 104). Le Bon occasionally just rephrases Renan's statements: "There is no example in ancient or modern history of a negro people having reached a certain level of civilisation" (p. 104).

The next race up, for Renan, is the "intermediate" race—that is, yellow: Chinese and Japanese, Tartars and Mongols. Once again, its characteristics are derived from its name: it is capable of being civilized, but only up to a certain point; it is inherently incomplete, having gone from a period of infancy straight into old age without ever achieving a true maturity. "China, that shriveled old child" (*Histoire du peuple d'Israël* [History of the People of Israel], p. 33). In its turn China rejoins the nonhuman part of humanity: "China is a sort of non-perfectible Europe" ("Histoire de l'instruction publique en Chine," p. 577). Even the Chinese language has "an inorganic and incomplete structure" (*L'Origine du langage* [The Origin of Language], p. 99), and "we find Chinese civilization incomplete and defective" (*Histoire générale*, p. 588). The value judgment leaves no room for doubt: "China . . . has always been inferior to our West even in its worst days" ("The Future of Religion in Modern Society," p. 342). A given language and culture are clearly being measured here by the yardstick of another language and culture; hence, every difference is perceived as a lack. But what justifies the choice of one particular language and culture as a norm? Renan does not linger over this; he is dealing with self-evident facts, and he does not seek out supporting arguments. These intermediate races are not only relatively unproductive; they also present a potential danger for the superior races: "The Tartar races . . . have acted only as natural scourges to destroy the work of the others" ("The Share of the Semitic People in the History of Civilization," p. 153).

Those races that Le Bon calls "average" occupy the third level in his hierarchy: "the Chinese, the Japanese, the Mongolians, and the Semitic peoples" (*The Psychology of Peoples*, p. 27). Here again, the Japanese and the Arabs are linked only by criteria involving civilization: Le Bon has drawn the logical conclusion from Renan's subdivision of the white race into Aryans and Semites, and from the latter's self-evident inferiority; he has thus added them to the representatives of the yellow race.

At the top, for Renan, we have the "superior," or white, race, which has beauty on its side, subject, as was already the case for Buffon, to absolute judgments. These two races, Aryan and Semitic, "have in common, and are alone in possessing, the sovereign characteristic of *beauty*" (*Histoire générale*, p. 576). These races have never known the savage state and they have civilization in their blood. "These two races appear everywhere with a certain degree of culture . . . We must therefore suppose that the civilized races have not gone through the savage state and that they have borne within themselves, from the very beginning, the seeds of future progress" (p. 581). Civilization is innate in some races, inaccessible to others: one could hardly ask for a clearer way of disavowing the unity of the species and submitting to the verdict of Providence. The proof, for Renan, is historical: only the various representatives of the white race have contributed to the development of world civilization. "One after another, the Jews, the Syrians, and the Arabs have entered into the project of general civilization and have played their role as an integral part of the great perfectible race; this cannot be said of the Negro race, nor of the Tartar race, nor even of the Chinese race, which has created a distinct civilization for itself" (p. 577). The inferior races are thus relegated to a kind of subhumanity.

With Le Bon we find only one human group left at the top: "Only the Indo-European peoples can be classed among the superior races" (p. 27). As was the case for Buffon, the criterion that makes this classification possible for Le Bon is reason and its consequences, technological inventions. "Among the primitive and inferior races . . . a greater or lesser incapacity to reason is always met with" (p. 29); among the superior races, on the contrary, we find "great inventions in the arts, the sciences, and industry . . . , it is they who have discovered steam and electricity" (p. 28). The difference between the top of the scale and the bottom is immense. Renan had already declared that, "as for the inferior races . . . , an abyss separates them from the great families of whom we have just been speaking" (*Histoire générale*, pp. 580–581), and Le Bon repeats: "The mental abyss that separates them is evident" (*The Psychology of Peoples*, p. 28).

The idea of the inequality of the human races is a constant in Renan's thinking, even if he does not always pay much attention to it. This is because for him it goes without saying. "Men are not equal; races are not equal. The negro, for instance, is made to serve the great enterprises that have been willed and conceived by the white man" (*Philosophical Dialogues and Fragments*, p. xxix). And he imagines with horror what would result from the opposite position: "The lack of sound ideas regarding the inequality of races may bring about a general debasement . . . Fancy what a spectacle the earth would have presented, had it been peopled solely with negroes, subordinating everything to individual enjoyment in the midst of a general mediocrity" (pp. 36–37).

This view accounts for Renan's reaction to Gobineau's book: despite major reservations to which we shall return, and even if we allow for the prevailing conventions of politeness, Renan sends Gobineau a letter full of revealing praise: "You have produced a most remarkable book, highly vigorous and original" ("Lettre à Gobineau" [Letter to Gobineau], p. 203); "power, loftiness, logic that I unhesitatingly judge admirable! Your concluding pages are truly astonishing in their forcefulness and liveliness: I shall quote them" (pp. 204–205). This last promise, which must have been a supreme compliment in Renan's eyes, was never kept, and Renan avoided all public reference to Gobineau's work, perhaps in order to avoid tarnishing his own reputation (which does not mean that he plagiarized Gobineau: their writings are contemporaneous, and both in fact drew from the same ambient "common sense"; for Renan, Gobineau was a rival—perhaps a somewhat compromising one, for he was not a good philologist—rather than a source).

In 1890, when Renan wrote a preface to *The Future of Science* (a work written in 1848), one of the major criticisms he made of his own youthful text was that it had not adequately stressed the hierarchy constituted by human societies. "I had not a sufficiently clear perception of the inequality of races" (p. xiv). This is no longer the case when he writes his preface: "The onward course of civilization has been made manifest in its general laws. The inferiority of certain races to others is proved" (p. xv). However, from our own vantage point, this idea of inequality was not entirely absent from the texts Renan wrote around 1848, *L'Avenir de la science, L'Origine du langage*, and *L'Histoire générale et système comparé des langues sémitiques*. What might these texts have contained if Renan had been enlightened earlier? Between 1848 and 1890, Renan had not forgotten his own principles, either: "We reject as a fundamental factual error the equality of human individuals and the equality of races; the higher components of humanity must determine the lower ones" ("Nouvelle Lettre à M. Strauss," p. 455). After this, can one really call oneself a relativist, as Renan does, and assert that all values are socially and historically determined? The relativist façade hides a baldly ethnocentric construction.

This vision of the races quite naturally entails some practical consequences. In *The Future of Science*, Renan imagines an educational project that retains some traces of the spirit of the Enlightenment (Helvétius or Condorcet): "The scientific and experimental study of the education of barbarous races will become one of the most striking problems offered to the mind of Europe" (p. 359). However, at roughly the same time, in *L'Origine du langage*, a different project is emerging, one that has to be recognized as imperialistic: "Since the Aryan race and the Semitic race . . . are destined to conquer the world and restore unity to the human species, the rest of the world counts, alongside these races, only as experiments, obstacles, or auxiliaries" (p. 115). Obviously Providence is still assigning roles to the various populations of the globe. The white race alone is endowed with the dignity of the human subject, while the other races are restricted to instrumental functions: they do not exist in themselves but exist only as objects of the imperial program to which the white race is predestined.

Renan makes this vision somewhat more explicit in "La Réforme intellectuelle et morale de la France" [Intellectual and Moral Reform in France]: "Nature created a race of laborers, the Chinese . . . ; a race of field-workers, the Negroes . . . ; a race of masters and soldiers, the European race" (p. 390). He conceives of a world state (the master race would "restore unity to the human species") in which races would replace classes, but his vision is less generous than that of Auguste Comte, who may be one of his sources of inspiration. Everything is the work of nature; it is futile to protest. Humanity has no common ideal; there are as many models for happiness as there are races. "The life that disgusts our workers would make a Chinaman or a *fellah* happy, for these creatures are in no way military. Let everyone do the work he is intended to do, and all will be well" (p. 391). One might wonder how an entire people could be destined for a single function. Renan does not encumber his text with proofs; when something occurs to him, he does not hesitate to imagine what he needs: "The man of the people is almost always, among us, a nobleman who has lost his status" (p. 390): apparently, in the beginning, France—all of Europe perhaps— was populated exclusively with noblemen; some remained noble, while the others, impoverished, gave birth to "the people"!

If the function of triumphant military mastery exists in nature, then expansionist wars are entirely legitimate, provided that they do not erupt between "masters" but allow the conquest of worker and peasant peoples; in other words, the perfect war is a colonial war. Colonial wars have a further advantage, one particularly important to Renan: they allow us to study the conquered peoples at our leisure. "The scientific exploration of Algeria will be one of France's claims to glory in the nineteenth century, and the best justification for a conquest" ("La Société berbère" [Berber Society], p. 550).

And Renan is not disquieted by the future submission of the inferior races, any more than he is shocked by their past extermination: "The conquest of a country of inferior race by a superior race that settles there to govern it is not at all shocking" ("La Réforme," p. 390). Renan is fond of saying, as we shall see, that the results of scientific inquiry must not dictate political decisions. Yet here in fact it is science—philology or ethnology—that establishes the superiority or inferiority of the various races; thus, science is what allows us to call an act shocking or, on the contrary, acceptable, even desirable (tending in the direction of nature or progress). It is clear that "natural laws" and "science" have become the modern synonyms for "Providence" or "destiny." On the one hand, there are the superior races and countries, whose destiny is to spread beyond their borders; on the other, there are the inferior races and countries, those of workers and peasants, which are predestined to play a complementary role by welcoming the victorious warriors. Renan thus points toward universal concord, and he is right to invoke Providence: "Just as conquests between equal races must be condemned [Germany is wrong to conquer France], the regeneration of the inferior or bastardized races by the superior races is in the providential order of humanity" (ibid.).

At other points, Renan is not satisfied to imagine the transformation of the social life of the other races, but also suggests their physical transformation, through the contribution of superior blood: a eugenicist project thus parallels the imperialist one. Writing to Gobineau, Renan counters the latter's pessimism: "A very small quantity of noble blood infused into a population suffices to ennoble it" (p. 204); his assertions about the need to regenerate the inferior races, in "La Réforme intellectuelle et morale," are contemporaneous with the earliest formulations of eugenicism by Darwin's cousin Galton. In his letter to Gobineau, Renan specifies that he has in mind not the very lowest races (the blacks, and so on) whose situation is desperate and who are destined for extermination, as we know from other texts, but rather the intermediate races or the inferior strata of the white race itself. But does the high degree of importance granted to Providence still leave room for human will, which Renan is so fond of praising elsewhere?

Le Bon's position is distinguished by its tendency to identify the hierarchy of race with the hierarchies of sex and class (although Renan, too, was beginning to make the latter association, as we have seen). There is no need to go to Africa to observe the inferior races: we can simply study the workers at home. "The lowest strata of the European societies are homologous with the primitive men" (*The Psychology of Peoples*, p. 29). "It would suffice . . . to allow time to act to see the superior grades of a population separated intellectually from the inferior grades by a distance as great as that which separates the white man from the negro, or even the negro from the monkey" (p. 43). Within each country, some part of the population does not lend itself to civilization; Le Bon sees this threat hanging over the United States, a country that has absorbed too many members of inferior races into its work force.

And there is no need even to go to factories or farms to see how primitive mentalities work: it suffices to go into the kitchen and take a quick look at that inferior being who is your own wife (Le Bon's reader is necessarily male). Between observer and observed, then, there is a "great mental separation . . . The man and the woman may have common interests and sentiments, but never like chains of thought. The difference in their logical faculties is alone sufficient to create between them an insuperable gulf" (p. 36). We can see that, in Le Bon's eyes, the civilized white man leads a dangerous life, surrounded as he is by so many abysses. The proof of female inferiority, and of the similarities between women and Negroes, is provided by craniology, another of Dr. Le Bon's specialties. White skulls are larger than black skulls—but only in men; male skulls are larger than female skulls—but only in whites. "The average of the skulls of female Parisians classes them among the smallest skulls with which we are acquainted, almost on a level with the skulls of Chinese women, and scarcely above the feminine skulls of New Caledonia" (p. 49). What else is there to say!

Scientific Determinism

Racialist doctrine, as we have seen, is linked from the outset to the rise of science, or more precisely to scientism—that is, the use of science to establish an ideology. The fact that both Buffon and Diderot contributed to the *Encyclopedia* is no accident. We shall rediscover the two doctrines even more tightly interwoven in the second, culminating period of racialist thought, during the second half of the nineteenth century. Thus, we need to examine the scientistic premises of racial doctrine in the works of its most zealous proponents: Taine, Renan, and Gobineau.

Scientism is essentially based, as we have seen, on two postulates: integral determinism and the subordination of ethics to science. Hippolyte Taine, the great prophet of determinism in the second half of the nineteenth century, was also one of the most influential racialists. If we take him at his word, no event occurs without a cause; our very ways of thinking and feeling, not to mention our acts, are dictated by completely identifiable and extraordinarily stable causes. This determinism is integral, first of all in the sense that it concerns even the smallest elements of every phenomenon: "Here, as elsewhere we have but a mechanical problem; the total effect is a result, depending entirely on the magnitude and direction of the producing causes" (*Histoire de la littérature anglaise*, in English *History of English Literature*, p. 23). But it is also integral in that it concerns all forms of activity: "And so for every kind of human production—for literature, music, the fine arts, philosophy, science, the state, industries, and the rest. Each of these has for its direct cause a moral disposition, or a combination of moral dispositions: the cause given, they appear; the cause withdrawn, they vanish" (p. 31).

It is incumbent upon science to reveal just how this determinism works. "Here [in psychology] as elsewhere we must search out the causes after we have collected the facts. No matter if the facts be physical or moral, they all have their causes; there is a cause for ambition, for courage, for truth, as there is for digestion, for muscular movement, for animal heat. Vice and virtue are products, like vitriol and sugar; and every complex phenomenon arises from other more simple phenomena on which it hangs" (pp. 10–11). Science is nothing but knowledge of causes, and morality does not constitute a realm apart. We are reminded of one of Helvétius' formulas: "I imagined that morality ought to be treated like all the other sciences, and founded on experiment" (*Essays on the Mind and Its Several Faculties*, p. iii).

In a world so thoroughly predetermined, is there any room left at all for the exercise of freedom? Taine would like to think there is: "An analogous discovery [analogous to the discovery of laws in the natural sciences] ought to provide men with a way of foreseeing and modifying the events of history to a certain extent" (*Histoire de la littérature anglaise*, p. xxiii). But to what extent? Taine seems to get around the problem by bringing "moral dispositions" or "historical forces" into play at two distinct moments: first as sources of individual activity (in which case they allow for no exceptions); then as the outcome of the actions of many individuals (in which case they are subject to influence).

The fact remains that the individual as such determines nothing, and there is no place for an autonomous ethics: once we have come to know causes, there is no more room for personal choice. "The right to govern human beliefs has shifted entirely to the side of experience, and . . . precepts or doctrines, instead of authorizing observation, receive from those beliefs their entire credibility" ("Préface" to the second edition, *Essais de critique et d'histoire* [Essays in Criticism and History], p. xxi). It is obvious here that for Taine the relation between knowledge and morality is simply an inversion of the relation that had prevailed before the Enlightenment. Then, doctrines had the role of authorizing the observation of experience; now, the role of observation is either to invest moral precepts with its prestige or else to deny them any validity. And in a commentary on Théodule Ribot's *L'Hérédité*, a work that falls into the category of social Darwinism (the survival of the fittest), Taine concludes: "Science leads to morality, by seeking only truth" (*Derniers Essais de critique et d'histoire* [Last Essays in Criticism and History], p. 110). Morality is merely a supplementary product, delivered free of charge to patient seekers after truth.

It is already apparent that for Taine there is no difference between the natural world and the human world: the same causality is at work in both contexts, producing vitriol or vice accordingly. When he describes the world of men, Taine's favorite metaphors come from the vegetable realm: works of art have seeds that fall upon a certain soil, to be swept away by the wind, chilled by frost; then they sprout, grow, flourish. "There are similarly connected data in the moral as in the physical world, as rigorously bound together, and as universally extended in the one as in the other. Whatever in the one case produces, alters, or suppresses the first term, produces, alters, or suppresses the second as a necessary consequence" (*History of English Literature*, p. 31).

As a result, there are no significant differences between the natural sciences and the human sciences: witness the countless formulas in which psychology is presented as parallel to chemistry, or history to physiology. This is hardly surprising: "A career similar to that of the natural sciences is open to the moral sciences; . . . history, the most recent arrival, can discover laws like its elders; . . . it can, like them and in its own province, govern men's conceptions and guide their efforts" (*Essais*, p. xxviii). Thus, it is no longer enough for science to discover humanity's goals as a secondary product of its activity; science is to take over the role of social guide directly. If there is any difference at all between the natural and the human sciences, it does not lie in the character or mechanisms of their respective subject matters, but in the relative ease and precision with which observations can be made in each realm.

The reason for the unity of scientific disciplines clearly lies in the oneness of the world; Taine's professed materialism is as thoroughgoing as his determinism. "One could list many other analogies between natural history and human history. This is because their subject matter is similar" (p. xxvii). This postulate will be spelled out in several examples—which, however, are none too convincing. In both cases, phenomena are naturally classified as individuals, species, and genres (!).

In both cases, the object undergoes continual transformation. In both cases, molecules are transmitted by heredity and are modified only slowly under the influence of the environment. What is common to the two forms of history or science is clearly only the *vocabulary* Taine has chosen to use. He is thus quite pleased to note that others around him have established similar correlations between the physical and the moral realms. Our ancestors had skulls smaller than ours by one-fortieth, and their ideas were not as clear as ours. "This one-fortieth capacity added to the vase indicates the perfecting of the contents" (*Derniers Essais*, p. 108).

In all this, Taine comes across as a faithful, if hyperbolic, disciple of the materialism and scientism of the Encyclopedists, Sade as well as Helvétius and Diderot. And yet he is a resolute adversary of the Enlightenment, since he sees it only as the dissemination of the "classical spirit" that he lambasted in *Les Origines de la France contemporaine (The Origins of Contemporary France)* and that led to the French Revolution. How can we account for this? The answer is that Taine has settled on an implicit compartmentalization: from the Enlightenment he accepts faith in determinism and all that ensues, while he rejects universalism, faith in the essential unity of the human race, and the ideal of equality. Taine holds onto materialism and discards humanism. Early in the *History of English Literature* he rejects the universalist credo as follows: "[People of the eighteenth century] thought men of every race and century were all but identical; the Greek, the barbarian, the Hindoo, the man of the Renaissance, and the man of the eighteenth century as if they had been turned out of a common mould, and all in conformity to a certain abstract conception, which served for the whole human race. They knew man, but not men; . . . they did not know that the moral constitution of a people or an age is as particular and distinct as the physical structure of a family of plants or an order of animals" (p. 8).

Rousseau wanted us to know men in their diversity, the better to know man (it is true that he himself did not devote much time to the first stage). Taine for his part dismisses the second stage: man does not exist, only *men*, in their historical and geographical diversity; human groups differ from each other as much as animal or vegetable species do. Taine thus distances himself not only from Rousseau but also from Diderot (who still believed in a universal human nature), to rejoin Voltaire, partisan of polygenesis. Universalism, which had provided the constitutive framework for scientistic philosophy, has clearly been abandoned; thus, we discover that universalism was not a necessary condition for scientism but only a contingent circumstance, since scientism (faith in determinism, subordination of ethics) can be combined—indeed, is preferentially combined, in the nineteenth century—with relativism and the rejection of the unity of the human race, with the racialist and nationalist doctrines that find their source of inspiration in Taine.

The Reign of Science

If Taine subscribed above all to Diderot's thoroughgoing determinism, Renan, another crucial influence in the history of racialism, became the high priest of the cult of science, even though he also tended to recognize the action of free will alongside that of transindividual causes. His career began in 1848 with an encomium to science entitled *The Future of Science*. The book was not published until 1890, but Renan never abandoned the major tenets of the doctrine he professed in that first text, and in the writings he published in the interim he often drew examples and arguments from his earliest work. Science is humanity's noblest feature, its greatest claim to glory. "The progress of positive research is the brightest acquisition of humanity . . . A world without science is slavery, it is man turning the millstone, subjected to matter, no different from a beast of burden" ("L'Instruction supérieure en France" [Higher Education in France], p. 70). Without science, humanity would not deserve our respect. "We love humanity because it produces science; we cling to morality because only honest races can be scientific races" ("Examen de conscience philosophique" [Philosophical Examination of Conscience], p. 1179). Science warrants this place, for science alone leads us toward solutions to humanity's enigmas; its role is to provide "the final explanation to mankind of the meaning of things, the explanation of man to himself" (*The Future of Science*, p. 17). In other words, science—and science alone—can show us the truth. In the presence of science in Europe, coupled with its absence in the Orient and in America, we have at once the index and the cause of Europe's superiority and the others' inferiority. "The foundation of a civilized nation is science" ("Discours prononcé au Collège de France" [Speech Delivered at the Collège de France], p. 876).

If science is hoisted up to the place of honor, what becomes of morality? How is the good to be situated with respect to the true? At first, Renan seems to belong to Rousseau's line rather than Diderot's. To be sure, like Diderot, Renan holds that nature is immoral. "The sun has witnessed the most glaring inequalities without turning away, it has smiled on the most heinous crimes." But this does not justify deducing a different morality (an "amorality") from nature; on the contrary, this argument leads Renan to assert the autonomy of the ideal with respect to the real, the autonomy of what ought to be with respect to what is. "But a sacred voice arises in man's consciousness and speaks to him of a wholly different world, the world of ideals, truth, goodness, and justice" ("Letter to M. Adolphe Guéroult" ["Lettre à M. Adolphe Guéroult"], p. 136).

Consequently, science and ethics have to remain autonomous. Reworking a statement made by Alexander von Humboldt (which itself refers to an already extensive philosophical tradition), Renan writes the following in one of his earliest books, *Histoire générale et système comparé des langues sémitiques:* "For science to be independent, it must not be constrained by any dogma, just as it is essential that moral and religious convictions be protected from the results to which science may be led by its deductions" (p. 563). Renan does not ask himself here whether, beyond the requisite autonomy, science and morality might not find a common foundation; he is content to denounce the dangers of close contact: "The greatest mistake philosophy and religion can make is to allow their truths to depend upon some scientific or historical theory" ("Discours de réception à l'Académie française" [Reception Speech at the French Academy], p. 747). Autonomy is likewise in the interest of science: "To avoid falsifying science, let us abstain from giving advice upon these problems, in which so many interests are involved. You may be sure that if science is charged with the duty of furnishing the elements of diplomacy, it will be, in many cases, found to be in the gravest error. It has better work to do; let us simply demand of it the truth" ("Qu'est-ce qu'une nation?" in English "What Is a Nation?" p. 75). Truth and good remain rigorously separate here.

But there is something paradoxical about such a state of affairs. How is it possible to assert at one and the same time that science occupies the pinnacle of human values and that the behavior of individuals, like that of communities, eludes its grasp, must be subordinated to an entirely independent morality or politics? In a second phase, then, while Renan recognizes the theoretical separation between the two domains, and even their complementarity, he *observes* an established fact (but refrains from passing judgment on it): in our day, science is triumphant, whereas religion and philosophy, which are supposed to reign over morality, are languishing. "I can descry the future in store for the historical sciences; it is immense . . . I can descry also the future of the natural sciences; it baffles all attempts to estimate it . . . But I cannot descry any future for philosophy, in the old sense of the word" ("La Métaphysique et son avenir," in English "Metaphysics and Its Future," p. 143). Whence a temptation to shift toward a new sense of the word. "The true philosophers have become philologists, chemists, physiologists . . . In place of the old attempts at explaining the universe, there have been substituted a series of patient investigations into Nature and History" (p. 144). And where human affairs are concerned, the human sciences in particular are the ones that take the place of philosophy. "The historical sciences especially seem to me called to replace the abstract philosophy of the academy in the solution of the problems that weigh most heavily on the human spirit today . . . History, I mean the history of the human spirit, is in this sense the true philosophy of our time" ("M. Cousin," pp. 73–74; cf. *The Future of Science*, p. 255).

If science has in fact replaced philosophy, must we not turn toward science rather than toward the former occupant of its position to seek advice about human affairs? That is indeed the next step, and Renan does not hesitate to take it: "The philosopher is only interested to know the direction in which the world is going, to see clearly the consequences involved in actual facts" ("The Future of Religion in Modern Society," p. 385). If the consequences follow inexorably from the facts, if the only thing the philosopher can do is note in what direction the world is headed, it is hard indeed to see why he would not give up his place to the scientist, who is infinitely better equipped for the task of observing the world. Ethics is then reduced to a province ruled by science. Thus, we see Renan embracing the most important postulate of scientism (while publicly distancing himself from Auguste Comte and his doctrine).

At the end of his investigation, Renan finds himself faced with a problem: the philosophy, the morality, and the religion to which he adheres postulate the unity of the human race and equal rights for all human beings. Now science (his science) has "demonstrated" to him the inequality of the races. What is to be done? "It is obvious that this faith in the religious and moral unity of the human species, this belief that all men are children of God and brothers, has nothing to do with the scientific question that concern us here" (*Histoire générale*, p. 563). Having thus paid homage to morality, Renan the scientist deems that he has a free hand to *observe* the absence of unity and the impossibility of equality, both within the white race and among the three major races (white, yellow, black), as we have seen. "It would be taking historical pantheism too far to put all races on an equal footing and, on the pretext that human nature is always beautiful, to seek in its diverse combinations the same plenitude and the same richness. I am thus the first to recognize that the Semitic race, compared to the Indo-European race, actually represents an inferior combination of human nature" (pp. 145–146).

The separation between science and ethics advocated by Renan operates in fact in one direction only: moral dogmas (in this instance the doctrine of equality among human beings) must not be allowed to prevent science from doing its work properly. But it is not enough to declare that science and ethics have nothing in common: if science says the races are unequal and ethics says they are equal, can one still claim that the juxtaposition is unproblematic? In reality, Renan does not fail to reestablish the bridge between the two, but he uses it only to go in the opposite direction: science, for its part, may guide human beings or justify their behavior, thus occupying the place of ethics. Lacking this, what would legitimate Renan's wish to see "the destruction of the peculiarly Semitic element" ("The Share of the Semitic People in the History of Civilization," p. 164)? What would allow him to assert simultaneously that the Aryan race has distinguished itself from the dawn of history by "its profound morality" (*Histoire générale*, p. 584), and that these same Aryans exterminate the half-savage races they find in their way (p. 585)? What leads him to note that the conquest of an inferior race by a superior race is not at all shocking, if not the postulate according to which, when science speaks, the business of ethics is done? Has he not been telling us that morality takes its full value from the fact that the honest races alone can produce scientific works? Renan's homage to virtue barely veils the submission of the good to the true (or to what is believed to be true), and thus of ethics to science; the so-called autonomy of these disciplines is actually the camouflage of a new subordination, the inverse of the one imposed on science under the tutelage of religion.

It is not only a particular individual judgment that finds its support in science, it is politics as a whole. Here again, Renan starts from what might appear to be a Rousseauistic principle: one must submit to the general will and not to the will of all; in other words, one must submit to what is appropriate according to reason and not according to the wishes of a malleable majority. "As the greatest good of humanity should be the aim of every government, it follows that the opinion of the majority is only entitled to impose itself when that majority represents the most enlightened reasons and views . . . The only sovereign by divine right is reason, the majority only has power so far as it is supposed to represent reason" (*The Future of Science*, p. 321). That is just what happened in 1789, he believes: "Condorcet, Mirabeau, Robespierre are the first instances of theorists meddling with the direction of affairs and endeavouring to govern humanity in a reasonable and scientific manner . . . The principle involved in all this admits of no controversy, intelligence alone must reign, intelligence alone; in other words, sense must govern the world" (pp. 19–20). That is why it is essential to choose society's direction and thus its goals: "The dogma which must be maintained at any cost is that the mission of intellect is the reforming of society according to its own principles" (p. 24).

But we now know that, for Renan, reason is best embodied in science: the two terms are interchangeable in this context. "I still believe that reason (that is, science) will succeed again in creating strength (that is, government) in humanity" ("L'Eau de jouvence" [The Fountain of Youth], preface, p. 441). This means not only that reason will become strong, but also that government must rely upon science. Renan spells out this idea in somewhat greater detail on another occasion: "Science is the very soul of a society; for science is reason. It creates military superiority and industrial superiority. Some day it will create social superiority—that is to say, a state of society in which the amount of justice compatible with the essence of the universe will be attained. Science gives force for the service of reason" ("L'Islamisme et la science," in English "Islamism and Science," p. 102).

And what if the opposite were true? What if science could put reason at the service of force? Freed of all philosophical or religious tutelage, discovering all by itself "the essence of the universe" and making sovereign determinations as to the dose of justice it is appropriate to inject, preoccupied with an efficacity of which it alone possesses the criteria (military, industrial, and social superiority), is science really a trustworthy guide? Is it not in the very nature of science, to the extent that it seeks truth, to be mistaken sometimes, or often? Is it wise to base a politics upon the racial inequality "proven" by Renan's science? Did Robespierre's "science" always turn out to be a wise counsellor? Let us go further: Is it legitimate to see science as the unique mistress of truth? And is it right to reduce reason to science, and to dismiss philosophy along with religion, and to throw wisdom into the trash cans of folly? Would not reason be the element that is common to the scientific spirit and to universal ethics, and that would thus have the right to pass judgment upon the results of scientific inquiry, rather than allowing those results to rule us, whatever they may be?

The experience of humanity during the century that has passed since Renan's day casts some doubt on the answers he gave to those questions. But Renan himself, as we shall see later on, had already imagined that the reign of science might have disastrous consequences.

The Higher Morality

In many respects, Gobineau's itinerary parallels that of his contemporaries Taine and Renan. Like Taine, he was an enemy of Enlightenment humanism, of the ideals of the French Revolution and the forms of democracy to which they gave rise (in this he also resembles Renan); hostile to modernity, he nevertheless fully subscribed to the determinism and materialism that resulted from the Enlightenment, and he put his entire faith in science (or what he took to be science)—even though science is an integral part of that same modernity.

For Gobineau, men's behavior is entirely determined by the race to which they belong, and it is transmitted by bloodlines; an individual's will is helpless against it. Societies "impose their ways of life on populations, confining their members within limits that these blind slaves have no inclination—and would not have the power—to transgress. Societies dictate their members' laws, inspire their wishes, designate their loves, stoke their hatreds, govern their contempt" (*Essai sur l'inégalité des races humaines* [The Inequality of the Human Races], p. 1151). The individual thinks he is acting, while in reality he is acted upon by forces that transcend him. "Thus, above any transitory and voluntary action emanating either from the individual or from the multitude, generative principles are deployed that produce their effects with an independence and an impassivity that nothing can perturb" (p. 1149).

Under these circumstances, there is very little the individual can do. "It is not the will of a monarch or his subjects that modifies the essence of society; it is, by virtue of these same laws, a subsequent ethnic mix" (p. 1151). "Imagine the strongest, most enlightened, most energetic of men: the length of his outstretched arm is but a trivial thing . . . In the eyes of his contemporaries, it is a great deal; but for history, most often the results are imperceptible" (p. 1145). The best one can do is observe the course of history, understand it, and resign oneself to it. If we look at the careers of great men, we notice that they "are made not of invention but of comprehension. Here ends the historical power of man acting under the most favorable developmental conditions" (p. 1146).

In this respect there is no more difference for Gobineau than there was for Taine between the natural world and the human world. Throughout Gobineau's book, this idea is suggested by the presence of organic metaphors: civilizations are male or female, they are born, they live, they die, they have seeds and roots and can be grafted. "To make my thinking clearer and easier to grasp, I shall begin by comparing a nation, any nation, to the human body" (p. 163). Hence, there is not (there must not be) any qualitative difference between the natural and the human sciences. "It is a matter of bringing history into the family of natural sciences" (p. 1152). "Ethnology follows the same pattern as algebra and the science of a Cuvier or a Beaumont" (p. 1153)—that is, biology.

The moral qualities of the individual are entirely determined by his physical dispositions: it is thus vain to place any faith in the effects of education. In this, too, Gobineau was followed by Taine, who was fond of telling a story about a little black child from the Philippines adopted in the United States at the age of three and educated at the best schools. On the surface, nothing set him apart from other Americans. But one day the vagaries of travel led him to Manila, where he disappeared mysteriously, only to be discovered by a naturalist some years later: he had turned back into a little black peasant. "The primitive instinct, covered over in vain by our varnish, breaks through" (*Derniers Essais*, p. 106). As for the Europeans, they are civilized in advance, and in their case reason is innate rather than acquired. Taine, like Gobineau, disagreed with the Encyclopedists on this point, for they believed in the virtues of education and in the possibilities of progress for the individual as well as the species.

Gobineau is in fact strongly opposed to theories of progress (like Condorcet's): "Humanity is not infinitely perfectible," says the title of his thirteenth chapter (I, p. 287). The white race, although superior, is no exception to this rule: like the other races, it has not known continuous progress in science or philosophy or poetry. There have been some successes, to be sure, but there have also been lapses and losses. "In short, we proceed differently. We apply our minds to different goals, to projects different from those elected by humanity's other civilized groups; but in changing terrain we have not been able to conserve in their full fertility the lands that those groups were already cultivating" (p. 290). The same thing is true of social evolution: slavery has been abolished, to be sure, but modern slaves, the proletarians, are still with us. Generally speaking, Gobineau refers to a unitary scale of values; confronted with the need to contest the idea that progress is possible, he opts for relativism. And this, he believes, is one of the main reasons his book was contested and rejected, in the century that took the idea of continuous progress as its gospel.

Such a determinist vision of history obviously leaves little room for morality. Gobineau takes particular care, in an initial phase, to distinguish his undertaking from any sort of moral reflection. But the separation exists not only in his book; it is inherent in the world Gobineau is examining. "As the existence of a society is, in the first instance, an effect that does not depend on man for its production or prevention, it entails no results for which man is responsible. Society thus implies no morality. A society is, in itself, neither virtuous nor vicious, neither wise nor foolish; it simply is" (p. 1150). Here Gobineau returns to Diderot's position: in the face of history, ethical judgments are irrelevant.

However, a break as radical as this disturbs Gobineau somewhat, for he sees himself as the defender of certain values embodied in Christianity or in the institutions of the Old Regime; thus, he decides that a small free—and therefore moral—space must be maintained. Societies leave to individuals, he says, "(and with no reservations, this point is all-important) the merits of a morality whose forms they [societies] have determined themselves" (p. 1151). What does this mean? Once it is based on ethnology—that is, on knowledge of races—history "will distinguish what science can merely observe from what justice must grasp. From its superb throne will henceforth descend judgments without appeal and salutary lessons for clear consciences . . . Its decrees . . . will make the free will of each individual rigorously responsible for the value of each of his acts" (pp. 1152–1153). The tone is solemn, but the content is as vague as ever; all Gobineau needs is to be able to say, with the appearance of legitimacy, that Robespierre is an "immense scoundrel" (p. 1153), a declaration that would be meaningless in a world lacking ethical judgments.

Criticized by Tocqueville on this very point, Gobineau assumes a more extreme position in their correspondence, but it is a position we have already encountered in Taine and one that was not foreign to Renan. Society may be amoral, but its knowledge is not; the good stems from the true, and science conveys an ethics to which all must submit. "If truth and morality are not connected, I shall be the first to agree that my book is devoid of the latter, but then it is also devoid of anti-morality, as are geology, medicine, archaeology. My book is research, exposition, presentation of facts. These facts exist or they don't. There is nothing else to say" (Tocqueville, "Lettres à Gobineau," in English *"The European Revolution" and Correspondence with Gobineau,* p. 286). Once again, ethnology is likened to geology; Gobineau overlooks the fact that stones are indifferent to the results of science, while men are not. This is because he believes, in the last analysis, that there is a higher morality in the work of science—just as, during the same period, Renan believed he had found a higher morality in works of art.

Here is an additional reason, Gobineau thinks, for the poor reception accorded his book: its detractors are people who dare not look at naked truth—the truth of science—head on; those who "have always been the world's poorest when it comes to scientific matters" (p. 288). For we must not forget that Gobineau claims the status of science for his work: "If I am wrong, nothing will remain of my four volumes. If I am right, the facts will not be subdued by the desire of those who do not want to face them" (p. 285). In which Gobineau is mistaken once again, for he is indeed wrong in his four volumes, and yet something of them remains—here is proof that what he is doing is not science. The fact is that Gobineau opposes science to ethics, and chooses the former, unlike one of his antagonists whom he describes as follows: "He proposed not to know and to state the truth of things, but to reassure philanthropy" (*Essai,* p. 1169). Gobineau believes he is doing the opposite; in reality he is doing exactly the same thing, except that he has put a different ideology in philanthrophy's place.

In his letters to Gobineau, Tocqueville attacks him both on the level of science and on the level of morality, as Rousseau had done with Diderot. Regarding these doctrines, Tocqueville writes: "I believe that they are probably quite false; I know that they are certainly very pernicious" (*Correspondence with Gobineau*, p. 227). We shall look more closely later on at the details of Tocqueville's arguments; for the time being let us focus on the fact that, according to him, Gobineau's resolutely materialist and determinist position leads to "a vast limitation, if not a complete abolition, of human liberty" (ibid.). Tocqueville believes just the opposite: he affirms the existence of liberty, and thus the possibility of education. "I, too, believe that our contemporaries have been badly brought up and that this is a prime cause of their miseries and of their weakness, but I believe that a better upbringing could repair the wrongs done by their miseducation; I believe that it is not permissible to renounce such an effort . . . To me, human societies, like persons, become something worth while only through their use of liberty" (p. 309). Tocqueville's position is thus very precisely modeled on Rousseau's.

But even if we were to suppose that Gobineau had got it right, the specialist in human societies can only be led astray in claiming to conform to the concern for truth alone: by making his "discoveries" public, he accomplishes an *act*, and that act can be judged, like any other, by the standard of good and evil. Science must not be confused with philanthropy: its only guide must be the search for truth. However, its results are not miraculously exempt from the requirements we impose on other human actions. Gobineau's conclusions can only be "pernicious." Tocqueville continues: "What purpose does it serve to persuade lesser peoples living in abject conditions of barbarism or slavery that, such being their racial nature, they can do nothing to better themselves, to change their habits, or to ameliorate their status?" (pp. 228–229). "A book which tries to prove that men in this world are merely obeying their physical *constitutions* and that their will power can do almost nothing to influence their destinies is like opium given to a patient whose blood has already weakened" (p. 270). After discussing knowledge, Tocqueville goes on to examine the question of interest: if the results the scientist has achieved are detrimental to society, it would be better to suppress them.

We do not actually need to go along with Tocqueville on this last point, even if we accept the rest of his argument. Deciding that ethics may require us to suppress the results of science entails some serious disadvantages. We are well aware today that certain scientific discoveries—nuclear reactions, genetic manipulations—are potentially dangerous, but it is neither possible nor necessary to conceal these discoveries. It is enough to remember what Tocqueville knew—namely, the falsity of the scientistic postulate according to which what ought to be stems from what is. If we were to assume that the human races are unequally endowed, it would not follow that they do not have the same rights (and indeed this is how we treat differences in physical strength, which for their part are undeniable). Even if the determinism governing human behavior were much more extensive than it is believed to be today, we would not thereby gain the right to reduce human beings to slavery. From another point of view, Tocqueville does not distinguish here between two phases of science, knowledge of nature and the transformation of nature. The second phase is the one that produces dangerous results (apocalyptic weapons, mutation of the species). This phase is no longer governed by the quest for truth; it is governed by the quest for effectiveness, whose definition depends entirely upon our value judgments. The restrictions proposed by Tocqueville should apply to this aspect of scientific work and not to the initial phase of acquiring knowledge about what already exists.

Tocqueville did not turn out to be mistaken, in any event, about Gobineau's destiny. In the latter's own lifetime, his work met with some success when it was translated in the United States, a phenomenon that did not fail to surprise its author, who had a poor opinion of the country of democracy and ethnic mixtures and did not understand how his own work could apply. Tocqueville enlightens him on this point: "Those Americans whom you mention and who translated your book are known to me as perfervid leaders of the anti-abolitionist party. They translated the part of your book which suits their prejudices, the part which tends to prove that the Negroes belong to another, to a different and inferior race" (p. 294). In the next century, the twentieth, Gobineau's work would be welcomed by the Nazis, as we know; Tocqueville, clairvoyant once again, had predicted it: "Your book is fated to return to France from abroad, especially from Germany. Alone in Europe, the Germans possess the particular talent of becoming impassioned with what they take as abstract truths, without considering their practical consequences" (p. 294). Thus it is that Gobineau, who does not defend slavery any more than he recommends the extermination of the inferior races, will have contributed, through his work, to the reinforcement of these causes—because he was naive enough to believe that one could be passionate about what he took to be the truth without concern for the political and moral effects of this passion. In this, too, Tocqueville is his opposite number, since the latter chooses, as he says, to look into "the practical consequences of these philosophical doctrines" (p. 227)—that is, also to inquire into the morality of science.

Gobineau

Popular Racialism

Turning now toward Gobineau's original contribution to racial theory, let us begin by noting that he evinces a degree of broadmindedness difficult to reconcile with his racialist reputation. He cannot be accused of narrow chauvinism, or of fomenting colonial warfare, still less of promoting the extermination of inferior races. Perhaps because of his service as a professional diplomat, Gobineau is capable of appreciating foreign cultures, and his critique of blind ethnocentrism puts him squarely in Helvétius' lineage. He writes with irony, "The most nobly developed man will be, for each of us, the one who holds the same ideas as we do about the respective duties of governing bodies and subjects, whereas the unfortunate wretches who hold different views will be barbarians and savages" (*Essai*, p. 216). Xenophobia is not spared: "From the fact that on the surface their civilization bears no resemblance to the corresponding facets of our own, we are often led to the hasty conclusion either that they are barbarians or that they are less worthy than ourselves. Nothing is more superficial, and nothing should be more suspect" (p. 224).

From another standpoint, however, Gobineau's writings manifest a racialism that is faithful to the major current of thinking about race that we can follow from Buffon and Voltaire to Renan and Le Bon. Like Buffon, Gobineau sees a qualitative difference between men and animals, consisting in the presence or absence of reason ("of an intellectual department," p. 288). But once he has formulated this statement of principle, Gobineau nevertheless sees radical differences among the various groups of human beings, and he refuses to grant the notion of "man" any content other than biological; thus, he borrows De Maistre's well-known formula for his own purposes while modifying its meaning:

"There is no ideal man; *man* does not exist . . . In the field, I know someone who speaks Finnish, others who have mastered the Aryan system or the Semitic combinations, but I do not know *man* in the absolute" (pp. 316–317). This awareness of disparities leads him to claim that some races are perfectible while others are not. "Do all men have, to an equivalent degree, the unlimited power of progressing in their intellectual development? . . . I say no" (pp. 288–289). For example, "the fact that certain Tahitians may have helped repair a whaler does not mean that their nation is civilized. Just because some man from Tonga-Tabou may have treated foreigners well, he is not necessarily open to all forms of progress" (p. 288). There is thus no real unity within the human race, and Gobineau in fact subscribes to Voltaire's belief in polygenesis, even though he tries to appear respectful of the Christian doctrine of monogenesis: he is all too conscious of "the eternal separation of the races" (p. 274).

Not only do the races differ, but they are also arrayed along a single hierarchical scale. Here again Gobineau is inventing nothing; he is content to trot out the old procession of classifications and characteristics. The three major races, black (or melanian), yellow (or Finnish), and white, identified by physical marks such as ruddiness, hairiness, cranial form, and facial features, are evaluated according to three criteria, beauty, physical strength, and intellectual capacity, always with the same result. *Beauty:* Unlike eighteenth-century "relativists" such as Montesquieu or Helvétius (but in agreement, once again, with Buffon), Gobineau believes that "beauty is an absolute and necessary idea that cannot be applied optionally" (p. 286); and human beauty is embodied by the white race. Another author, Meiners, settled for dividing all the races into two groups: "The *beautiful* one, that is, the white race, and the *ugly* one, which would include all the others" (p. 242). Gobineau finds this thesis simplistic, but in fact his own is not very different; without discussion he posits an equivalence between "beauty" and "European type," and he does not go beyond measuring the distance, great or small, that separates the other races from this ideal: "I have already observed that, of all the human groups, those that belong to the European nations and their descendants are the most beautiful" (p. 285); but on what is this "observation" based, if not custom? As for the other races, they "also differ to the extent that they are close to or remote from the model proposed" (p. 286). *Physical strength:* The yellow race is completely feeble; "clearly the Creator was only making a sketch" (p. 559). Just as surprisingly, "blacks also have less muscular strength than whites," and thus "honors go to our people of the white race" (p. 286). Finally, *intellectual capacity* (the moral goes hand in hand with the physical): In blacks, the "mental faculties are mediocre or even nonexistent" (p. 340); in yellows, "in all things, there is a tendency toward mediocrity" (p. 341); everything thus converges to prove "the immense superiority of the whites, in the whole realm of intelligence" (p. 342). And Gobineau attempts to confound his egalitarian adversaries with the following ironic argument: "Thus, the Huron's little brain contains the seeds of a mind just like that of the Englishman or the Frenchman!" (p. 174). In a word, "from the beginning, the white race has had a monopoly on beauty, intelligence, and strength" (p. 344).

Race and Civilization

All this is quite banal and Gobineau would not warrant special consideration if he had not gone beyond this *n*th reiteration of a commonplace. The interesting aspect of his speculations lies elsewhere: not in his views on race, but in his ideas about what he calls civilization (as it relates to race, to be sure). However, here again some precautions are in order. Gobineau uses the word "civilization" in a new and idiosyncratic sense; nevertheless, despite what his repeated diatribes against purely material and technological progress might lead us to suppose, he never breaks entirely with the meaning the word has had since the Enlightenment. He is not above using this theme to establish the superiority of the white race: the poor Hurons, indeed, did not discover "either printing or steam," they failed to offer history "either a Caesar or a Charlemagne," they never produced "a Homer or a Hippocrates" (p. 174). In another passage, Gobineau evokes once again, and to the same effect, "printing," "our sciences," "our discoveries," "our philosophies," "political systems, a literature, arts, books, statues, and paintings" (p. 210): if we were to leave military leaders aside for the moment (this is in fact crucial to Gobineau's argument), we could easily take him for a defender of scientific, technical, and artistic progress— whereas precisely the opposite is true.

Let us look a little more closely, then, at the specific meaning the notion of civilization takes on in his work. To do this, we need to begin with the two somewhat similar hierarchies he sets up among the various forms of human society. According to the first schema, societies have three stages: tribe, people, and nation. A *tribe* is a completely independent and self-sufficient human group that lives in total ignorance of its neighbors. A *people* results from violent encounters between two tribes: one has conquered the other and reduced it to slavery. Their separation, formerly "horizontal" (territorial), has become "vertical" (based on class), but it is nevertheless maintained: there is no more communication between the two strata than there was between the two tribes from which they arose. Finally, a *nation* results from the genuine fusion of formerly isolated tribes: their lands are joined, their populations merge. The feature that makes it possible to identify these phases of human evolution is thus the relation to others: ignorance is the lowest degree, interaction the highest (pp. 164–166).

The second hierarchy has to do with the status and role of ideals in the life of a society. At the lowest level, the ideal cannot be distinguished from the real, or at least has no influence on the real; the population is thus condemned to immobility. At the second level, the population has an ideal, and this ideal allows it to modify its current status. At the third level, finally, not only does this ideal influence the population within which it has arisen, but it also influences other peoples; then "over vast countries spreads the unchallenged domination of a more or less well-coordinated set of ideas and facts, in a word what may be called a *civilization*" (p. 220). Thus, we find that the same ability to unify populations that were originally distinct provides the very definition of the word "civilization."

When he reaches the point of identifying and characterizing the various forms of civilization, Gobineau resorts to criteria that once again emphasize intermixing. It is worth noting here that Gobineau's categories are not valorized as such: they are presented rather as the poles of a continuum, and the highest degree consists in their successful equilibrium, not in the exclusive presence of one or the other. Take, for example, the opposition between stability and mobility, permanence and change. Gobineau's definition of "civilization" begins with the words "a state of relative stability" (pp. 224–225). The "oriental" civilizations are too stable, but ours is too mobile, and the advantage easily becomes a liability: "Our civilization, thus rendered incapable of maintaining a firm faith in itself, therefore lacks the sort of stability that is one of the principal characteristics" of civilization. "That is one of the advantages that these [oriental] civilizations have over ours. There, everyone agrees on what is to be believed in the political realm" (p. 237). A moderate mobility, then, but mobility nonetheless: to ensure lasting success, a civilization must be capable of absorbing new elements.

The male-female axis, another of Gobineau's categories, is just as impossible to reduce to a simple gradation. Aware of the customary associations of the terms "male" and "female," Gobineau takes care to specify that the notions are to be used only on condition that "by these words simply an idea of reciprocal procreation should be included, without praise for the one side or blame for the other" (p. 221), "unrelated to any idea of supremacy for one or another of these foyers" (p. 1150). The masculine, or male principle, is the predominance of the material, the utilitarian, the objective; the feminine, or female principle, is the predominance of the mental, the contemplative, the subjective (this resembles the opposition between *yin* and *yang*, although the associations are not the same). The exclusive presence of just one of these poles is harmful; however, their perfect equality is not desirable either. The best solution is for one to dominate without completely effacing the other: "It is only in races adequately supplied with one of these two elements, without ever being completely deprived of the other, that the social state can achieve a satisfactory degree of culture, and consequently of civilization" (p. 222).

As vague as these evocations may be (but biological metaphors are heavily invested with meaning for Gobineau), we can still see that they have a common feature by which they are related to the three degrees of society identified earlier. This is because intermixing is preferable to the simple and pure state; nations, like civilizations, are constituted through the absorption of heterogeneity. Stability and mobility, male and female must be present simultaneously, and the white race itself, the acknowledged crowning glory of the human species, is in fact a "happy medium"; it succeeds in avoiding the excesses of the black races (which are a bit too "female") and the yellow (too "male"); it is a mixture, on the conceptual level at least. Gobineau draws out the implication of his arguments quite clearly: civilization is nothing but a successful blend. Not all peoples are capable of it; but the best of them can be recognized by means of this key. There has always been "a secret repugnance for racial mixing," but those who manage to surmount it "form what is civilizable in our species" (p. 167). "As soon as an individual regime manages to get itself accepted [by the others], there is a nascent civilization" (p. 223). This is what gives the white race its strength: "The essentially civilizing tendencies of this elite race have continually driven it to mix with other peoples" (p. 283). In a word, summing up universal history: "Thus mixed, mixed everywhere, always mixed, there is the clearest, most assured, most durable work of the great societies and powerful civilizations, the work that, unquestionably, lives after them" (p. 1159).

Intermixing, certainly, but only under certain conditions: the truly civilizing regime is the one that manages to "get itself accepted" by the others, that imposes "its unchallenged domination." It is clearer now why Caesar and Charlemagne were high on the list of representatives of European civilization, along with scientists and artists: the common feature of all these personalities is that they were able to subjugate others, in body or mind. Such is also the latest major manifestation of civilizing superiority, of "aggregative work," the expansion of the German race: "We have seen it, almost in our own day, discover America, mixing with the indigenous races there or else reducing them to oblivion; we have seen it drive the Slavs back among the last tribes of Central Asia, through the impulse it gave to Russia; we have watched it pounce down amidst the Hindus and the Chinese; knock on the doors of Japan; ally itself, along the entire circumference of the African coastline, with the native peoples of that great continent" (p. 1161). But is this way of reducing others to oblivion, driving them off, pouncing down among them or knocking at their door, anything but military conquest, European imperialism? Gobineau is fond of presenting things as if military power always had to be associated with spiritual superiority, but counterexamples come readily to mind. The spread of Christianity has not always been accompanied by advancing armies; conversely, "barbarian" invasions have often been victorious, but can we therefore maintain that they have always brought a superior civilization along with them? Only if civilization has already been equated with power. From this point on, Gobineau's assertion is merely tautological. He does not say that the strongest are the most civilized, nor that the most civilized are the strongest, but only that the strongest are the strongest.

Thus, if Gobineau can speak of "civilization" throughout his book, it is by a misuse of the term (a misuse rendered almost imperceptible by his occasional use of the word in its conventional sense). Here and there Gobineau hints that civilization is not what interests him; for example, he writes: "The intervention of an ethnic agent of considerable strength was required, an agent that resulted from a new marriage of the best human variety with the already civilized races" (p. 1160). But if the "best" have to marry the "civilized," this means that excellence does not reside in civilization. Another sentence makes things clearer still: Gobineau affirms Austria's worth "not according to the yardstick of civilization, but according to the yardstick of vitality, which is the only thing with which this book is concerned" (p. 1098). Here is a substantial acknowledgment: Gobineau's discourse indeed becomes much more comprehensible once we are aware that the object of his book is not civilizations but only societies, and that he uses the term "civilization" as a synonym for "vitality." In a movement running counter to Enlightenment universalism, then, Gobineau abandons the search for a common framework that would allow him to situate the respective models of "progress" achieved by the various peoples on the path toward (the one and only) civilization. At certain points, he even abandons the attempt to valorize our own society in the name of a spiritual superiority: "We have, it seems to me, changed the methods used in an earlier day to approach the secret. We have not taken a single step forward in its obscurity" (p. 290). His critique of modernity notwithstanding, Gobineau is a relativist—for the relativist position is the only one compatible with the acclamation of power.

Gobineau is proposing a theory of social history, and he postulates that a society's quality must be judged by its capacity to assimilate other societies, to subjugate by absorption. Alongside this first assertion we now have a second—namely, that civilization is an effect of race and race alone. All the other factors that can influence it act only on the surface; in reality, the quality of a people is "a fact resulting from race" (p. 1168). Correspondingly, the hierarchy of civilizations is rigorously parallel to that of the races. "The inequality of the races . . . suffices to explain the entire unfolding of the destinies of peoples" (p. 138). This is what Gobineau calls his "axiom": "Whatever the value of the mixture obtained [mixing of blood, of race], that was the value of the human variety produced by this mixture" (p. 1170). We shall not be surprised to note that the quality of a race is measured by means of a criterion closely related to the one used for evaluating a civilization: again it is a matter of power, sometimes also called "energy" or "vitality." Thus, "the Aryan is superior to other men, chiefly by virtue of his intelligence and his energy" (p. 981), and "the Germanic race was supplied with all the energy of the Aryan variety" (p. 1161).

Race and History

Gobineau's second thesis thus posits a high degree of solidarity between civilization and race. Now races themselves evolve. They do so, to be sure, for reasons other than those ordinarily suggested: neither institutions nor climate have any effect on their evolution (Gobineau contests both Buffon and Montesquieu on this point), nor do general geographical conditions (the territory). A historical race (that is, one belonging to a period about which some information is available) is already a mixture of blood; but it is a stable mixture. The race can be modified—here is another tautology—only through a modification of this cocktail, a new mixing of blood. "The contemporary races succeed in losing their major features only in the wake of, and through the power of, intermixings" (p. 268).

This second thesis invites numerous objections. In his letters to the author of the *Essai,* Tocqueville had already put his finger on the weak point in the argument. It concerns the nature of proofs: Gobineau always tends to explain the known by the unknown, the observable features of civilization by the supposed mixtures of yesteryear: "What, in this whole world, is more difficult to find than the place, the time, and the composite elements that produced men who by now possess no visible traces of their mixed origins?" (*Correspondence with Gobineau,* p. 228). In practice, Gobineau finds himself continually inclined to construct "facts" on the basis of his hypothesis: to find proofs, he postulates what he ought to observe, while declaring suspect any documents that seem to contradict his thesis. This is the case with his assertion that the white race has been able to impose its way of life upon others. When he is faced with a contradictory fact (a given black population has subjugated certain other black populations), Gobineau finds himself obliged to postulate prior contact with whites. "These are only the distant results of an ancient alliance with the white race" (p. 1156), a fact for which he supplies no corroboration whatsoever. Thus, even supposing that the "mixture of blood" had some meaning, it remains useless as an explanation of the past: by virtue of trying too hard to prove his thesis, Gobineau renders it properly "unfalsifiable." The only way to get around these objections would be to set aside all the "sanguinary" and physical imagery (although this imagery clearly plays a crucial role for Gobineau) and observe that not only are "civilization" and "race" judged by means of one and the same criterion, but that this criterion is finally applied to one and the same object—namely, society. "Race" determines "civilization" only because the two terms have become synonymous for Gobineau: what is at stake in each case is society, considered from the standpoint of its "strength," its "energy," or its "vitality."

But here is where things become complicated. In fact, from the perspective of race, any intermixing is a degradation. Gobineau goes even further: every degradation results from a mixing of blood. That is what he calls his "fundamental claim." "Peoples only degenerate as a result of, and in proportion to, the intermixings they undergo" (p. 345). What does "degenerate" mean, moreover? (We have already come across this term in Buffon.) "The word *degenerate*, applied to a people, must mean and does mean that this people no longer possesses the intrinsic value it once had, because it no longer has in its veins the same blood, for successive alloys have gradually modified its value" (p. 162). If "degenerate" means "having modified the composition of its blood," does that not mean that any (new) intermixing amounts to degeneration? Gobineau says just this, over and over again: it is a "misfortune that the intermixings do not end" (p. 344), for intermixing "leads societies to the oblivion that is without remedy" (p. 345); the life of a race is made up of "an infinite series of intermixings and thus of blemishes" (p. 1163).

Now we can appreciate the paradoxical character of Gobineau's thesis. According to him, "race" and "civilization" are intimately inter-connected entities; indeed, they are perhaps merely two aspects of a single entity called "society." But, viewed as a civilization, a society is all the stronger for having been able to assimilate other, different societies; whereas, from the standpoint of race, the more mixed the race, the weaker it is. We need to remember one thing: those who succeed in overcoming their repugnance for mixing constitute the civilizable element of our species; but where race is concerned, every intermixing is a blemish leading to degeneration. What we have here is not a contradiction in Gobineau's thought, but rather a tragic paradox that weighs upon the human race. As soon as a society is strong enough, it tends to subjugate others; but as soon as it subjugates others its own identity is threatened, and it loses its strength. The source of evil lies in the presence of good, and at bottom people really only have a choice among the means of their own destruction. The weak perish under the dominion of the strong, and the strong perish corrupted by the weak, owing to an encounter that was the inevitable result of their strength itself.

"A people," Gobineau writes, "would never die if it could remain forever composed of the same national elements" (p. 170). The assertion can never be verified, but it is important to add a reciprocal proposition: a people that remained forever composed of the same elements, in an absolutely stable state, would never become a nation or a civilization; it would not even live. It comes down to a choice, as it were, between death and nonlife. Any proof of strength is a guarantee of weakness; any success is a step toward failure: "As the nation grows, whether by force of arms or treaties, its ethnic character is increasingly altered" (p. 168). Now ethnic character is indissociable from the nation!

It is clear that Gobineau's philosophy of history is profoundly pessimistic. Humanity's best days are already behind us; the races today are irremediably mixed and the definitive extinction of the species will come about in just a few thousand years. The end of the world, as Gobineau sees it, will take the form of a generalized entropy, a universal indistinction resulting from the acceleration of contacts and the proliferation of intermixing. "The definitive goal of the fatigue and the suffering, the pleasures and triumphs of our species is to arrive one day at the supreme unity" (pp. 1162–1163). A unity at the opposite pole from that of the original races: instead of being the juxtaposition of homogeneous and distinct entities, the world will be a magma of monotonous heterogeneity, "the final term of mediocrity in all genres, . . . we may almost say nothingness" (p. 1163). An enemy of equality and a defender of difference, partial to the hierarchies of the Old Regime and contemptuous of modern democracy, Gobineau nevertheless believes that the advent of that nothingness is unavoidable. For him it is a hateful prospect; thus, he settles for describing the apocalypse that awaits us.

If we wanted to take this vision of history as a scientific hypothesis, we could marshal two series of arguments against it. On the one hand, the facts do not seem to tend in the direction Gobineau envisions. Take, for example, the United States, which horrifies Gobineau: not only is it a democratic country, but it is also a dreadful mix of populations. "As for the creation of a higher or at least a different civilization, . . . these are phenomena that are only produced by the presence of a relatively pure and young race. This condition does not exist in America" (p. 1142). Now whether we understand the term "civilization" in the usual sense or in Gobineau's special sense (the ability to dominate other peoples), in the years since 1855 the United States has demonstrated a "vitality" superior to that of many other countries. The twentieth century's superpowers are multiethnic states: this fact has not seemed to concern them overmuch. If we were to believe Gobineau, moreover, the population of the globe would have to be in constant decline (owing to the exhaustion of the vital principle): "China has never had fewer inhabitants than it has now; central Asia was an anthill, and now there is no one there" (p. 1164). Truly no one?

On the other hand, there is something fragile in the very form of Gobineau's argument. It is Tocqueville again who first noticed this. To account for the present, Gobineau resorts not only to an inaccessible past, but also to the future in its entirety. "But that these tendencies, that these capacities should be insuperable has not only never been proved but no one will ever be able to prove it since to do so one would need to know not only the past but also the future" (*Correspondence with Gobineau*, pp. 227–228). Tocqueville's critique is addressed to a certain type of philosophy of history, of which Gobineau's is only one example among others: the philosophy that predicts the entire future of human- ity, and that requires these predictions in order to establish its own truth and value!

But quite obviously this is not how Gobineau's text works. If it could be proved false, this would have been done (has been done) long since; in reality, the text is unfalsifiable, closer in this respect to myth and fiction than to science. As myth and vision it has had a powerful impact, and could have such an impact again. Its notions are sufficiently vague, its ambitions sufficiently vast, that a well-disposed reader might take it as the point of departure for a new reverie on the history and future prospects of humanity. Will the world perish from an excess of com- munication and exchange, as Gobineau thought (but also, nearer our own day, as Segalen and Lévi-Strauss thought)? The question seems destined to go unanswered. The German interpretation of Gobineau's

book, in the nineteenth century, and the Nazi interpretation in the
twentieth, illustrate the possible dangers of such a reverie. It is certain
that in large measure this interpretation constitutes a misreading: the
pessimistic and fatalistic Gobineau ought not to have spawned any
political activists proposing to rid the world of inferior races, and his
praise of the "Germans" is not really a glorification of the Prussian
state; as for "popular racialism," we find as much or more of it in Renan
and other contemporaries. In short, Gobineau is the victim of his own
literary talent, which made him racialism's most illustrious representative.

Renan

Linguistic Races

So long as he was focusing on the division of humanity into three races,
Renan was a willing practitioner of popular racialism, as we have seen.
However, when he turned to the superior (white) race and its subdivisions, his attitude changed. He himself noted the presence of a qualitative difference: his own reasoning begins, he says, "by setting aside
the wholly inferior races, whose blending with the major races would
only poison the human species" ("Lettre à Gobineau," p. 204). In his
specific analyses, this is the way he always proceeds. In order to study
religion, for example, we have to begin by "setting aside" more than
half of humanity: "The whole world, if we except India, China, Japan,
and tribes altogether savage, has adopted the Semitic religions. The
civilized world comprises only Jews, Christians, and Mussulmans"
("The Share of the Semitic People in the History of Civilization,"
p. 159). The civilized peoples clearly constitute a distinct species.

   Thus, once he finds himself on the terrain of the superior race,
Renan embarks on a new path. He begins by observing that there are
no pure races, given the countless intermixings that have marked their
earlier existence (here the term "race" obviously no longer applies to
the three major races, but corresponds to the population of the various
European states). Pure race is a chimera. All the European nations are
the product of intermixing; it is even apparent (here Renan rejoins
Michelet, but also, in a way, Gobineau) that "the noblest countries,
England, France, Italy, are those in which the blood is most mixed"
("Lettre à Gobineau," p. 204).

By virtue of this intermixing the races have neutralized one another, and thus in today's world they are without influence. Here is where Renan's position differs radically from Gobineau's. The difference lies not in the hypothetical reconstruction of the historical process (both think that the races were pure in the beginning and will be totally intermixed in the end), but in their attitudes toward this process. For Gobineau, race is power; its waning is thus tantamount to degeneration. For Renan, as also for Michelet, race represents the physical realm, and the lessening of its impact liberates humanity from material determinism. "The phenomenon of race is immense in the beginning," Renan writes to Gobineau, "but it gradually loses its importance, and sometimes, as in France, it ends up vanishing entirely. . . . I see in the future a homogeneous humanity, in which all the original streams will flow together in one great river, and in which all recollections of diverse origins will be lost" (p. 204). Much more than by blood, modern men are motivated "by a great force that is superior to race and destructive of local differences, a force called civilization!" (*Histoire générale*, p. 139; cf. "La Société berbère," p. 570). The principal gulf between animals and men (white men, at least) is located here: the latter are exempt from biological determinism. "Human history is essentially different from zoology. Race is not everything, as it is in the case of the rodents and felines" ("What Is a Nation?" p. 74).

The entities known as England, France, and Italy, formed by the intermixing of diverse races but also by a history unique to each one, are nothing other than *nations*, or so one might think. The common mistake that Renan uncovers among his contemporaries consists in crediting race with characteristics that belong to nations. In the modern period, races no longer exist; nations do. And racial (biological, material) determinism brings us closer to the animals, whereas national (spiritual, historical) determinism marks our superiority among living creatures. Thus, we have to defend the one and combat the other. "So far as the national principle is just and legitimate, so far is the primordial right of races narrow, and full of danger for true progress" (pp. 70–71).

Such is the first part of the critical analysis to which Renan subjects the concept of race. But this radical separation between race and nation, inherited from Michelet, is not intrinsically satisfying to Renan. He deals with the problem by subjecting the concept of race to a new examination, one that leads him, paradoxically, to reaffirm its pertinence—except that he uses the term in a new sense. He takes pains to point out that the word has two meanings, and that he is rejecting one of them and focusing on the other. There is physical race, and there is cultural race; language plays a dominant role in the formation of a culture. And one must be careful not to confuse the two. "The divisions to which comparative philology leads do not coincide with those to which we are brought by anthropology properly speaking" (*L'Origine du langage*, p. 102). "The word 'race' is taken by the philological historians and by physiological anthropologists in two totally different senses . . . The words *Brachycephalus* and *Dolichocephalus* have no place in history or philology" ("What Is a Nation?" pp. 72–73). The meaning of the word has been radically transformed: "Language is thus almost completely substituted for race in the division of humanity into groups, or rather the word 'race' changes meaning. Language, religion, laws, mores brought the race into being much more than blood did" ("Histoire du peuple d'Israël," p. 32). Taken to the extreme, this use of the word can be seen as a simple homonymy: "One can draw virtually no conclusions from the science of language for the science of anthropological races: there are linguistic races, if I may be allowed the expression, but they have nothing to do with the anthropological races" ("Des Services rendus aux sciences historiques par la philologie" [On Services Rendered to the Historical Sciences by Philology], p. 1224).

The Semitic race and the Aryan race, which hold Renan's attention for years on end, are thus not physical races but linguistic races. "The separation between Semites and Indo-Europeans, for example, was created by philology and not by physiology" (*L'Origine du langage*, p. 102). "As the individuality of the Semitic race has been revealed only by the analysis of language, an analysis particularly well corroborated, it is true, by the study of mores, literatures, and religions [but not, let us note, by the study of blood or cranial structures], as this race has been in some sense created by philology, there is really just one criterion for recognizing Semites, and that is language" (*Histoire générale*, p. 180). Judaism is a matter of religion, not race, Renan asserts in another text ("Le Judaïsme comme race et comme religion" [Judaism as Race and Religion], pp. 925–944). The same holds true for the subdivisions of these large families: "What is philologically and historically called the Teutonic race, is assuredly a very distinct family of the human species. But is it a family in the anthropological sense? Certainly not" ("What Is a Nation?" p. 73). "Races are molds for moral education more than a matter of blood" ("La Société berbère," p. 571).

A linguistic race is not a physical race. It does not correspond exactly to a nation, either: several languages may be spoken within a single nation, as in Switzerland, and several nations may speak the same language, as with English; nevertheless, linguistic races are much closer to nations than to the earlier "races." Attempting to define the content of this notion more precisely, Renan writes: "From the point of view of the historical sciences, five things constitute the essential assets of a race, and give us the right to speak about that race as an individual entity within the human species. These five documents, which also prove that a race is nourished by its own past, are a separate language, a literature with identifiable characteristics, a religion, a history, and a civilization" (p. 553). It is almost surprising that Renan does not hit upon the word "culture," which would have gotten him out of his difficulty: entirely separate from the physical "race," located on neighboring territory (historical) and yet distinct from that of the "nation" (the cultural is distinct from the political), "culture" is the common action of language, literature, religion, and mores.

But it may be that Renan deliberately chooses not to use a term that would lack any hint of a connection with physical race. It may be that on the contrary he needs to maintain the subterranean relationship of the two meanings of the word, for the break between them is not as complete as it might have seemed, either in synchrony or in diachrony. When Renan writes, in *L'Origine du langage*, "The race that speaks Sanskrit [is] an aristocratic and conquering race, distinguished by its white color from the darker shades of the former inhabitants [of India]" (pp. 109–110), we can attribute the aristocratic and conquering spirit to culture; but can we do the same for light and dark skin?

The same holds true for history. Language accounts for the spirit of a nation, or so Renan asserts in the wake of Wilhelm von Humboldt. "The spirit of each people and its language are very closely connected: the spirit creates the language, and the language in turn serves as formula and limit for the spirit" (p. 96). But can the spirit, as a product of the language, really create the language? Does it do so all by itself? Renan's answer, in the same passage, is "no": "It is in fact in the diversity of races that we must seek the most effective causes of the diversity of idioms" (ibid.). We cannot have it both ways: either the word "race" is used here in its "linguistic" sense, and then the statement is a pure tautology (the diversity of idioms leads to the diversity of idioms)—but it is hard to believe that Renan would not have noticed this; or else the word retains its "physical" sense, and then the sentence declares the existence of a pertinent relationship between the two meanings of the word, between (anthropological) races and languages. Or else, when Renan recalls "that great axiom which we have often proclaimed, that the worth of religions is to be determined by the worth of the races that profess them" ("Islamism and Science," p. 104), he must no longer be using the word "race" as he had said he was using it—that is, as a term encompassing "religion" along with literature.

At the very beginning of his career, in *The Future of Science*, Renan wrote: "All the grammatical processes proceed directly from the manner in which each race treated ideas" (p. 253). If race is the origin of grammar, then race is not identical to grammar. In his last great work, *L'Histoire du peuple d'Israël*, Renan declared: "As language is, for a race, the very form of its thought, the use of a common language over the centuries becomes, for the family encompassed by it, a mold, a corset, as it were" (p. 32). This statement not only asserts linguistic (and cultural) determinism, it also asserts a relation between language and race, a relation that attests first to the noncoincidence between the two and then to their solidarity.

The treatment to which Renan subjects the concept of "race" now appears more complex than he suggested, even if we confine ourselves exclusively to the white race and its subdivisions. Far from separating language (and culture) from "race," Renan on the contrary legitimizes the production of "linguistic races" through the ambiguous use he makes of the term "race." "Linguistic races," he says, are the products of philology alone, but these products are (physical) "races" nevertheless. The "linguistic race" is the tourniquet that allows him to bring "race" into communication with language. Far from jettisoning the concept of "race," Renan's work gives it a new footing, since it is with Renan (and certain of his contemporaries) that the terms "Aryan" and "Semite" cease to designate language families and begin to apply to "races"—that is, to human beings. The same results are achieved, as we shall see, by the work of many of Renan's contemporaries and successors, such as Hippolyte Taine or Gustave Le Bon. Gobineau, who believes that races are based on differences of blood, is something of an exception in the second half of the nineteenth century. But this change in the meaning of the notion in no way prevents Renan and Le Bon, as we have seen, from remaining racialist (Taine is a different story): they simply transpose onto culture the prejudices that are commonly attached to race.

And the determinism they profess is no less inflexible for being cultural rather than physical. A member of a race, according to Renan, can never escape its domination; education does not make much difference. "All the progress of modern science leads us, on the contrary, to envision each race as confined to a characteristic type that it may or may not achieve but from which it cannot escape" ("Le Désert et le Soudan," p. 541). Kant and Goethe were already present among the primitive Teutons; the Africans for their part can never reach the apex of civilization. This division of humanity into mutually impermeable cultures harmonizes fully with Renan's relativism: values are part of culture. There is still a need to explain by what miracle science itself escapes: as the work of Indo-Europeans alone, logically speaking it ought to be of value only for them. How can a particular culture produce something that is truly universal, such as science?

Thus, Renan's speculations on cultural difference are, most of the time, only the direct expression of his own "prejudices." In reality, like almost all relativists, Renan makes an exception within his own doctrine for himself and his positions. The general law is illustrated only by others. If, for example, a contemporary Jewish writer were to develop a thesis, that thesis would devolve from the properties of the Semitic race. The opinions of a M. Salvador on religion hold no surprises for Renan: "He brought to his task what we may call an endowment of race, that sort of political insight which has rendered the Semites alone capable of great religious combinations" ("The Future of Religion," p. 346). Conversely, if one is fortunate enough to speak "Indo-European," one benefits from all the qualities of that race. In his play *Caliban*, Renan has Ariel say to the tamed savage: "Prospero taught thee the Aryan language, and with that divine tongue the channel of reason has become inseparable from thee" (English, p. 18).

If—on top of all that—one speaks *French*, one is invested with a special spirit, here again quite apart from the intentions of the speaking subject: "It [the French language] will say quite diverse things, but always liberal things . . . It will never be a reactionary language, either . . . This language improves [those who learn it]; it is a school; it has naturalness, good-naturedness, it can laugh, it conveys an agreeable

skepticism mingled with goodness . . . Fanaticism is impossible in
French . . . A Musulman who knows French will never be a dangerous
Musulman" ("Conférence faite à l'Alliance pour la propagation de la
langue française" [Lecture Given at the Alliance for the Propagation
of the French Language], pp. 1090–1091). Could we not believe we
are reading Renan's self-portrait? After this, we can hardly be astonished that Renan, although he claimed to be suspicious of the illusions
of patriotism, ended up recommending the universal use of French:
Why deprive others of the best language in the world? "The preservation and propagation of the French language are important for the
general order of civilization" (p. 1088).

Science versus Religion

Renan devoted his life to the description of the "Semitic" language,
religion, and history, always comparing this "race," more or less explicitly, with the other great white "race," Indo-European or Aryan. His
comparative portraits of Aryans and Semites give us an excellent opportunity to see how he uses the concept of "linguistic race."

Some of the forms in which Renan presents the opposition might
lead us to believe that he has used up his hierarchical categories in the
description of the "three races," and that he is content here to point
to nonhierarchical differences. All the oppositions that he identifies can
indeed be reduced to a single one, the opposition between reason and
faith, between truth and revelation, between philosophy (or science)
and religion. "The premeditated, independent, severe, courageous—in
one word—philosophical search after the truth seems to have been the
inheritance of that Indo-Germanic race" (*The Future of Science*,
pp. 266–267; cf. *L'Origine du langage*, p. 98, and *Histoire générale*,
p. 145; Renan likes the sentence so much he repeats it three times). As
for the Semitic "race," on the other hand, "It is par excellence the race
of religions, destined to give birth to them and to propagate them"
(*L'Origine du langage*, p. 97). This opposition governs numerous others—for example, that of multiplicity (Aryan) versus unity (Semitic) (cf.
Histoire générale, p. 146). Now are not these two qualities equally necessary to the human spirit?

But the illusion of equilibrium and impartiality—religion for some,
philosophy for others—cannot last. Renan's comparison is always also
a condemnation. To begin with, unity and multiplicity only appear to

be a symmetrical pair: as we might have expected from a partisan of relativism, only multiplicity and diversity are presented as desirable. Unity in politics means Rome—which died of it; diversity means Greece, whose legacy modern Europe has inherited. "Uniformity is despotism" ("Philosophie de l'histoire contemporaine" [Philosophy of Contemporary History], p. 37); conversely, "division is the condition of freedom" ("The Future of Religion," p. 351). "If the Christian nations constituted a unitary world, analogous to the *orbis romanus,* decadence would be inevitable, since outside of this closed circle there would be no element of regeneration. But the principle of diversity and individual vitality that created in Europe an invincible obstacle to any universal domination will be the salvation of the modern world" ("M. de Sacy et l'école libérale" [M. de Sacy and the Liberal School], p. 53). There is no room to hesitate between two options so unequally endowed with hope.

Or again, let us take languages themselves (the basis for race). "The Aryan language was highly superior, especially as regards verb conjugations. This marvelous instrument, created by the instinct of primitive men, contained the seeds of all the metaphysics that would be developed later on by the genius of the Hindus, the Greeks, or the Germans. The Semitic language, on the contrary, got off to the wrong start where verbs are concerned. The greatest mistake this race ever made (because the most irreparable) was to adopt such a niggardly mechanism for treating verbs that the expression of tenses and moods has always been imperfect and awkward in its language. Even today, the Arabs are still struggling against the linguistic error committed by their ancestors ten or fifteen thousand years ago" (*Histoire du peuple d'Israël,* p. 35). On the one hand, Renan is clearly talking about imperfection, error, defect, even niggardliness; on the other hand, he is clearly practicing a cultural determinism at least as rigid as Gobineau's biological determinism. If today's Arabs are wretched while Germans are prosperous, the fault lies with their ancestors, who created (?) their languages some fifteen thousand years ago. In this light, it is a mockery to speak of individual liberty or, in a different perspective, of equality among peoples, since everything depends on language, and languages are not equal.

If this is true of languages, it is all the more true of cultures. The Semitic peoples are always described negatively in Renan's texts—that is, by what they lack in comparison to the Indo-Europeans; except for the marks of disapproval, we might think we were reading Montaigne's description (to which we shall return) of the Golden Age, a description similarly deduced through an inversion of the features observed, with no attempt to present the other society on its own terms. "Thus, the Semitic race can be recognized almost entirely by its negative features: it has no mythology, no epic, no science, no philosophy, no fiction, no plastic arts, no civic life; in all things, there is an absence of complexity, of nuance, there are exclusive sentiments of unity" (*Histoire générale*, p. 155). "In every respect, as we see, the Semitic race appears to us as an incomplete race by virtue of its very simplicity. It is, if I may say so, to the Indo-European family what *grisaille* is to painting, what plain-chant is to modern music" (p. 156). More generally speaking, "the East has never produced anything as good as we have" ("The Future of Religion," p. 351).

With this inferior equipment, we can hardly be astonished to learn that the Semites have managed to make only a modest and limited contribution to the history of civilization—namely, the introduction of monotheistic religions. "From the day when they committed the Bible to European science . . . they have had nothing more of consequence to do" (p. 348). Once this day was past, the Semites were destined to play a subordinate role, or even to disappear. "Once this mission was accomplished, the Semite race declined rapidly, and left the Aryan race to walk alone at the head of the destinies of the human race" (*Histoire générale*, p. 587). In the present day, every step away from Semitic culture is a step ahead. "At the present time, the essential condition of a diffused civilization is the destruction of the peculiarly Semitic element" ("The Share of the Semitic People in the History of Civilization," p. 164). "In all departments progress for the Indo-European people will consist in departing farther and farther from the Semitic spirit" (p. 165). And that is more especially true of the evolution of Christianity: "The future perfection of Christianity will consist in a further and further remove from Judaism, to give predominance to the genius of the Indo-European race" ("The Future of Religion," p. 349).

At first glance, Renan's predictions and recommendations are nothing but a reiteration of the Enlightenment project: he comes out against prejudices, in favor of reason. "Judaism and Christianity will disappear. The Jewish work will reach its end; the Greek work—that is, science, rational and experimental civilization, without charlatanism, without revelation, civilization based on reason and liberty—will on the contrary continue forever, and, if this globe ever fails to fulfill its duties, there will be others to take the project of all life to the limit: enlight-enment, reason, truth" (*Histoire du peuple d'Israël*, p. 1517). What does not reflect the Enlightenment spirit, however, is the identification of one population (the Greeks, the Indo-Europeans) with civilization, and another with superstition. For Renan, the triumph of reason finally signals nothing other than the victory of the Indo-Europeans. "The great Indo-European race [is] obviously destined to incorporate all the others" (*Histoire générale*, p. 587), he writes, once again introducing Providence into history, and by the same token reducing the freedom of action of individual subjects. He thus expects to see the time come when, "after thousands of years of efforts, the Aryan race will have become master of the planet it inhabits" (*L'Origine du langage*, p. 115).

The superiority of Aryans over Semites is thus expressed in terms rigorously parallel to those used to describe the superiority of the white race over the others—whereas in the latter case physical races were in question, and in the former, linguistic races! The Aryans are to the other white races (that is, to Semites—Jews or Arabs) what the white race is to the other two races, namely the people destined to rule the world. Once again, we note that it was not without cause that Renan argued in favor of the separation between science and ethics: the ethical dogma of universal equality or the Christian dogma of the unity of the human race must not keep "science" from establishing the real inequal-ity that prevails among human groups. However, are "linguistic races" really the issue?

Faith in Reason

One puzzle remains for the reader of Renan's texts. Why did the author devote his life to the study of the Semites and of religion (for him these amount to the same thing), which he held in contempt, rather than to the study of the Aryans and of science, which he venerated? Toward the end of his life, he wrote: "If I could lead a second life, I would certainly devote it to Greek history, which is even more beautiful, in some respects, than Jewish history" ("Le Judaïsme comme race et religion," p. 937). But these words do not express any regret, and Renan can also write, without contradicting himself: "All things con-sidered, I should not, if I had to begin my life over again, with the right of making what erasures I liked, change anything" (*Recollections of My Youth*, p. 318). It is not *in the place of* Jewish history that Renan would like to write that of the Greeks, it is *in the wake of* that history, in a second lifetime—the first having sufficed for him to settle the Semitic question. There is thus a significant continuity, since the project that came to fruition with Renan's last great work, *L'Histoire du peuple d'Israël*, was announced in his very first work, *The Future of Science*, some forty years before.

It was indeed in his earliest work that Renan first formulated the ideas to which he would devote his entire life. In *The Future of Science* he first sets forth a task worthy of general attention, an impersonal and noble project. "The history of the *Origins of Christianity* written by a critic who would go to the direct sources would undoubtedly be a work of importance" (p. 172). He elevates the tone a little further on: "The most important book of the nineteenth century should bear the title of 'A Critical History of the Origins of Christianity.' Oh, the admirable book, the author of which I envy" (he then becomes much more personal) "and which will be the work of my ripe old age" (p. 261). However, in these same pages, Renan does not hesitate to pass unfavorable judgments on the works he uses as his sources: one (the Talmud) is "a very curious monument of moral depression and extravagance," the others are "insipid" works "pervaded by a suave mediocrity" (p. 170). "Those books do not contain a single line of sense; they are simply so much raving composed in a barbarous and indecipherable style" (p. 171); they are "utterly insignificant books" (p. 172). How is it that the least brilliant matter can lead to the most important book?

Renan gives the following explanation. The perfection of any object consists in the equilibrium of its elements; but that state of equilibrium and moderation also renders them hard to perceive, and thus hard to comprehend. Imperfection, on the contrary, consists in the excessive development of one constituent at the expense of the others; but, by the same token, imperfection is easy to grasp. If one wants to study and understand humanity, one must not focus on what is most perfect about it—the Greeks, science, reason. "Scientific works, therefore, can in no way convey an idea of the originality of human nature nor of its proper character" (p. 259). On the other hand, "the most insignificant works are often the most important in so far as they energetically depict one aspect of things" (p. 170). Such is the law of knowledge: "It is easier to study diverse natures in their crises than in their normal condition. The regularity of life only shows one surface and conceals in its depth the inmost mainsprings; in a state of ebullition, on the other hand, everything rises in its turn to the surface" (p. 171). Just as psychology draws its greatest insights from the study of madness, so history finds its object of predilection in religion. "Religions, therefore, are the purest and most complete expressions of human nature" (p. 258).

It is well known that in his early youth Renan broke with Christianity and opted for science (and we have seen what hyperbolic praise he offers of the latter). He finds his dispositions confirmed the day he visits Athens for the first time: this place that embodies for him the spirit of science inspires the most powerful impression of his life, gives him the feeling of being in contact with perfection; next to that, all the rest is mere barbarity. But he does not valorize just any science. He does not choose to study nature, or even the Greeks and reason; he takes as the object of his scientific research precisely religion and the Semites, as if the very progression of his investigations were to bring proof that he had made the right choice. His assertion of the superiority of Aryans over Semites is only an anthropomorphic transposition of the superiority of science over religion, which he affirms with a relentlessness bordering on obsession, reducing religion to the status of object and elevating science to a position of mastery, thereby repeating on a daily basis the gesture that had determined his destiny.

But if religion must be endlessly immolated (and thus the Semites humiliated), Renan's science itself does not seem to differ from religion as much as it ought to for the purpose of contrast. Renan lived his relation to science the way others live their relation to God: with passion rather than reason. He himself actually compared the two experiences, describing his relation to science as superior in terms ordinarily reserved for religious experience. "I have tasted in my childhood and from early youth the purest joys of the believer, and I say from the bottom of my heart that these joys are nothing by comparison with what I have felt in the pure contemplation of the beautiful and the passionate search after truth" (p. 299).

When Renan speaks of his intellectual experience as a scholar, he consistently uses religious terminology. The project of his first book, *The Future of Science*, is "to inculcate . . . faith in reason" (p. 407). It is not reason versus faith, Aryans versus Semites, but faith *in* reason, religious experience integrated into the practice of science. "The ancient faith is impossible, but there remains faith by science, the critical faith" (p. 416). The unique result of science, he concludes, is to give man, "in the name of the sole legitimate authority which is the whole of human nature itself, the symbol of the creed which religion gave him ready made and which he can no longer accept" (p. 17). Throughout his entire life Renan continues to use this sort of imagery, thus translating his secular ideals into sacred terms. Referring to his friend Berthelot, he declares: "We had . . . the same religion. That religion was the cult of truth" ("Discours à la conférence 'Scientia'" [Speech at the "Scientia" Conference], p. 859). At another point he says: "When I want to typify what an unexampled pair of friends we were, I always represent two priests in their surplices walking arm in arm" (*Recollections of My Youth*, p. 299). "The final resurrection will be brought about by science," he writes to the same friend ("Les Sciences de la nature et les sciences historiques" [The Natural Sciences and the Historical Sciences], p. 650). But by dint of stating that the new religion is truth, doesn't one risk making truth into a new religion? Is the goal of science and reason really to lead to faith? By slipping into the shoes of religion this way, rejoicing at having so easily ousted the previous occupant, doesn't science end up borrowing many of its features?

Renan's ideal goal in fact is not to see reason triumph over faith but to bring about their ultimate reconciliation. For that it suffices to rid religion of its paraphernalia of superstition. "The scientific spirit is not, for religion thus conceived, an enemy that must be mistrusted. It constitutes part of religion itself, and without it no one can be a true devotee . . . I consider that, by following a purely scientific line, I am serving the cause of the true religion" ("La Chaire d'hébreu au Collège de France" [The Chair in Hebrew at the Collège de France], p. 170). Science provides a means for attaining the objectives of religion. "The world improved by science will be the realm of the spirit, the reign of the sons of God" ("L'Instruction supérieure en France," p. 70).

It is easier now to understand why Renan chooses as his vocation not science in general but the science of religions. "I endeavoured, therefore, on leaving St. Sulpice to remain as much of a St. Sulpice man as possible . . . One only [sic] occupation seemed worthy to absorb my life, and that was the pursuit of my critical researches upon Christianity by the much larger means which lay science offered me" (*Recollections*, p. 302). Renan repeats this over and over in his *Recollections*: by giving up the priesthood, he did not give up the priestly vocation, but only its outward signs, which had become outmoded. "For a long time, my programme was to abandon as little as possible of Christianity, and to hold on to all that could be maintained without belief in the supernatural" (ibid.). This choice corresponds to his deepest inclinations: "I was born to be a priest, as others are born to be soldiers and lawyers" (p. 139). But what has happened to Renan's faith in the virtues of education? He looks back on his time at Saint-Sulpice as the turning point of his life, and he believes he has never betrayed the ideal he conceived there. "Thus it may, upon the whole, be said that I have come short in little of my clerical promises . . . I have been truer to my engagements than many priests apparently more regular in their conduct" (p. 317). This is how Renan became the high priest of science.

Thus, religion—which Renan also identifies with morality, and sometimes even with political doctrines such as socialism—is never presented as truly autonomous; even within its own domain, that of faith, it is outstripped by science—which, in the process, acquires certain features of religion and morality, and begins to provide goals for human society and to indicate how they are to be achieved. Perhaps this explains better than Renan himself did why he devoted his efforts to what he claimed to respect so little: religion and its inventors. In so doing he rejoins mainstream scientism as found in authors for whom he professed contempt, such as Saint-Simon and Auguste Comte. The scientistic doctrine consists in effect not only in denying human freedom and in proclaiming the undivided reign of determinism (something Renan does without acknowledging it), and in subordinating ethics to science (something he does openly), but also in requiring a religious attitude toward scientific achievements: science is transmuted into a Church. Reason becomes the object of faith: this is the logical outcome of scientistic philosophy—and, at the same time, the step that leads it to turn its back definitively on science.

The Paths of Racialism

Historical Races

The most significant change in the notion of race in the late nineteenth century is its transposition from the physical to the cultural plane, under the influence of such authors as Renan, Taine, and Le Bon. Having looked at Renan's "linguistic" races, let us now consider the notion of "historical" race shared by Taine and Le Bon.

Hippolyte Taine's place in the history of racialism is somewhat difficult to pin down. His influence is quite considerable, although his

writings include only a few pages devoted to the issue of race. Moreover, there is a troubling discrepancy between his programmatic
exposés and his own practice. Like Renan, his contemporary, Taine in
fact swings back and forth between physical and cultural interpretations
of the word "race," thus authorizing his disciples to find arguments in
his writings in support of contradictory theses.

In his statements of principle, as we have seen, Taine aligns himself
with an integral determinism (this is not the case with his practice). In
his introduction to the *History of English Literature*, Taine's systematic
presentation of the factors governing human behavior reduces them to
three: race, surroundings, and epoch—that is, what man contributes in
himself, what the external environment imposes on him, and finally the
results of the interaction of these two factors. The "epoch" *(le moment)*
is not actually the result of the era in which one lives, but rather the
result of the phase of an internal evolution proper to each human
group; in other words, it combines the two preceding factors, yet it
becomes a determining factor in turn. "With the forces within and
without, there is the work which they have already produced together,
and this work itself contributes to produce that which follows" (p. 21).
But just what does the contribution from "within" (called "race") consist of? What are its nature and its scope?

In "The Philosophy of Art in the Netherlands" ("Philosophie de
l'Art dans les Pays-Bas"), Taine attempts to draw a rigorous distinction
between race and nation (or people), but he does so with the help of a
metaphor that leaves room for a certain interpretive license. "I shall
first show you the seed, that is to say the race, with its fundamental
and indelible qualities, those that persist through all circumstances and
in all climates; and next the plant, that is to say the people itself, with
its original qualities expanded or contracted, in any case grafted on and
transformed by its surroundings and its history" *(Philosophie de l'art*, in
English *The Philosophy of Art*, II, p. 168). But just what do these vegetable images yield when they are transposed onto the human species?

When he sets out to illustrate the influence of race, in the *History of
English Literature*, Taine resorts to an example that seems to confirm
the foregoing distinction. "A race, like the old Aryans, scattered from
the Ganges as far as the Hebrides, settled in every clime, and every
stage of civilization, transformed by thirty centuries of revolutions,
nevertheless manifests in its languages, religions, literatures, philosophies, the community of blood and of intellect which to this day finds

its offshoots together" (p. 17). Let us note here that while Taine may be talking about "blood" and "intellect," his list includes only intellectual products, languages and literatures, religions and philosophies; the common denominator of activities as numerous and varied as these can hardly be very powerful. In any event, race is presented here as a supranational entity.

However, the same text also includes statements that tend to identify race with nation. Races, according to Taine, "vary with various peoples" (p. 17). Why, then, are two terms needed instead of just one? He goes on to give examples of "regulating instincts and faculties implanted in a race" (p. 20) that involve the Germanic, Hellenic, and Latin races—or rather Spain, England, and France, which is to say nations and not races. In another passage, where he lists "the fundamental causes" that govern human behavior, Taine specifies that he means "nationality, climate, temperament" (p. 34); here "nationality" appears again as a synonym for "race." At the same time, Taine says he intends to complete the task Montesquieu had set for himself: the description of "the special psychology of each special formation" (p. 33)—that is, the spirit of nations. And it must be said that in practice, physical characteristics play only a small part in Taine's analyses; thus, contrary to what his own distinctions imply, his races are nations, understood as "cultures."

We find the same ambiguity in the description of "race" itself. Race is what is innate; but is what is innate modifiable? Is it radically distinct from what is acquired? On the one hand, Taine implies that race is a stable entity. "There is one [fixed element], a character and spirit proper to the race, transmitted from generation to generation, remaining the same through cultural change, organizational shifts, and variation in products" (*Essais*, preface to the second edition, pp. xviii–xix). These are "the universal and permanent causes, present at every moment and in every case, everywhere and always acting, indestructible, and finally infallibly supreme" (*History of English Literature*, p. 12). So much for the immutable side.

But at the same time, Taine makes precisely the opposite claim. The brief passages in the *History of English Literature* that describe the entity called "race" are oddly focused on the search for the *origin* of races—which is nothing other than an adaptation to the surroundings. The inside that was supposed to be opposed to the outside is only a slightly older outside. "As soon as an animal begins to exist, it has to reconcile itself with its surroundings; it breathes and renews itself, is differently affected according to the variations in air, food, temperature. Different climate and situation bring it various needs, and consequently a different course of activity; and thus, again, a different set of habits; and still again, a different set of aptitudes and instincts" (p. 18). It is no longer race and surroundings that are in opposition, but long and short time periods. "The race emigrates, like the Aryan, and the change of climate has altered in its case the whole economy, intelligence, and organization of society" (p. 16). Taine then falls back on another comparison in which he has given up the qualitative difference between seed and plant: the race is "a kind of lake, a deep reservoir wherein other springs have, for a multitude of centuries, discharged their several streams" (p. 19). Certain waters flow out of the lake, and others flow into it; but there is no difference in nature between them.

When he turns to the study of the "surroundings," Taine mentions the climate and geographical features, political circumstances, and social conditions as being among the most powerful environmental forces that act on men; taken together, "these prolonged situations, these surrounding circumstances" produce "the regulating instincts and faculties implanted in a race—in short, the mood of intelligence in which it thinks and acts at the present time" (p. 20). Thus, race no longer produces history, but rather history produces race (or the spirit of the nation). Moreover, by modifying the institutions or forms of social life, one can transform race: such actions "are to nations what education, career, condition, abode are to individuals" (p. 21). The possibility of an educational project alluded to here is at the opposite pole from racialist thought, and it allows us to measure the full ambivalence of Taine's position (although properly speaking there is no contradiction, and Taine was probably conscious of the apparent inconsistency).

In his books *(Philosophie de l'art, Essais de critique)*, Taine deals at length with "the spirit of nations." He uses the term "race," but he often leaves the impression that the word is only a substitute, sometimes synonymous with "nation," sometimes with "essential element" or "dominant faculty." Whatever the case, starting with Taine the word "race" comes into play with renewed vigor.

In the transformations that Renan and Taine, or even Le Bon, bring to racialist doctrine, we can see a prefiguration of its contemporary outlines. The term "race," having already outlived its usefulness, will be replaced by the much more appropriate term "culture"; declarations of superiority and inferiority, the residue of an attachment to the universalist framework, will be set aside in favor of a glorification of difference (a difference that is not valorized in itself). What will remain unchanged, on the other hand, is the rigidity of determinism (cultural rather than physical, now) and the discontinuity of humanity, compartmentalized into cultures that cannot and must not communicate with one another effectively. The period of classical racialism seems definitely behind us, in the wake of the widespread condemnation of Nazi Germany's policies toward Jews; thus, we can establish its chronological limits with a precision that is unusual in the history of ideas: from 1749 (Buffon) to 1945 (Hitler). Modern racialism, which is better known as "culturalism," originates in the writings of Renan, Taine, and Le Bon; it replaces physical race with linguistic, historical, or psychological race. It shares certain features with its ancestor, but not all; this has allowed it to abandon the compromising term "race" (and thus the first "proposition" of classical racialism). Nevertheless, it can continue to play the role formerly assumed by racialism. In our day, racist behaviors have clearly not disappeared, or even changed; but the discourse that legitimizes them is no longer the same; rather than appealing to racialism, it appeals to nationalist or culturalist doctrine, or to the "right to difference."

Racialism as Scientism

As we have observed from the beginning of this discussion, racialism flourishes in the shadow of science, for it borrows from science the determinist outlook, which it carries to the extreme. The inexorable determinism of race: this is the feature common to racialist theories that differ in other respects, such as those of Gobineau, Renan, and Taine. The individual is powerless before the fact of race; his destiny is decided by his ancestors, and the efforts of educators go for nought. From this scientific "certainty," the racialist draws conclusions in the form of a set of precepts concerning practical life, for morality must be subject to science—unless science itself produces a higher morality. And these precepts will in the end be revered just as religious dogmas are revered. Once again, this set of ideas is digested and popularized for the benefit of the larger public in Dr. Gustave Le Bon's *The Psychology of Peoples*.

Le Bon is no less a determinist than Taine, but he modifies Taine's causal hierarchy. For Taine, as we have seen, what is innate (race) and acquired (surroundings) maintain a certain equilibrium and are even inextricably intertwined. Le Bon, more like Gobineau in this respect, considers the influence of surroundings entirely superficial, and he deems race, or heredity, wholly determining (but we have also seen that Taine could make the same case on occasion). There are thus two facets to Le Bon's argument: one critical, or negative, combating the idea that mentalities can be modified; the other positive, asserting the relevance of hereditary factors.

In particular, Le Bon does not believe in the idea, so widespread in the mid-eighteenth century, that one can act on the mores of a people by transforming its institutions. "Tocqueville and other illustrious thinkers have imagined that they have discovered in the institutions of various peoples the cause of their evolution. I, on the contrary, am persuaded . . . that institutions are of extremely slight importance as regards the evolution of civilization" (*The Psychology of Peoples*, p. xix). Le Bon regards this opinion as scientifically established. "I believe . . . that it is scarcely elsewhere than in the obtuse brain of the masses and the narrow minds of some few fanatics that the idea can persist that important social changes are to be brought about by legislative acts" (p. 91). What was still excusable in Helvétius' era (and Tocqueville's?) is no longer excusable in Le Bon's: the time has come to yield to the facts. Helvétius declared peremptorily: "Examining the effects which nature and education may have upon us, I have perceived that education makes us what we are" (*Essays on the Mind*, p. 240). Le Bon argues strenuously against the educational project, "one of the most baneful illusions that the theoreticians of pure reason have ever brought into existence" (*The Psychology of Peoples*, p. 37), but he does so, it must be said, while relying upon a determinism that comes to him precisely from eighteenth-century philosophical materialism, and thus also from Helvétius, who was no less a determinist than Le Bon himself but who believed in the power of acquired rather than innate characteristics.

Education in particular is impossible as soon as one crosses national boundaries. The only thing Europeans can give others, according to Taine, is a veneer of civilization. Le Bon uses the same metaphor: "A negro or a Japanese may easily take a university degree or become a lawyer; the sort of varnish he thus acquires is however quite superficial, and has no influence on his mental constitution . . . Our negro or our Japanese may accumulate all possible certificates without ever attaining to the level of the average European" (p. 37). For education has no influence over character or modes of thought. "It is possible to drill an army of negroes in accordance with European military principles and to teach them to handle rifles and canon, but their mental inferiority and the consequences it involves will not be modified on this account" (p. 85, note 1). Is civilization really what is at issue here? Yes, if we are to believe Le Bon, who continues: "The varnish of European civilisation boasted at present by Japan in nowise corresponds to the mental condition of the race. It is a trumpery borrowed garment which will soon be rent by violent revolutions" (ibid.). To date, Le Bon's prophecies do not seem to have come true.

Not only does European education have no positive impact on non-European peoples, but it actually corrupts them, for it destroys what they had without putting anything in its place; to use the later expression of apologists for colonialism, it leaves these child-peoples stranded "in the middle of the ford." "If it be sought, by means of education, to spare a people these stages, all that is done is to disorganise its morality and its intelligence, and to reduce it in the end to a level inferior to that it would have reached if it had been left to itself" (p. 82).

For this mistaken view of history and social action, Le Bon means to substitute another, one he has in common with Gobineau: the idea that race determines everything. However, Le Bon's idea of race is borrowed from Renan and Taine: it is a matter of cultural traditions rather than bloodlines. This is Le Bon's main thesis, repeated tirelessly, although—need we add?—never supported. "It will be easy for us to prove this statement by a few examples," Le Bon says (p. 130). However, examples have obviously never proved anything; at most, they serve to illustrate and to seduce. What is the value of Taine's anecdote about the little Filipino who returned to "savagery"? Is it true? Is it representative? What are the actual circumstances? We do not know, we cannot know, and the author knows we shall never know. Le Bon's statements are only incontestable when they are reduced to meaningless tautologies: "It is the mental constitution of races that determines their conception of the world and of life" (p. 35). But where does this get us, this reiteration of "mental constitution" by "conception of the world"?

When such a strong claim is made in favor of collective determinations (the individual is merely the representative of his race), no room at all is left for individual freedom—a result that does not give Le Bon pause. Man "has perceived that what he used to term liberty was merely

ignorance of the causes of which he is the slave, and that in view of the
inexorable necessities of which they are the puppets, to be slaves is the
natural condition of all living beings" (pp. 215–216). He could not
make himself any clearer. Race—that is, all those who have gone before
us in our lineage—decides for us: "The dead, besides being infinitely
more numerous than the living, are infinitely more powerful" (p. 11).
For the dead act through our collective (racial) unconscious, and the
unconscious rules man: this is why Freud reserves such high praise for
Le Bon.

Once again, science (Le Bon's science) makes ethics superfluous. It
has brought to light, he thinks, "the immovable rock of natural inequalities" (p. xx); it "has proved the vanity of the theories of equality"
(p. xv). Henceforth it must serve as the basis for our behavior: "a close
study" of "the psychological constitution of peoples" must become "the
basis of politics and education" (p. 137). Any other attitude would
amount to knuckling under to religion once again: "the immortal
principles" of 1789 are "the only divinities that survive to-day" (xv).

Scientism and Totalitarianism

Our contemporary reading of racialism is inevitably influenced by our
knowledge of its historical destiny (from the Dreyfus affair to apartheid) and more particularly by our knowledge of its influence on Nazi
doctrine, which led to the extermination of several million human
beings—one of the greatest racial crimes in the history of humanity.
The author of *Mein Kampf* in fact professed doctrines that were not
noticeably different from those of our nineteenth-century racialists,
whom he is known moreover to have read. For Hitler, too, nature was
omnipotent and one had to be content to obey its laws. Now these laws
teach us that life is struggle and warfare, and that only the fittest—that
is, the strongest—survive: for Hitler as for Gobineau, civilization was
identified with military superiority. This kind of power arises in turn
from race: all of history is there to prove it, for good as for evil, as
Hitler declared in harmony with Le Bon, even though he understood
the notion of race in Gobineau's sense—that is, as a matter of blood
instead of culture. For the races are endowed with unequal strengths:
Aryans are at the top, blacks and Jews at the bottom. If this degradation
of Semites is new in terms of the theories with which we have become
acquainted up to now, Hitler's portrait of the Semites nevertheless owes

a good deal to Renan. It is on these "scientific" bases that Hitler decided to build his policies, intended to prevent racial mixing, as Le Bon and Barrès also sought to do, and to purify the race by a rigorous selection process along with the elimination of the least perfect individuals (we saw the eugenic project surface with Renan). Thus, in characteristic fashion Hitler combined faith in the ineluctable laws of nature, and therefore a certain fatalism, with a highly energetic activism, since the state, the party, and the leader must struggle constantly to attain this ideal.

We are both right and wrong to project recent history against an earlier history in this way: right, because we cannot overlook the practical consequences of an ideology (and even if we are uncertain about the exact role ideology played, there is no doubt that its role was extremely important); wrong, because Buffon and Gobineau, Renan and Taine themselves never envisioned the extermination of inferior races in gas chambers. But the juxtaposition remains legitimate: it is less a matter of *explaining* the horrors of Nazism by Hitler's ideas, and these by the racialist theories of the previous era, than of *evaluating* these theories in the light of Nazi ideology, with whose equivalent in acts we are all too familiar. Without seeking to impute to nineteenth-century authors what was going to happen in the twentieth century, we have to observe that the pernicious implications of these doctrines are not entirely absent, either, from the minds of the French racialists. Evidence of this can be found, once again, in Renan, who devoted a lengthy and striking passage to this topic in the third of his *Philosophical Dialogues*.

This dialogue, whose principal speaker is called Theoctistes, deals with the nature of the ideal to which one ought to aspire, with what could be the perfection of the universe. The universe, and not humanity: this first point is important, and it is explicitly stressed by Theoctistes: the point is, "in short, to assign to the universe a purpose superior to it" (p. 49). In other words, we shall not ask what makes human beings happy or what is best for them, but, as Lévi-Strauss does later on, we shall try to uncover suprahuman or transhuman intentions so as to attempt to conform to them in the future. Such a way of posing the problem dismisses at the outset the response most commonly offered in Renan's day as to the nature of that ideal, a response that can be linked to the philosophical and ideological tendency of individualism: it is in effect unreasonable to think that the entire universe is designed so as to contribute to the earthly happiness of a particular individual. "The principle that society exists only for the well-being and liberty of the individuals composing it, does not seem consistent with the plans of Nature—plans in which the species only is taken into account, and in which the individual seems to be sacrificed" (p. 56). To begin with, then, we have to shed "our superficial individualism" (p. 71). Theoctistes justifies this gesture in two ways. First, the subordination of the small to the large, the individual to the general, is in the nature of things: we can see this merely by looking around. "The nation, the church, the commonwealth exist more truly than the individual, since the individual sacrifices himself for these entities, which yet a gross realism regards as mere abstractions" (p. 51). The second justification involves not facts but what is right: such a subordination is not only omnipresent but just. "The sacrifice of a living creature to an end desired by Nature is justifiable" (p. 72), the reason being that a general good justifies an individual evil.

The nation, the community, or even the state and royalty, as they currently exist, are indeed transindividual entities to which individual wills submit, or are expected to submit. But what we have here is only a highly imperfect state of affairs; the ideal requires us to go much farther down this path. A way to do this imposes itself; it is presented by Theoctistes, moreover, not as a means but rather as an integral part of the goal itself—namely, the reign of the best. Not everyone can become perfect at the same time; thus, those who are already perfect must be favored, and they must govern the others. "The essential point is that high culture establish itself and become mistress of the world, by making the less cultivated portions feel its benign influence" (p. 54). "The mass is devoted to labour; a few perform for them the high functions of life; this is humanity" (p. 72). Thus, in passing from the cosmic to the human perspective, one can transpose "the perfection of the universe" to "the reign of the best." "The purpose prosecuted by the world, far from being a levelling of the mountain summits, must, on the contrary, be to create gods, superior beings, such as the rest of conscious beings shall adore and serve, and feel happy in serving" (p. 57). "The aim of humanity, in a word, is to produce great men" (ibid.).

Once this equivalence has been established, Theoctistes wonders—in fact somewhat hypocritically—what form of government would allow it to be achieved. He imagines three possibilities: the rule of one person, or monarchy; the rule of several, or oligarchy; and the rule of all, or democracy. The monarchical solution is somewhat beside the point, and is not directly relevant to our topic; the crucial opposition here is between oligarchy and democracy. Now the outcome of the contest is in fact preordained, since the one but not the other conforms to the elitist ideal of humanity. It is nevertheless worthwhile to look at Theoctistes' criticisms of democracy and the consequences he imagines for oligarchy.

His critique of the democratic solution is in fact twofold. On the one hand, the democratic ideal of equality is incompatible with the desired goal, the rule of the best: there is thus a disparity between function and form. But alongside this argument based on what is right, we find another argument based on facts: even if one were to try, one would never reach the goal, for democracy equals impotence. "We can hardly imagine a high culture reigning over one portion of mankind, unless another portion serve it and share in it in a subordinate manner" (p. 54). "A scholar is the fruit of the self-denial, the earnestness, the sacrifices of two or three generations; he represents an immense economy of life and strength"; the ground must be prepared if he is to emerge (p. 57). Thus, we have to choose between scaling the heights or sharing in misery with everyone else; it is an illusion to think that the entire set of human beings can reach perfection. "If the ignorance of the masses is a necessary condition for this end, so much the worse" (p. 58). "Reason and science are products of humanity, but to seek for reason directly for the people's sake and through the people's agency is chimerical" (p. 55). In fact the democratic solution is handicapped from the start, since Theoctistes had chosen to adopt not the perspective of humanism and individualism, of which democracy is the political expression, but rather the perspective of a kind of naturalism.

Oligarchy is offered unmistakably as the most appropriate form for progressing toward the ideal. For Theoctistes, the reign of the best signifies the reign of scholars. "A select body of intelligent beings, possessed of the most important secrets of reality, would rule the world by the powerful agencies at their command, and establish the sovereignty of the largest possible amount of reason" (p. 59). From this point on, the reign of an elite over the rest of the population is fully justified. "Then the idea of a spiritual power, that is to say, a power having intellectual superiority as its basis, would be a reality" (pp. 59–60). It is for this reason that the efforts of all must contribute to producing such (intellectually superior) beings. Science is thus politically marked: it is on the side of the "positivist tyrants" (p. 62), and it is opposed to the regime of universal suffrage. "The great work will be accomplished by science, and not by democracy" (p. 57). Science must become mistress of the world, for scientists embody the highest principle of humanity—that is, reason.

Theoctistes and through him Renan dream of the final convergence of knowledge and power. "Truth will one day be power" (p. 63). This means not only, as we have seen, that power will belong to scientists, but also that science will produce the power that will allow it to reign everywhere. "Theory will be verified by its applications. A theory which shall lead to the invention of terrible engines, overpowering and subjugating all, will establish its truth by irrefragable evidence" (ibid.). Not only does truth supply power, but in addition power proves truth; the winner cannot be wrong. In this, too, oligarchy is preferable to democracy: the means at democracy's disposal for changing the world—namely, discussion and persuasion—turn out to be very inefficient. Much faster progress is possible if we can proceed by an "act of faith" (p. 56): we note that here as elsewhere, with Renan, science abandons one of its own principles and edges closer to religion.

By what concrete means will the scientific elite impose its dictatorship—on its fellow citizens first of all, then on the rest of the world? We can point to three in particular. The first is terror. The old religions sought to frighten gullible men by threatening them with hellfire; but, now that they are rid of their superstition, men are no longer afraid. The government of science can do better: "An authority will some day have hell at its command, not a chimerical hell of whose existence there is no proof, but a veritable one" (p. 60). The existence of such a place—such a prison, such a camp—would strike true fear into people's hearts. "The being possessed of science would set up unlimited terror in the service of truth" (pp. 62–63). That is indeed a powerful tool, and with its use "the very idea of revolt would disappear" (p. 63). If there were nevertheless some individuals who refused to submit, they would simply be eliminated: "Whoever shall offer any resistance to it, that is to say, shall not recognise the reign of science, will have to atone for his offence on the spot . . . All disregard of that power [that of reason] will be punished with instant death" (pp. 63–64). For the execution of these tasks, the scientific government would have at its disposal a special corps (janissaries, Chekists, SS troops), "obedient machines, unencumbered by moral scruples and prepared for every sort of cruelty" (p. 62).

The second means of acting on society is eugenics, or the improvement of the species (Theoctistes rejoins Renan on this topic). "A broad application of the discoveries of physiology and of the principle of selection might lead to the creation of a superior race, deriving its right to rule not only from its science, but from the very superiority of its blood, its brain, and its nerve" (pp. 64–65). Power and science are at each other's service: science supplies power, but also, through a reversal, it grants those who hold power a still greater advantage over others; by this very token their rule is better assured. In place of the current aristocracy, whose superiority is purely fictitious, will come the true nobility, scientifically produced beings who will be as different from the other inhabitants of the earth as man is from the animals. Imitating botany and zoology in this regard, human biology will contribute to the fabrication of a more perfect species, by eliminating all defective specimens and by favoring the development of the essential features of the organism. "It is possible that means may be found one day of concentrating in the brain the entire power of the nervous system, and of transmuting all nerve-energy into brain-energy, by atrophying, if we may say so, the opposite pole" (pp. 65–66). Such a transformation would immediately be put at the service of the "positive tyrants."

Finally, the third major means is the ultimate weapon. For the reign of truth to be assured, truth must have adequate technical means at its disposal. "A spiritual power will be really strong only when it is furnished with arms, when it has in its hands a material force belonging exclusively to itself" (p. 60). Now the creation of a weapon assuring mastery is within the grasp of science; as soon as it has been produced, the whole world will have to submit to the nation that owns it. "By a wider and wider application of science to the art of war, a universal sovereign government will become possible; and this government will be secure in the hands of those who shall direct the armaments" (p. 59). "The day when a few persons favoured of reason shall really possess the means of destroying the planet, their supremacy will be established; these privileged persons will rule by means of absolute terror, because they shall have in their hands the life of all" (p. 63). All those who would then challenge the right of science to rule would be threatened with immediate annihilation.

The realization of this dream, a modern and macabre version of Plato's *Republic*, is not going to come about tomorrow, Theoctistes acknowledges. But starting at once, it is possible to analyze the world in terms of its probable or desirable future, and we can discern certain elements that allow us to spell out future accomplishments. Thus it is that Theoctistes imagines, for reasons similar to those Tocqueville gave Gobineau, that the rule of science will first be established in Germany. "The government of the world by reason, should it ever come to pass, seems more suited to the genius of Germany, which shows little anxiety for the equality, or even the dignity, of individuals, and which aims before everything at increasing the intellectual powers of the race" (p. 67).

The chief justification of this project comes from the fact that it is, as we have seen, in harmony with nature. "It is Nature's sole care, at every step, to gain a superior end at the expense of inferior individualities" (p. 71). Nature is not concerned with victims: "Nature is not stopped in her course by such considerations; she sacrifices entire species in order that other species may find the conditions essential to their existence" (p. 58); nature itself is thus oligarchic and anti-democratic. Now anything that serves nature's designs is legitimate, and there is no reason to issue moral condemnations on this point. In any event, the fact that something exists proves it is supposed to exist, and "the desire to exist" has priority over "our proprieties and . . . our laws" (p. 52). The laws of nature, it goes without saying, are discovered by scientists, who nevertheless do not hesitate to go beyond them if they deem nature's accomplishments too timid. "It is for science to take up the work where Nature has left it" (p. 65). Certain plants, certain animals would not exist without the voluntary intervention of men (scientists); these are, however, the most useful ones of all. The race of superior beings that science will be charged with producing is not in nature; it is even "a being in antagonism to Nature" (ibid.). It is nevertheless justified by principles drawn from "nature"!

We need to ask at this point to what extent Theoctistes' "dream" is a utopia or a "dystopia" (a negative utopia), or, from another standpoint, to what extent Renan assumes responsibility for the ideal he formulates in this text. In his preface to the *Dialogues*, he keeps his distance—but only in the sense that he does not want to endorse personally any particular idea developed in his work; he is just as adamant about refusing to condemn any of them. "Each of these characters represents . . . the successive aspects of a free thought; not one of them is a pseudonym which I would have chosen" (p. xxiv). Within the *Dialogues* themselves, he presents Theoctistes' position as an exaggeration—but a perfectly consistent exaggeration—of what everyone believes; that is why "rays of light do occasionally break forth" (p. 48). After listening to him, another protagonist compares him to Columbus glimpsing America in an era when people still did not know it existed; from the gathering of dreams, says the same protagonist, one day the truth will spring up. Renan's text is comparable in this respect to P. Joly's *Dialogue de Machiavel et Montesquieu aux enfers* (Dialogue of Machiavelli and Montesquieu in Hell). But the commentary that sheds the most light on Renan's attitudes with respect to these ideas is found in another of his own texts, a text written at the same time as the *Dialogues* but not in dialogue form: "La réforme intellectuelle et morale de la France." The path to which Theoctistes points is more or less the one that is being followed, in Renan's view, by contemporary Germany (this accounts for the localization of the dream). Renan wonders whether this path is appropriate for France and concludes that it is not: given the character of the country's inhabitants and the vicissitudes of its history, the French path must be a compromise between that ideal and historical reality—that is, as it happens, democracy. We must resign ourselves to maintaining universal suffrage, but we could make it indirect; we must give up wars in Europe, but colonial wars are beneficial; we must provide for instruction, but must not give it over to the State; and so on. This was a position Renan had already put forth before the war, in "La Monarchie constitutionnelle en France" (Constitutional Monarchy in France); and to the end of his life he supported the same political options: the only thing that separates him from his friend Berthelot, he says in his *Recollections*, is that he, Renan, prefers the rule of an informed tyrant to democracy.

It has to be acknowledged that Renan succeeds in evoking, in these few pages, a large number of the problems that have become familiar to twentieth-century readers: totalitarian states, police terror, nuclear weapons, Nazi eugenics. We have not (yet) reached the point where we can create superior beings with chemistry (the subject remains the preserve of science fiction); but in a perhaps more insidious manner we are beginning to accept the legitimacy of genetic manipulations and other techniques of intervention in the process of human reproduction. We are not far from seeking to eliminate imperfect embryos, or to choose the sex, and even the type of intelligence, of our children. In an era when science has become the embodiment of the highest authority, Theoctistes' reveries have become very real problems: if science and technology are developed without external constraints, guided solely by concern for their own advancement and not by what is best for humanity, or—worse—if they are put at the service of political and personal aims that endanger the lives of part of humanity, then the consequences Renan imagined are not at all implausible, and, although he presents them calmly, we are right to find them frightening.

Does science really have to be held responsible for these future or present misfortunes? Theoctistes' reasoning is based on a double supposition: that science itself is infallible, and that those who represent it, the scientist-kings, the positivist tyrants, are disinterested beings, uniquely concerned with the pursuit of their ideal, the harmonious universe. That is why Theoctistes warns his interlocutors, "The class of ideas with which I am now dealing, refers but imperfectly to the planet earth" (p. 64), and he specifies: "It is clear that the absolute reign of one portion of humanity over another is odious, if we suppose the governing body to be swayed only be personal egoism or by class egoism" (p. 62). But he is content to declare that he himself does not endorse this hypothesis.

These two dangers are in fact more real than Theoctistes—or Renan—was willing to admit. Renan's own raciology, which seemed to him to lead to indubitable facts, has proved eminently fragile. From the standpoint of today's science, it has to be categorized alongside astrology and alchemy; it informs us about its subject, the scientist, much more than about its object, human populations. Not only is science not always perfect; one is tempted to say that it is never perfect: it is in the very nature of scientific knowledge that none of its results must be taken as definitive. As for the individual human beings that represent so-called scientific policies, it is well known that they have difficulty remaining above all suspicion: bureaucrats in totalitarian systems, who are supposed to be in charge of these policies, are considerably more concerned about their personal advantages than about what is good for humanity, or even for their homeland.

But even if we suppose, with Theoctistes, that these two obstacles may be removed (reasoning in the abstract, as it were), the responsibility of science does not appear to be clearly established. "Evil" has not waited for science to appear: what is specific to the twentieth century is not the emergence of evil but the fact that it can use scientific techniques, from highly efficient crematorium ovens to atomic bombs, as well as the organization of the state according to the principles of historical materialism. In other words, science is not to blame, but rather the uses made of it—which end up completely distorting the scientific project. It is not science but scientism that, leaving no room for the exercise of human will or human freedom, purports to subordinate ethics and politics to science; when this happens, as we saw with Renan, scientific utterances take on the status of declarations of faith—that is, they become the opposite of what they were intended to be. It is not true that science dictates politics and ethics in totalitarian states (to suppose this is to be taken in by propagandistic arguments): once again politics and ethics dominate science, but the scientific camouflage allows them to pursue goals that would otherwise be judged contrary to the well-being of humanity.

If any doubt remained, it would suffice to observe the fate of scientific undertakings in totalitarian countries. They are subject to ideological ukases and to arguments based on authority; we need only recall the lamentably celebrated "Lysenko affair." In order to advance, science needs to be free of all constraints (even if it is appropriate, in a second phase, to judge its results from an ethical standpoint); science achieves consensus only by rational arguments and by dialogue. Now in totalitarian society, there is no discussion with people who "think differently"; they are deprived of their jobs, locked up in asylums, thrown into prisons or work camps; in the best cases they are exiled. Even declarations that are scientific in form are endowed with the status of articles of faith; but it is illegitimate to use the term "science" for what is only a new dogma, and to hold science responsible for the advent of totalitarianism. Is the ultimate proof not found in the fact that Stalin and Hitler, who presided over nations supposedly subject to the demands of reason and science, were individuals whose own behavior gave indications of mental illness?

Scientism is not science. And we hardly need add that scientism is not humanism. Even if it is true that humanism and scientism coexist for certain Enlightenment philosophers, we would have to be exceedingly myopic, or utterly dishonest, to see the two as one. Renan was well aware of this, moreover, for he begins Theoctistes' dream with a rejection of the humanitarian ideal, which he replaces with the project of perfecting the universe according to nature's design. To fail to distinguish between the two is to ignore the arguments between Rousseau and Diderot, between Tocqueville and Gobineau, and many others like them. It was scientism and not humanism that helped establish the ideological bases of totalitarianism. Racialist theories, as we have seen—those of Gobineau, Renan, Le Bon, and others—paved the way for Hitler's anti-Semitic delirium and conditioned the European populations to accept it; scientistic principles have justified inhuman political systems. Even when the determinism professed by these theories leaves our biological nature aside and focuses exclusively on social forms, it is just as dangerous; this has been amply demonstrated by the existence of totalitarian regimes based on the laws of history (Stalinism and its avatars). Claiming that the differences among human beings are social rather than physical in nature does not lessen the resolve to exterminate some of them. The relation between scientism and totalitarianism is not limited to this justification of acts through so-called scientific necessity (biological or historical): one must already be a practitioner of scientism, even if it is "wild" scientism, to believe in the perfect transparency of society and thus in the possibility of transforming society in function of its ideal by revolutionary means. Utopianism (certain forms of which have engendered totalitarian systems) in turn presupposes the scientistic viewpoint.

Even so, scientism does not necessarily lead to totalitarianism. But that fact makes it more dangerous, not less. Indeed, in democratic states as well, since the collapse of the spiritual power of the Church, science tends to occupy the Church's place: Comte's dreams and Renan's have actually come to pass. Decisions made by governments and assemblies cannot come up with any better justification, it seems, than the one they derive from the norms of "scientific progress" or "technological efficiency." We do not yet inhabit a world run like a laboratory, but the temptation is not far off. If we want to avoid this, we have no choice but to resist not only the most glaring forms of scientism, those we can see at work in totalitarian regimes, but also the insidious forms of scientism that pervade democratic life. And this struggle implies that ethics must regain the place usurped by scientistic ideology.

3

Nations

Nations and Nationalism

Distinctions and Definitions

Shifting our focus now away from races, or groupings based on physical similarity, back to the problem of universal and relative judgments, we may recall the commonplace fact that human beings do not exist simply as isolated individuals: they also belong to social groups of varying sizes. From our perspective, two types of groups are of special interest: ethnic entities and political entities. On the one hand, all of us belong to communities that speak the same language, inhabit a common territory, have certain shared memories, and follow the same customs (this is the sense in which anthropologists use the word "culture," making it synonymous with "ethnic group"). On the other hand, all of us belong to communities that guarantee our rights and impose obligations on us—communities of which we are citizens, communities that may enter into armed conflict with one another. On the one hand there are cultures, on the other there are states.

As for nations, they are both political and cultural. Whereas cultural and political entities have always existed, the nation as such is an innovation introduced in Europe in modern times. Antonin Artaud clearly distinguished between two types of nationalism based on these two aspects of nationhood, while noting his own preference. "There is cultural nationalism, in which the specific and distinguishing quality of a nation and its works is asserted; and there is what we may call civic nationalism, which in its egocentric form ends up as chauvinism and is translated by customs restrictions and economic conflict, if not all-out

warfare" (*Messages révolutionnaires* [Revolutionary Messages], p. 106).
Not only do the forms of nationalism based on each of these aspects
of nationhood differ from one another, but in certain respects at least
they are opposites. Cultural nationalism (that is, attachment to one's
own culture) is a path that leads toward universalism—by deepening
the specificity of the particular within which one dwells. Civic nationalism, as Artaud argues, is a preferential choice in favor of one's own
country over the others—thus, it is an antiuniversalist choice.

Montesquieu (whose positions we shall examine at greater length
later on) sought to interpret the nation as a cultural entity. In the vast
project of *The Spirit of the Laws*, what he calls the "'general spirit' of a
nation" (p. 308) plays an essential role (roughly half of the book is
devoted to its analysis). This spirit is the outcome of a whole series of
factors: forms of government, traditions, mores, geographical conditions, and so on. In what sense does the spirit of the nation lead to
universality? In his *Pensées* [Thoughts], speaking of religions, Montesquieu suggests a response that could be applied just as well to nations.
"God is like the monarch that has several nations in his empire: they
all come to pay him tribute, and each speaks in her own language"
(2117). This aphorism establishes parallels among three series of terms.
(1) God is unique and universal, while religions are multiple and diverse; there is no contradiction, however, for each religion constitutes
a different path for advancing toward the same point. (2) Languages
are multiple, yet for someone who knows more than one language, the
same meaning can be revealed through each. (3) Several nations may
have the same king, and all may pay him tribute: while they may be
materially different, these tributes are equivalent in the monarch's eyes
(just as money translates the value of all goods onto a single scale). Now
religion, language, and political institutions are all elements of the spirit
of a nation (of its culture): we may thus reasonably suppose that the
same relationship is found there. Culture is like a language that provides access to universals; one culture is not, *a priori*, better or worse
than another. "The various characters of the nations are mixtures of
virtues and vices, of good and bad qualities" (*The Spirit of the Laws*,
XIX, 10, p. 313). But it is absolutely essential to have a culture: without
language, there is no access to meaning.

The civic or political sense of the word "nation" is entirely different.
As a first approximation, we may say that this sort of nationalism arises
from the expressed preference for one's "own" over all "others," a

phenomenon that seems to have been recognized from earliest antiquity as a characteristic of all human groups; it is what might be called their patriotism. In his *History*, Herodotus describes the Persians as follows: "They honor most of all those who dwell nearest them, next those who are next farthest removed, and so going ever onwards they assign honor by this rule; those who dwell farthest off they hold least honorable of all; for they deem themselves to be in all regards by far the best of all men, the rest to have but a proportionate claim to merit, till those who dwell farthest away have least merit of all" (Book One, 134, I, p. 175). But at this rate, who among us is not Persian? Patriotism of this sort would merely be the transposition of individual egocentrism to the level of the group. And just as egocentrism seems to be, if not a universal human trait, then at least an inevitable one during a certain developmental stage (childhood), the privileged treatment of one's "own" people at the expense of "others" characterizes at least certain phases of the history of peoples. In short, egocentrism is a spontaneous reaction that arises prior to any education; we shall refer to it here as "the rule of Herodotus." But we have not yet encountered modern nationalism.

How are we to evaluate patriotism, understood in this way? We might say, on the one hand, that there is not much to be proud of in an attitude that is after all rather self-centered. However, we must also note that, in passing from the individual to the group, self-centeredness does not come out unscathed. There is a radical difference between "taking care of oneself" and "taking care of one's own." The valorization of the group has a double aspect: it implies turning one's back on the lesser entity (the self) as well as on the greater entity (other groups, humanity as a whole). Attachment to the group is at once an act of solidarity and an act of exclusion.

True schools for solidarity are found in groups smaller than the nation: the family or clan, then the village or neighborhood. Here is where children learn to overcome their own innate egocentrism. The exclusion of others is entirely relative. A child knows that other families exist, and cannot imagine life without them, but she also learns that a higher loyalty binds her to her own: this loyalty involves both a right to receive help and a duty to give it. The earliest notions of morality are acquired here, and we may wonder whether this mode of acquisition is not also the only one solid enough to be able to endure and spread. Auguste Comte thought so, at all events; he believed that familial affections constituted "the only real transition from egocentric instincts to universal sympathies" (*Système de politique positive*, I, p. 396), and he thought that any other path to morality would turn out sooner or later to be illusory: "Any attempt to orient moral education toward its own direct flowering that skips this intermediate step has to be deemed radically chimerical and profoundly disastrous" (I, p. 94). Love of humanity is not worth much if it does not begin as love of one's neighbors. This latter sentiment is thus not to be condemned; quite the contrary: it must be present if it is to be extended, through individual development, from people who are close at hand to the whole of the human race, as the principles of morality dictate.

But a nation is not the same sort of spontaneously formed group. First of all, nations are much larger than families or neighborhoods, and this fact entails two consequences. On the one hand, any given nation is too large for anyone to know all its members (one's compatriots), or even to have a great deal in common with them. On the other hand, it is large enough to give individuals the illusion of infinite size (and thus it bars the way to "universal sympathies"). It is neither a genuine school for solidarity (moreover, it requires that family loyalties be abandoned) nor a useful transitional stage in the evolution toward respect for humanity in all its forms. That is why history is full of examples in which family devotion coexists with tolerance for foreigners, whereas nationalism never leads to universalism.

It is important to distinguish between the two meanings of the word "nationalism," for, like Artaud himself, we shall be inclined to judge them differently. But are we really dealing with a simple case of homonymy? Is there no significant relation between the two uses of the term? A relation does of course exist, but it resides in the object itself, not in the concept that encompasses the object. As it happens, the nation as culture, the set of individuals who have a certain number of features in common, partially *coincides* with the nation as state, a country separated from others by political borders. And in reality the two are quite often connected: it is because a national cultural consciousness exists that the idea of political autonomy can evolve; conversely, the state (nation) can allow the culture (nation) to assert itself and flourish. The fact remains that the concepts themselves are independent, and to a certain extent opposed, since the universal is the contrary of the particular. What is more, the common culture is not necessarily national in scope (generally speaking it is smaller in scale, but it may also be transnational), and the existence of an autonomous state is neither sufficient nor necessary for the survival of a particular culture. But if state and culture are not rigorously interdependent on the level of logic, their interdependence may become imperative under certain historical circumstances.

Here we need to introduce another distinction between two meanings of the word "nation," both of them political in nature. The first sense, which we might call "internal," took on considerable importance on the eve of the French Revolution and in its immediate aftermath. The nation is a space of legitimation, and as a source of power it is opposed to kingly or divine right. People act in the name of the nation, instead of referring to God or monarch; they cry "Long live the nation!" instead of "Long live the king!" This space is then perceived as a space of equality: not the equality of all inhabitants, to be sure (women and the poor are excluded), but the equality of all citizens; people turn to the "nation" in order to combat social privilege or regional self-aggrandizement. The second, or "external," sense of the word "nation" is quite different: here one nation is set in opposition to another nation rather than to the king, or the aristocracy, or geographical regions. In this sense the French constitute one nation and the English another.

Once again the two meanings of the word are not unrelated, but once again the relationship is limited to the (possible) identity of the object. Under the Old Regime in France, individuals did not identify strongly with their country. As Renan put it, "the handing over of a province was only a transfer of property from one prince to another; the inhabitants remained largely indifferent" ("La Réforme intellectuelle et morale de la France," p. 453). How can anyone identify with one country in preference to another, if a royal marriage is all it takes to bring about a change in citizenship? How can anyone believe that a war is of personal concern when it results from the whim of a prince? On the other hand, as soon as the nation, in the sense of its citizenry as a whole, has become the locus of power, each of its members may consider the state as his own; this is how modern "external" nationalism is introduced. Voltaire had already noted this: "A republican is always more strongly attached to his own country than a subject is to his; and for this good reason, too, that men have a greater regard for their own property than for that of their master" ("Pensées sur le gouvernement," in English "Thoughts on the Public Administration,"

The Works of Voltaire, p. 232). The fact remains that the intention underlying the two concepts is once again different and even opposed, since the "internal" nation proceeds from the idea of equality, while the "external" nation implies on the contrary a preferential choice in favor of one's own country over all the others, thus implying inequality.

It is precisely the encounter between these two meanings, internal and external, cultural and political, that has given rise to the specifically *modern* entities of nation and nationalism. They are characterized by the fusion of what I am trying to keep separate here. Legitimation via the nation instead of God has been viewed as inseparable from preference for one's own country at the expense of universal principles; membership in a culture—which is undeniable and unavoidable—has come to justify the requirement that cultural and political entities should coincide. Still, what concerns us here is less modern nationalism in its full extent than patriotic feeling (which has existed from time immemorial) in its recent manifestations.

Man or Citizen

In its relation to values, is patriotism a form of absolutism or of relativism? The patriot has an undeniable preference for certain values—but not in the name of an absolute system. A consistent patriot ought to recognize that everyone is entitled to prefer the values chosen by her own country. Patriotism is thus a form of relativism, but a tempered relativism. The radical relativist refuses to pronounce any value judgments at all; the patriot agrees that any reference to absolute and universal criteria must be rejected, but he introduces an alternative basis for judgments: to paraphrase Pascal, one might say that a person born on one side of the Pyrenees owes an absolute allegiance to French values, while the same person born on the other side of the Pyrenees would owe just as strong an allegiance to Spanish values. As Charles Maurras, one of the best-known theoreticians of French nationalism, pointed out, from this perspective it is necessary to look for the good; yet "this good will be not absolute Good but the good of the French people" ("L'Avenir du nationalisme français," p. 530). In this respect patriotism is the perfect mirror image of *exoticism*, which also forswears an absolute frame of reference but does not give up value judgments; exoticism is the opposite of patriotism in that it valorizes what does *not* belong to one's own country. In the abstract, like any relativist, the patriot may proclaim equality among peoples (we all have the right to prefer our own country to others, as La Bruyère would have it, or Diderot's protagonist in his reflections on Bougainville's *Voyage*); still, in practice, the patriot is almost always also an ethnocentrist. No sooner has my relativist judgment been pronounced than I render it absolute: being a Frenchman, I declare that France is superior to all countries, not just for me but for everyone.

A national value may coincide with a value that claims universality; in many instances patriotism is not opposed to universalism. It is nevertheless always possible to conceive of a situation in which the two conflict and in which it is necessary to choose between universal values and national values, between love of humanity and love of country. The state of war, in particular, multiplies the opportunities for this sort of conflict. Two questions then arise. Is it possible to reconcile patriotism with cosmopolitanism, attachment to national values with love of humanity? And if not, which of the two should we prefer?

In the eighteenth century, Helvétius, Voltaire, and Rousseau offered negative answers to the first question in their writings. Helvétius denies the existence of natural law, since justice is only what best suits a given community (a state). "In all ages and nations, probity can be only a habit of performing actions that are of use to our country" (*Essays on the Mind and Its Several Faculties*, II, 13, p. 66). Universal probity is thus a contradiction in terms: one cannot imagine an action that is useful in exactly the same degree to all nations; humanitarian virtue, like all other universals, "is nothing but a Platonic chimera" (II, 25, p. 122). Patriotism and universal love are thus incompatible: "It is evident that a spirit of patriotism, a passion so desirable, so virtuous, and so worthy of esteem in any citizen, is, as is proved by the example of the Greeks and Romans, absolutely exclusive of the love for all mankind . . . It is necessary that the private interest of nations should submit to a more general interest, and that the love of our country, becoming extinguished in the heart, should give place to the more extended flame of universal love: a supposition that will not be realized" for a very long time (ibid.).

Which of the two passions is preferable? Given that one of them is impossible, there can be no doubt about how Helvétius responds: humanitarian sentiment, which is only a personal illusion, must be sacrificed to civic virtue. "Everything becomes lawful, and even virtuous, that procures the public safety" (II, 6, p. 41). Thus, in a ship that has been cast adrift, it may become necessary for some of the voyagers to eat one of the others in order to survive: the act appears cruel, but it is nonetheless justified. In certain countries, the food supplies available to the population are limited; the young, then, "making their old men mount the oaks, . . . shake the boughs with great violence, on which most of the old men falling, they are in a moment massacred" (II, 13, p. 68). Here again, no fault is to be found: the young spare their parents the suffering of a lingering death, and at the same time they ensure the survival of the group.

Voltaire takes the opposite tack. He, too, believes that love of country and love of humanity are incompatible, and this troubles him. "It is sad that men often become the enemies of the rest of mankind in order to be good patriots . . . This, then, is the human condition: to wish for the greatness of one's country is to wish evil to one's neighbors. The man who would wish his country never to be either larger or smaller, richer or poorer than it is, would be the citizen of the world" (*Dictionnaire philosophique*, in English *Philosophical Dictionary*, XII, p. 413). But of the two terms in question, Voltaire places a higher value on the universal, even though he knows that, especially as they age, people become sentimental about their fatherland and prefer bread at home to biscuits abroad.

As for Rousseau, who read and pondered Helvétius' text, he warrants a more extensive look. In his writings, the opposition centers on the terms "citizen" and "man," the latter term designating, sometimes ambiguously, both the human being viewed as inhabitant of the universe and the private individual. The citizen's path and the man's do not coincide, for obvious reasons. Their endeavors have different goals: the happiness of the group in the one case, that of the individual in the other. In order to make the difference clearer, Rousseau chooses characters who embody each path and who are equally admirable. In "Dernière Réponse," a text appended to his *Discours sur les sciences et les arts*, the role of citizen is played by Brutus, who "had his children put to death after they had conspired against the State" (p. 81); the other role is not attributed, but when Rousseau evokes Brutus in another text, he contrasts his position with the spirit of the Christian religion by recalling the way Brutus was condemned by one of the Church Fathers, Saint Augustine (*Fragments politiques* [Political Fragments], V, p. 506). The antithesis is developed in greater detail in the *Encyclopedia* article entitled "Economie politique"; the characters who embody the two poles are now Cato and Socrates. Each is an exemplary figure, but for different reasons. The first sees only men around him; he does not distinguish between his compatriots and others; he aspires to personal virtue and wisdom. The second, on the contrary, is never concerned with himself but thinks only of his fellow citizens, and he works toward the common good rather than his own.

Rousseau comes back to this distinction in the chapter of *On the Social Contract* devoted to "civic religion." This time it is the citizen who is not named; as for the man, he is no longer Socrates but Christ, and the difference lies between "the religion of man and that of the citizen" (IV, 8, p. 127). But the substance of the terms remains the same: the universalism of one of these religions is opposed to the patriotism of the other. Owing to its universalism, the Christian religion is incompatible with the objectives of nationhood. "Far from attaching the citizens' hearts to the State, it detaches them from it as from all worldly things" (IV, 8, p. 128). "Since the Gospel does not establish a national religion, a holy war is impossible among Christians" (IV, 8, p. 130).

We cannot say that one of these terms is valorized here at the expense of the other; rather, there are two independent value systems at work, and we cannot simply eliminate one of them. If we were to give up citizenship, we could no longer guarantee the application of the law (the universe is not a State); if we were to forget about humanity, Rousseau suggests, we would be denying our own most intimate feeling that tells us, when we see another human being, whoever he or she may be, that we belong to the same species. The universality of the Christian religion has already contributed to marking the difference between the two systems, by "separating the theological system from the political system" (IV, 8, p. 126); it must be said that this theology turned universal is nothing other than ethics. Politics and ethics thus cannot be confused. (It is true that Rousseau often uses identical terms to designate separate realities: he speaks of "virtue" in both contexts, whereas *civic* virtues do not necessarily coincide with *humanitarian* virtues, just as he speaks of "justice" without specifying whether it is exercised with respect to national laws or to universal principles—in which case it would be better to speak of "equity.")

Rousseau does not stop at indicating the difference between these two paths; he declares that they are radically incompatible. At least, this is his outlook while he is writing *Emile:* "Forced to combat nature or the social institutions, one must choose between making a man or a citizen, for one cannot make both at the same time" (I, p. 39). The success of civism is in inverse proportion to that of "humanism." "Good social institutions are those that best know how to denature man" (p. 40): here the word "denature" concerns "natural man" (or "man"), insofar as he is opposed to the citizen. "The legislator who seeks both [these virtues] will not get either one: this harmony has never been seen; it never will be seen, because it is contrary to nature, and because one cannot give a single passion two objects" (*Lettres écrites de la montagne* [Letters Written from the Mountain], I, p. 706). Rousseau's vision is dramatic: where others note a divergence, he sees an irreducible opposition.

In a further complication, Rousseau is convinced that this contradiction, like any contradiction, moreover, is a source of irreparable unhappiness (he presents the nostalgia inspired by loss of unity as an axiom, without arguing the case); it is even the main source of unhappiness in human beings. "What causes human misery is the contradiction . . . between nature and social institutions, between man and citizen . . . Give him over entirely to the state or leave him entirely to himself, but if you divide his heart you destroy him" (*Fragments politiques*, VI, p. 510). As composite beings, we cannot achieve either ideal; by dint of serving two masters, we are no good either to ourselves or to others. "Make man whole, you make him as happy as he can be" (ibid.). "To be something, to be oneself and always one, a man must act as he speaks . . . I am waiting to be shown this marvel so as to know whether he is a man or a citizen, or how he goes about being both at the same time" (*Emile*, I, p. 40).

Just what features are derived from the position of citizen? The latter is wholly defined on the basis of the notion of fatherland; "man," on the other hand, is the one who does not wish to privilege his own people at the expense of the rest of humanity. Civic education has as its primary function the inculcation of patriotism. "The newly-born infant, upon first opening his eyes, must gaze upon the fatherland, and until his dying day should behold nothing else"; a citizen is a patriot or he is nothing at all. "That love makes up his entire existence: he has eyes only for the fatherland, lives only for his fatherland; the moment he is alone, he is a mere cipher; the moment he has no fatherland, he is no more; if not dead, he is worse off than if he were dead" (*Considérations sur le gouvernement de Pologne*, in English *The Government of Poland*, p. 19). To make education more effective, each state must add education via cultural nationalism to its civic nationalism. It must protect and encourage national institutions, traditional customs, costumes, ceremonies, games, festivals, spectacles: all these are forms of social life that help attach the citizen to his country (so long as they are forms specific to that country and to no other), by making the cultural and the political coincide. Rather than feeling like a "man," the citizen formed in this way will feel like a Pole, or a Frenchman, or a Russian; and since patriotism will have become his "governing passion" (p. 16), all his values will be derived from the national values: "This is to say: you must turn a certain execrable proverb upside down, and bring each Pole to say from the bottom of his heart: *Ubi patria, ibi bene*" (p. 14).

The obverse of this love for everything that belongs to one's country is a certain contempt for whatever does not belong to it, and especially for foreigners. The ideal classical city-states provide examples: the Spartan ensures that equality reigns at home, but he becomes inequitable as soon as he crosses the borders of his homeland; similarly, "the humanity of the Romans extended no further than their domination" (*On the Social Contract*, Geneva ms., I, ii, p. 162). The reign of equality at home does not prevent people from practicing slavery or colonialism abroad: such is the logic of patriotism. "Every patriot is harsh to foreigners. They are only men. They are nothing in his eyes. This is a drawback, inevitable but not compelling. The essential thing is to be good to the people with whom one lives" (*Emile*, I, p. 39). Thus, if today's Poles want to follow the classical example, they need to manifest their "instinctive distaste for mingling with the peoples of other countries" (*The Government of Poland*, III, p. 14). Once again, this reasoning is not at all paradoxical; it might even be considered trivial: to defend and exalt one's fatherland means preferring it to other countries (and to humanity). Such is the logic (and the ethics) of the citizen: Cato is a better citizen than Socrates. But is that really what Rousseau believes? In other words, is he on the side of patriotism or of "cosmopolitanism"?

A number of references to cosmopolitanism can be found in Rousseau's writings, and they have sometimes been used to argue that Rousseau's position was subject to change. This is not in fact the case. His earliest declarations on the subject appear in the "Discourse on the Origin of Inequality," where he sings the praises of "a few great Cosmopolitan Souls" who rise above national frontiers and who "embrace the whole of Mankind in their benevolence" (*The First and Second Discourses*, p. 184). Thereafter, although he no longer uses the word "cosmopolitan" in the same sense, Rousseau maintains the same principle: virtue and justice are on the side of humanity (but it would be more accurate to speak of humanitarian virtues, or equity).

What are we to make, then, of the texts in which Rousseau appears to denigrate cosmopolitanism? Let us take a closer look. Rousseau in fact attacks "those supposed cosmopolites who, justifying their love of the homeland by means of their love of the human race, boast of loving everyone in order to have the right to love no one" (*On the Social Contract*, Geneva ms., I, ii, p. 162). But it is clear that his criticism is directed toward self-professed cosmopolites rather than real ones: what he is actually condemning is the dissociation between words and deeds that characterizes the "philosophers" (we would call them intellectuals) who hide their self-centeredness behind general pronouncements (the conservative Burke, in England, the utopian Comte, in France, are in this respect Rousseau's faithful disciples, even though they see themselves as his opponents). Rousseau makes the same accusation later on, but this time the word "cosmopolitan" designates only the latter form of love of one's fellow man: "Distrust those cosmopolitans who go to great length in their books to discover duties they do not deign to fulfill around them. A philosopher loves the Tartars so as to be spared having to love his neighbors" (*Emile*, I, p. 39). How much easier it is to defend remote worthy causes than to put into personal practice the virtues one is professing: the love of distant peoples is less costly to the individual than the love of his nearest neighbor. This does not mean that one must love only one's neighbors, but that one must love foreigners as well as—and not instead of—one's own people.

In reality, Rousseau never retreats from his attachment to universalist principles. However, he does shift back and forth between the citizen's perspective and the individual's (again, both roles are worthy of respect), and he explores the logic of both positions in order to describe their various characteristics. When he says, referring to contempt for foreigners, that "this drawback is inevitable but it is slight," Rousseau is speaking not for himself but for the citizen (Helvétius); when in the first version of *On the Social Contract* he speaks of universalism as "healthy ideas" (Geneva ms., I, 2, p. 162), it is the man, not the citizen, who is speaking. There is no contradiction here.

But Rousseau goes still further. Not satisfied to present two equally coherent systems of values between which one might make an arbitrary choice, he explores the relation between them and concludes that man must be placed above citizen. "Let us first find the cult and the morality that will belong to all men, and then when we need national formulas, we shall examine their foundations, their relationships, their conventions, and after having said what belongs to the man, we shall then say what belongs to the citizen" ("Lettre à Beaumont," p. 969). The man takes precedence over the citizen: such is the order dictated by reason—which does not prevent circumstances from dictating the reverse order. "We do not really begin to become men until after we have been citizens" (*On the Social Contract*, Geneva ms., pp. 161–162). We are born in a particular country; it is only through an effort of will, by rising above ourselves, that we become "men" in the full sense—that is, inhabitants of the world. Rousseau is even more categorical in one of his autobiographical texts: "In general, any party man, by that alone an enemy of the truth, will always hate J.J. . . . Now there is never any disinterested love of justice in these collective bodies. Nature engraved it only in the hearts of individuals" (*Dialogues*, in English *Rousseau, Judge of Jean-Jacques: Dialogues*, III, p. 237, note).

Patriotism, then, has an inherent flaw. By preferring one segment of humanity over the rest, the citizen transgresses the fundamental principle of morality, that of universality; without saying so openly, he acknowledges that men are not equal. Moreover, a Spartan or a Roman has a limited sense of equality even within the community, since women and slaves are excluded; in Poland—a modern Sparta—as well, everything that is feminine is avoided. Now true morality, true justice, true virtue presuppose universality, and thus equal rights. And yet in order to be able to exercise one's rights one must belong to a state, and thus be a citizen: there are no rights except within a juridical space underwritten by the establishment of a frontier separating inside from outside. The expressions "rights of man" and "world citizen" thus both entail internal contradictions. In order to have rights, one must be not a man but a citizen; yet—with apologies to Voltaire—only states have citizens, not the world. To be in favor of rights thus implies being on the side of the citizen, and yet the best principle of justice is that of universality.

If Rousseau is to be believed, the opposition is radical, irreducible. And yet we are all both men and citizens, or ought to be. What are we to do? The response Rousseau seems to suggest involves several phases.

We must first take advantage of all the situations in which the two
"passions" tend in the same direction; we must then be lucid as to their
incompatibility in all other instances, rather than being misled by good
intentions; finally we must aspire to modify the laws of the nation in
the name of the laws of humanity, while continuing to remember that
we always remain citizens of a particular state whose laws we must obey.
Rousseau is by no means a revolutionary: the path he recommends in
Emile is that of an obedient but potentially critical citizen. Correspondingly, in order to be acceptable, a society need not resemble the one
described in *On the Social Contract*; all that is required is that individuals
be able to exercise their judgment freely in that society and be able to
act according to that judgment. Rousseau is not at all an "idealist,"
either: he knows perfectly well that only a compromise can meet these
contradictory requirements, and he prefers lucidity to the euphoria of
illusions.

The Evolution of Nationalist Doctrines

Rousseau's response thus amounts to a judgment that the conflict is
insoluble and nevertheless inevitable. We are necessarily men *and* citizens, yet it is impossible to succeed in both capacities simultaneously;
this impossibility leads to a dramatic or even tragic view of the human
condition. But it is clearly also possible to choose one of the two terms
and forget about the other: there are happy patriots and happy cosmopolitans.

On the cosmopolitan side, we find on the one hand philosophers,
concerned with transcending narrow egocentrism as well as all collective determinism, where there would be no more room for personal
will, and on the other hand Christians, for whom unity before God
takes precedence over differences among nations. Thus Montesquieu,
author of the celebrated formula: "If I knew something of use to my
nation that were ruinous to another, I would not propose it to my
prince, because I am a man before I am a Frenchman, (or else) because
I am necessarily a man, and I am only a Frenchman by chance" (*Pensées*,
10). Dom Ferlus, a Benedictine of Saint-Maur, for his part condemns
"virtue that would be harmful to humanity," and asserts that "if patriotism could only exist in a country in order to make its inhabitants
enemies of other peoples, only to cement that country's power through
bloodbaths, there is no doubt about it, my brothers, it would have to

be banished from every heart" (*Le Patriotisme chrétien* [Christian Patri-
otism]). But being a Christian does not suffice to bring about a renunciation of patriotism: witness Ives of Paris, a Capuchin priest who
declares that it is a duty "not to allow many foreigners into a country,
unless they enter, as Plato recommended, as servants, to do the tasks
that the natural inhabitants are not willing to perform [here is a
prefiguration of immigrant workers coming in for hire to carry off our
garbage]. Otherwise, one would be putting one's goods at risk and
putting bastards in the place of legitimate leaders" (*Morales chrétiennes*
[Christian Morality], p. 419). Is it a coincidence that a passage like this
refers to Plato's *Republic* rather than to the Gospels?

These are clear choices, after all. However, most of the time a
different attitude prevails, one that consists in seeking to satisfy the
requirements imposed on the man and the citizen simultaneously. This,
finally, will be the solution preferred by good souls, Christian or otherwise. Examples abound; this is what Bossuet recommends, for example, when he writes: "The division of property among men, and the
division of men even into peoples and nations, ought not to alter the
general society of mankind" (*Politique tirée des propres paroles de l'Ecriture
sainte*, in English *Politics Drawn from the Very Words of Holy Scripture*, I,
5, p. 24). And also: "If we are obliged to love all men, and as it is true
to say that to a Christian there is no such thing as a stranger, it is more
reasonable that we should love our fellow citizens" (I, 6, pp. 27–28). It
is clear that Bossuet is simply refusing to reckon with the latent conflict;
he prefers to close his eyes to it so as to enjoy the harmony he requires,
and he is satisfied to declare what men *ought* to do. But will they do it?
The lay version of this attitude is found in the *Encyclopedia* article
entitled "Patriotisme" [Patriotism], written by the Chevalier Jaucourt:
"The most perfect patriotism is the patriotism one possesses when one
is so thoroughly imbued with the rights of the human race that one
respects them with regard to all the peoples of the world." But can this
still be called patriotism? Similarly, Diderot and d'Holbach imagine a
"general society" of which the individual countries would be the inhabitants; this utopia allows them to maintain a serene view of relations
among the various countries. Condorcet does not even want to imagine
that such a moral scandal as the opposition between patriotism and
humanism can exist in the world: "Nature could not have wished to
found the happiness of one people on the unhappiness of its neighbors,
nor to set in opposition two virtues that it equally inspires: love of the

fatherland and love of humanity" ("Discours de réception à l'Académie française," in English "Reception Speech at the French Academy," pp. 10–11).

Those very voices that claimed affinity with Rousseau in 1789 turn out to be impervious to his teaching: the Revolution aims to satisfy both man and citizen. No conflict between the two is thinkable, even if their noncoincidence is noted. Thus, in *Qu'est-ce que le tiers état? (What Is the Third Estate?)* Sieyès identifies readily with natural reason, or natural law, whereas his discourse in fact starts with the idea of the nation. When he distinguishes between the two, it is in order to link them in an apparently unproblematic sequence: "The nation is prior to everything. It is the source of everything. Its will is always legal; indeed it is the law itself. Prior to and above the nation, there is only *natural* law" (p. 124). And if the two were not in agreement?

That question does not trouble Sieyès. It is true that he is thinking first and foremost about the "internal" meaning of the word "nation," but his formulas also allow for an interpretation in the "external" sense. All the more so in that the reference to natural law is not always maintained: "The national will . . . never needs anything but its own existence to be legal. It is the source of all legality" (p. 126). What Sieyès wants to dispense with here is divine right, or the rights of kings, or any legitimation based on privilege, but at the same time he affirms the nationalist credo: the nation is always right; being "the source and the supreme master of positive law" (p. 128), it cannot itself be judged. Failing to differentiate between the two "nations" thus also amounts to opting for the nation over humanity, for patriotism over cosmopolitanism.

The fact that the first Declaration of Rights, written in August 1789, is the one known as "of Man and of the Citizen" is already paradoxical for anyone aware of the distinctions Rousseau established and the incompatibilities he disclosed. The seventeen articles of the Declaration never envisage a potential conflict between the rights of each party. Taking up Sieyès' idea, Article 3 says: "The principle of all sovereignty resides essentially in the Nation"; but it is the "internal" sense of the word that is invoked here, as the remainder of Article 3 suggests: "No body, no individual can exercise authority that does not emanate directly from it" (*Les Constitutions de la France* [The Constitutions of France], pp. 33–34). In the constitution itself, which dates from September 1791, Title VI is devoted to "Relations of the French Nation with Foreign Nations"; the question of conflict is at least evoked here, and it is settled in the sense of a preference for humanitarian principles. "The French nation renounces the undertaking of any war in view of making conquests, and will never use its forces against the freedom of any people" (p. 65; this is the rewriting of a decree dated May 20, 1790). In other words, in deciding whether or not a war should be fought, the question is not whether the war is useful to France but whether it is right in itself—that is, whether it is right from the standpoint of humanity.

Under the impetus of the revolutionary developments, a certain reflection on the relations between France and the world was elaborated. Clubs of foreigners favorable to the Revolution were founded, and even a club of foreign patriots (!); a confederation of "Friends of Truth throughout the World" was established in France. On June 19, 1790, a delegation of foreigners appeared before the National Assembly. The delegation was led by Anacharsis Cloots, a German baron who had lived in France for many years and who transmitted to those present the fervent congratulations of the universe. "The trumpet that sounds the resurrection of a great people has reverberated in the four corners of the earth, and the songs of joy of a chorus of twenty-five million free men have woken people long buried in slavery. The wisdom of your decrees, Gentlemen, the union of the children of France, this ravishing picture gives despots cause for concern, and it gives legitimate hopes to the enslaved nations" (*Procès-verbal de l'Assemblée Nationale* [Transcript of the National Assembly], XXII, pp. 21–22). The next day, during an outdoor meeting, "M. Danton . . . said that patriotism should have no limits but the Universe; he proposed to drink to the health, freedom, and happiness of the entire Universe" (ibid.). Cloots gave himself the title of ambassador (or orator) of the human race and he dated his letters from "Paris, headquarters of the world." And Durand-Maillane wrote in 1791, in his *Histoire apologétique du Comité ecclésiastique* [History and Defense of the Ecclesiastic Committee], that the new constitution "has to make the people of France happy, and, by imitation, all people" (p. 48).

Similar formulations, however empty or naive they may seem to us, in fact prepared the way for a certain interpretation of the relations between man and citizen, cosmopolitan and patriot, that we shall encounter again in Michelet. France and more specifically the French Revolution became exemplary incarnations of the route of the universe (rather as philosophy finds its exemplary embodiment in fifth-century B.C. Greece). The liberation of the French showed the way to the rest of humanity, and French decrees or the French constitution came to serve as models for all other countries. Patriotism and cosmopolitanism thus could conflict only for people who came from countries other than France, since as patriots they owed allegiance to their own country and as men they owed allegiance to France, the incarnation of humanity! The French, on the other hand, could be patriots with a clear conscience, for in working for France they were defending the interests not of a particular country but of the entire universe.

We find the same ideas even in the draft of a declaration that Robespierre presented on April 21, 1793, though he himself was hardly tender-hearted toward foreigners as a general rule: "Men of all countries are brothers and the various peoples must help each other according to their abilities, like the citizens of a single State [here we see the return of the fallacious analogy familiar to the Encyclopedists]. He who oppresses a single nation declares himself the enemy of all" (*Les Constitutions de la France*, p. 72). The constitution of June 1793 postulates, in Article 118, that "the people of France are the friend and ally of free peoples" (p. 91), which leaves us with the corollary supposition that, as Robespierre says, oppressor peoples are France's enemies. Is France thus to be charged with the universal mission of making liberty reign throughout the world? It is true that Article 119 also says that the people of France do not "involve themselves with the government of other nations," which amounts to requiring them simultaneously to take part and to remain neutral; but it is perhaps characteristic of constitutions to authorize a variety of behaviors . . .

In fact, at the time of the Revolution itself, the behaviors at issue were not exempt from ambiguity. Certain revolutionary declarations gave an interventionist cast to universalist principles. One decree, adopted by the Convention of November 19, 1792, granted "fraternity and aid to all peoples seeking to recover their freedom," thus opening the way to future "exportations" of the Revolution. Cloots himself also chose the policy evoked in Article 118: in the name of the rights of man, he wanted to make war on all other countries, until Revolutionary ideas finally triumph. "Our situation requires the scalpel of Mars; the abscess that troubles us must be lanced with bayonet blows." The result was supposed to be the installation of a single State, and the submission of all to the same perfect laws (Condorcet's dream). "I propose an absolute leveling, a total reversal of all the barriers that interfere with the interests of the human family," Cloots wrote (*La République universelle* [The Universal Republic], p. 17). "I defy anyone to show me a single article of our Declaration of Rights that is not applicable to all men, in all climates" (p. 40). Cloots, himself a foreigner by origin, often sounded more chauvinistic than the French, and his universalism was only another name for his Francophilia; as for the Revolution, it became dictatorship when it was exported.

The rights of man can thus serve, in certain instances, as pretexts and weapons of war, somewhat as the Christian religion served the Crusaders. In other circumstances, the revolutionaries appealed to abstract equality among nations, and thus preferred Article 119 to Article 118; such was the position of Danton and Robespierre in particular. But what is perhaps more telling is that, in order to defend their own country, the incarnation of the revolutionary victory, the French had to turn against outsiders. Robespierre's violent diatribes against the English are familiar: "I do not like the English, for my part, because that word makes me think of an insolent people who dare to make war on the generous people that has reconquered its liberty . . . I have hope only in our soldiers and in the profound hatred the French have for that people" ("Discours du 30 janvier 1794" [Speech, January 30, 1794], pp. 348–349). By the same token, all foreigners living in France found themselves under accusation: they were to be arrested and imprisoned. In a logical—and absurd—conclusion, their supporters were also to be accused: Cloots himself was attacked by Robespierre, who reproached him for belonging to the "foreign party" and for wanting to be called a "world citizen" rather than a "French citizen" ("Discours du 12 décembre 1793" [Speech, December 12, 1793], p. 248). And Cloots ended up on the scaffold.

Thus, despite their common attachment to universalist ideas, and despite their disagreement as to which concrete policies to follow (export the Revolution or come to terms with neighboring governments), Cloots and Robespierre in fact converged in their preference for the French over other peoples; the difference is that Robespierre practiced this preference at home, whereas Cloots wanted to impose it abroad. For both, then, patriotism won out over universalism. From this point on, the price of ignoring Rousseau's wisdom would be hypocrisy or inconsistency.

Let us now leap more than one hundred years forward to the end of the nineteenth century, a period whose way was paved by the French Revolution. The final years of the century, marked by the Dreyfus affair, witnessed the constitution of two "leagues": the League for the Rights of Man, in February 1898, and the League for the French Fatherland, in January 1899. It is hardly necessary to add that the goal of the second league was to combat the first. Man and citizen, humanitarian and patriot found themselves on opposite sides of the barricade, as Rousseau had predicted, and contrary to the hopes of the nineteenth-century republicans. It was not these republicans who turned out to have understood Rousseau but rather Charles Maurras, who hated him, and who declared: "A fatherland is a union of families constituted by history and geography; its principle excludes the principle of the liberty of individuals, of individual equality," in other words, it excludes humanitarian principles ("Mes Idées politiques" [My Political Ideas], p. 264).

In these conflicts between patriots and humanitarians, some chose the camp of "man" and may have paid dearly for it, like Jaurès (whose thinking was not exempt from ambiguity on this point, however). Others preferred the "citizen": Maurras was one of the more eloquent among the second group. Criticizing the revolutionary amalgam of man and citizen, he wrote: "It is a doctrinal truth, in a philosophy very remote from daily life, that the fatherland is in our day the most complete and the most coherent manifestation of humanity . . . ; one can and must say that the national ideal represents the human race, French nationality moreover having a special claim to represent it [here the narrow ground of agreement between Robespierre and Maurras is evident]. However, these are the theses of a scholar sitting at his desk. If one is seeking an active value in this order of things, one must proceed differently and declare that patriotic feelings exist; humanitarian feelings do not exist, or have so little existence that they are scarcely conceivable except in opposition to the national idea: instead of motivating it, they get in its way" (pp. 264–265). Maurras is perhaps wrong to argue for the superiority of patriotism on the basis of its greater extension in the world (it is right because it is a fact); but he still remains faithful to Rousseau (we become men whereas we are born "nationals"), and he is right to denounce the illusion of continuity between man and citizen.

At least since the Second World War, nationalist discourse has become the specialty of antirepublican and antidemocratic movements.

These two tendencies were already reconciled during the war of 1940, but only because German fascism was the enemy (thus an enemy on two counts); the recent colonial wars, on the contrary, bring the conflict clearly to light. When Maurras says that patriotism, "conceived in its historical marrow, in its hereditary essence, . . . resembles all the ideas against which democracy has risen up in all times" (p. 271), he forces the issue without betraying it; his heirs, today's nationalist movements, oppose the entire array of democratic parties. This obviously does not imply any sort of withering away of nation-states. These exist as an effect of modern social structures, and they will disappear only with the disappearance of those structures; the nation easily outlives nationalism. But the existence of a nation-state does not require the adoption of a patriotic ideology. This was not readily recognized between the Revolution and the First World War, when all possible means were attempted to establish continuity between humanism and nationalism, as we shall now be able to observe in detail.

Tocqueville

Against Slavery

Alexis de Tocqueville's nationalist sentiments come to light chiefly in the speeches and reports he prepared in his role as statesman dealing with the Algerian question. But we should begin by stepping back to look at the broader picture. During his travels in America, Tocqueville was able to see the suffering of the black slaves at first hand. After returning to France, he was elected to the Chamber of Deputies, where he participated in commissions that were debating the issue of slavery and preparing to abolish it in the former French colonies, for example in the West Indies. In his speeches on the subject, Tocqueville invokes the humanitarian principles inherited from Enlightenment philosophy. Slavery is rejected and condemned in the name of natural law, in this case the principle of equality. "Man has never had the right to possess man, and the fact of possession always has been and still is illegitimate" ("Rapport" [Report], p. 54). "That odious institution . . . is . . . contrary to all the natural rights of humanity" ("Rapport sur l'Algérie" [Report on Algeria], p. 330). Thus, Tocqueville never asks whether or not slavery is to be abolished, but only under what conditions its abolition should be carried out.

The postulate of equality among human beings, independent of any considerations of origin or race, becomes explicit in this context: Tocqueville does not believe "in the so-called differences among the instincts of the various human races" ("L'Emancipation des esclaves" [Emancipation of Slaves], p. 98), and he knows that declarations made on this subject are actually justifications invented after the fact by supporters of slavery. The problem is nevertheless widespread: "Might one not say that the European is to men of other races what man is to the animals?" (*De la Démocratie en Amérique*, in English *Democracy in America*, I, part II, ch. 10. p. 292). Tocqueville never doubted that "the Negro is civilizable" rather than belonging to "an intermediate species between man and monkey" ("Intervention" [Speech], p. 122). Similarly, in America "the success of the Cherokees proves that the Indians have the capacity to become civilized" (*Democracy*, I, part II, ch. 10, p. 304); if their "success" is not more widespread, there are sociological and historical explanations for this fact that have no bearing on the principle of equality among men.

According to Tocqueville, this concept of humanity is undeniably Christian in origin: "Christianity is a religion of free men" ("Rapport," p. 45), and it is a "Christian idea that all men are born equal" ("L'Emancipation," p. 88). But either because Christians have been exhausted by the difficulty of the struggle or because they have settled for equality before God, the principles of equality and liberty have fallen into disuse. Thus, it has been necessary to bring them back to life, to infuse them with new vigor and bring them closer to the earthly preoccupations of human beings: this is the task accomplished by the French Revolution. "It is we who have given a definite and practical meaning to the Christian idea that all men are born equal, and we have applied it to the realities of this world" (ibid.). "It is we who, by destroying the principle of castes and classes throughout the world, by rediscovering, as has been said, the rights of the human race that had been lost, it is we who, by spreading throughout the universe the idea of the equality of all men before the law, as Christianity had created the idea of the equality of all men before God—I maintain that we are the ones who are the true authors of the abolition of slavery" ("Intervention," pp. 124–125). The French thus have the special merit of having originated the movement, and they also have an obligation: for the institution of slavery has not yet been abolished, in France or elsewhere in the world.

Such is the ethical view of the question. But slavery is not merely an abstract problem that can be put to the philosopher, nor is it merely an individual problem for someone confronting its consequences; it is also a social institution with very far-reaching economic and political implications. Now as an elected deputy charged with reporting to a parliamentary commission, Tocqueville's stance is that of a statesman rather than that of a moral philosopher. It would be best, of course, if morality (or submission to general principles) and politics (or defense of particular interests) were to coincide, and Tocqueville had the impression that in his day such a thing was possible. He was already convinced of this during his trip to America. "Christianity destroyed slavery by insisting on the slave's rights; nowadays it can be attacked from the master's point of view; in this respect interest and morality are in harmony" (*Democracy*, I, part II, ch. 10, p. 320). And once back in France, he continued to hold the same view: "Humanity and morality have often, and sometimes even imprudently, called for the abolition of slavery. Today this is required by political necessity" ("Rapport," p. 48). Let us note several things here: first, that the two viewpoints are clearly distinguished; second, that politics evaluates morality and not vice versa; and finally, that it is possible to be an abolitionist "imprudently," by paying no attention to the political consequences. Must we conclude that it is possible to justify taking an antiabolitionist position?

Tocqueville probably would not go that far. But he would at least like to see the application of the humanitarian principle subjected to political constraints of time and place. He asserts repeatedly that one must not proceed with abolition without taking all sorts of precautions, making the former slaves go through intermediate stages between subjugation and freedom. In this context it is permissible to bend the principle of equality before the law in certain respects: for example, Negroes must temporarily be denied "the right to become property owners" ("L'Emancipation," p. 105); morality is thus once again subordinated to politics. At the same time, and this is characteristic of Tocqueville's position, it is essential to ensure that certain rights granted to the former West Indian slaves do not infringe on the enjoyment of rights previously acquired by others. "If the Negroes have the right to become free, it is undeniable that the colonials have the right not to be ruined by the Negroes' freedom" (ibid.). The right "not to be ruined" is a defense of property. But if the freedom of a human being is inalienable and if man has never had the right to possess man, to use Tocqueville's own terms, can one still assert that the slaveholders' wealth is legitimate property? Is being rich an unconditional right? "It is equitable to grant the colonials . . . an indemnity representing the venal value of the freed slaves" (ibid., p. 107). In order to abolish slavery, is the State really obliged to compensate former slaveholders? In other words, must the State make the citizenry as a whole pay for the loss it is imposing on a particular group of citizens?

Here we confront a conflict between two requirements of different origins. The right to compensation is based on a consideration of individual well-being. The individual must not be allowed to suffer from the action of the group; this is, as Tocqueville also says, "guaranteed." The illegality of slavery arises, for its part, from a universal consideration—namely, the equality of human beings. Despite the similarity of the terms, "disposing freely of oneself" and "disposing of one's property whatever its origin" do not refer to the same principle. It is this conflict—sometimes only a latent one—that Tocqueville wants to avoid, by requiring the intervention of the State. Here it is no longer a matter of politics imposing constraints on morality, but of one principle of law confronting another; things have to be worked out in such a way that both are respected.

In order to ensure that the abolition of slavery in the former French colonies will not have harmful effects (the ruin of property owners, a decline in the level of industry), although individuals will be free the territories they inhabit must be maintained in a state of submission. In other words, colonialism must replace slavery. "For France is working toward the creation of civilized societies and not savage hordes" ("Rapport," p. 59). In this way Tocqueville becomes one of the first French ideologues of colonization.

In Support of Colonies

Tocqueville sometimes sought to justify colonization by the humanitarian principle of spreading civilization (in Condorcet's style, as we shall see). Thus, writing to an English friend about the occupation of India: "I have . . . never for an instant doubted your triumph, which is that of Christianity and of civilization" ("Lettre à Lord Hatherton," in *Selected Letters on Politics and Society*, November 27, 1857, p. 359). "Your loss of India could have served no cause but that of barbarism" he writes to another correspondent ("Lettre à Senior," in English *Correspondence and Conversations of Alexis de Tocqueville with Nassau William Senior,* November 15, 1857, p. 191), apparently writing off the interests of the Indians as an autonomous population. But it must be added at once that he never resorts to this argument in any of the cases with which he was personally acquainted; what is more, he explicitly denies the pertinence of the argument. Thus, regarding the colonization of North American Indians: "The European tyranny . . . [made] them more disorderly and less civilized than they had been before. At the same time, the moral and physical condition of these peoples has constantly deteriorated, and in becoming more wretched they have also become more barbarous" (*Democracy*, I, part II, ch. 20, p. 293). The same thing is true for the outcome of the French colonial conquest of Algeria: "We have made the Musulman society much more wretched, more disorderly, more ignorant, and more barbarian that it was before it knew us" ("Rapport sur l'Algérie," p. 323).

Tocqueville rejects the civilizing argument, at least in his explicit reasoning, and yet he remains an unshakable partisan of colonization in Algeria. On what grounds? In the name of the interests of his own country, France. "The conservation of the colonies is necessary to the strength and greatness of France" ("L'Emancipation," p. 84). He judges the war of conquest from just one viewpoint: "I have no doubt that we can erect on the coast of Africa a great monument to the glory of our fatherland" ("Lettre sur l'Algérie" [Letter on Algeria], p. 151). If the colonies were to be abandoned, it would be the sure sign of our decadence, which other countries would not fail to exploit; if they are retained, on the contrary, if they increase in number, "our influence in the general affairs of the world will be greatly increased" ("Travail sur l'Algérie" [Project on Algeria], p. 215). This is the lesson of the British conquest in the Indies: its brilliance "shines over the whole nation" ("L'Inde, plan" [Plan for India], p. 478).

As a general rule, national feeling strikes Tocqueville as all the more precious in that it is the only aspiration that transcends individual interests and has some chance of surviving in a democracy. The danger of the democratic regime, as Tocqueville proclaims over and over, is that each individual may be exclusively preoccupied with his own interests, and that citizens may no longer aspire to any collective ideal; the danger, he writes in a letter to John Stuart Mill, lies in "the taste for material well-being and softness of heart . . . , the gradual softening

of mores, the abasement of the mind, the mediocrity of tastes" ("Lettres
à J. S. Mill," in English *Selected Letters*, March 18, 1841, pp. 150–151).
The only remedy, under these circumstances, is to revitalize national
pride. "It is necessary that those who march at the head of such a nation
[a democratic nation] should always keep a proud attitude, if they do
not wish to allow the level of national mores to fall very low" (ibid.,
p. 151). It would have been preferable "that such men should come to
adopt a language that raises again and sustains the nation's heart and
seeks to check it in this enervating taste that drags it more each day
toward material enjoyments and small pleasures" (ibid., pp. 151–152).
It is not certain that Tocqueville's analysis is accurate: Is nationalism
the antidote for, or on the contrary the product of, individualism (or
industrial society)? Does the nation as an entity bear a close resemblance to earlier communities or not? But even if we assume he is right,
we may wonder whether the remedy may not be more dangerous than
the malady it is supposed to cure. Tocqueville does not seem concerned
about this.

It is striking to see that Mill, in his reply to Tocqueville's letter,
showed much greater awareness of the nationalist peril. "I have often,
of late, remembered the reason you gave in justification of the conduct
of the liberal party in the late quarrel between England and France—
that the feeling of orgueil national is the only feeling of a public-spir-
ited & elevating kind which remains & that it ought not therefore to
be permitted to go down. How true this is, every day makes painfully
evident . . . Most heartily do I agree with you that this one & only
feeling of a public, & therefore, so far, of a disinterested character
which remains in France must not be suffered to decay . . . But, in the
name of France & civilization, posterity have a right to expect from
such men as you, from the nobler & more enlightened spirits of the
time, that you should teach to your countrymen better ideas of what it
is which constitutes national glory & national importance, than the low
& grovelling ones which they seem to have at present" (*The Earlier
Letters of John Stuart Mill*, Letter 366, August 9, 1842, p. 536).

What Mill put his finger on, respectfully but also firmly (this is one
of the few letters he addressed to Tocqueville in English, perhaps not
by coincidence), is the relativism of a purely nationalist position. If one
is prepared to exalt national pride without subjecting its content to any
examination, one will end up recognizing as many ideals as there are
nations. Mill, for his part, does not hesitate to observe what a distress-

ing situation results when national transcendence is the only transcendence possible; he does not forget that it is necessary to pass judgments not only in the name of France but in the name of civilization. In short, he recognizes that some national feelings may be worthy of respect while others are not; and he reminds Tocqueville that he expects to see him act not only as a Frenchman but also as an enlightened and noble human being. Mill concludes: "I would like to see crucified the first man who dared to speak ill of another people before the tribune of his own" (Letter 388, February 20, 1843, p. 571; in French in original). But this is a point of view that Tocqueville the politician does not want to hear: "It is madness," he says later in their correspondence, "for a public figure to seek any reward but respect and justice for his own country" ("Lettres à Mill," p. 343). Barrès could have written that sentence.

But let us come back to the colonies. When he wrote his major report on Algeria for the Chamber of Deputies, Tocqueville asked just one question: "Is the dominion we are exercising over the old Regency of Algiers of use to France?" ("Rapport," p. 311). He does not ask whether this dominion is in conformity with the interests of humanity, still less whether it conforms to those of the Algerian population; national interest is the only thing that counts. The question he does raise is purely rhetorical, moreover, for Tocqueville views the affirmative response "as a proven truth." This is because, while the colonies' economic usefulness may be open to discussion, their usefulness as a component of political power is virtually a tautology: victory is the unmistakable sign of power. Now this is indeed the sort of usefulness Tocqueville has in mind: "The chief merit of our colonies is not in their markets but in the positions they occupy around the globe" ("L'Emancipation," p. 85).

It is this position of principle—the nationalist argument—that explains Tocqueville's reactions in any particular case. During his trip to Algeria, he witnessed a peroration that he reports in the following terms: "There is nothing, Gentlemen, except force and terror, that works with these people . . . After killing five or six men, I spared the livestock . . . An Arab who was under suspicion was brought to me. I questioned him and then I had his head cut off" ("Notes de voyage" [Travel Notes], p. 216). Tocqueville does not approve of such behavior. But here is his commentary: "And listening sadly to these things, I wondered what could be the future of a country turned over to such men and where this cascade of violence and injustice would end up, if not with the revolt of the natives and the ruin of the Europeans?" (p. 217). Tocqueville's sadness does not cause him to abandon his nationalist outlook for an instant: such acts will bring about the ruin of the colonials—that is, of the interests of France; but on the part of the "natives" he foresees only revolt. The question of *their* ruin, for example, or even their death, does not arise.

Or let us consider another occasion: In 1846, a French newspaper in Algiers declared that certain "human races" are "destined for destruction by a decree of Providence." Applied to the Arabs, this led to the following conclusion: "The extinction of this guilty race is a harmony." Now here is Tocqueville's commentary: "I do not want the natives to be crushed, I especially do not want them to be exterminated . . . , but I think that trusting to the good will of the natives in order to maintain our presence in Africa is a pure illusion that it would be folly to cherish" ("Travail," pp. 293–294). While he disagrees with the means proposed by the Algiers newspaper, Tocqueville nevertheless supports the project of occupation; he rejects the two extremes—extermination on the one hand, expression of the free will of the Algerians on the other—and recommends a tranquil position of strength.

Thus, there is no occasion to take into account the "good will of the natives." Tocqueville does not think that the French in Africa are simply struggling against the ill will of a few leaders: "We first recognized that we were facing not a true army, but the population itself . . . It was less a matter of conquering a government than of holding back a people" ("Rapport sur l'Algérie," pp. 316–317). It may seem somewhat surprising that he makes so little of this opposition. Indeed, he knows perfectly well that the distinction between natives and foreigners is purely relative: let us recall that for him "instincts" do not differ from one race to another. Now Tocqueville always expressed the greatest intransigence regarding any amputation whatsoever of individual rights (his "guarantees"), and particularly of the individual's political freedom. Moreover, he repeatedly recalled this in the colonial context: "We need in Africa as much as in France, and even more than in France, the essential guarantees of man living in society; there is no country where it is more necessary to establish individual freedom, respect for property, the guarantee of all rights than in a colony" ("Lettre sur l'Algérie," p. 150). He thus never failed to react with indignation when he observed that "in Algeria the first of all civil liberties, individual liberty, is not assured" ("Travail," p. 263).

What leads to this apparent contradiction is the reference to membership in a nation, and the hierarchically superior role it occupies with respect to membership in humanity. Individual liberty and equality are inviolable principles. However, this is not the case for states or peoples: dominion over others, which is illegitimate on the individual level, becomes acceptable as soon as we are dealing with groups. However, these groups are still composed of individuals! So by virtue of this detour we end up with a defense of inequality between persons—so long as the persons in question belong to different communities. "It is neither in our interest nor our duty [political principles always take precedence over moral principles, but here they happen to be in agreement, from Tocqueville's perspective] to allow our Musulman subjects to hold exaggerated ideas as to their own importance, nor to persuade them that we are obliged to treat them in all circumstances exactly as if they were our fellow citizens and our equals" ("Rapport sur l'Algérie," p. 324). So Musulman subjects will not be subjects like any other, and there is an "extreme of benevolence" that must be avoided.

Thus, even though he invokes the principle of equality before the law, Tocqueville recommends that justice not be the same for all. As far as the "natives" are concerned, "war councils may be established for them. This is of secondary interest . . . But what is not secondary is providing the European, invited into Africa, with all the legal guarantees, both civil and criminal, that he is used to regarding as necessities of civilized life" ("Travail," p. 280). Is civilization then appropriate only for those who already possess it? Similarly as to the distribution of lands: "In certain places, instead of reserving for Europeans the most fertile lands, the best irrigated, the best prepared lands of the territory, we gave them to the natives" ("Rapport sur l'Algérie," p. 321). Tocqueville is indignant about this, forgetting perhaps that before the lands could be "given" they had been taken, by force of arms, from these very natives. But equality is clearly no longer at issue. Whereas Tocqueville had traveled across America himself in order to prepare his study, sharing the lives of the "natives," he recommends quite a different sort of scientific behavior here: "One can only study barbarian peoples with weapons in hand" (p. 309). Renan learned this lesson well, as we have seen.

This is why the only injustices Tocqueville denounces in his travel narrative are those to which the colonials are subjected. One day, for instance, a civilian director noted the inanity of a military decision concerning the Arab population. He decided to lodge a complaint; lengthy proceedings ensued; the decision was revoked only much later. "During this time a month had gone by, a month during which a good number of blows had been administered to the Arabs. These anecdotes," Tocqueville comments, "amused us but taught us nothing, for what is the poor civilian functionary to do in the face of the French insolence that has a sabre behind it?" ("Notes de voyage," p. 204). The only character in this "anecdote" that arouses Tocqueville's pity is the civilian employee; he has not a word to say on behalf of the Arabs who had been beaten.

States—or peoples—thus do not enjoy the treatment reserved for individuals, and individuals, by virtue of inhabiting a state, ultimately lose the rights they warranted as human beings. Tocqueville, who was wont to denounce the ownership of one man by another, saw no problem with the ownership of one state by another. "France today possesses . . . colonies in which 200,000 men speak our language, share our mores, obey our laws," he writes without turning a hair ("L'Emancipation," p. 87). In Tocqueville's position is there a simple inconsistency, a failure to extend a principle (or even a contradiction, as most of Tocqueville's commentators believe), or rather an accepted discontinuity, a matter of principle, as it were?

In order to be able to answer this question, it is first necessary to recall a classic distinction between two kinds of individual rights. On the one hand, there are rights that may be called positive, or substantive; these rights stem essentially from the principle of equality. All citizens have a right to the same privileges (which thereupon cease to be privileges)—for example, equal status before the law, or the right to vote. On the other hand, there are also rights that are in some sense negative (or formal), rights consisting in the establishment of a boundary beyond which the group has no business intervening (thus a boundary that divides an individual's life into public and private spheres). These rights consist essentially in an exercise of freedoms: freedom of thought, of religion, of speech, the freedom to educate one's children as one sees fit, and so on. The two groups of rights are not contradictory but complementary. However, they sometimes come into conflict, as we have seen with regard to the right to autonomy on the one hand

and the right to benefit from one's property, whatever its origin, on the other. Stress on positive rights, extended to all members of the group, characterizes "socialism" in the broad sense (or should we perhaps speak of "societism"?), whereas insistence on the negative rights of each member of the group is characteristic of "liberal" thought.

We are now in a position to reformulate the preceding question. Is the analogy between individual and State justified, especially insofar as the various rights of each are concerned? If we want to believe that Tocqueville's views are consistent, we have to suppose that his answer to this question would be negative. What he suggests is that states, like individuals, have spheres in which they act in terms of their will alone (negative rights); but, unlike individuals, states do not have to conform to a code that attributes positive rights to them, for the simple reason that such a code does not exist. In fact, in order for rights to exist, there has to be a social space within which the collectivity can impose the application of the law (this is precisely the state of law). Now, contrary to what the idyllic reveries of the Encyclopedists suggested, there is no such thing as a "general society," or universal social space, endowed with "policemen" who would ensure the application of planetary law. The only rule of international behavior is thus liberty—that is, the absence of rules (the "law of the jungle"); which amounts to saying that the only principle governing behavior between states is nationalism. Universal morality stops at the threshold of international relations.

Far from being in contradiction with the general principles Tocqueville identified in the individual's sphere, nationalism would then be the projection of one of those principles, liberalism, onto the scale of interstate relations. The liberal principle is, for the life of the individual, an indispensable corrective to the action of the "general will"; but in the absence of such a will it reigns alone, and its meaning is thereby transformed. Liberalism proclaims the right of the individual to do as she likes within certain limits established by the group; nationalism does the same for states, but on the basis of the observation that no such limits exist. Liberalism encourages individuals to profit from their own abilities and strengths; but the individual's sphere of action is restricted by what is considered to be in the common interest of the group. Nationalism is a politics of power proper to the State, a *Machtpolitik* that is restrained not by any "society of nations" (because such a society is nonexistent or ineffective) but only by the power of neighboring states.

Tocqueville had begun to deal with this problem in *Democracy in America*, observing that the internal and external politics of a nation could not be based on a common principle. It might be said that the goal of internal politics is to achieve a high degree of "civilization," with all that that word implies. Now one of these implications is renunciation of war. "I think one can accept it as a general and constant rule that among civilized nations warlike passions become rarer and less active as social conditions get nearer to equality" (II, part III, ch. 22, p. 621). War is a politics of force, not of justice; it is thus contrary to civilization. But if a state applies the same principle in its external politics, it simply becomes easy prey for its neighbors. "No matter how greatly such nations may be devoted to peace, they must be ready to defend themselves if attacked, or in other words, they must have an army" (ibid.). Not only must one not extend the same principles to the whole set of actions of a state, but it is imperative to apply contrary principles, without which the efforts expended internally would be nullified by vulnerability to the outside world. "What does comfort or freedom profit a nation if it is in daily danger of being ravaged or conquered? . . . Therefore force is often for nations one of the primary conditions of happiness and even of existence" (I, part I, ch. 8, p. 126).

While defending the rights of individuals (and especially their negative rights to freedom) at the same time that he is advocating colonial expansion, and thus the subjugation of other countries, Tocqueville remains at least superficially consistent. Internal liberalism favors— within the sphere exempt from social control—the strong and the rich; external liberalism, transformed into nationalism, does the same. Liberalism seeks to guarantee to each individual the free exercise of his abilities; thus, colonizers have the right to colonize. Tocqueville's colonialism is merely the international extension of his liberalism. The only acceptable criticism, from his perspective, would be one that demonstrated that colonial expansion is not useful to France (this will be the core of Raymond Aron's argument concerning the Algerian war a century later).

Conviction and Responsibility

Tocqueville's position thus has a kind of consistency; but this does not mean it is beyond reproach. If we have accurately reconstructed his argument, it can be criticized for its simplicity, its tendency to dismiss differences that are in fact quite significant. We may recognize that the international situation of a country requires it to maintain an army in order to "avoid war" or to prevent conquest; the argument is no longer acceptable if we are talking about a war of conquest. Even if one wants one's own country to be strong, as the logic of nationalism would dictate, one is not obliged to treat all means of expansion as equivalent, and, for example, to judge war and commerce by the same standards (this distinction, proposed by Montesquieu and amplified by Benjamin Constant, was nevertheless familiar to Tocqueville). In a situation of warfare, finally, not all means for reaching victory are equally acceptable. In other words, even if one accepts as a fact the absence of an effective "society of nations," one can continue to call upon reason and rational norms to control and restrain the use of force.

Tocqueville starts with a declaration that he presents as if it were an established fact: "The idea of possessing Africa, of maintaining Africa with the aid and support of the native population, an idea that is the dream of noble and generous hearts, is chimerical, for now at least" ("Intervention," p. 293). "There is nothing but war" ("Travail," p. 226). War is presented as the only means that will allow France's goals to be achieved; the assertion is open to criticism, whether or not one agrees with the goals in question. Once this step has been taken, another follows: since we have chosen to adopt the single vantage point of effectiveness, we will agree to wage war whatever the means deployed. "Once we have countenanced the great *violence* of conquest, I believe we must not recoil before the specific acts of violence that are absolutely necessary to consolidate it," Tocqueville wrote to General Lamoricière on April 5, 1846 ("Lettre à Lamoricière" [Letter to Lamoricière], p. 304). Field-marshal Bugeaud must have followed the same reasoning when he defended himself before the Chamber of Deputies from the criticisms that were being addressed to him about the means he had used: "These mutterings would seem to be telling me that the Chamber finds these means too barbarian. Gentlemen, one does not wage war with the sentiments of a philanthropist. He who desires the end must desire the means; when there are no means other than the ones I have indicated, then these must be used. I will always prefer French interests to an absurd philanthropy toward foreigners who are cutting off the heads of our captured or wounded prisoners" ("Discours" [Speech], pp. 67–68). Here "philanthropy" is obviously a pejorative synonym for humanism: a morality that does not understand the first thing about politics.

With Tocqueville some of these "means" are political or social. Thus, the French would find it advantageous to pretend, in a first phase, that they were adopting the mores of the country in order to win the confidence of the inhabitants and thus to succeed more easily, in a second phase, in Frenchifying the Arabs. Or they ought to try to sow dissension among the various groups that occupy Algerian soil, in order to facilitate their subjugation. But other "means" belong to the category of pure repression, like the famous *razzias* inaugurated by Bugeaud and Lamoricière, which consisted in burning all the villages and harvests of the Algerian population in order to break down all resistance and bring the inhabitants to surrender. Bugeaud theorized about this as follows: "It counts for little to cross the mountains and fight the natives once or twice; to bring them under control, you have to attack their interests. You cannot do this by rushing through; you have to make your presence felt on each tribe's territory. You have to arrange to have adequate food supplies so you can stay long enough to destroy the villages, cut down the fruit trees, burn or pull up the harvests, empty the silos, search the ravines, rocks, and caves to seize the women, children, old people, livestock, and personal property; this is the only way you can make these proud mountain-dwellers capitulate" ("De la stratégie" [On Strategy], p. 112). As it is easy enough to imagine, under such circumstances no one bothered to keep track of "accidental" deaths.

This policy was not unanimously approved in France. Tocqueville thus undertook to challenge its detractors: "I have often heard men in France whom I respect but with whom I disagree deem it bad to burn harvests, empty silos, and seize unarmed men, women, and children. In my view these are unfortunate necessities; any people seeking to wage war against the Arabs will have to use them" ("Travail," pp. 226–227).

We can also observe Tocqueville's reactions to some specific situations. Bugeaud's troops had pursued the undefeated Arabs, trapped them in the Dahra caves and exterminated them by asphyxiating them with smoke. Colonel Saint-Arnaud, one of Bugeaud's subordinates, reported an operation of this sort in the following terms: "The same day, the 8th, I pushed through a reconnaissance of the caves or rather caverns, 200 meters in use, five entrances. We were greeted with rifle fire . . . The 9th, beginning of the siege works, blockades, mines, explosions, requests, demands, entreaties to come out and give up. Response: insults, curses, gunshots . . . fire lit . . . One Arab comes out on the 10th, urges his compatriots to leave; they refuse. On the 12th, eleven Arabs come out, the others shoot. Then I have all the exits hermetically sealed and I make a huge cemetery. The earth will cover the corpses of these fanatics for all time. No one went down into the caves; no one . . . other than myself knows that there are 500 brigands under there who will no longer cut the throats of Frenchmen. A confidential report told the Maréchal everything, simply, without terrible poetry or images" (*Lettres* [Letters], II, p. 37). Bugeaud must have appreciated his colonel's simplicity; had he not been outraged, some months earlier, at the protests aroused in France by an earlier operation? He had written to Thiers: "You have seen the outburst of insults that the press and even the Tribunal of Peers have been spreading in recent days about the business of the *Ouled Riah;* they have made us deeply indignant . . . Very few people in France are able to comprehend the cruel necessities of this inextricable war . . . For a long time yet it [the conquered people] will keep trying to throw off the yoke; it will try all the more often to the extent that the repression is philanthropical. The disastrous incident of the caves will prevent a lot of bloodshed in the future . . . The country will find many advantages in it; it can offer us some comfort against the outrages that people are hurling in our faces" ("Lettre à Thiers" [Letter to Thiers], pp. 212–213).

Tocqueville does not pick up the argument of lesser cost (which will be invoked years later to justify the use of the atomic bomb in Japan); for the rest, the difference between his text and Bugeaud's is merely stylistic. I do not think, he says, that "the dominant merit of M. le Maréchal Bugeaud is precisely that he is a philanthropist; no, I do not believe that; but I do believe that M. le Maréchal Bugeaud has rendered a great service to his country on the soil of Africa" ("Intervention," p. 299). Here the massacre is not only excused but glorified: what might look like a crime against humanity becomes a praiseworthy action, by virtue of the fact that it is undertaken in the service of the nation. Tocqueville writes elsewhere: "I think that all means for devastating the tribes must be used. I except only those that humanity and the law of nations reject" ("Travail," p. 227); but one wonders what this last restriction might mean, given the examples of what is allowable. Is it anything but a rhetorical formula?

Tocqueville's positions in this context cannot fail to arouse some astonishment in the reader of *Democracy in America*. The author of that work indeed devotes an acerbic chapter to the history of the relations between the Anglo-Saxon colonizers and the Indians. Commenting on an official report about the Indians, he wrote: "One is astonished at the facility and ease with which, from the very first words, the author disposes of arguments founded on natural right and reason, which he calls abstract and theoretical principles" (*Democracy*, I, part II, ch. 10, p. 312, note 29). But is it not Tocqueville himself who swept aside with the back of his hand the considerations of respectable men, of noble and generous hearts, of philanthropists (considerations that Bugeaud, more crudely, called "sentimental hogwash"—p. 213), to recognize only the inexorable logic of "unfortunate necessities"? He writes with irony: "The Americans in this part of the Union look jealously at the lands occupied by the natives" (I, part II, ch. 10, p. 308); but is it not Tocqueville himself who will be indignant at seeing that some of the best lands had been "given" to the Arabs? The desperate fate of the Indians weighs on him and horrifies him; yet he does not see any problem in imposing the same fate on the inhabitants of Algeria. Reflecting in general terms on the political motivations of peoples, he is unsparing in his treatment of "patriotism, which is most often nothing but an extension of individual egoism" (p. 337); once he becomes a politician, he erects this same patriotism into the sole guiding principle of his behavior. As a visitor on the American continent, he sees independence as the highest goal of every people: "Never have I felt more convinced . . . that the greatest and most irremediable ill in a people is to be conquered" ("Voyage aux Etats-Unis," in English *Journey to America*, "Visit to One of the Civil Courts of Quebec," August 27, 1831, p. 188). Back in France, he casts himself as an apologist for the conquest of others.

It may be that there is no inconsistency here either. Tocqueville's discourse does not have equivalent status in the two different contexts, and consequently it does not rely on the same principles. The philosopher-scholar makes the trip to America, a foreign country; he analyzes and judges it in the name of his "ethics of conviction," an ethics that happens to be humanistic: a "natural" (that is to say, rational) law, based on the rightful equality of human beings. The deputy-statesman, for his part, adopts a political discourse: he writes reports, letters, speeches for the Chamber, texts that are intended to influence the political orientation of the State. His frame of reference is an "ethics of responsibility": he is seeking the good of his country, not conformity with some abstract principles. Politics is not morality: this is the lesson to be drawn from the juxtaposition of Tocqueville's various writings. Morality must be universal; politics cannot be. As people have been saying since Max Weber, the "ethics of responsibility" is a politics, not an ethics. Now a humanitarian politics is in a sense a contradiction in terms. Of course. But does that mean we have to dismiss the one as soon as we begin to practice the other? By instituting a radical dichotomy between morality and politics, Tocqueville seems to have neglected what his customary lucidity had nevertheless made him feel, and which he formulated in the shape of a prediction (one more!): "If . . . we were to act in such a way as to show that in our own eyes the former inhabitants of Algeria are only an obstacle that must be pushed aside or trampled underfoot; if we were to surround their populations not in order to lift them up in our arms toward well-being and enlightenment but to choke and stifle them, the question of life and death would be posed between the two races. Sooner or later, believe me, Algeria would become a closed field, a walled arena, in which the two peoples would be locked in merciless combat, and one of the two would inevitably succumb" ("Rapport sur l'Algérie," p. 329). Tocqueville is no more attentive to this warning than his contemporaries; a century later, the merciless battle will break out.

Michelet

France and the Universe

Jules Michelet was heir to the revolutionary and humanitarian ideal. Throughout his life he never ceased to proclaim principles of justice, equality, liberty, and universal love. At the same time, he was an outspoken partisan of the idea of nationhood. How did he manage to reconcile these contradictory requirements?

Michelet seems to have begun by observing that the principle of nationhood, far from withering away (as certain utopian minds in the revolutionary period had assumed it would), was more powerful than ever in the middle of the nineteenth century. "The barrier of nationalities which you thought had been swept away remains almost intact" (*The People*, p. 21, note 6). It was even being reinforced: "Nationalities are so far from disappearing that I see them every day developing profound moral characteristics, and becoming individuals instead of collections of men as they once were" (p. 179). And several decades later, in *La France devant l'Europe (France before Europe)*, a heated reaction to the Franco-Prussian War, Michelet confirmed his diagnosis: "Humanitarians are fools to believe that the walls, hedges, barriers, which were between them of old, are done away with. On the contrary, a few antiquated prejudices may have died out; but a growing personality separates more and more nations and individuals" (p. 59).

Michelet might be thought to have regretted this state of affairs. Not at all; at least not at the time he was writing *Le Peuple (The People)*. The separation of the world into nations is a gift from heaven: "The most powerful means employed by God to create and develop distinctive originality is to maintain the world harmoniously divided into those grand and beautiful systems which we call nations" (p. 180). Michelet sees himself as a product of the national spirit: "All our various works have sprung from the same living root: the feeling of France and the idea of the fatherland" (p. 3); and he stresses that he finds his inspiration in love for the fatherland: "My light, . . . which will not deceive me, is France. The feeling for France, the devotion of the citizen to the native land, is my standard for judging these men and these classes" (p. 92). The ultimate values are national, not universal.

Michelet's *The People* thus takes aim at all the nation's adversaries. In practice, these come in two categories: those who support the interests of groups smaller than the (French) nation, and those who prefer a foreign country to their country of origin (there are internal and external enemies, as it were). Against the first set of enemies—the regionalists—Michelet evokes once again the inexorable movement of history. "It is quite clear that internal dissension is declining in every nation. Our French provincialism is rapidly disappearing" (p. 178). For all that, he does not hesitate to recommend that history be helped a bit in its inexorable march—for example, by the imposition of a truly common instructional system: "The first institution that can make [our people] live and endure is this harmonious education, which would found the country in the very heart of the child, and which should be given to *everyone*" (p. 193). As for the second set, the external enemies, Michelet castigates them in particular in the person of certain French writers (he has in mind George Sand, Eugène Sue, Balzac) who are critical of France and who reserve their praise for foreigners. "Who is the ridiculous man in these [two French novels]? The Frenchman—always the Frenchman! The Englishman is the admirable fellow—the invisible yet ever-present Providence who saves everything" (p. 187).

And Michelet muses about the appropriateness of certain sanctions that might be imposed: "It would be worthwhile examining whether these French books which have so much popularity and authority in Europe truly represent France, or whether they have not exhibited certain exceptional and very unfavorable aspects of character. And these pictures, where people seldom see anything but our vices and our defects, have they not done our country an immense disservice among foreign nations?" (p. 6).

But these enemies, or rather these rivals, are less to blame than is the world view that opposes patriotism—namely, cosmopolitanism or humanism. While the philosophers preach universal love, "the peasant alone has preserved the tradition of salvation; to him a Prussian is still a Prussian, an Englishman still an Englishman. His common sense has been right in spite of all you humanitarians!" (p. 21). What is the most harmful act one can accomplish? "From being a Frenchman he falls to the level of a cosmopolitan, of just any man, and from there to the level of a mollusk" (p. 94). Whatever may be made of this last transition, Michelet summarizes his own undertaking in *The People* as follows: "I have also sacrificed another religion—the humanitarian dream of philosophy, which believes it can save the individual by destroying the citizens, denying the nations, and renouncing the fatherland. The fatherland, my fatherland, can alone save the world" (p. 210).

The humanitarians' mistake, Michelet explains, is that they misjudge man's social dimension. Thus, Michelet identifies humanism with individualism. As soon as "the flower of nationality grows pale," we have "the pure egotism of the calculator who has no fatherland" (p. 93); "the hardheartedness of individualism" (p. 171) leads to the singleminded preoccupation with accumulating wealth (the theme was already present in Tocqueville); Michelet can then condemn the "cosmopolitan utopias of material enjoyments" (p. 185). Man is a social being: individualism is not only immoral, it is antinatural. "I see at a glance that even from his birth [man] is a sociable being. Before he has his eyes open, he loves society; he weeps as soon as he is left alone. Why should we be surprised at this? On the day we call his first day, he leaves a society already quite old, and so pleasant!" (p. 158). One can obviously respond to Michelet, as to all those who make similar associations (Michelet, an admirer of the Revolution, reasons no differently here from the counterrevolutionary Bonald), that, in the first place, individualism cannot be reduced to materialism, in the sense of an exclusive concern with material goods (the individualist may also be ascetic); and that, in the second place, humanism is not a disguised form of individualism, in the sense in which the term is used here: respect for all human beings is not equivalent to pure concern for oneself. And if it is true that human beings are always social, it is on the other hand false that the nation is the only possible form of community: there are infranational entities (like the family, the locality, the region) and also supranational ones (a group of countries, like Western Europe or the Maghreb)—that can satisfy the human need for belonging just as well.

Up to this point, we might have thought that Michelet, conscious of the potential conflict between patriotism and humanitarianism, had simply chosen the first term, without taking the trouble to coordinate this portion of his work with his other writings, in which he advocates universal love. But in fact the picture is more complex: it is within his "patriotic writings" themselves that he attempts to reintroduce humanitarianism! In his first major text, his *Introduction à l'histoire universelle* (Introduction to Universal History), Michelet lays the groundwork for this tour de force by positing the equivalence of France and the universe (and thus, potentially, the equivalence of a *French* patriotism like his own and humanitarianism): "This little book," his first sentence says, "could just as well be called *Introduction à l'histoire de la France* [Introduction to French History]; France is its culminating point" (p. 227). France is destined to be "the pilot ship of humanity" (ibid.) as it leads the modern world "down the mysterious road of the future" (p. 258).

What is the basis for this equating of France with the universe? Michelet explains his view at greater length in *The People*. Since the Revolution (and indeed starting long before), France has built its identity on the principles of liberty, equality, and fraternity; these are the universal values par excellence. That is why France's laws, like its legends, "are only those of reason itself" (p. 190), for it is reason that tells us that Revolutionary motto is the best in the world. As Michelet adds in his *Histoire de France (History of France)*, this trend had already begun with the Gauls, a race set apart by mobility and flexibility—in other words, by freedom, or perfectibility. This race is "the most sympathetic and the most perfectible of human races" (I, 1, p. 1). What Rousseau deemed the distinctive feature of the human race—its ability to acquire knowledge and to improve itself—here becomes a specifically French trait. France incarnates humanity in humanity's most specifically human aspects. France is that contradiction in terms, a "universal fatherland" (*Introduction*, p. 229). Thus, Michelet declares that he prefers his own patriotism to the humanitarianism of others; but in order to establish its superiority, he relies on arguments drawn from humanitarian doctrine! On this basis every feature of the French nation can be seen as a manifestation of universality, and thus as a value. This identity "makes the history of France that of humanity"; at the same time, France is "the moral ideal of the world" (p. 228) and it has proclaimed "the future common law of the world" (pp. 217–218). France is the country "that has best merged its own interest and destiny with those of humanity" (p. 229). It is France's vocation to "deliver the world" (p. 75), to "help every nation be born to liberty" (p. 217). Thus, France is a midwife.

This possibility of simultaneously embodying the particular and the universal is obviously open only to the French, since other peoples, as they move in the direction of patriotism, do not reinforce universalism but contest it. Except that those other peoples, who are not so dull-witted after all, have noticed this, and they have secretly chosen France as their second fatherland, often preferring it to the first. "What is holy in France, whatever it may be, is holy to all nations: it is adopted, blessed and mourned by the human race. For any man, an American philosopher said impartially, his first country is his own, and his second is France" (p. 228). Other peoples "sympathize with the French genius, they become France; if only by their silent emulation, they award it the pontificate of the new civilization" (*Introduction*, p. 257). This is why Michelet thinks he is safe from any charge of bias: if he defends France, it is not because France is his own country, but because he loves goodness and truth. "And this is not fanaticism. It is the overly condensed summary of a considered judgment based on long study" (*The People*, p. 192).

There is an obvious paradox in Michelet's reasoning. The defense of the principle of equality is to France's credit. But if this principle is just, it forbids us to favor one people at the expense of others. The content of the assertion contradicts the actual meaning that Michelet seeks to draw from his statement. "No doubt every great nation represents an idea important to the human race. But great God! how much more true is this of France!" (p. 183). When we realize that the "idea" in question is precisely that of equality, we can appreciate the risks of the assertion: some people do have to be more equal than others! Even if we assume that the universal good and the political program of France have coincided at some particular historical moment, this confers no lasting privilege on France, since it may change its course at any moment (as it has of course done many times). Only universalism can judge whether national passions are worthy of praise in a given era (and unworthy at some other point). Or, to reverse Michelet's formula (p. 92), it is the humanitarian sentiment that will be the yardstick for measuring "the citizen's devotion to the fatherland."

We must also make it clear that, when Michelet refers to the universe, he is in fact thinking of Western Europe. Not that he refuses to apply the same criteria to other peoples; but only the European nations have come close enough to these ideals to deserve reward. In *France before Europe*, he exclaims: "Workers, creators, indefatigable producers, stand together as one people. Preserve for the world the sacred source which produces all its wealth . . . I appeal to Englishmen, Frenchmen, Belgians, Dutch, Swiss. I appeal to Germans [and also to North America: may she devote herself] to the great cause of human progress, closely allied to the civilized West" (preface to the first edition, p. xix). Outside the civilized West there is no salvation; Michelet evokes with alarm "yonder giant masses which are darkening the horizon" (p. 111)—that is to say, in the case in point, the Russians.

The Determinism of Freedom

How can we account for France's rise to this place of honor? Michelet has an answer to this question, which he presents in his *Introduction à l'histoire universelle* and puts into practice in his *Histoire de France*, especially in the early volumes.

To justify his assertions, Michelet proceeds to develop a theory of social evolution. His first postulate is that progress consists in liberation from the determining factors that nature brings to bear upon human populations, inside and outside the human body. "Human will stiffens against the influences of race and climate" (*History of France*, p. 229). In a spirit not far removed from the central tendencies of Enlightenment thinking, Michelet thus conceives of humanity's evolution as, on the one hand, an increase in freedom at the expense of any biological or geographical determinism, and, on the other hand, as a victory of the social, the artificial, the complex, over a supposed natural simplicity. This book, he says later, presents "universal history as the struggle of freedom, its constant victory over the fatal world" (*Histoire de France*, "Préface de 1869," p. 15).

As a result, the closer a country is to its original state, the less civilized it is, for its physical determinations have not yet been neutralized. Such is the case with several European countries. "In Germany and in Italy, . . . moral freedom is prevented, oppressed by the local influences of race and climate. In those countries man also bears the sign of fatality in his personal appearance" (*Introduction*, p. 246). Man is blended with earth and nature; he remains alone, and thus wild. "The man of the earth and of strength . . . , rooted, localized in his fief, and by that very token dispersed over the territory, tends to isolation and barbarity" (p. 250). One might almost deduce all of Barrès from these lines, through a simple inversion of signs.

The unmixed populations, or pure races, thus turn out to be at a more primitive stage in their development. This is the lesson of the English. "That inflexible pride of England has put an eternal obstacle in the way of racial fusion and social leveling" (p. 252). For it does not suffice for the various "races" to be in contact; they must actually blend. Now "in such lands there will be a juxtaposition of diverse races, never an intimate fusion" (p. 247).

On the contrary, the mixing of races equates with progress. "The crossing of races, the mixing of contrasting civilizations, is . . . the most powerful auxiliary of freedom. The diverse fatalities that they contribute in such blendings cancel and neutralize each other." And here is where we grasp the reasons for French superiority. For France is nothing less than this fortunate mixture, this absence of physical determinations, this state of maximum distancing from original simplicity. "What is least simple, least natural, most artificial, what is least fatal, most human and most free in the world, is Europe; what is most European is my country, France" (p. 247). What others take as an absence of characteristic features is in reality the feature constitutive of this country's identity: "Its proper genius lies precisely in what foreigners, even provincials call insignificance and indifference, and which rather ought to be called an aptitude, a capacity, a universal relativity . . . Here is central France's superiority over the provinces, the superiority of France as a whole over Europe. This intimate fusion of the races constitutes our nation's identity, its personality" (p. 248).

France is not entirely alone in this exceptional position. On two occasions, in the past, other nations have already played similar roles.

From the perspective of the chosen nation in relation to all the others, the example of ancient Greece comes to mind. "Every solitary thought of the nations is revealed by France. It speaks the Word of Europe, as Greece did for Asia" (p. 257). On the religious plane, the comparison with the birth of Christianity is self-evident. "It is at the point of contact among races, in the collision of their contrasting fatalities, in the sudden explosion of intelligence and freedom, that from humanity bursts forth this celestial flash that is called the Word." The religion of man, revealed by the Revolution, is to modern times what the Christian religion was to antiquity. "At the point of the most powerful blending of the Oriental races, the bright flash shone over the Sinai . . . At the point of the most perfect blending of the European races, in the form of equality in freedom, the social Word burst forth. . . . It is up to France both to bring this new revelation to light and to explain it" (p. 257). We see here why France can henceforth be viewed as a "religion," why the French Revolution is a *revelation*. "It was necessary that God should have a second era and appear upon earth in his incarnation of 1789" (*The People*, pp. 176–177). "France is a Religion" (p. 190).

The result of this liberation from primitive determinations is the flowering, in France, of what Michelet calls its "social genius." Internally, this genius is equivalent to the "liberty within equality" that constitutes Michelet's ideal. In relations among countries, this same genius is manifested "with its three apparently contradictory characteristics, the ready acceptance of foreign ideas, the ardent proselytism with which it spreads its own ideas abroad, and the organizational strength that summarizes and codifies both" (*Introduction*, p. 249). Michelet's discourse here goes beyond apology and becomes a pertinent description of France's distinguishing cultural features: the French may not *be* the most universal people on earth, but it is certain that they *think* of themselves in such terms. "The Frenchman wants especially to imprint his personality on the vanquished, not because it is his own, but because it typifies the good and the beautiful; this is his naive belief. He believes that he can do nothing more beneficial to the world than to give it his ideas, his mores, and his fashions. He will convert other peoples to his ways by the sword, and after the battle, partly out of fatuousness and partly out of sympathy, he will show them all they have to gain by becoming French" (p. 249). It is rather remarkable to see Michelet using terms like "naive belief" and "fatuousness" here to characterize the very sort of projections from the particular to the general that he himself customarily practices.

Some years later (1833), Michelet began to construct his monumental *History of France* on the basis of principles established this way. He himself explained in the preface he added later (1869) that one of the essential motives of his enterprise was to combat the conception of history being illustrated at that time by the work of Augustin Thierry, who was in fact trying to explain the history of France by the persistence (and the conflict) of two races, Franks and Gauls, who had been subsequently reincarnated in two classes, aristocrats and peasants (this hypothesis had already been popular in the eighteenth century). Michelet decided to work "against those who pursue that element of race and exaggerate it in modern times" (p. 13); unlike Thierry, he declared that the races, originally influential forces, had been neutralized as a result of their intermixing. Now any lessening of material determinism is a victory for man, and a sign of his superiority. "The more this race isolated itself, the more it preserved its primitive originality, the more did it decline and fall. To remain original, to keep clear of foreign influence, to repel the ideas of others, is to remain incomplete and feeble . . . Woe to the obstinate individuality which persists on belonging to itself alone, and refuses to enter into the community of the world!" (*History of France*, I, 4, p. 75). The superiority of the nation over the primitive familial clan lies precisely in this capacity to integrate foreigners.

If we formulate the requirements that the ideal nation might be asked to meet, we cannot fail to observe that France satisfies them better than any other country, according to Michelet. "No doubt our country owes much to foreign influence; all the races of the world have contributed to endow this Pandora" (I, 4, p. 66). "Race upon race, people upon people" (I, 4, p. 68). Michelet held onto his conviction that the French are a chosen people, but he did not continue to maintain his preference for mind over matter and for liberty over determinism. His sympathy for the people led him first to break off writing his *History of France* and plunge into the history of the Revolution; after which, in *The People*, he renounced many of his earlier convictions. In that work he in fact proclaimed his attachment to very different values. The artificial, the intellectual, the civilized, which he had favored earlier, square poorly with his praise for the instinctive, spontaneous, unreflective people—a people ever so superior to the drawing-room philosophers.

Geographical determinism, whose previous role had been quite modest, now serves to explain the differences between nations. Finally, racial mixing, earlier a source of progress, no longer seems to be held in esteem; from this point on, Michelet believes, like any consistent nationalist, that "if fortune changes, so much the better; but let nature remain" (*The People*, p. 118). Interactions and borrowings are henceforth condemned. "You take from a neighboring people this or that which is a living thing among them, and you place it on yourselves no matter what, in spite of the repugnance of a frame that was not made for it. But it is a foreign body that you are grafting to your flesh, an inert, lifeless thing. It is death that you are adopting" (p. 186). The Romantic has gotten the upper hand over the heir to the Enlightenment.

But over and beyond Michelet's personal evolution and the question of the opposition between the two texts, there remains a problem even within the theory presented in the *Introduction à l'histoire universelle*. France is applauded to the extent that it has distanced itself from the physical factors that originally defined it. As Michelet says, "France is not a race, like Germany; it is a nation" (*Introduction*, p. 253). This means, as we now know, that human freedom and will have won out over the fatality of natural causes. The defining characteristic of a nation (and France is the nation par excellence) is that it has created itself, by a "work of self on self," an effort of self-engenderment. "France has made France . . . It is the daughter of its own freedom" (*Histoire de France*, "Préface de 1869," p. 13). The raw materials count for nothing. The only thing that counts is the work that goes into fashioning them; thus, the only thing that counts is the nation's history. "An acorn is a little thing compared to the gigantic oak, which is sprung from it. Well may it be proud, that living oak, which has cultivated, which has made and makes itself" (*History of France*, I, 4, p. 68). In this, France is simply exemplifying the fate of all humanity: "Man is his own Prometheus" ("Préface," p. 13). But if emancipation from determinism is the distinctive feature of the French, there is no longer any guarantee that the French will act in one way rather than another, since they are, precisely, free—or, in any event, freer than others. Now this is a consequence that Michelet obviously does not want to contemplate. If his reasoning were to be pursued, no common characteristics whatsoever could be attributed to the French: freedom does not really count, since freedom is precisely the absence of all constraint. Michelet believes, on the contrary, in the decisive determinism of shared membership in the nation: all French people benefit from the advantages pertaining to France. In other words, even if, in its content, a nation is not identical to a race (the latter is a biological entity, the former historical), the two are one in terms of their role, that of determining individual behavior. Just as he sought to prove superiority through equality, Michelet is now seeking to produce determinism on the basis of liberty itself.

Good and Bad Nationalism

Michelet would like to profess a humanitarian and egalitarian nationalism, which is a contradiction in terms. We may assume that his practice leads him to betray one or the other of those two terms, but which one?

The image that Michelet seeks to give of France belongs, we discover, to the purest ethnocentric tradition, which consists in attributing superlative qualifications to one's own group, without attempting to justify them. We have already seen—and Michelet repeats it in *The People*—that "This nation is above all others a *true society*" (p. 8, note 2). "Endeavor to grasp for once the meaning of these words,—*Organic Unity*. It is the unity of one nation,—of France" (*France before Europe*, p. 97). But France is also an exceptional nation, since "she sees in the darkest night when others see nothing" (*The People*, p. 189). To tell the truth, France is in fact unique in every respect. "Who has a literature [that] still sways the mind of Europe? We do, weak as we are. Who has an army? We alone" (p. 20). Likewise as far as the country's history is concerned: "No other people has anything like it . . . Every other history is mutilated: ours alone is complete" (p. 191). And as for legends, only the French ones are of good quality: "It would be very easy for me to show that the other nations have only peculiar legends, which the world has not accepted" (p. 192). And which, finally, is the most magnanimous of nations? "I have read many histories. But I have never read of so brave, yet humane a revolution, so generous towards its barbarous enemies, and shewing such clemency even to treason" (*France before Europe*, preface to the second edition, p. xxiii). No topic has given rise to a greater profusion of ineptitudes than national pride.

As for the way other nations are represented, this does not take us far from the xenophobic clichés we encounter everywhere. The Russians are "barbarous masses" (*France before Europe*, preface to the first edition, p. viii), in the grip, we shall not be astonished to learn, of a "barbaric joy" (p. vii), and what we hear from them is "a concert of wild beasts" (p. ix); in short, Russia is nothing but a "monster" (p. 85). Speaking of the Germans, Michelet says in *The People* (1846): "As for books in German, who reads them except the Germans?" (p. 6). After the Franco-Prussian war, intellectual condescension persisted, and Michelet evokes "the smoke-distorted visions which fill a German brain between his stove, his tobacco, and his beer" (*France before Europe*, p. 29). But hatred is added to the mix: "This absolute faithfulness [which characterizes Germans] . . . is a barbaric virtue" (p. 33); "the inherent barbarism of their race, hitherto latent, has revealed itself" (p. 67). Here we can pick up an echo of the *Introduction à l'histoire universelle*); in short, "the hour of the savage beast" has arrived (*La France devant l'Europe*, p. 577). There is not much difference, finally, between Germans and Russians. And let no one suggest that the French were guilty of starting the war; this war was in fact only the response to a different war, started by the Germans.

The other nations come off almost as badly. "We are not Italy, thank God" (*The People*, p. 8). England is a weak, bloated giant (p. 20). The Jews, a landless people, are an eternal threat, sowing terror everywhere by means of banking and usury (here Michelet manifests his solidarity with the anti-Semitic pamphlet of the Fourrierist Toussenel): "The Jews, whatever be said of them, have a country—the London Stock Exchange; they operate everywhere, but they are rooted in the country of gold" (p. 93, note 1). And if France has had some misfortunes in spite of everything, its foreign ministers are surely at fault (pp. 28–29).

In practice, Michelet's nationalism is thus much more conventional than his theory might have suggested. He becomes lucid with respect to nationalism only when that of others is in question. German nationalism, as he describes it, is not very different in its aims from French nationalism, however: it is the aspiration to make Germany's own defining characteristics universal. "All people have these moments [of divine delirium], and then they are blind . . . At such moments in the unity of one's country one would embrace the unity of the world. So Italy and Germany, through Rome and the Holy Empire, in their dreams absorbed all" (*France before Europe*, p. 9). But when he is talking about others, Michelet knows that this dream proceeds from blindness and has harmful results. "Drunkenness leads to wickedness" (p. 10).

And the final product of these exacerbated nationalisms can only be hatred between peoples: "M. de Bismarck takes the ground that between France and Germany, an eternal hatred will ever subsist, and that all good policy must always be grounded on that fact" (p. 11).

In his own dreams, Michelet wanted love of country to serve as a springboard to love of humanity, refusing to see that the two are not only not connected—they are incompatible. In the reality of history, he discovers that nationalism leads to war, hatred, and suffering. But is he aware that that devastating effect is in part due to his own teaching? He never gives the slightest indication that he is.

Renan and Barrès

Freedom versus Determinism

Renan's thinking on the subject of nationhood may look, at first, like a simple adaptation of humanist philosophy—as found for example in Rousseau—to factual realities. However, as is always the case with Renan, his thinking undergoes a series of inflections along the way that modify its direction profoundly.

Renan states that he does not believe in an integral national determinism. Before giving serious thought to the question (prior to the war of 1871), he had confined himself to more traditional views, to be sure. "Peoples do not exist except insofar as they are natural groups formed by the approximate community of race and language, the community of history, the community of interests" (preface to *Questions contemporaines* [Contemporary Questions], p. 2). Thus, it was against his own earlier ideas as much as against those of his contemporaries that he spoke out in 1878, in a talk entitled "Des Services rendus aux sciences historiques par la philologie." In this text, Renan opposes all efforts to reduce human behavior to the various external causes that put pressure on man. "Above language and race—even above geography, natural frontiers, divisions resulting from differences in religious beliefs and practices—there is something that we place above all of these: the respect for man viewed as a moral being" (p. 1231). Individual will is more important than anything else. "Man, Gentlemen, belongs neither to his language nor to his race; he belongs to himself above all, for he is above all else a free and moral being" (p. 1232). Will is thus a principle that triumphs over the reign of necessity.

Given that Renan is such a faithful disciple of Enlightenment philosophy, it is not surprising to find him capable of recognizing the
opposition between man and citizen, between humanism and patriotism. "With the collection of those qualities which constitute what is
called *a great nation*, one would make a most detestable individual," says
one of the characters in his "philosophical drama," "Le Prêtre de
Némi" (*The Priest of Nemi*, p. 56); and another character illustrates this
idea with the most telling example of all, that of war: "Real virtues
become disadvantageous in war. Those virtues which we call warlike
are all either faults or vices" (p. 64). In his "Lettre à M. Strauss" [Letter
to M. Strauss], Renan had already written the following: "War is a
tissue of sins, a state contrary to nature, in which we are told to carry
out certain actions deemed praiseworthy that at any other point we
would be ordered to avoid as vices or faults" (p. 447). After which,
Renan does not hesitate to valorize humanism at the expense of patriotism. It is in support for the idea of universal man that he discovers—
rightly—the characteristic feature of modern philosophy. "The idea of
humanity is the grand line of demarcation between the ancient and the
new philosophies" (*The Future of Science*, p. 161).

Thus, he indignantly rejects Joseph de Maistre's famous statement—
"'I know Frenchmen, Englishmen, Germans,' he says; 'I do not know
men'" (p. 473, n. 79)—interpreting it as an attack on the abstract idea
of humanity. "We outsiders are under the impression that the aim of
nature is enlightened man, be he French, English, or German" (ibid.;
de Maistre's formula, to which we shall return, is from *Considérations
sur la France*, [Considerations Concerning France], VI, p. 64). What is
common to men is precisely, over and above their divergent material
conditions, a common moral conscience. "All men bear within them
the same principles of morality" (*The Future of Science*, p. 318). "Beyond
anthropological characteristics, there are reason, justice, truth, and
beauty; and these are the same in all" ("What Is a Nation?" p. 74). The
nationalist's pride, on the other hand, is nothing but ethnocentric
prejudice, an error in perspective. "Can you believe that your country
has a particular excellence, when all the patriots of whatever nation in
the world are just as blindly convinced that their country has the same
advantage? But what is patriotism in you, you term prejudice and
bigotry in the others. You must be blind as a mole not to see that they
will pass the same judgment upon you" (*Caliban*, pp. 26–27).

If one must choose, consequently, between French identity and human identity, there is no room for hesitation. Speaking of himself, Renan rejects what he calls "exaggerated patriotism," and espouses a motto that, according to Rousseau, any consistent nationalist would have to reject: "Where I see good, beauty, truth, there is my country" ("Lettre à M. Strauss," p. 443). The reasons for this choice are clear: "Man is a reasonable and moral being before being allotted to such and such a language, before being a member of such and such a race, an adherent of such and such a culture. Before French culture, German culture, Italian culture, there is human culture" ("What Is a Nation?" p. 77). Nationalism cannot have anything but provisional usefulness, when it coincides with a higher aspiration. "We only appeal to the principle of nationality when the nation oppressed is superior intellectually to that which oppresses her. The absolute partisans of nationality can only be narrow-minded people. Humanitarian perfection is the aim" (*The Future of Science*, pp. 63–64).

The nation has only relative and historical value. Nations are good when they are at the service of freedom, bad when they favor tyranny, whereas the principles of morality are absolute (Renan is prepared to abandon his relativism here). "The great common interests . . . are, after all, those of reason and civilization" ("Lettre à M. Strauss," p. 446). Nationalist passions have played a major role in the nineteenth century, but this is a transitory phenomenon, and Renan thinks he can already make out the premonitory signs of its decline. The reason for this is the expansion of the same philosophy that places man at the center of the universe: "The nation lives by virtue of the sacrifices individuals make to it; ever-increasing egocentrism will find unbearable the requirements of a metaphysical entity that is no one in particular, of a patriotism that entails more than one prejudice, more than one error. Thus, we shall witness throughout Europe the weakening of the national spirit which made such a forceful appearance in the world eighty years ago" (preface to *Mélanges d'histoire et de voyages* [Miscellany: History and Travel], p. 314). "The terrible harshness of the proceedings by which the ancient monarchial States obtained the sacrifice of the individual will have become impossible in free States . . . In fact, it has become too clear that the happiness of the individual is not in direct proportion to the grandeur of the nation to which he belongs" (*The Future of Science*, preface, p. xvii). Here Renan is reasoning like a pure individualist, for whom the social entity is only a hindrance; and he imagines modern men subject to the pleasure principle alone. In this

respect he rejoins Tocqueville, according to whom the taste for individual well-being is opposed to the national spirit; but unlike his predecessor, Renan unhesitatingly chooses the former over the latter.

The Nation as Will

Such is the Renan of ideals. But in 1871, as it happened, France
underwent a crushing defeat in the war against Prussia, and lost the
provinces of Alsace and Lorraine. Even if he was striving to be an
unbiased scholar, Renan remained a Frenchman. He reacted at once
by publishing "La Réforme intellectuelle et morale de la France," in
which he attributed responsibility for the defeat to the democratic and
individualist spirit that prevailed in France. But that solved only part
of the problem. Renan's thoughts on this subject, sketched out initially
in his letters to Strauss during the war and reformulated on several
later occasions, found their most definitive expression in 1882, in the
celebrated speech entitled "What Is a Nation?" In order to maintain
his attachment to Enlightenment values, and thus to the primacy of
will and liberty, without betraying his country at a painful moment,
Renan took the route of affirming that one belongs to a nation by the
exercise of one's free will alone. From this point on, one can be a
nationalist and a humanitarian at the same time in good conscience:
the national attachment is the proof of the triumph of the will—and
thus of what creates the unity and identity of humanity—over material
constraints. "A nation . . . is summed up . . . by a tangible fact—consent, the clearly expressed desire to live a common life. A nation's
existence is . . . a daily plebiscite" ("What Is a Nation?" p. 81). What
about the foreign countries Renan consigns to colonization? He does
not seem to recall them in this context, any more than his followers
will, when they find nothing to criticize in French imperialism. But we
now know that, for Renan, the races are not equal.

Renan was not the first, in France, to formulate this definition of
nationhood. The ideologues of the Revolution, for whom man was a
blank slate and human will all-powerful, had preceded him along the
same path. Sieyès saw the nation as "a legitimate, that is to say voluntary
and free, association" (*What Is the Third Estate?* p. 127); in his view,
legitimacy could arise only from the free exercise of the will. The
nation is thus conceived here as a political (rather than a cultural) entity,
although this conception is not thereby reduced to a new version of

patriotism, of preference for one's own at the expense of others. Artaud's alternative between political and cultural nationalism seems to have been abandoned. But does this view correspond to the way things really are? Do the concerted actions of a few individuals give birth to nations? Sieyès seems to believe this, and he even reproaches others for not seeing the issue clearly. He imagines human beings first wandering in solitude over the surface of the earth and then one day deciding to form a nation. "In the first period, we assume a fairly considerable number of isolated individuals who wish to unite; by this fact alone, they already constitute a nation: they enjoy all the rights of a nation" (p. 121). Let us skip over the image (a caricature of Rousseau?) of men as originally asocial; but can one say that any association at all is equivalent to a nation? Joseph de Maistre was right to reply, "No assembly of men whatever can create a nation" (*Considérations sur la France*, in English in *The Works of Joseph de Maistre*, p. 78). Nevertheless, Renan takes up this very idea. Like Michelet, he distinguishes nation from race—the first is to the second what freedom is to determinism—and does not hide his preference for the first. Now one cannot base nationhood on race (multiracial states exist) any more than on other physical factors or factors that are simply independent of individual will, as we have just seen. "A nation is . . . a spiritual principle" ("What Is a Nation?" p. 80). What does that mean? This principle is nothing but the expression of the free will of individuals, their agreement to live together. "The will of nations is then the only legitimate criterion; and to it we must always return" (p. 82). If one chooses to use the past as a justification, one is condemned to an infinite regression, which leads to the absurd. "With this philosophy of history, there will be nothing legitimate in the world except the rights of orangutans, unjustly dispossessed by the treachery of civilized creatures" ("Nouvelle Lettre à M. Strauss," p. 454). As soon as we abandon the "healthy principle of free adherence" (preface to *Discours et conférences* [Speeches and Lectures], p. 720), we are paving the way for the worst evils. From here Renan readily takes the next step: not only must each individual be able to choose his own country freely, but the nation itself is nothing but the result of a free decision; it arises from "the right of populations to decide their own fate" (p. 721). For Renan, the right to national self-determination stems from the right of the individual to free choice.

This shift, in turn, poses problems. If my choice of where to live can in fact be considered as a case in which I have exercised my free will, and harmonizes in this way with humanist philosophy (Voltaire wrote, in *Annales de l'Empire*, "Man is born with a natural right to choose his own party"—*Annals of the Empire*, p. 214), it still does not follow that the nation is simply the union of a few individuals who have expressed similar wishes, or that the legitimacy of the individual wish is perpetuated when that wish becomes collective. The individual has (or ought to have) the right to remain in the country where he was born, or else to emigrate; but what does it mean to say that he has the right to create a state? New nations are certainly not created through the mechanical multiplication of the desires of several individuals to choose their country freely. They are created by the action of a culturally homogeneous group that occupies a subordinate position in the existing state and that decides to seize the dominant position. Far from being the miraculous unison of individual free choices, the nation has to do with distribution of power within a state, sometimes implying a redistribution of the state's lands.

The right of populations to decide their own fate, and thus eventually to found a new state, raises yet another problem. Recognizing this right in fact implies that one is able to delimit with absolute certainty the contours of the "population" or the "people" in question. Now one cannot have it both ways: either such terms are camouflaged synonyms of "nation," and the affirmation, somewhat tautological, is that nations have the right to live as nations (but this supposes that the problem being addressed has been solved: the nation is a cultural *and* a political entity; so long as the political entity—the State—does not exist, there is no "nation"); or else the terms are understood in the sense of "homogeneous cultural entity" (such entities obviously exist prior to nations). But it is absurd to declare that each culturally homogeneous group has the *right* to establish a new State. Culture, in fact, is an entity with variable dimensions: one speaks of a culture by identifying a certain number of features with certain persons, and by discounting the divergent features; but the choice of level of generality is not at all automatic. One culture may be embedded in another and cultures also sometimes overlap: there exists a Western culture, a European culture, a Latin culture, a French culture, an Occitan culture—and the latter also has its own minorities, which in turn are made up of even smaller and more homogeneous groups. To say that any culture has the right to become autonomous in its own State is meaningful only if one has established the appropriate size for a State in advance; the issue would then be decided on political rather than cultural grounds.

But this is not how Renan manages to claim Alsace-Lorraine for France without abandoning his principles: according to all the other criteria—now repudiated—the Alsatians and the Lorrains may be closer to Germany; but their desire is to remain French. In this way, what is most human about men is valorized; finding one's justifications in assorted determinisms, or in history, amounts to privileging what men have in common with animals. In short, according to Renan, one has the choice between two ways of conceptualizing nations. One may think of a nation as if it were an animal species, and thus a race; the destiny of nations is then to give themselves over to merciless wars, "wars of extermination . . . analogous to those battles for life waged by the various species of rodents or carnivores" ("Nouvelle Lettre à M. Strauss" [New Letter to M. Strauss], p. 456). Now such an assimilation of men to animals, derived from social Darwinism, is not only immoral—it is also false, as is proved for example by the fact that "animal species do not team up against one another" ("La Guerre entre la France et l'Allemagne" [The War between France and Germany], pp. 434–435). The alternative is to define the nation as the voluntary consent of its subjects, in which case a new international horizon opens up, no longer that of war but of federation between adjacent and complementary nations: Renan is already dreaming of a United States of Europe that will be able to stand up to the American and Russian giants, and that will be at the same time the triumph of reason.

There would be nothing to criticize in such a program if it did not remain a purely intellectual approach to the problem. Even discounting the logical and ethical difficulties that are posed by the passage from individual expression to the collective will, no nation has ever been created on the strength of deliberation alone. In Sieyès' wake, Renan dismisses the problem; he does not resolve it. And yet he knows perfectly well that an individual decision does not suffice to make someone French, in the full sense of the term, from one day to the next; it suffices still less to create the French nation. He thus decides to add a second criterion to the first: paradoxically, this is the existence of a past common to the members of the nation—the very past that Renan up to this point has been endeavoring to present as irrelevant. "Man does not improvise. The nation, like the individual, is the outcome of a long past of efforts, and sacrifices, and devotion. Ancestor-worship is therefore all the more legitimate; for our ancestors have made us what we are. A heroic past, great men, glory,—I mean glory of the genuine kind,—these form the social capital, upon which a national idea may be founded" ("What Is a Nation?" pp. 80–81). Our judgments themselves are determined by our past: "We love in proportion to the sacrifices we have consented to make, to the sufferings we have endured. We love the house that we have built, and will hand down to our descendants" (p. 81). And when he has to describe himself, Renan cannot help recalling the ancestors who are speaking through him: "They led . . . for thirteen hundred years an obscure existence, storing up sensations and thoughts the capital of which has devolved upon me. I can feel that I think for them and that they live again in me" (*Recollections of My Youth*, pp. 81–82).

But the cohabitation of these two "criteria" is obviously problematic. If man does not improvise himself, if he is determined by his past, if it is his ancestors who are expressing themselves through him, can one still speak of his entrance into the nation as an act of free adherence, an exercise of free will? If our ancestors have made us what we are, can we still hold the individual responsible for his acts, can we make him answer to moral requirements? And if I love my home not because it is a good one but because it is mine, can I still claim that patriotism is governed by universalism? Following some necessary adjustments of his doctrine, Renan here rejoins the scientistic position that he defended elsewhere, leaving no more room for ethics or individual freedom. The political criterion (free will) avoids the dangers of patriotism; but the cultural criterion (the common past) is, on the contrary, interpreted in an egocentric manner, rather in the fashion of Diderot's character: my house is the best one of all. That does not prevent Renan from presenting the two "criteria" of the nation as being harmoniously united. A nation, he writes, is constituted "by the feeling on the part of its people that they have done great things together in the past and that they have the will to do more in the future" ("Des Services rendus," p. 1232). Now the past is determinism and the future freedom: can one claim that what is at issue here is one and the same thing? Which of the two takes precedence in case of conflict? One feels that Renan, as he himself says, would like to privilege the living at the expense of the dead (unlike Barrès, as we shall see); but his "realism" prevents him from finding any consistency.

There is nevertheless a measure of truth in each of Renan's assertions. The common past is relevant to the discussion, as is the will for the future. Where exactly does the argument break down? If there is a contradiction when each "criterion" is justified in itself, it is that Renan, who has avoided reducing "civic" nationalism to patriotism, does not manage to untangle another aspect of nationhood: he does not distinguish between its political and cultural components, and he interprets the "cultural" in a patriotic sense.

Political Nation, Cultural Nation

We have already noted a similar confusion in Michelet's case. Even while clinging fundamentally to the political sense of the word "nation," Michelet formulated a certain number of statements that could only be applied to the nation understood as a culture. The nation, he said, needs to recognize itself within a certain geographical framework, in certain rivers, certain hills. He thought his predecessors had not taken this factor sufficiently into account. The earth, he wrote in his *Histoire de France*, "is not only the theatre of action. Through food, climate, and so on, it influences the action in a hundred ways. Like nest, like bird. Like fatherland, like man" ("Préface de 1869," p. 13). Or, in another passage: "Like land, like race" (*History of France*, I, 4, p. 74, note). Similarly, a nation must be able to refer to its own past, for place and past become features shared by all its inhabitants and constitute their national identity. These formulas must not be understood in an overly deterministic sense; it is enough to tell oneself that the nation can satisfy its needs "in defining itself, in carving for [itself] a piece of time and space, and in feeding on something of its own in the midst of indifferent and dissolving nature, which always wishes to mix things together" (*The People*, p. 180). The spirit will limit itself in order to grow deeper. The nation is "a living education" (p. 181); it teaches us a particular way of relating to the world. Nations will always be needed, much as thought has always needed language (here is the tradition of Montesquieu).

Thus, whereas love of nation in the political sense can lead only exceptionally to love of humanity, knowledge of the particular does lead to knowledge of the general; or rather there is no fruitful means of access to the universal except by way of the particular. "The more man advances, the more he enters into the spirit of his country and the better he contributes to the harmony of the globe" (p. 181). The world

in turn can exist only owing to the multiplicity of cultures that constitute it; it would be immobilized if there were no longer the friction
produced by diversity. "If the impossible occurred and diversities were
to disappear, if unity were established with every nation singing the
same note, then the concert would be at an end . . . The world,
monotonous and barbarous, might then perish without even causing a
regret" (p. 181). Here Michelet is arguing against the scientistic universalists (the tradition of Condorcet) while managing not to fall back
into patriotic exaltation.

We find a variation on this theme in Renan, who was a devoted
reader of Michelet. It is no longer to the nation as political entity but
to the nation as culture that he is referring when he writes: "Each
nation, with its temples, its divinities, its poesy, its heroic traditions, its
fantastic beliefs, its laws and its institutions represents a unity, a way of
its own of taking life, a separate tone in humanity, a distinctive faculty
of the great soul" (*The Future of Science*, p. 163). And, like Michelet, he
thinks that the absence of difference signifies death: "Uniformity
would, as things now are, be the extinction of humanity" (p. 382).
Moreover, he even picks up the concert metaphor: "By their diverse
and often antagonistic faculties, the nations take part in the common
work of civilisation; each brings a note to that great chorus of humanity,
which in sum is the highest ideal reality to which we attain" ("What Is
a Nation?" p. 82).

When Renan says that the nation is an affair of will, he is placing
himself on political ground. And he is right, provided that he limits
himself to individuals and does not extend the formula to groups. In
fact, nothing prevents me, in the abstract, from leaving my country of
origin and adopting another; if I have done so, I am not required to
have grown up in this very spot, or to share the memories of my new
fellow citizens. But nationality that is acquired on the political level by
the power of a simple decree requires long years of apprenticeship on
the cultural level. From the perspective of nation as culture, it is in fact
essential to have a common past, or rather a common knowledge about
this past (which also means sharing a certain forgetfulness, as Renan
points out)—and also knowledge of place: a culture is learned like a
language. To say, as Renan does, that there is a "human culture" *before*
there is French or German culture is to play on the double sense of
the word "culture," which is both descriptive and prescriptive, anthropological and educational: culture (in the sense familiar to Renan,

culture as a set of characteristics and behaviors) is always particular, even if certain characteristics common to the entire species make the species well-suited for the acquisition of cultures.

But we are now familiar with Renan's ideas about cultures (or "linguistic races," or "historical races"), and in particular we have seen to what extent, for Renan, belonging to a culture inhibits the free exercise of will. The same gesture is repeated in both contexts: in his theory of races, Renan also began, as we saw, with the radical opposition between (physical) race and nation; then, as if struck by remorse, he introduced the mediating concept of "linguistic race"—that is, approximately, of culture. What Renan gives with one hand (freedom—within a nation) he takes away with the other (determinism—within a culture): such is the effect produced by the amalgam between culture and politics.

A Tendentious Disciple

It may be useful to say a few words here about one of nationalism's most famous spokesmen, Maurice Barrès, who identified himself, during part of his life at least, with that passion. "For my part, only one thing interests me, and that is nationalist doctrine," he writes in *Scènes et doctrines du nationalisme* (I, p. 71). The importance of Barrès' nationalism nevertheless stems from the influence it exercised much more than from the originality of his ideas: Barrès is in fact at once a docile and a tendentious disciple of Renan and (especially) Taine.

Like Michelet and Renan, Barrès knows that races no longer exist, that France is a nation. "We are definitely not a race but a nation" (I, p. 20). But unlike his predecessors, he regrets this state of affairs. "Alas! There is no French race, but a French people, a French nation" (I, p. 85). "What is a nation?" Renan asked himself in 1882, and he replied: a cult of ancestors and "the will to preserve worthily the undivided inheritance which has been handed down" ("What Is a Nation?" p. 80). "What is a nation?" Barrès asks, and, faithful disciple that he is, he replies (though without attribution): "A nation is the shared possession of an ancient cemetery and the will to continue to maintain the prominence of that undivided heritage" (*Scènes*, I, p. 114). However, unlike Renan, Barrès places the full weight of his assertion on the determinist side of the formula—that is, on the common past.

What counts for a nation, in Barrès' favorite formula, are its Land and its Dead. Or, in nonmetaphoric language: "Everything we are arises from the historical and geographical conditions of our country" (I, p. 132). This twofold determination comes from Taine, who had insisted on the role of race and environment; Barrès writes that Taine "sought the characteristics of the national house that nature and history have built for us" (I, p. 84). Nature and history: here is yet another translation of the Land and the Dead. In practice, Barrès pays little heed to the influence of the geographical milieu; he concentrates on the determining role of the past. This historical determinism is perceived in turn as both natural and cultural: it acts as much through the blood that flows in our veins as through the education received in our "early youth when we are as malleable as soft wax" (I, p. 45); which leads Barrès to declare: "With a professorial chair and a cemetery, we have the essence of a fatherland" (I, p. 45). "A common language, shared legends—this is what constitutes nationalities," Barrès also asserts (II, p. 203). Now languages, like legends, are learned in childhood. But of course nature is stronger than culture, and one cannot change one's nationality at will: "If I were to be naturalized as a Chinese and conform scrupulously to the prescriptions of Chinese law, I would not stop forming French ideas and associating them in French" (I, pp. 43–44). Barrès thus constantly manipulates the metaphor of blood, and his "nations" hardly differ from the "races" of his contemporaries.

Barrès borrowed from Taine not only the subdivision between the Land and the Dead, but also the determinist principle itself. "The historical sense, the lofty naturalist feeling, the acceptance of a determinism—this is what we mean by nationalism" (II, p. 52). The nationalist feeling thus consists in saying that an individual is entirely determined in his acts by the nation to which he belongs. Whence, once again, the frequent comparison with the vegetable world, and the endlessly repeated metaphor of rooting or uprooting: the soil determines the plant, the nation determines the individual, an uprooted plant dies, an individual without a country withers. "My tree needs to be cultivated with care so it will be able to bear me aloft, a fragile little leaf like me" (I, p. 132). But is there really no difference between a man and a plane tree? To judge by his interpretations of individual behavior, Barrès leans toward a negative response. "That Dreyfus is capable of betrayal, I conclude from his race" (I, p. 161). "What is M. Emile Zola? I am looking at his roots: this man is not a Frenchman" (I, p. 43). "An opposition cannot count on Gallieni. He is an Italian, a calculator" (II, p. 111).

The individual being is wholly ruled by external factors. The dead act through the living. Barrès borrows this theme from Renan and, beyond him, from all those in France who believe in the primacy of the social over the individual, whether they are "progressists" like Comte or conservatives like de Maistre. "There is not even freedom of thought. I can live only according to my dead" (I, p. 12). The very notion of the individual originates in blindness: "More and more disgusted with individuals, I am inclined to believe that we are automatons" (I, p. 118).

Collective forces dominate the individual. The collectivity par excellence is the nation, but it is not the only one; that is why Barrès, unlike Michelet, readily welcomes regionalism, as an application of his nationalist principle on a smaller scale. "To national feeling do not hesitate to add local feeling . . . One will never love one's country so much as if one enters into contact with it, by belonging to a region, a city, an association" (I, p. 79). And if the nation and the region are in conflict? Barrès does not raise that question; he postulates their necessary harmony. "The French nationality is made up of provincial nationalities" (I, p. 80). He even goes so far as to invent the paradoxical notion of decentralized centralism: "We shall multiply points of centralization throughout the territory" (ibid.). The logic may be shaky, but Barrès is intent upon ensuring the support of regionalists, who like himself are determinists and conservatives; he chooses to ignore the conflict, which Michelet had clearly identified, between the nation and all the smaller groups: families, corporations, regions.

The result, in Barrès, is a constant critique of individualism: he sees the individualist view of man as false in a first phase, harmful in a second, for it hinders the natural course of history. "Our deep misfortune is to be divided . . . by a thousand individual imaginations. We are splintered" (I, p. 85). The remedy is obviously a reinforcement of the social bond; it is "to substitute for the present individualist disorder a *social* organization of work" (II, p. 159). Here again, Barrès prolongs—perhaps unwittingly—the tradition of French social thinkers. He readily identifies himself as a "socialist" (but, as we saw with regard to Tocqueville, "societist" would be a more appropriate term: what is involved is the priority of group over individual). Socialism and nationalism are thus occasionally synonymous for Barrès: "I never hesitate to insist on the union of the socialist idea and the nationalist idea" (II, p. 53). This "societism," which requires protection of the national group, is opposed to "absolute liberalism" based on "laissez-faire" and "laissez-passer" (II, p. 158).

For Barrès, intellectuals are the embodiment of the individualist ideology. As a general rule, they are cut off from life; they reason as logicians about a subject matter arising from the vicissitudes of history rather than from the laws of reason (this is yet another echo of Taine's attacks against the classical spirit and Jacobinism). But intellectuals are also, more specifically, people who believe in individual freedom. Barrès for his part takes his determinism to the point of deeming it necessary to abandon the very idea of an ideal distinct from reality that might serve as stimulus to the desire to change that reality. "We are determined to take as our point of departure what is and not some ideal in our mind" (I, p. 87). He does not seem to notice the contradiction inherent in his plan: since everything that exists is supposed to exist, it is illogical to resist revolutionaries, volontarists, or activists: they all exist just as fatalists do. Whoever says "plan" and "political action" (and Barrès is a politician who drafts plans) has already accepted the possibility of modifying the world in view of an ideal.

By dint of practicing determinism, Barrès thus ends up with pure conservatism: any change is bad. "Our national character (and this matters very much to me) will be the better maintained to the extent that the conditions in which we live continue to resemble the ones that formed our ancestors" (I, p. 129). It is enough for Barrès to note that something *is*, in order to conclude at once that it ought to be: such is the logic of conservatism. Thus, one of the great arguments in favor of nations is precisely their contemporary importance. The classical and medieval periods were cosmopolitan, whereas the modern period is nationalist; that proves it should remain so. "Evolution toward nationalism has come about over the centuries" (II, p. 173). It suffices to look around to note that, everywhere in Europe, nationalism is being reinforced. "Nationalism is the law that dominates the organization of modern peoples, and at this moment you see that in all of Europe measures of national protection are being studied" (II, p. 204). What better argument can be found to demand that this protection be carried a little further? Barrès is in fact playing here on the two meanings of "nationalism." It is true that nationalism, as an aspiration to fuse a cultural and a political entity, is a specifically modern phenomenon. That in no way justifies the doctrine that advocates that "we" be privileged and the "others" mistreated.

Barrès is thus opposed to all reformers, not to mention revolutionaries. This brings him to reject not only the activism of the "left," that
of Jaurès and the socialists, but also, significantly, that of the "right,"
represented by Maurras and the Action Française. Addressing Jaurès,
he exclaims: "You would prefer that the phenomena of heredity did not
exist, that the blood of men and the soil of the land had no impact,
that the species were in harmony and frontiers were gone. What are
your preferences worth against necessities?" (II, p. 174). Barrès does
not even discuss the value of the Jaurèsian ideal: it is an ideal, and that
suffices to discredit it. But his reply to Maurras is not finally very
different: when Maurras invites him to come militate in favor of a
restoration of the monarchy in France, Barrès replies that there are not
many royalists in France, that there is no real aristocracy, that the
Revolution and the Republic are accomplished facts. Rather than modifying the real in the name of an ideal, one must adapt the ideal to the
real—that is, abolish the ideal. "Being unable to get what appears
reasonable to you accepted by all, why do you not try to make what
the majority accepts reasonable?" ("Lettre à Maurras," p. 3). At bottom,
Barrès suggests, Maurras is inconsistent: he wants to impose conservatism by revolution, whereas with Jaurès there is continuity between
means and ends. But the two have common ground in voluntarism,
activism, and artificialism, all of which Barrès vehemently rejects.

All the features of Barrès' nationalism are borrowed from other
ideologues of his century. He inherits his determinism from Taine, his
"societism" from Comte or de Maistre, his conservatism also from
Taine or de Maistre; Renan's formulations are never quite forgotten
either. But the combination is new, and Barrès thus becomes the first
important spokesperson for conservative nationalism—although he
does not condemn the Revolution or militate in favor of reestablishing
the monarchy, as his contemporary Charles Maurras will do at the head
of Action Française.

Péguy

Justice and War

In the years immediately preceding World War I, Charles Péguy undertook to base his nationalism, and in particular his support of France's
claim to the provinces of Alsace and Lorraine, on the doctrine of the

rights of man. How could this be? This is the question one wants to ask when one knows that Péguy formulated the following requirement with respect to the texts he himself was reading: "What I require of doctrines, systems, parties, is above all that they be consistent—that is, that they hold together" (*L'Argent suite* [Money: Sequel], pp. 137–138). Here is an initial response: Péguy brought this off by conjoining an ethical principle with an analysis of world history (or rather a hypothesis about the nature of human affairs).

The ethical principle that was Péguy's starting point is best seen at work in his condemnation of pacifism. Pacifism, or the preference for peace above all other values, he declares, is contrary to a system of thought based on justice: the defense of peace is nothing but an exclusive attachment to the preservation of life. "It is a well-known system, one that has always been called the system of peace at any price. It is a scale of values in which honor is held less dear than life" (p. 143). Péguy thus develops an opposition between two "systems," which he calls the "peace" system and the "rights of man" system. "The idea of peace at any price . . . , the central idea of pacifism . . . , is that peace is an absolute, . . . that peace with injustice is better than war for justice. This is diametrically opposed to the system of the rights of man, in which a war for justice is better than peace with injustice" (p. 150). It is thus illegitimate to demand peace in the name of the rights of man. "It is folly to seek to connect pacifism with the Republic and the Revolution and the rights of man. Nothing is more contrary" (p. 145).

Péguy has a tendency to confuse several different realities under a single label. On the one hand, he uses the expressions "rights of man" and "honor" as if they were synonymous, whereas the meaning of the former goes back no further than the Revolution, while the latter evokes the value system of the Old Regime above all. On the other hand, Péguy claims to believe that "peace at any price" is a univocal expression, whereas it can be seen to have at least two meanings, one equivalent to the formula "Better red than dead," and the other to "Thou shalt not kill" (the reluctance to die and the reluctance to kill, in Simone Weil's terms). In fact, declaring my own life sacred and declaring someone else's life sacred are not the same thing; refusing to *submit* to death is different from refusing to *inflict* it. Péguy clearly reckons only with the first interpretation, in which one gives up everything rather than risk one's own life; he never considers the second possibility, although it corresponds better to pacifist philosophy: according to this second interpretation, I can put my own life in danger in the name of an ideal cause (militant pacifists do sometimes get killed, as we know), but I refuse to serve that cause by killing.

Péguy's recriminations are thus justified only if we confuse honor with the rights of man, on the one hand, and conflate "Thou shalt not kill" with "Better red than dead," on the other. "Order (I mean material order) has infinite value in the *peace* system. And rights have infinite value in the *rights of man* system" (p. 152). But, even in this case, from an accurate assertion Péguy immediately draws extreme consequences. From the fact that peace is not the supreme value, he seems to deduce that war, its opposite, *is* the supreme value; he thus confuses contraries and contradictories, by postulating that whatever is not peace is war. More precisely, he equates war with justice, considering that a preference for justice leads inevitably to war (since efforts will be made to impose justice). "One must be what is politely called a dolt or, less politely, an imbecile to believe that one can present and seek to introduce any justice whatsoever, any point of justice on the surface of the earth, without giving rise, at the same time, by the same token, indissociably, to a point of war" (p. 146). "Justice does not make peace; it makes war. And justice is not often produced by war, but it is still less often produced by life" (p. 164).

The Declaration of the Rights of Man, more particularly, is nothing but a charter for preparation for war: with this conviction, Péguy is a faithful disciple of Anacharsis Cloots. "What folly to seek to link a declaration of peace to the Declaration of the Rights of Man. As if a declaration of justice were not in itself and instantaneously a declaration of war" (p. 147). "There is in the Declaration of the Rights of Man . . . the basis for waging war on everyone until the end of time" (p. 149).

But is it true that every demand for justice means war? To ask the question differently, is there no middle course between peace at any price and war at any price? Is there no way but war to try to bring an ideal into reality? Péguy declares in fact that "the temporal is essentially military" (p. 92), that everything else boils down to this: he perceives "money itself as a military power" (p. 93). He clearly does not have much use for all the nuances that make for distinctions among various forms of action on behalf of a goal, particularly between commerce and warfare (the same thing was true for Tocqueville). The end alone counts, for Péguy, in establishing the identity of an action; the means are irrelevant. It could be objected that what lies outside the "peace system" is called struggle, and that not every struggle is war, nor is every change an instance of violence; Gandhi's example (albeit unknown to Péguy) comes readily to mind and keeps us from implementing that amalgam: Gandhi refused to put others' lives in danger but did not hesitate to risk his own. In the same context we might also evoke the struggle of women (the "suffragettes") to obtain the right to vote, in Péguy's own day: a struggle, undeniably, but one that did not cost a single life. The rightness of the cause is one thing; the equivalence of any and all means for achieving it is quite another. These are commonplace truths, but Péguy appears to overlook them. In the course of history, humanity has seen all too many noble causes compromised by the means adopted to ensure their success.

Péguy evokes the problem of means and ends in his polemic against Pressensé, a pacifist who was president of the League for the Rights of Man. Pressensé is for justice, provided that it does not lead to war. Or, in Péguy's incisive but obviously tendentious presentation: "Pressensé is for justice against power when power is not powerful" (p. 143); in other words, he is afraid of the bad guys and abandons his principles as soon as he finds himself facing someone stronger than he is. But this is an outrageous oversimplification of the problem. First, one cannot overlook all differences between offensive and defensive wars, as Péguy would do—and as would the wholesale pacifism with which, paradoxically, he shares his presupposition. (The socialists, at whom his discourse is aimed, maintain the distinction, even if their practice does not always live up to their theory.) Offensive wars are to be condemned in principle. The fact that the cause for which one is fighting is proclaimed a just one does not mean much: special interests weigh too heavily in such cases for us to expect perfect clairvoyance. Most of the colonial wars waged by European countries had a higher justification in the eyes of those who started them: to propagate the Christian religion, which is naturally the best one of all, and to spread Western civilization, purported to be *civilization* pure and simple. The same holds true for exported revolutions: does the supposedly just cause for which the French Revolution was fought justify the Napoleonic Wars? Does the Russian Revolution justify Soviet expansionism?

We might assert without fear of contradiction that no human enterprise produces more victims than the one that consists in seeking to impose good on others. Even if we suppose genuine sincerity on the part of the people involved, and the real superiority of their cause, war generally has the result not of making that cause victorious but of annihilating it. Fraternity is certainly superior to slavery, but does the extermination of masters and slaves still constitute fraternity? In order to liberate, one must be prepared to kill, Péguy suggests; but one will not have led people to what is right and good if one has had to kill them first: corpses don't get much satisfaction from freedom. If, in order to "liberate" Alsace-Lorraine (assuming that the region has been subjugated and that French domination will bring about freedom's reign), the lives of the majority of the inhabitants of these provinces have to be sacrificed, then it is better not to go to war. Offensive war is the perfect example of a behavior in which the nature of the means cancels out the objectives, no matter how lofty the latter may be.

Furthermore, defensive war itself is no simple matter, not because defense is not legitimate—it is, and constitutes, in principle, a duty on the part of each citizen (including female citizens, once women have succeeded in gaining recognition as citizens)—but because the border-lines of the notion of "defense" are not easy to trace. Recent history supplies many test cases which boil down to matters of conscience. The Americans' landing in France, at the end of the Second World War, was after all a violation of the territorial integrity of a foreign country; if we justify it, we do so in the name of a principle other than legitimate defense. Was opposing the German invader during that war the same thing as attacking, several years later, the government that the invader had set up? For how long a time after a defeat can one still speak of legitimate defense? Could the Germans, obliged at the end of the Second World War to pull out of various eastern regions, invoke that principle today if they were to engage in combat? Or the Palestinians, expelled from the territory that became Israel? These are all questions that cannot be answered with reference to the principle of defense alone, but that require us to take into consideration the nature of the regime in each country, whether or not there has been a displacement of populations, the status of the population conquered, the length of the occupation, and so on.

All these considerations show that one cannot settle the question as Péguy did by declaring that all wars waged in the name of a just cause are good, without taking into account the various elements involved (any more than one can uniformly condemn all wars, as pacifists do). Such a distinction between offensive and defensive wars does not suffice in itself to forestall errors of judgment (the failure of the socialists in the face of the First World War would be proof enough, if proof were needed); but without such a distinction, the risks are even greater. Here we come to the second premise of Péguy's nationalist doctrine, which is not only an ethical principle (the superiority of justice over life) but also a hypothesis about the human condition; this premise thus has to do with truth and falsehood, as well as with good and evil. Péguy's reasoning can be broken down into three propositions, which he presents in a relation of rigorous implication: (1) Spiritual goods are the most precious thing in the world. (2) The spiritual cannot be imposed without the simultaneous imposition of the temporal. (3) The temporal is essentially military. However, the validity of each of these assertions can be questioned.

Let us begin with the third one. The truth of life is war, says Péguy in effect—and he is obviously not the only one who believes this. "It is the soldier who measures the temporal cradle" (p. 93). But he offers no argument in support of his assertion. For the argument he advances in *Notre Patrie*—namely, that the population loves anything military—cannot be taken seriously: not only is this hardly a proven fact, but even if it were proven, it would not establish the legitimacy of the requirement (the fact that a population supports the death penalty, for example, does not make the death penalty legitimate). It is certain that conflicts and wars have always existed; but are they alone in giving the measure of the temporal, in defining its essence? If by "political" we mean the defense of the interests of a group (including those of a nation), we might say that conflict is in the very nature of political activity: the concern I express in favor of one group can always lead to action against the interests of other groups. But the political does not coincide point for point with human life. Alongside and sometimes in the place of political concern, the human being is engaged on the one hand in an inner and private life, and on the other hand in a life in which he judges others not by virtue of their belonging to the same group, but by virtue of their common participation in humanity. Therein lies the principle of moral life. Now private life and moral life are no less real than political life.

The spiritual, Péguy continues, cannot be imposed without the temporal. "The military infrastructure is the temporal cradle in which mores and laws and arts and even religion and language and race can then, but only then, lie down in order to grow" (*L'Argent suite*, p. 92).

"It is the soldier who measures the amount of temporal ground that is *the same* as the spiritual ground and the intellectual ground" (p. 93). "The temporal constantly guards, and constantly governs, the spiritual" (p. 101). Péguy's metaphors are modeled on the content of his assertions. He is able to line up a few examples, of course—but we can easily imagine others that would point in the opposite direction. He himself evokes the example of the Jewish religion, only to set it aside at once ("this people is always and in everything an exception"—p. 98). Is the pope really powerless now that he has no more military divisions at his disposal? Have intellectual discoveries had to be backed up by weapons in order to spread? We have come a long way from Bossuet, according to whom "hands raised toward heaven bring down more battalions than hands armed with spears."

But even if it were true that the spiritual cannot be imposed without the temporal, and that the temporal is essentially military, the question would remain open: If the price of promoting the spiritual is war, is the game still worth the candle? Must we be prepared to sacrifice everything in favor of spirituality? Does one immortal page justify Verdun? Péguy says: "It is the French soldier and the cannon of '75 and temporal force that have marked off, that have measured, that are still measuring at each moment the amount of land where French is spoken" (p. 101). Suppose we grant this. It is certain that French writers feel frustrated to be addressing only forty million French speakers, rather than eighty million. But in the first place, souls won for the French language are so many souls lost for some other language, and there is thus, for humanity, no gain. (But is Péguy concerned about this?) And then, in order to accede to spirituality, is it really indispensable to understand French and to read French writers? Does not God, who speaks to Péguy, speak all languages? Finally, do laws and arts and religions warrant the immolation of human beings? As Las Casas said in the middle of the sixteenth century, "it would be a great disorder and a mortal sin to throw a child into a well to baptize him and save his soul, if he died of it." The right to life may not be situated at the pinnacle of spiritual values; but can one conclude from this that any sort of spiritual gain at all is worth the sacrifice of human life? We may be allowed to entertain doubts, moreover, as to Péguy's attachment to the works of the spirit, since we read in a letter to his friend Millerand, who had just been named minister of war: "May we have under you that war that has been our sole thought since 1905; not just have it, but wage it. I would give my complete works, past, present, future, and my four limbs to enter Weimar at the head of a good division."

Rights of Peoples and Territorial Unity

The bases for Péguy's argument are thus much more fragile than he would have us believe: he seldom avoids the pitfalls of extremist thought. Yet it is on these bases that he goes on to construct his nationalist doctrine, which he justifies in two ways. Let us take the example of Alsace-Lorraine. Its attachment to France, Péguy says, is doubly motivated: from the point of view of its inhabitants, it is justified by the right of peoples to self-determination; from the point of view of the French, it is justified by the need to keep the Republic one and indivisible. But are these two motivations legitimate in turn? And do they stand up together in that consistent way that Péguy demands of the systems of others?

Regarding the right of populations to self-determination, Péguy asserts that this right is based on the rights of man. "If there is a system in which the right of populations to determine their own fate is an absolute, and a primacy, and a given, immediate, it is surely the system of the Declaration of the Rights of Man" (p. 123); thus, one cannot decently both be president of the League for the Rights of Man and abandon Alsace-Lorraine, which is the case of his adversary Pressensé. In short, Péguy is making the same argument as Renan: human will is inalienable, freedom of choice is a natural human right, and self-determination is only an extension of this right to the level of the nation. But this extension is problematic, as we have seen. The rights of men are individual rights. What does it mean to talk about the rights of a people? Are we to conceive of peoples existing in advance, patiently awaiting their independence? Would every cultural group have the right to self-determination? At this rate, every village might want to secede, or even—why not?—every family.

From another standpoint, how does one manage to know the will of a people? Assuming that it is the will of the majority, the minority will have to yield; in so doing, its members, far from exercising their free will, will have to give it up. In practice, the demand for self-determi-nation can never be attributed to a people (it is rare that the majority of a population becomes passionately concerned about such abstract causes); it can be attributed only to a political group that is currently playing a subordinate role in the country and seeks to take on a different, dominant role. The real problem here is the problem of the protection of the rights of the individual, or individuals, if they turn out to belong to a subordinated minority. The solution is not the nation-state, but the State of justice, which prevents the individual from being penalized simply because her culture is different. Any identification of the State with one particular cultural group clearly signifies the oppression of other groups ("minorities"). The definition of the "people" through the popular will alone also raises considerable difficulties, as we have seen. We may wonder whether such an appeal to the "right of the peoples" can be anything but demagogy. That is what Tocqueville thought it was, in any case: "'The will of the nation' is one of the phrases most generally abused by intriguers and despots of every age" (*Democracy in America*, I, part I, ch. 4, p. 51).

The Declaration of the Rights of Man does not mention the rights of peoples. The spirit of the declaration does require, rather, a good balance between justice and freedom—that is, the application of certain universal principles, and not the label "France" or "Germany" that may be attached to this agenda. But by its constant reference to "man and citizen," as if their convergence were taken for granted, the declaration does its part to help maintain the confusion. Now the interest of the nation coincides neither with that of humanity nor with that of the individual. Péguy is right to denounce the inconsistency of the humanitarians who, in his day, use the principles of self-determination to justify their support of the cause of certain peoples but refuse to apply it universally, and most notably to the "peoples" of Alsace and Lorraine. But he is wrong to demand that the principle of self-determination be generalized in the name of a more complete application of the Declaration of the Rights of Man. If humanitarians support a cause, it will be in the name of justice and freedom, as people used to say, not because every association of individuals has the *right* to establish a State, as Sieyès claimed. Neither "French Algeria" nor "Algerian Algeria," but democratic Algeria: there is an agenda to which a defender of the rights of man ought to be able to subscribe.

The rights of the individual risk being infringed upon by the rights of the community: here is a reality that does not escape Péguy. But it does not trouble him; on the contrary. His admiration for Robespierre and the Committee for Public Safety is motivated by the severity with which they were able to repress discordant voices and the "foreign party" (the poor Cloots) in a dangerous situation. "Woe to the party that does not subdue the enemies within" (*L'Argent suite*, p. 116). "In time of war there is only one policy, and that is the policy of the National Convention" (p. 127)—that is, the execution of traitors. "In time of war, there is only one regime, and that is the Jacobean regime . . . In time of war, there is nothing but the State. And it is *Vive la Nation*" (p. 131). The observations are keen. But are we still in the realm of the rights of man? The fatherland gets its due, but not humanity. Péguy is then wrong to go on in the same breath as follows: "It is in the system of the rights of man (and in this the system has my full endorsement), the right of peoples to dispose of themselves . . ." (pp. 152–153). Péguy accepts the rights of man only by completely reversing them.

He then adds an argument that we have seen in Bugeaud: "Nothing is as destructive as weakness and cowardice. Nothing is as human as firmness. Richelieu is the one who is literally human, and Robespierre" (p. 129). But such an argument evokes more the omnipotence of the monarch by divine right, who disposes of his subjects' lives for his own loftier purposes, than the freely exercised will of individual subjects, which has been viewed by general consensus, since the Enlightenment, as the distinguishing feature of humanity. If I am to defend my country, I do so as a citizen, not as a man: I renounce the exercise of my personal will so that the collective will can be accomplished. The conduct of a war has nothing to do with humanitarian principles, even if those principles lead me to judge that one war is just and another is not.

The claim that peoples have the right to self-determination was invoked when Péguy adopted the viewpoint of the inhabitants of the Alsace-Lorraine region. If we adopt the viewpoint of France, the reasoning is different: the requirement of territorial unity then comes to the fore. "*The Republic is one and indivisible*—that is what emerged from the Declaration of the Rights of Man and Citizen," Péguy reminds us (p. 145), and he is right: this formula appears in a declaration of September 1792, and it heads the constitution of 1793. But does everything found in these declarations and these constitutions derive from thinking about the rights of man? We may have our doubts. Moreover, the preceding constitution, from 1791, said in Article One: "The Kingdom is one and indivisible" (*Constitutions*, p. 37), and we have the sense that the difference between those two propositions is not decisive. Péguy himself says as much: "Nothing is as monarchical, and as royal, and as old France as that formula" (*L'Argent suite*, p. 145). But then why invoke the spirit of the declarations of rights?

This continuity between the Old Regime and the new, cherished by Péguy (it constitutes the theme of the volume entitled *L'Argent*), is based on other than humanitarian values: the cult of work, dignity, honor, honesty, heroism, courage—values which are not called into question by the break that the Revolution represents. Here again Péguy recalls Michelet, who saw a continuity between Jeanne d'Arc and Robespierre. "The person who does not give up his ground may be as republican as he likes, and as secular as he likes . . . He will be no less the cousin of Jeanne d'Arc. And the person who does give up his ground will never be anything but a scoundrel, even if he should be warden of his parish. (And even if he were to have all the virtues. Virtues are not what a man of war is required to have)" (p. 135). Péguy now agrees with Renan about the fact that war and virtue are incompatible, but, unlike his predecessor, he chooses war over virtue.

The requirement to defend the "one and indivisible" republic (or monarchy) at any price also raises the problem of consistency. Is this principle really compatible with that of the self-determination of peoples? Only if the people of Alsace and Lorraine indeed desire to remain attached to France. If on the contrary they were inclined to seek autonomy and wanted to found a new State, thus joining the ranks of the Basque, Breton, or Corsican separatists, the two principles would be in contradiction, and Péguy would have to choose (he would no doubt prefer the raison d'Etat to the exercise of free will). The maintenance of the integrity of the State at any price implies the submission of individual will to the interests of a higher, abstract entity. If the Declaration of Rights proclaimed simultaneously the axiom of territorial unity (which it does) and that of self-determination (which it does not do clearly), it would contradict itself; moreover, both axioms are foreign, not to say contrary, to the principle of the rights of man.

Heroism and Pity

Péguy would like to believe that he has overcome the antinomy of humanism and patriotism. "Our socialism . . . was not in the least anti-French, not in the least anti-patriotic, not in the least *anti*-national . . . Far from reducing or weakening the race, it exalted it, strengthened it" (*Notre Jeunesse* [Our Youth], partly translated into English as "Memories of Youth," in *Temporal and Eternal*, p. 61). "It is clear that it did not and could not endanger the legitimate rights of nations, but . . . could but serve the most essential interest of the nation and the legitimate rights of the people" (p. 70). Péguy's "internationalism" certainly does not harm the nation, it even contributes to the affirmation of the nation's rights. But in what respect does it then amount to internationalism and humanism? Is this continuity anything but a way of begging the question? If it were not, would Péguy have needed to fall back on sophistic distinctions that one would expect to find rather in a text by Lenin? "*Internationalism,*" he writes, "which was a system of political and social equality and temporal justice and mutual freedom among peoples, has become in their hands [the hands of socialists like Jaurès] a sort of vague and vicious bourgeois cosmopolitanism" (*L'Argent suite*, p. 161). Cosmopolitanism *is* internationalism; Péguy simply uses the first term when he notices the conflict with his nationalism, and the second when he does not.

Péguy is prepared to recognize that every people is in the right when it is nationalist: this is the sole internationalist aspect of his nationalism. His enemies are less the German nationalists—after all, they are only doing their duty—than the French humanitarians, traitors to the national cause. "The Prussians were never anything but soldiers, vanquishers and conquerors. They brought into play power, the power of war, of victory, of conquest. But I scorn and I hate, I bear a grudge against those wretched Frenchmen who sold off two provinces in order to have peace" (p. 126). Here is what results from a consistent nationalism (though this form is rare), a nationalism that assumes the—national—relativity of values.

But can one profess this sort of nationalism and at the same time believe in such things as chosen peoples? Péguy seeks to bring off this tour de force. "That there are entire peoples who have a price, a proper value, that are marked for history, . . . and that entire peoples, so many other peoples, the immense majority of peoples, are marked on the contrary for silence and shadow . . . , that there are . . . entire peoples temporally chosen and perhaps more—this is certainly perhaps the greatest mystery of the event, the most poignant problem of history" (*Notre Jeunesse*, pp. 3–4). Péguy is prepared to see that there is a problem, but not to question the idea of chosen peoples. Now among these peoples, France—this will hardly surprise us—occupies first place: going further than Michelet, Péguy sees France as a unique example, as much in secular history as in the history of Christianity (and he could not care less that the very idea of a "chosen people" is profoundly alien to Christianity). France must today fulfill "its vocation of Christianity and its vocation of freedom. France is not only the eldest daughter of the Church . . . ; it also has, in secular terms, a sort of unique parallel vocation; it is undeniably a sort of patron and witness (and often a martyr) to freedom in the world" (*L'Argent suite*, p. 166). Apart from the content of the ideal, which is freedom, it is hard to see how, having come to this pass, Péguy's nationalism differs from any other ethnocentric and chauvinistic nationalism: as soon as it gives up its internal consistency to integral relativism, Péguy's nationalism no longer has any distinguishing features.

Humanism sets up a certain individual freedom as a principle. By putting the interest of the nation at the top of his scale of values, Péguy denies that freedom and breaks with humanistic principles. For he believes not in individual liberty but in national determinism. "A man is not determined by what he does and still less by what he says. But at the deepest level a being is uniquely determined by what it is" (*L'Argent* [Money], p. 40). But what is a man? "A man is made of his background, a man is made of what he is. He is not made of what he does for others" (p. 41). Now man *does* by his own will, and he *is* by virtue of his origins; if being takes precedence over doing to such an extent, there is not much left of free will.

In a well-known passage Péguy takes on Kantian morality, which holds that the value of an action lies in the possibility of universalizing it. "Kantianism has clean hands, *but it does not have any hands*" (*Victor-Marie, comte Hugo*, p. 246). "How many of our actions could not be set up, *geschickt*, as universal laws, for which this *envoi* does not even have any meaning; and these are the ones to which we are most attached, the only ones to which we are attached no doubt; actions of trembling, actions of fever and shivering, not at all Kantian, actions of mortal uneasiness; our only good actions perhaps" (p. 247). Péguy is certainly right when he says that the universalist principles of ethics cannot account for a great part of our existence—a part that we must not only not give up, but that we must cherish, for it is the part in which we live the most intensely, in feverish trembling. What good does it do to want to have clean hands if we proceed to lose all contact with life? But can we claim more, for those undoubtedly exciting actions, than the epithet "good"? The fact that there is something other than ethics in life does not mean that there is no room left for ethics, or that that other thing, whatever it may be, must replace ethics. Unless we change the meaning of words radically—but it is hard to see what we would gain by doing so—intensity does not signify goodness; it could rather be said that goodness (or, in other circumstances, justice) must serve to contain, to limit, the principle of intensity that on its own cannot regulate the life of a community.

In the great opposition—to use Péguy's language—between the life system and the justice system, Péguy, contradicting himself yet again, finally chooses the life system, in which intensity (trembling) is at the pinnacle. This is a scale of values in which justice is worth less than life, in which heroism, war, and ecstasy no longer need be concerned with what is good or what is right. Péguy's writing mirrors this choice: it is passionate, febrile, vibrant—and contradictory, biased, unjust. In life as in death, he opted for intensity over reason. "The contest is not between heroes and saints; the fight is against the intellectuals, against those who despise heroes and saints equally" ("Memories of Youth," p. 34). One hundred fifty years earlier, in *The Spirit of the Laws*, Montesquieu had already criticized warriors and saints, contrasting them not with intellectuals but with the spirit of moderation, which he preferred. "Extremely happy men and extremely unhappy men are equally disposed to harshness: witness monks and conquerors. Only the middling sort, and the mixture of good fortune with bad, offer gentleness and pity" (VI, 9, p. 83). The Péguy system is in essence a system in which gentleness counts for less than febrility.

Consequences of Nationalism

Nationalism versus Humanism

We can see to what extent nationalism has departed from humanitarian ideals, once again, in the example of Maurice Barrès. "Contre les étrangers" (Against Foreigners) is the title of a pamphlet he published in 1893, and used again in *Scènes et doctrines du nationalisme*. He starts with an alarmist reference to "the height of the flood that is about to submerge our race" (II, p. 189). There are too many foreigners in France. Now for a nationalist, the condemnation of foreigners (not of Italians in Italy but of Italians in France) is something of a tautology.

"The foreigner, like a parasite, is poisoning us" (II, p. 161), since he is making the French deviate from the path to which they are destined by their own tradition. Given this situation, a twofold reaction is called for. On the one hand, the French have to be more severe with foreigners. Barrès thus advocates "the expulsion of all foreigners who become the responsibility of Public Assistance" (II, p. 198), believes that those who remain in good health and who manage to stay must be prevented from being naturalized, and claims that those who do succeed in being naturalized should not benefit from any civil rights (such rights should be available only to their descendants). In a word, "the idea of fatherland implies an inequality, but at the expense of foreigners, and not, as is the case today, at the expense of nationals" (II, p. 193). On the other hand, therefore, and this is the positive side, the native population is to be privileged. "Hospitable France—it is a fine phrase, but let us first be hospitable to our own" (II, p. 188).

Barrès' point of departure is not shocking in itself; a state cannot allow itself not to distinguish at all between its own citizens and foreigners, once it imposes certain duties on, and grants certain rights to, the former but not the latter. But this administrative distinction obviously does not imply that foreigners are poisoning French blood, or that they are parasites. We cannot expect Barrès to give up his xenophobia in the name of humanitarian principles, however: xenophobia exists, and whatever is must be. "The ideas we have just presented *against foreigners* are in harmony with the deepest feelings of this country" (II, p. 205).

Barrès' Judeophobia is even more irrational. The physical signs of Jewishness seem to him to be recognizable from a distance; the moral features of Jews, the opposite of those of the French, are quite simply abject. Jews are guilty of not blending into the nation, of remaining cosmopolites in every country; for a Jew, being a foreigner is not a transitory state but an essence. Not only are Jews not at home, like Italian or Polish émigrés, but they have no home; they are people without a fatherland—whereas human beings are only what the fatherland makes them; Jews are thus nothing at all. (Unless one maintains, as Toussenel and Michelet did, that their fatherland is the London Stock Exchange.) "The Jews have no fatherland in our sense. For us, the fatherland is the soil and the ancestors, it is the land of our dead. For them, it is the place where they can make the highest profit" (I, p. 67). If necessary, Barrès could justify his Judeophobia still further by the presence of this "passion" in the French population: thus, he himself reports a scene that takes place in a courtroom. Here is "Mme de Martel, . . . a perfect model of French kindness and spontaneity . . . *M. le Président:* Your profession? *Response:* Anti-Semite" (I, p. 268).

Barrès' xenophobia and Judeophobia stem from his nationalism. Nevertheless, he would like to demonstrate that his doctrine is equally in harmony with the humanitarian principles of 1789. How does he proceed? Barrès knows perfectly well that these principles support universalism. "The role of eighteenth-century philosophy and of the French Revolution was to establish society upon the basis of natural right—that is, upon logic. Philosophers and lawmakers declared that all men were the same everywhere, that they had rights as men: whence the *Declaration of the Rights of Man and the Citizen*" (II, p. 171). But this principle, which Barrès is prepared to recognize, does not have any implications, in his view, for the way people organize their lives. Now history has shown that nationalities (and nationalisms) flowered in the wake of the Revolution and under its influence. How can we account for this fact? The explanation is that the Revolution "established the principle of the right of peoples to govern themselves" (II, p. 53). This is the argument we have already seen in greater detail in connection with Renan and Péguy, an argument based, as we now know, on a fallacious analogy between an individual and a people. But even if it were valid, it would not justify this interpretation of the nationalist principle in the sense of contempt for and rejection of others. There is not the same relationship of implication between nationalism and humanism as there is between nationalism and xenophobia.

Nationalism and racism have in common a hostile attitude toward others. But the differences between nationalism and racism are nonetheless significant. Nationalism leads naturally to xenophobia (the very title of Barrès' pamphlet, "Against Foreigners," and its inclusion in his book on nationalism, attest clearly to this). The notion of foreigner, however, says nothing about the physical characteristics of the incriminated individual: all those who are not *citizens*, quite simply, are foreigners. The racist, on the other hand, sees the *man*, not the citizen: American blacks or Jews belong to the same nation as Ku Klux Klan members, but not to the same "race." One can change one's nation, not one's race (the first notion is moral, the second physical). The nationalist operates on a single plane, even if he changes sector: he attaches moral judgments to differences in political status and cultural membership. The racist, for his part, establishes a relationship between two different planes, by assimilating the moral to the physical. These conceptual differences are important even though, on the affective and evaluative levels, nationalism and racism often go hand in hand. It is not because he is a nationalist (a xenophobe) that Barrès ceases to be a racist (an anti-Semite); and he is not alone in this—far from it.

The example of Barrès, the last in a series that began with Sieyès, shows the fundamental incompatibility between patriotism and human-ism—even though the spokespersons for each position attempt to con-vince us of the contrary. Sieyès decided arbitrarily that national needs were necessarily in harmony with natural law. The revolutionaries found themselves obliged to abandon their humanitarian rhetoric as soon as they thought the interests of the country were at stake; the flirtation with the "foreign party" did not last long. Tocqueville saw no problems with patriotism, first because he judged it contrary to the excessive self-interest of individuals in a democracy; then because he transposed the principle of individual liberty to relations among groups, without taking into account, here, the absence of a "general will"; this led him in practice to contradict the theory of *Democracy in America*, in his speeches on the subject of Algeria. Michelet declared that France was the pure and simple incarnation of universal values. Renan rejected patriotism, but he did not distinguish between the political and cultural aspects of the nation, and he thus found himself demanding not only that the members of a nation have the will to act in common in the future, but also that they have a common past. Péguy illegitimately deduced the right of peoples to self-determination from the rights of man; he added the requirement that the Republic must remain "one and indivisible," a requirement that contradicts the preceding "right" but that cannot be deduced from the rights of man either. Finally, Barrès, who also confused the cultural and political elements, equated the already problematic right to self-determination with the most in-tolerant patriotism, amounting to racism and xenophobia. Having thus surveyed the most compelling ideologies of nationalist doctrine in France, we may conclude that no legitimate way of deducing patriotism from humanitarian principles has yet been found.

But should we not evaluate patriotism on its own terms, apart from any humanist justification? If we agree to understand patriotism not as interest in one's own culture nor as an expressed desire to live in a given country and thus to obey its laws, but as a preference for one's own

people over others (the "national preference")—if, in other words, we
agree to dissociate the various meanings of the word "nation"—then
this evaluation becomes problematic. For we cannot forget that nationalist passions were at the origin of all the wars waged by France during
that same period: as Péguy's example (rather than his statements)
shows, a patriotic declaration readily leads to a declaration of war. If
we extend the field of observation to Germany, we must note that
nationalism was also one of the main ingredients of the ideology that
led to the Second World War. But let us stick to France. A century of
bloody wars went by between the Napoleonic campaigns and the end
of the First World War: these wars were accepted all the more easily
in that they were presented as invested with the prestige of the French
Revolution and the humanitarian ideal. Ideology may not cause wars,
but it can help make them popular, acceptable to all.

We ought to add here that "humanitarian" patriots bear a particularly
heavy responsibility. A patriot who is only a patriot acts openly: it is
obvious from the outset with whom one is dealing. A patriot who
proceeds under cover of republican virtues and humanitarian principles, in a country where these values are venerated, deserves to be
doubly condemned. As soon as love of country comes to mean rejection
of others, it becomes a potential source of conflict. Michelet and
Maurras held opposing views on the ideal political regime (republic or
monarchy); but their nationalisms were equivalent. However, from the
ethical viewpoint, the difference reappears: it arises from the degree of
lucidity (or sincerity) encountered on each side; and this matters.

But as Artaud (among others) said, what is true of "love of country"
does not necessarily apply to the attachment to a national culture. In
the French tradition, even including Montesquieu or Taine, there has
been relatively little reflection on the role of culture, no doubt because
this tradition likes to see itself as a direct (and thus privileged) incarnation of the universal; it would have been better, however, if the
patriotic passions had been used for the enhancement of knowledge
and the enrichment of that national culture. If the individual spirit were
really a blank slate, individuals would never be capable of getting their
bearings in the infinite variety, simultaneous and successive, of the
world, nor could they go very far in their attempts at conceptualization.
Fortunately for us as individuals, we do not enter the world directly
but enter it by way of a culture—that is, an interpretation of the world,
thus an order; in this way an immense part of the work that awaited us

has already been carried out. Culture is a classification of the world that allows us to get our bearings in it more easily; it is the memory of the past that belongs to a community, which also implies a code of behavior in the present, and even a set of strategies for the future. And just as one cannot learn "universal" love without passing through the stage of loving one's neighbors, one cannot gain access to the universal spirit except through knowledge of a particular culture: what is true for affect is also true for cognition.

It is thus clear that an individual who possesses a culture in depth has an advantage over someone who does not know it at all; and it is clear that a richer cultural tradition represents an asset for the individual. This does not mean that the individual must meekly comply with tradition, or that he or she must never transgress its codes; moreover, the very desire to escape from the codes can arise only from one's consciousness of their existence. The example of poetry is eloquent here. The cultural vein mined by poets is language. Now the more familiar a poet is with all the resources of the language, the further she can go in carrying out her task. Such a plunge into the particular might become a goal in itself (the collection of rare expressions, or idiomatic phrases); but with the great poets it is the immersion itself, and this alone, that leads to universality. Endowed with a maximally rich English vocabulary, a vast and thorough knowledge of the English language, Shakespeare is nonetheless one of the most universal authors in the history of literature.

The loss of one's culture is thus a misfortune. Barrès was wrong to project the human into the vegetable realm by speaking of "uprooting" (just as Simone Weil, in a reflection that is, however, infinitely more generous, was wrong to use the same term); but it is true that the problem of *deculturation* exists. It is not a specifically national phenomenon, for, as we have seen, culture itself is often infra- or supranational. In addition, the causes of deculturation are not, as is sometimes claimed, necessarily connected with the ease of international communication that characterizes the modern world. It would be wrong in any event to suppose that human beings are originally monocultural: geographically, cultures are embedded one within another, to be sure, but socially they overlap, and each of us necessarily belongs to several subsets—by virtue of origin, profession, age group, and so on; the plurality of cultures cannot astonish us, or degrade us. That is why the *project* of a multicultural state, about which there is sometimes talk today, is rather futile: multiculturalism is neither a panacea nor a threat, but simply the reality of all existing states. Unlike patriotism, which requires loyalty to a single state, cultural membership can be multiplied. Moreover, the émigrée often preserves her culture all the more fiercely in that she is distant from it, and the traveler does not necessarily leave his habits behind because he has become acquainted with those of others. As Simone Weil says, a painter worth her salt who visits a museum comes away with a heightened originality; a culture is enriched by contact with others. Mobility within a given country, a corollary of industrialization, contributes strongly, on the other hand, to the destruction of local cultures. To be sure, a new culture and new traditions are established in suburban bedroom communities; but at the outset, at least, they are infinitely poorer than the ones they replace.

Acculturation is the rule, not the exception. One is not born French (in this sense of the word); one becomes French. And one can acquire a culture between the ages of twenty and forty, even though it is easier to do so during the first two decades of life. In her new culture, the individual may be as much at ease as in her culture of origin, or even more so, profiting from the dual status of participant and observer. This possibility is limited simply by the duration of human life: it takes much longer to learn a culture than a language. During a lifetime one can acquire two cultures, perhaps three, not more. It is easy to see the difference between the acculturated person, at ease in two cultures, and the decultured person, who has forgotten his first language but has not learned the language of his adopted country. The acquisition of a second culture does not bring about a radical change in the initial situation; the loss of one's unique culture, on the contrary, leads to the impoverishment, if not the disappearance, of one's own universe.

We begin to glimpse here what directions "cultural nationalism" might take. But let us go back for one more look at "civic nationalism."

Legitimations of Colonialism

Patriotism has perhaps been, since the nineteenth century, the source of European wars; but is it also the source of the specific form of conflict known as colonial warfare? France, as we know, stands out in this realm (from the occupation of Egypt and Leclerc's macabre expedition to Haiti, through the wars in North Africa, sub-Saharan Africa, and Indochina, to the "pacification" of Morocco). In a first phase, we can observe that the advocates of colonization are prepared to use any tools at their disposal, including whatever ideology they have at hand, without any troubling scruples over consistency. The work of Paul Leroy-Beaulieu, author of *De la colonisation chez les peuples modernes* (On Colonization among Modern Peoples) and a great theoretician of French expansion, provides an example of this sort of eclectic accumulation of arguments which would be incompatible in any logic (Leroy-Beaulieu draws his original inspirations from Renan's appeals to imperial conquest in "La Réforme intellectuelle et morale de la France"). But let us rather look at these arguments one by one, as developed by those partisans of colonization who remain internally consistent.

First of all we need to note that a *universalist* ideology of colonization exists. It can already be identified in some authors—prior to the great campaigns—who play a direct role in Enlightenment philosophy, such as Condorcet or the Ideologue de Gérando. Condorcet is convinced that there is a unique scale of civilizations at whose pinnacle one finds "that state of civilization which is the most enlightened, the freest, and the least burdened by prejudices, such as the French and the Anglo-Americans have attained already" (*Sketch for a Historical Picture of the Progress of the Human Mind*, p. 173); whereas there is a "vast gulf that separates these peoples from the slavery of nations under the rule of monarchs, from the barbarism of African tribes, from the ignorance of savages" (pp. 173–174). Progress, for Condorcet, is a gradual liberation from prejudices, and his contemporary compatriots are the ones who have gone the farthest in this direction.

In 1800, when he drafts his memoir intended for travelers in remote countries, *The Observation of Savage Peoples*, Joseph-Marie de Gérando expresses in turn what the Ideologues have preserved of the Enlightenment heritage. It is self-evident for de Gérando that there exist "peoples at very different degrees of civilization or barbarity" (p. 60), and he proposes "to construct an exact scale of the various degrees of civilization" (p. 63). On this scale the peoples close to their origins will be distinguished from those who tend toward perfection; the criteria will be once again rationality and sociability, thus also technological development: "As for fire, ignorance of it attests without doubt a state furthest removed from civilization" (p. 96).

De Gérando does not despise savages for their lack of civilization, but he is condescending toward them, exactly as we may be toward our own ancestors, who are of the same species as ourselves and yet inferior.

The identification of savages with ancestors (which goes back at least as far as Thucydides) takes on an entirely new impact here. By associating with savages, "we shall in a way be taken back to the first periods of our own history . . . The philosophical traveller, sailing to the ends of the earth, is in fact traveling in time; he is exploring the past; every step he makes is the passage of an age." That is indeed why it is worthwhile to devote oneself to the study of savages; among them, our own characteristics "are bound to emerge much more prominently" (p. 62).

However, as consistent men of the Enlightenment, Condorcet and de Gérando believe in the necessity of establishing equality for all; they are therefore "voluntarists" and, more specifically, reformists and educators, seeking to export European civilization in order to have it propagated throughout the world. Addressing himself to blacks, Condorcet proclaims: "Nature has formed you to have the same mind, the same reason, the same virtues as the whites" ("Réflexions sur l'esclavage des nègres" [Reflections on Negro Slavery] p. 63), and in his *Sketch* he proclaims that "men of all races are equally brothers by the wish of nature" (VIII, p. 105), which implies "the abolition of inequality between nations" (X, p. 173).

Condorcet's dream, as we have seen, is that of a progressive unification of the universe: he dreams of a uniform legal code for all nations, a homogenization of humanity. The way to achieve this universal and homogeneous State is by spreading enlightenment. "Having spent a long time meditating on the ways of improving humanity's lot, I have not been able to keep from thinking that there is really only one: it is to accelerate the progress of enlightenment," Condorcet writes ("De l'Influence de la révolution d'Amérique sur l'Europe" [On the Influence of the American Revolution on Europe], p. 30). And this is how the modern colonialist project is born, a project that resembles missionaries' dreams more than the practices of the sixteenth-century conquistadores. Its goals are not to occupy and subjugate but to integrate the colonized countries into a universal project, and to raise them up by this means to the level of the motherland. This project goes hand in hand with Condorcet's desire to see utopia established at home; and both projects arise from his conviction that social structure is transparent and can therefore be easily acted upon: for every cause there is one and only one corresponding effect.

It is the noble mission of the European nations to eliminate savagery from the face of the earth. "Will not the European population in these colonies, spreading rapidly over that enormous land, either civilize or peacefully remove the savage nations who still inhabit vast tracts of its land?" (*Sketch*, p. 175). Civilize or remove! This project is not to be confused, however, with the extermination practiced by the conquistadores, nor with the institution of slavery, which still has its partisans at the time: it is a matter of making these populations more like our own. The action will be undertaken by colonizers, "men of industrious habit"; from this point on, what are at present "the counting-houses of brigands will become colonies of citizens propagating throughout Africa and Asia the principles and the practice of liberty, knowledge, and reason, that they have brought from Europe" (p. 177). Which would obviously fall in line with the interest and desire of the populations in question, these "large tribes who need only assistance from us to become civilized" (p. 177).

For de Gérando, too, it is an act of "philanthropy" to offer "a hand to them to raise them to a happier state" which will contribute to "re-establishing . . . the august ties of universal society" (pp. 63–64). For there is no other way they can have access to progress: "our help is almost indispensable in this process" of leading the people to civilization (p. 97). The savages must be taught agricultural techniques, their countries must be opened up to free trade, and no one will regret seeing "these peoples of Europe . . . expanding at pleasure in more beautiful terrain" (p. 103), since de Gérando addresses them in the following terms: "You [colonizers] aspire only to the good of all, to the glory of being of use!" (p. 104). Here again, colonization is distinguished from the wars waged by the "greedy conquerors": it is the work of new "pacifiers and friends" (p. 103). This is because the means deployed are themselves entirely different; it is no longer a matter of destroying or reducing to slavery, but of "exercising a gentle and useful influence on these abandoned Peoples" (p. 97). Moreover, they themselves cannot fail to invite us to intervene: "Witness . . . of our superiority, he will perhaps . . . call us among his people to teach them how to reach our own condition" (p. 97).

These words were written before the great period of modern colonialism, and it would be all too easy today to ironize over the naiveté of the project. Why did colonization not develop along the lines of Condorcet's and de Gérando's idyllic visions? Among the various reasons, let us single out three. In the first place, our philosophers were unacquainted with the conflict between man and citizen, and they imagined that the states would enact policies that would be in the interest of the universe—a likelihood that is, as it were, excluded by definition. In the second place, their image of the universal is strongly tinged with ethnocentrism: the culture of others is perceived essentially as a lack with respect to our own, not as an internally consistent entity. In the third place, finally, and in consequence, each culture is presented as the accumulation of a certain number of isolated features, rather than as a structure: it is thought to be possible to modify some particular feature (for example, to contribute an agricultural technique) without necessarily changing the others, or to entrust power to the colonizers so they can build roads, without fearing that they will use this power toward other ends. De Gérando gives the following advice to future colonizers: "Bring them our arts, and not our corruption, the standard of our morality, and not the example of our vices, our sciences, and not our scepticism" (p. 64). This is how the undeniably good intentions of Condorcet and de Gérando finally prove quite sterile.

Alongside the "humanist" justifications for colonization, we find many others. We saw that *scientism* was not to be confused with humanism; now we encounter arguments of the scientistic type in the writings of Jean-Marie Antoine de Lanessan, a theoretician and practitioner of colonization (he served as governor in Indochina while continuing to hold a position as botanist and professor at the Faculté de Médecine in Paris). He goes back very far, all the way back to human nature. "It is natural curiosity that drives man to cross the borders of the land where he was born in order to explore the rest of the world; it is the desire each people has to increase its sphere of influence; it is finally the pursuit of the physical and intellectual pleasures procured by victories and conquests and the whole abuse of power in which man satisfies his need for domination and glory" (*Principes de colonisation* [Principles of Colonization], pp. 1–2).

Where it is only a question of natural needs and desires, any value judgment would obviously be misplaced. "In every era, the human races have shoved and jostled each other in a ceaseless struggle that always ends with the destruction of the oldest and less perfected races, and with the triumph of the youngest and more perfect ones. I am not arguing the case; I am noting a law of life" (*L'Indo-Chine française* [French Indochina], p. 53). In this tableau, influenced as much by racialist theories as by social Darwinism, only the best-adapted can survive. It would be futile to revolt against an inviolable law of nature: it is a "fatality of things" (*L'Expansion coloniale de la France* [France's Colonial Expansion], p. xxi), a "fatal and necessary manifestation of the life of these nations" (p. xxiii).

From this viewpoint, the history of humanity is confused with that of colonization—that is, with migrations and exchanges; the contemporary struggle for new markets, for supplies of raw materials is only the end result—rendered harmless owing to its origins in nature—of that first step that led the human being to cross her own threshold. The most highly perfected race will unfailingly win, for perfection is recognized by its own ability to win battles (we saw this argument in more detail with Gobineau). "The more perfected a race, the more it tends to spread; the more inferior a race, the more it remains sedentary," Lanessan declares (*Principes de colonisation*, p. 60). "The world will one day belong to the race that will have spread most widely over its surface and the whole history of humanity bears witness to the fact that that race will necessarily be the most highly perfected of all those the earth has nurtured" (p. 48).

This way of hierarchizing races leads to a paradox, one that is also present in Gobineau (and made explicit, as we have seen, by Lévi-Strauss). The paradox consists in valorizing racial intermixing as a sign of superiority, and at the same time condemning it as a threat of decadence. Lanessan tries to get out of this by distinguishing the superior races, with their good mixtures of blood that are necessary to "the vitality of the race" (p. 129) from the inferior races; only the former are recommended, needless to say. Now everyone knows which is the superior race. "The European race . . . , anthropologically and without any possible argument the most highly perfected of all the human races, has already spread over all the points of the globe without exception" (p. 16). But if this is the best race, is it not the case that any intermixing can only do it harm? The pessimistic Gobineau is more consistent on this point. The fact remains that the politics of colonization here turn out to be based on a scientistic and racialist doctrine, opposed to humanist thinking.

Finally, and as surprising as it may seem, the theses of the *relativists* can also be adapted to the politics of colonization. Let us look at Barrès, who is characterized on the one hand by his praise of "rootedness," maintenance of the past, conservatism, and on the other hand by his support for the imperialist policies of colonialist countries like France, policies that undeniably contribute to national greatness but that at the same time uproot other peoples. "What hold can we have on nationalities and civilizations different from our own?" he wonders in "Une Enquête aux pays du Levant" (An Inquiry into the Orient, p. 469). "How will we form an intellectual elite with which we can work, from Asians who are not uprooted, who continue to judge by their own standards, who remain imbued with their own family traditions, and who thus form a connecting link between us and the native masses?" (p. 470). Here indeed is the squaring of the circle. How can we ensure that this elite will maintain its original standards even as we inculcate our own? How can we reconcile the disavowal of any uprooting with the praise of colonial conquest that provokes this disavowal?

The consistent nationalist, whom Barrès often manages to embody, is a relativist, and is thus opposed to any uprooting, even uprooting in favor of absorption by France. But the typical nationalist is not consistent: his ethnocentrism blinds him, and it introduces a small dose of absolutism into his system, one that allows him to exempt his own country from the general relativity of values. Faced with a concrete situation, Barrès will choose, despite these few scruples, the path of conventional nationalism. What he ends up observing and encouraging in it are "our masters who propagate Western civilization" (p. 102). Now this propagation is usually depicted in terms of hunting or fighting. "The net that we are throwing over the Alexandrian youth" (p. 114); "What varied regiments! What varied and cooperative action!" (about religious schools, p. 116). And Barrès knows perfectly well that—unlike the law Péguy thinks he observes—the spiritual carries the temporal along in its wake. "I am going into the Orient to verify the state of our spiritual power there," he declares upon leaving (p. 107), but he adds shortly afterward: "They [the religious congregations] ensure the prestige of our spirit, create a clientele for our industry, and furnish collaborators for our enterprises" (p. 454). France's mission is to colonize these countries, in Asia and in Africa.

Colonialism and Nationalism

Colonialism thus makes use of contradictory or incompatible ideologies in order to justify a policy that remains consistent in its overall outline. But the issue is still not settled. A distinction needs to be introduced here. The proponents of universalist theses usually defend a type of

colonization called *assimilation*, which seeks to make over the indigenous "races" in the image of France, out of a belief that France is the
perfect embodiment of universal values. An enemy of this policy,
Léopold de Saussure, cites the eloquent example of a French Republican leader: "Paul Bert, arriving in Tonkin, in order to 'attract' the
Annamites in his turn to our political beliefs, made it his first order of
business to have the Rights of Man posted in Hanoi" (*Psychologie de la
colonisation française*, p. 8); this is what Barrès ironically calls "a remote
burst of the Kantian spirit" (*Scènes*, II, p. 109). The relativists, and thus
the nationalists, to the extent that they are internally consistent, prefer
a different type of colonization, which they call *association:* this is the
approach practiced by Lanessan or by General Gallieni, an approach
defended by the same Saussure and applied on a large scale in Morocco
by Lyautey; it results in a protectorate, a form of colony in which the
mother country takes responsibility for military and economic control,
but leaves to local, indigenous power the responsibility for choosing
the most appropriate institutions and for managing everyday business.

What has to be said in particular is that all these arguments are
intended to reassure public opinion in the mother country (when it
gets riled up, for example) or else to attract investments. As for the
practice of the French leadership that decided on these colonial wars,
it actually obeys just one principle, the nationalist principle. A given
leader may be republican and humanist in other respects; this changes
nothing. Anacharsis Cloots, whom we saw as an ardent defender of
universal principles, modified his opinion as soon as he took into
consideration the interests of the country he had made his own, France,
and he came out—on the basis of nationalism—against the abolition of
slavery: "A hasty move would ruin France, and by seeking to liberate
500,000 blacks, we would have enslaved 25 million whites" (*Lettre à un
prince d'Allemagne* [Letter to a German Prince], p. 27). Napoleon did
not hesitate to send his expeditionary force against Toussaint-Louver-
ture, head of the colony of Saint-Domingue, even though the latter
claimed to be acting on behalf of revolutionary principles; Napoleon
set himself up as a champion of slavery, which had been abolished
earlier. We also saw this with Tocqueville and the conquest of Algeria:
the committed humanitarian had to shelve his principles in order to
support the colonial war; and Tocqueville did not hesitate to do just
this while he was deputy and minister, whereas he had condemned
these same practices when, as sociologist and philosopher, he was

writing *Democracy in America*. The ministerial function itself seems to have dictated the content of his thinking.

Another significant example can be found in Jules Ferry, the direct artisan of the conquest of Tunisia (since this was accomplished while he was prime minister), but also a defender and promoter of the entire French colonial policy, and at the same time a committed republican.

Attacked by the radicals (Clemenceau) on the government's colonial policy, Jules Ferry advances three arguments—economic, humanitarian, and political—to legitimize it. But the economic and the political arguments are simply two aspects of the same nationalist principle, according to which one must exert one's best efforts to make the country to which one belongs increase in power. These two aspects are closely related, moreover: "Where there is political predominance there is also the predominance of products, economic predominance" ("Discours" [Speech], July 28, 1885, p. 196). On the economic level, "surplus capital" or "excess goods" have to find natural outlets in the colonies. On the political level, "France . . . cannot only be a free country; . . . it must also be a great country, exercising over the destinies of Europe all the influence it has . . . It must spread this influence throughout the world, and everywhere where it can do so spread its language, its customs, its flag, its weapons, its genius" (p. 220). Future wars are justified by previous wars; power seems to secrete justice on its own. "A people that represents an organized force of 1,500,000 bayonets, at the heart of Europe, cannot detach itself from world affairs" (preface to *Tonquin et la mère-patrie* [Tonkin and the Mother Country], p. 554). "We have many rights on the surface of the earth: it is not for nothing that France is . . . one of the greatest maritime powers of the globe" ("Discours," p. 190).

Jules Ferry's vision of the terrestrial sphere is entirely dictated by French interests. "Look at the map of the world," he exclaims to the National Assembly, "and tell me if these stages in Indochina, Madagascar, and Tunisia are not necessary stages for the safety of our navigation?" (p. 216). This is how foreign countries are transformed into "stages" for French ships, and how French interests turn up more or less everywhere: "Egyptian business, in so many respects, is really French business" (p. 215). Jules Ferry would agree, if pressed, to let a few other European countries join this club of privileged members who determine the destinies of all the other countries in the world. A kind of reciprocity reigns among the members: if the French have occupied the Gulf of Tonkin, it is because the English beat them to Egypt; if the English have taken Cyprus, the French can take Tunisia; and so on.

Jules Ferry imagines a design of nature, or Providence, that transforms peoples into the building blocks of a world empire. "Alongside such a considerable natural capital [minerals], nature has placed the Chinese and Annamite work force, so inexpensive, and the wealth of a land that is good for anything" (preface to *Tonquin et la mère-patrie*, p. 549). The process of colonization seems to be an extension of the natural aspirations of men, and the greatest colonizer is rather like a sports champion. "An irresistible movement carries the great European nations along toward the conquest of new lands. It is like an immense steeplechase on the road to the unknown" (p. 555). This is why no moral condemnation is called for in the case of the modern colonizers (on this issue Jules Ferry agrees with Lanessan), even if they find themselves using the methods of the old conquistadores; on the contrary, the latter no less than the former illustrate the best thing the human race has done. We are invited to admire the "young heroes, at once scholars and soldiers, who are renewing in our day, in the land of the Annamites, the bold and prodigious actions of a Cortés or a Pizarro" (p. 548).

Alongside the nationalist argument there appears, however—and the coexistence is not simple—a humanitarian argument. There is definite continuity between Jules Ferry's politics of education—education that is free and obligatory for all, thus an elevation to the same cultural level for all—and his politics of colonization, which participates in the same "educational and civilizing mission." The civilized countries will be the masters of the young and uncultivated barbarian lands: what is at stake is a veritable "educational process," and the goal is not to exploit but to civilize and to raise up the "other races" to our own level, to spread the enlightenment that has been bequeathed to us; such is the meaning of the "progress of humanity and civilization" that Jules Ferry desires.

But the humanitarian ideal is subject to a peculiar interpretation in his writing. First of all, Jules Ferry seems to believe that the duty of civilization entails the right to intervene. "The superior races have a right vis-à-vis the inferior races . . . , because there is a duty for them. They have the duty to civilize the inferior races" ("Discours," pp. 210–222). It is by virtue of this right that wars and occupations will be justified, even though these acts no longer attest in any way to a superior civilization: the goal (assuming that there ever was one) is entirely blotted out by the means, which are not only distinct from the goal but in direct contradiction with it. Moreover, the initial duty seems to be fulfilled by the mere presence of the French, without a need for any particular actions on their part. "Can you deny, can anyone deny, that there is more justice, more material and moral order, more equity, more social virtue in North Africa, since France conquered it?" (p. 211). Tocqueville allowed himself to deny this, even though he never challenged France's colonial policy. But not Jules Ferry, whose humanitarianism is curiously tinged with racialism; for him, this duty is already fulfilled, and he thus pays attention only to the rights that ensue: any resistance must be immediately blocked, for otherwise "all civilization is compromised" (p. 185).

Jules Ferry's opponents in the parliamentary debate do not fail to point out to him the inconsistency of his position, for he finds himself inclined to justify barbaric acts in the name of civilization, and he forgets that "proposing and imposing are two very different things" (p. 210). He then falls back on another defense tactic that consists in opposing politics and morality (we saw Tocqueville do the same thing): such arguments, he says, "are not politics, or history either: they are political metaphysics." "I defy you," he exclaims, "to sustain to the end your thesis, which is based on the equality, liberty, and independence of the inferior races" (p. 209). He is right: nationalist politics is incompatible with humanitarian arguments. But then why introduce the latter into a political debate?

Reading what Jules Ferry said and wrote about the colonial issue, one cannot help questioning the sincerity of his humanitarian and legalistic arguments. To hear him tell it, one could imagine that the Europeans had been summoned by the local populations of distant continents, in view of a material and moral exchange that would be profitable to both parties; having subsequently broken the formal treaties, the natives placed themselves in a position of infraction and deserved to be punished. "We have only brought to bear our colonial expansion on the points where the failure to recognize our rights and the violation of the most formal treaties made it our duty to intervene by force of arms" (p. 183). Did he believe this himself? Was he really taken in as to the meaning of that "signature of their representatives at the bottom of the treaties" (p. 189)? It is just as though it were a matter of acting out a little comedy in which no one believes but which is the equivalent of buying an indulgence before the good Lord.

At the end of this process, nationalism indeed appears to bear the principal ideological responsibility both for the European wars, from the Revolution up to and including the First World War, and for the colonial wars of the same period and beyond. Even if a war has other than ideological causes, we may attribute to these doctrines, without fear of contradiction, the responsibility for the deaths of millions of human beings and for political situations whose resolution, in many instances, is not yet in sight.

4

Exoticism

On the Proper Use of Others

Exoticism and Primitivism

Ideally, exoticism is a form of relativism, just as nationalism is. However, the two forms are diametrically opposed. In each case, what is valorized is not a stable content but a country and a culture defined exclusively by their relation to the observer. If I am a nationalist, I proclaim that the values of my own country, whatever they may be, are superior to all others. No, the exoticist replies, the country with superior values is a country whose only relevant characteristic is that it is not my own. Thus, in both cases what is at issue is a relativism overtaken at the last minute by a value judgment (we are better than the others; the others are better than we are), but in which the definition of the entities compared, "ourselves" and "the others," remains purely relative.

The attitudes characteristic of exoticism thus offer the first instance we have encountered in which otherness is systematically preferred to likeness. But the way we have come to define exoticism in the abstract indicates that what is at issue here is less a valorization of the other than an act of self-criticism, less the description of a reality than the formulation of an ideal. No one is intrinsically other; an individual is "other" only because he is not myself. By saying of him that he is other, I have not yet really said anything at all; worse, I know nothing about him and do not want to know anything, since any positive characterization of him would keep me from confining him to the purely relative category of otherness. Exoticism thus invalidates what we have called, with reference to nationalism, the "rule of Herodotus." However, exoticism has its own claim to fame, for the first famous "exoticist" was none other than Homer. In Book 13 of the *Iliad*, Homer mentions the Abii, at that time the most remote population in the world known to the Greeks, and he declares them "the most righteous of men" (II, p. 3); in Book 4 of the *Odyssey* he supposes that at "the bounds of the earth . . . life is easiest for men" (I, p. 149). In other words, and as Strabo had already noted in the first century A.D., for Homer the most remote country is best: such is "the rule of Homer," exactly the inverse of the rule of Herodotus. From this standpoint we cherish the remote because of its remoteness: it would not occur to anyone to idealize well-known neighbors (the Anglophilia of the French in the eighteenth and nineteenth centuries is not exoticism). The best candidates for the role of exotic ideal are the peoples and cultures that are most remote from us and least known to us. Now it is not easy to equate unfamiliarity with others, the refusal to see them as they are, with a valorization of these others. It is a decidedly ambiguous compliment to praise others simply because they are different from myself. Knowledge is incompatible with exoticism, but lack of knowledge is in turn irreconcilable with praise of others; yet praise without knowledge is precisely what exoticism aspires to be. This is its constitutive paradox.

The classical descriptions of the Golden Age, and, as it were, the Golden Lands, are thus derived chiefly by inverting features observed at home—and to a much lesser degree by observing the others in question. Let us recall Montaigne's famous portrait of "cannibals." "This is a nation, I should say to Plato, in which there is no sort of traffic, no knowledge of letters, no science of numbers, no name for a magistrate or for political superiority, no custom of servitude, no riches or poverty, no contracts, no successions, no partitions, no occupations but leisure ones, no care for any but common kinship, no clothes, no agriculture, no metal, no use of wine or wheat. The very words that signify lying, treachery, dissimulation, avarice, envy, belittling, pardon—unheard of" ("Of Cannibals," *The Complete Essays*, I, 31, p. 153). The inhabitants of this nation, he adds elsewhere, are people "without letters, without law, without king, without religion of any kind" ("Apology," ibid., II, 12, p. 362). Thus, we learn a lot about what "cannibals" are not, what they lack; but in a positive sense, what are they like? What Montaigne says about them amounts to very little, for someone who prides himself on the fact that he has put together his portrait of "cannibals" on the basis of eye-witness observation. Where does the list of features they lack come from, since it obviously cannot originate in observation? Would it not be his own society? Montaigne in fact follows a rhetorical topos here: the evocation of the Golden Age is traditionally carried out in negative terms, precisely because it is simply the inverse of a description of our own era.

But it must be said at once that pure exoticism is as rare as consistent nationalism. In practice, the exotic preference is almost always accompanied by an attraction for certain contents at the expense of others; relativism often serves only as a means of access to the subject matter. These contents are customarily chosen along an axis that opposes simplicity to complexity, nature to art, origins to progress, savagery to sociality, spontaneity to enlightenment. There are thus, in theory, two symmetrical sorts of exoticism, depending on whether the culture or the people valorized are considered to be simpler or more complex than ourselves, more natural or more artificial, and so on. In practice, however, things happen a little differently. By and large, up to the end of the eighteenth century, western European authors considered themselves to be bearers of a culture that was more complex and more artificial than any other; they valorized others only as incarnations of the opposite pole. China may have been an exception to this rule, but it is an isolated case. In short, up to fairly recent times exoticism was necessarily accompanied by primitivism (in the cultural and not necessarily the chronological sense of the word). From the nineteenth century on, the opposite form has gained ground: first because certain ancient non-European traditions (Arab, Indian, Chinese, Japanese, and so on) have been valued more highly, and then because, more recently, western Europe has begun to consider itself "behind" with respect to other metropolitan centers such as New York, Hong Kong, or Tokyo (an exoticism of skyscrapers and electronics). The fact remains that primitivist exoticism is one of the most characteristic forms of European exoticism, responsible for the figure of the "noble savage" and its many avatars.

The primitivist interpretation of exoticism is as ancient as history itself. However, it received fresh impetus on a massive scale with the great sixteenth-century voyages, which—particularly with the European discovery of America—opened an immense territory on which to project ever-present images of a Golden Age long since past at home. In fact, an almost immediate identification was made between the mores of the "savages" observed in America and those of western Europeans' own ancestors; exoticism thus converged with a primitivism that was also chronological. Now it does seem as though all cultures (with the partial exception of modern European culture) have sought to valorize their own past, seeing it as a moment of plenitude and harmony; the present is always experienced as a fall. A full-blown idealization of savages is present in the very earliest travel narratives. More precisely, the first two well-known authors of such narratives, Christopher Columbus and Amerigo Vespucci, present two very different and, as it were, complementary forms of primitivism. Columbus, whose outlook is medieval in many respects, does not particularly exaggerate the merits of the savages, but he does believe he is about to discover the earthly paradise itself somewhere on the South American continent. Amerigo, much more a man of the Renaissance, has no faith in these old superstitions; at the same time, however, he depicts Indian life on the same South American continent as resembling what life must be like in paradise. This image plays a crucial role in Amerigo's celebrated letter of 1503 entitled *Mundus Novus* and destined to become the best-seller of sixteenth-century travel writing, owing to its literary qualities.

Amerigo's description of Indian mores deserves to be cited, so accurately does it foreshadow future portraits of the noble savage. "They have no cloth, either of wool, flax, or cotton, because they have no need of it; nor have they any private property, everything being in common. They live amongst themselves without a king or ruler, each man being his own master, and having as many wives as they please. The children cohabit with the mothers, the brothers with the sisters, the male cousins with the female, and each one with the first he meets. They have no temples and no laws, nor are they idolaters. What more can I say! They live according to nature" ("Letter . . . to Lorenzo Pietro Francesco di Medici," March [or April] 1503, *The Letters of Amerigo Vespucci*, pp. 46–47).

The society of savages, according to Amerigo, is characterized by five features: they have no clothes, no private property, no hierarchy or subordination, no sexual taboos, and no religion. All this is neatly summed up in the formula "they live according to nature." It must be added that these savages are endowed with exceptional physical qualities: the men are eight feet tall, and they often live to be one hundred fifty years old. We know that Montaigne's portrait of "cannibals" is largely inspired by this description. Montaigne does not mention the absence of religion, but he includes all the other features; he is content to add idleness and the absence of moral flaws, along with the absence of literacy and science. Before Montaigne, Thomas More had already found in Amerigo's description (among other sources, of course) the inspiration for his influential *Utopia:* he had conceived the idea after meeting one of Amerigo's travel companions in Antwerp, in 1515, and in his book he attributes the story about the island of Utopia to that character. Utopias in fact are only superficially opposed to the primitivist reveries: although the former look to the future and the latter to the past, their content is in large measure the same. Saint-Simon's celebrated formula—"The Golden Age of the human race is not behind us but before us" ("The Reorganization of the European Community," p. 68)—says the same thing in its way, since it does no more than note the temporal inversion. And once it has been decided that our own past is to be rediscovered in the present of others, utopian projects are regularly associated with exotic imagery, from More's *Utopia* and Campanella's *City of the Sun* (located in the Indian Ocean) right up to our own day. The noble savage is not only our past but also our future. In their turn, Thomas More and Montaigne influenced countless other writers.

In France, the first to put exotic material before the literate public was André Thevet, in 1557, with his *Singularitez de la France antarctique.* Thevet, as we know today, was only partially responsible for the narrative included in his book. It is true that he participated in the expedition of Villegagnon that brought the French into the bay of Rio de Janeiro, but he fell ill and promptly returned to France. The materials that make up his narrative derive instead—but this only increases their value—from "go-betweens," or interpreters, who knew much more than Thevet did about the Indians' lives. Thevet's role was no more important at the other end of the operation: he did not write the story himself. Instead, he entrusted it to a professional writer who had never left French shores, but who was quite familiar, on the other hand, with the humanist tradition: here again, its lack of originality makes the work all the more significant. And alongside the narrative of his trip, Thevet's work includes quite a long description of the mores of the Brazilian Indians, exemplary cannibals who will serve as the starting point for the exotic reveries of Thevet's contemporaries.

It is interesting to see that Thevet's text itself does not subscribe to the myth of the noble savage: precisely because it is based on authentic testimony, it does not idealize but combines praise with criticism. Never mind: Thevet's contemporaries needed a country and a people on which to project their dreams of a Golden Age; Thevet's narrative, read in the light of Amerigo's accounts, provided them with the indispensable elements. The Pléiade poets stand out in particular. An ode by Jodelle, included in the *Singularitez*, described the cannibals as less barbarian than ourselves; Ronsard wrote a "Discours contre Fortune" (Speech against Fortune) in which we find Amerigo's image mingled with echoes of Latin literature:

> . . . your America, where unknown people
> wander innocently all wild and naked
> as bare of clothing as of malice,
> not knowing the names of either virtue or vice
>
> . . . . .
>
> who do not disturb the earth with sharp knives,
> the earth which like the air is common to each
> and like the water of a river all their goods are shared
> without going to trial over the words Yours and Mine.

(p. 159)

The image of the noble savage is fleshed out and extended in the prose writings of Jean de Léry and Montaigne. Léry's *Histoire d'un voyage faict en la terre de Brésil (History of a Voyage to the Land of Brazil Otherwise Called America)* does not offer unconditional praise, but Léry prefers cannibals to the bad Christians he sees around him. Montaigne, who knows Thevet's and Léry's books as well as other Spanish, Portuguese, and Italian sources, takes a quite similar position. On the one hand, he uses the image of cannibals to criticize our own society, and thus he comes to idealize them. "It seems to me that what we actually see in these nations surpasses not only all the pictures in which poets have idealized the golden age and all their inventions in imagining a happy state of man, but also the conceptions and the very desire of philosophy" ("Of Cannibals," *Essays*, I, 31, p. 153). Perhaps the Golden Age was a myth, but these people are real, and they are better than anything we have been able to imagine. The explanation for this judgment is simple: in the beginning, man was natural; in the course of his history, he has become more and more artificial. Now "it is not reasonable that art should win the place of honor over our great and powerful mother Nature" ("Of Cannibals," I, 31, p. 152); thus, the earliest centuries were "the best and the happiest" ("Of the Resemblance of Children to Fathers," II, 37, p. 581). Today's savages resemble the men of the earliest ages, and therefore are closer to nature than we are. "They still enjoy that natural abundance . . . They are still in that happy state of desiring only as much as their natural needs demand" ("Of Cannibals," I, 31, p. 156). They are therefore superior to us: this is how the myth of the noble savage is constructed.

But from another standpoint Montaigne does not gainsay his own preference for Greek and Roman civilization (any more than Léry stopped preferring Christian values); he thus appreciates the cannibals only to the extent that they resemble Greeks and Romans. It is for this reason that he can praise their bravery in warfare, their deference toward women or their wholly "anacreontic" poetry. When he finds the resemblance inadequate, Montaigne becomes a partisan of colonization—provided it is carried out by the noble Greeks and Romans, rather than by his barbarous compatriots (or by Spaniards, Portuguese, and so on). Thus, Montaigne helps promote the noble savage even as he keeps his distance, insofar as his ideal is not simply primitivism.

The Noble Savage

The image of the noble savage played an important role between the sixteenth and eighteenth centuries, although it was not the only image of remote populations or even the dominant one. It was present, in particular, in travel narratives, a literary genre very much in vogue at the time. Recalling that era when travel was costly and dangerous, we may wonder whether there is not a natural inclination that leads travelers to praise what they have seen; otherwise how could they justify the risks, the exhaustion, the expense? This "natural" benevolence of the traveler of the day was likely to be accompanied by a critical view of his own country, preceding and in preparation for the journey; for if one is perfectly satisfied with everything at home, why leave? Conversely, if one is dissatisfied with one's life and wants to change it, one resigns oneself to acting on what can be most easily modified: the space one occupies (it suffices to leave). Travel through time is not yet available to us; as for modifying life at home, that requires a prolonged effort and a good deal of patience. For someone who dreams of changing lives, of changing life, travel is the simplest approach.

We shall not be surprised, then, to find the image of the noble savage and its obligatory counterpart, the critique of one's own society, amply represented in travel narratives. Such a choice is almost automatic; as proof, there is the fact that, for French travelers, all "savages" were alike. It mattered little whether they lived in America or Asia, whether they came from the Indian Ocean or the Pacific: what mattered in fact was whether or not they offered a contrast with France. Perhaps the purest example of the "noble savage" occurs in a work that appeared at the beginning of the eighteenth century, and which is also a travel narrative: a work by the Baron Lahontan, first published in 1703. The three volumes of this work are called *Nouveaux Voyages* (New Voyages), *Mémoires de l'Amérique septentrionale* (Memoirs of North America), and *Dialogues curieux entre l'Auteur et un Sauvage* (Curious Dialogues between the Author and a Savage).

The very existence of three titles is significant. These separate volumes refer in fact to a single voyage, and they include, on the whole, identical information about the Hurons. What is different is not so much the object of discussion but the attitude the author adopts toward that object. The first volume is made up of a series of letters; it constitutes the travel narrative itself, and gives us a close look at the traveler's first impressions. The second volume, although again presented as a letter, is more like a systematic treatise, in which separate chapters are devoted to the flora, fauna, and architecture of this part of the world, as well as the beliefs of the savages, their mores, illnesses, wars, and so on; there is a brief lexicon of their language at the end. Thus, a certain distancing from personal experience has already come into play. The third volume changes genre yet again: it is no longer a narrative or a treatise, but a philosophical dialogue between an astute savage called Adario, who has once visited France, and Lahontan himself. Thus, the same "ethnographic" material continues to be exploited, but it plays a less and less important role, constituting merely one argument among others invoked to establish Lahontan's theses. The author's use of the three genres provides a good illustration of the requirements of primitive exoticism: if one wants to idealize a society, one must not describe it in too much detail; conversely, a description that is even slightly detailed lends itself badly to idealization. Lahontan needed to leave aside certain details of his own initial description in order to portray the Hurons as truly noble savages.

Lahontan's book met with immediate success. In addition to reprintings, it appeared in 1705 in a new edition, substantially altered from the first one in its philosophical section (which became even more decisively independent of the ethnographic material); the changes are thought to be the work of a certain Gueudeville. The work remained well known throughout the eighteenth century, and Chateaubriand attested to its notoriety by borrowing numerous details from it for his own American epic. Taken one at a time, Lahontan's ideas have little originality: they can be found dispersed throughout many other sixteenth- and seventeenth-century narratives. His book has the merit, however, of pulling these ideas together and of taking them, as it were, to the extreme.

The general ideological framework within which Lahontan can be situtated is egalitarian and universalist. *"Since Men are all made of the same Clay there should be no Distinction or Superiority among them"* (*New Voyages to North America*, II, p. 8; in italics in source text). And Gueudeville goes further: "Nature makes no distinction, accords no preeminence in the constitution of individuals; thus, we are all equal" (*Mémoires*, p. 257). The same Gueudeville justifies the publication of the book by the pure usefulness of information about others: "We like to know what nature produces and what it does beyond the vast space that separates other countries from our own; we like to know the mental outlook, the religion, laws, mores, and customs of a number of men whom we do not think we resemble at all, and whom the great distance scarcely allows us to consider as individuals of our own species" (ibid., preface, pp. 85–86).

In reality, however, information recedes into the background as soon as Lahontan decides to turn the Hurons into an ideal for western Europeans' own use; and another remark by Gueudeville accounts much better for the real composition of the *Dialogues* as well as for a good portion of the *Mémoires*. The Huron Adario says to his interlocutor: "You are our true antipodes for mores, and I cannot examine our innocence without reflecting on your corruption" (p. 258). It would be more accurate to say that the innocent life attributed to the Hurons is nothing but the symmetrical inversion, the perfect polar opposite of a relatively realistic depiction of European "corruption." The portrait of the Hurons in the *Dialogues* does not teach us much, as it were, about the present existence of the others, and it has a great deal to say about the (desirable) future of our own society. Lahontan's exoticism is only a mask for his utopianism.

And yet the *Dialogues* deserve attention. In them we discover not, to be sure, a portrait of others, but a summary of the themes and motifs that are customarily associated with the image of the noble savage. In Lahontan's work, this image is comprised of three irreducible features: an egalitarian principle, a minimalist principle, and a naturalist principle.

Lahontan's egalitarianism, which is his explicit credo and his main justification for preferring the Hurons, has two facets, economic and political. On the economic side, it amounts—in the purest utopian tradition—to condemning private property. Lahontan declares at the outset, in his preface: "I take it, a Man must be quite blind, who do's not see that the property of Goods (I do not speak of the ingrossing of Women) is the only Source of all the Disorders that perplex the European Societies" (quoted from the *Dialogues*, in *New Voyages*, I, Preface, n.p.); from this point on we shall not be astonished to see the Hurons, their antipodes, characterized as "strangers to the Measures of *Meum* and *Tuum*" (I, Preface, n.p.). The formula, obviously not original with Lahontan, recurs endlessly; the suppression of private property is the radical remedy for all our ills. "Then indeed I shall hope . . . that a levelling of Estates may gradually creep in among you; and that at last you'll abhor that thing call'd Interest, which occasions all the Mischief that *Europe* groans under" (II, p. 138).

Economic equality is closely associated with political equality, for Lahontan: the absence of any hierarchy or subordination is, if we take his word for it, another characteristic feature of savage societies. (Such an assertion allows us to measure the distance between the reality of these societies and the portrait Lahontan paints of them; but this is obviously true for the rest of the portrait.) "These People are Strangers to a Military as well as to a Civil Subordination" (II, p. 75). The two forms of equality are inseparable, and Lahontan describes the savages as being "Strangers to *Meum* and *Tuum*, to Superiority and Subordination," as living "in a State of Equality Pursuant to the Principles of Nature" (II, pp. 36–37). The result of this second form of equality is freedom, understood as a complete absence of any subordination, and finally as the absence of all rules: Lahontan's Hurons live in an anarchic society. "I am Master of my own Body, I have the absolute disposal of my self, I do what I please, I am the first and the last of my Nation, I fear no Man, and I depend only upon the Great Spirit" (II, p. 124); and Lahontan himself would like to become a savage so he would "be no longer expos'd to the chagrin of bending the knee" (I, Preface, n.p.). The method Lahontan suggests for bringing France closer to that ideal is nothing less than a popular uprising: the spirit of the Revolution of 1789 is curiously present in these pages.

The second principle governing the lives of these noble savages is a certain minimalism, which may again be either economic or social. On the economic level, the Hurons are content with subsistence production, at the opposite extreme from the European's taste for luxury that leads Europeans to expend themselves in useless effort. The savages limit themselves to what is necessary; as a result, they can live an idle life. "The Savages are wholly free from Care" (II, p. 17). In France, "to be happy, one must always have somewhat in his view that feeds his Wishes. He that confines his Wishes to what he enjoys must be a *Huron*" (II, p. 148). The same is true on the cultural level: they get along without arts and sciences because they do not see a need for them; they undertake no studies, yet this does not keep them from having deep conversations; they are unacquainted with writing, which "[tends] to nothing" (II, p. 157).

The third major principle governing Huron behavior, finally, is conformity with nature. This requirement, which was already the basis for their preference for equality and liberty, is found in all aspects of life. The "natural" is sometimes what is reasonable, what conforms with "natural light." Thus, the Hurons have no written laws because they follow natural law alone, which arises from universal reason. "Why then, to observe the Law, imports no more than to observe the measures of Reason and Justice" (II, p. 122). This makes it possible to do without specific laws: "I should hope," Adario says, "that one day you might come to live without Laws as we do" (II, p. 136). The same holds true for religion, another subject that fascinates Lahontan: the Christian religion must be replaced by natural religion—that is, a religion in conformity with reason, and that turns out to be the Hurons' religion. "They maintain, That a Man ought never to strip himself of the Privileges of Reason, that being the noblest Faculty with which God hath enrich'd him" (II, p. 23); for them, "the Christian Faith was contrary to Reason" (II, p. 27). Not that everything in the Gospels is wrong: many of its principles are even excellent; but let us not forget that we can find the same principles in other religions. Furthermore, in the Christian doctrine they are mixed in with a lot of useless superstitions.

But alongside this rationalist interpretation of nature we find another, more properly "naturalist" (that is, biological) interpretation. What is natural is spontaneous behavior, subject to no social rules at all; what is natural is what originates in the physical characteristics of the species alone. This is the reason Adario condemns civility: "Do's not Civility consist in Decency and an affable Carriage? And what is Decency? Is it not an everlasting Rack, and a tyresome Affectation . . . And why would you Court a Quality that gives you so much trouble? . . . For what end must we lie upon all occasions, and speak otherwise than we think?" (II, p. 151).

The most important example of natural behavior involves sexuality. Here again, we must conform to instincts and not try to repress them with laws. Lovers' encounters are very simple. At nightfall, the young man visits the young woman of his choice, a lighted flare in hand. If the young woman accepts him, she blows out the flame; otherwise she hides under her blanket, and he withdraws. These couplings are made and unmade with no rule but mutual attraction. "'Tis allowable both for the Man and the Woman to part when they please" (II, p. 40). Fidelity is optional; jealousy, on the other hand, is unknown. European marriage is an aberration in their eyes: on what grounds would one impose a fidelity that is contrary to nature, and that applies moreover to women but not to men? The absence of clothes, which characterizes all noble savages, finds further justification here (it could also be motivated by contempt for the superfluous, or by the absence of hierarchical marks of distinction, or by the refusal of polite conventions). These attitudes taken together lead Lahontan to the following conclusion: "One may say, That they are wholly govern'd by Temperament, and their Society is perfect Mechanism" (II, p. 11), and his Adario confirms this: "We live quietly under the Laws of Instinct and innocent Conduct, which wise Nature has imprinted upon our minds from our Cradles" (II, p. 128).

If one chooses to live in accordance with these principles, it becomes possible to achieve the level of perfection of the Hurons, which extends to the physical realm as well as the moral. The savages are in fact exempt from most European illnesses, and the few that persist are resisted with perspiration; the Hurons are more robust than we are, and they live longer. But they also have a morality superior to ours: they are just, generous, disinterested, and cooperative with one another. All these qualities lead Lahontan to see them as being well advanced on the path toward paradise.

This portrait of the noble savage is found over and over throughout the eighteenth century, in more or less detailed form. Its most successful literary expression is perhaps the one Diderot offered in his "Supplement to Bougainville's 'Voyage,'" which bears clear traces of Lahontan's influence. The Tahitian savage is described as being "innocent and mild" (p. 192) and he is "happy"; civilized people, in contrast, are "corrupt," "vile," "wretched" (p. 195). The savage is generous; the civilized person is all greed, able to give nothing but death: "He gave you his fruit; he offered you his wife and daughter; he gave you his hut to live in—and you killed him" (p. 199). The savages are "healthy, straight and strong" (p. 197); even their food is "wholesome" and "frugal" (p. 202), whereas civilized people bring illnesses: "You have infected our blood" (p. 198). Beneath all these differences we find contrasting economic models: private property reigns in one place but not the other. "Here all things are for all, and you have preached to us I know not what distinctions between mine and thine" (p. 196). Private property is in fact limited to a strict minimum in Tahiti, whereas among the Europeans even "a woman came to belong to a certain man" (p. 231). This opposition is extended in turn to the opposition between a society based on a subsistence economy and a consumer society, a society of luxury in which people produce more than they need and consume for the sake of consumption. "We possess already all that is good or necessary for our existence. Do we merit your scorn because we have not been able to create superfluous wants for ourselves?" (p. 197). Diderot's Tahitians resemble Lahontan's Hurons point for point, and they obey the same minimalist principle. Behind Lahontan, we can always glimpse the shadow of Amerigo, who served as inspiration for utopians of various stripes. Each one selected from Amerigo's picture the features that suited him: Diderot retained the sexual freedom for which a rigorist like More had no use at all.

It follows, of course, that any intention of taking over the savages, even for their own good, is abandoned. Not only is Diderot hostile to slavery ("You are neither a god nor a devil—by what right, then, do you enslave people?"—p. 196), but the whole idea of a European civilizing mission is foreign to him: what would the savages have to learn from us, since they are already better than we are? The Tahitian chief's message to Bougainville can thus be summed up in a word: "Go!" (p. 201). If there are contacts among peoples, they must be based purely on reciprocity and equality: "You are both children of Nature—what right do you have over him that he does not have over you?" (p. 197).

To tell the truth, Diderot does not hide the fact that he is writing about our own society and not others. No sooner has the old Tahitian finished his harangue than A, one of the interlocutors in the dialogue, remarks: "In the midst of so much that is unmistakably abrupt and savage I seem to detect a few European ideas and turns of phrase" (p. 201); and when the interview between the chaplain and the Tahitian Orou is over, the same A notes that the latter's discourse is "cast somewhat in a European mold" (p. 226). Moreover, a reader of Bougainville's *Voyage* (and even though the "Supplement" remained unpublished in Diderot's lifetime, we can only suppose that his ideal reader would have read Bougainville's narrative) could not fail to notice several significant distortions: the "Supplement" presents the Tahitians as atheists and free from all illness, while the *Voyage* describes them as in the throes of superstition and suffering from syphilis. These disparities are overt indications that Diderot's aim was not to paint a faithful portrait of the Tahitians, but to use their case as an allegory in order to approach a more general topic: the necessity of submission to nature, an issue that Diderot, much more than Lahontan, supported and advocated, as we have seen. Less utopian than Lahontan (he does not share Lahontan's dream of an egalitarian society), Diderot is also more scientistic.

Natural Man

Jean-Jacques Rousseau's thought is traditionally associated with primitivism and the cult of the noble savage. In reality (and attentive commentators have been pointing this out since the beginning of the twentieth century), Rousseau was actually a vigilant critic of these tendencies. He himself is responsible, however, for sowing confusion among his earliest readers and interpreters, through the careless use he makes of some of his own ideas.

The traditional view derives Rousseau's primitivism from the opposition between natural man and civil man, and from Rousseau's preference for the former over the latter. But this image is much too simplistic, for several reasons. First of all, the state of nature (and thus natural man, the man of "nature" in this sense of the word) does not correspond, for Rousseau, to an actual period of human history that would be more or less remote from our own; Rousseau explained his views on this point clearly and at length in the preface to the *Second Discourse*. The notion of the state of nature is a mental construction, a fiction designed to make it easier to understand real phenomena, not a "phenomenon" comparable to others. The goal Rousseau sets for himself is "to know accurately a state which no longer exists, which perhaps never did exist, which probably never will exist, and about which it is nevertheless necessary to have exact Notions in order accurately to judge of our present state" (preface, p. 130). The deductive process upon which Rousseau embarks has nothing in common with a historical science. "The Inquiries that may be pursued regarding this Subject ought not be taken for historical truths, but only for hypothetical and conditional reasonings; better suited to elucidate the Nature of things than to show their genuine origin, and comparable to those our Physicists daily make regarding the formation of the World" (p. 139).

We might object that these formulas do not express Rousseau's thought, that they are there to protect him from the thunderbolts of religious censorship, which would not take kindly to the free rewriting of the history of the origins of humanity. But even if we suppose that for Rousseau this state of nature did exist once upon a time, there is no turning back: once man has passed through the "state of society," he can no longer go back to the "state of nature." Rousseau was always categorical on that point. "Never has a people, once corrupted, been known to return to virtue," he writes at the beginning of his career, in the "Observations" inspired by a response to his *First Discourse* (p. 51); and, at the end: "Human nature does not go backward" (*Rousseau, Judge of Jean-Jacques: Dialogues*, III, p. 213). Between the return to the primitive state and perfectibility, two incompatible notions, Rousseau resolutely chooses the second.

No misunderstanding has clouded Rousseau's thought longer than the one that attributes to him the goal of banishing arts and sciences from the community. That would do no good, he objects in one of his responses, for the harm has already been done. What is worse, an expulsion of that sort could not fail to have a negative effect, for to it would be added barbarity and corruption: although the sciences and the arts result from man's degradation, in the current state of affairs they are barriers against even greater degradation. The same is true of social life in general. "What, then? Must Societies be destroyed, thine and mine annihilated, and men return to live in forests with Bears? A conclusion in the style of my adversaries, which I would rather anticipate than leave them the shame of drawing it" (*First and Second Discourses*, p. 213). It is thus clear that Rousseau distances himself explicitly from the primitivist theses. Such a solution is inconceivable for society in general and unacceptable for Rousseau himself: "I am much too sensible in my own person of how difficult it is for me not to live with men as corrupt as myself" ("Letter to Philopolis," *First and Second Discourses*, p. 235).

Finally, to this second reason for rejecting the simplistic image that has Rousseau praising the noble savage, we need to add a third, which has to do with Rousseau's evaluation of the state of nature and natural man. It is true that Rousseau sometimes uses the two formulas in such a way as to suggest that he has a decided preference for that state. "The pure state of nature is of all states the one in which men would be the least wicked, the happiest, and more numerous on the earth" ("Fragments politiques," II, p. 465). On the other hand, in the state of society, there is "not a single People that does not rejoice at the disasters of its neighbors" (*First and Second Discourses*, p. 208). How could anyone have any tolerance for such a situation?

But within his own properly anthropological theory as it is presented in the *Discourse on the Origin of Inequality*, Rousseau's position is more nuanced. In the beginning, there was indeed a state of nature; but one cannot call that state admirable, for man was scarcely distinguishable from animals. If there is one point of doctrine on which Rousseau never wavered, it is this. In the state of nature, for want of communication among men, it is impossible to distinguish between virtue and vice; the sentiment of justice is thus unknown in the state of nature, and morality is absent. By this token, man is not yet fully man. "Limited to physical instinct alone, he is nothing, he is stupid" ("Lettre à Beaumont," p. 936). Only mutual contact develops reason, and the moral sense that is based on reason. "It is only on becoming sociable that he becomes a moral being" (*Fragments politiques* [Political Fragments], II, p. 477). There is no possible doubt about the judgment to be passed: this transition is "the happy moment that . . . changed him from a stupid, limited animal into an intelligent being and a man" (*On the Social Contract*, I, 8, p. 56).

At the other extreme, there is the state of society as we now know

it, and which is equally unsatisfying, although for other reasons. That
is why Rousseau refuses to use the label "Golden Age" for either of
these extremes. "Unfelt by the stupid men of earliest times, lost to the
enlightened men of later times, the happy life of the golden age was
always a state foreign to the human race, either because it went unrec-
ognized when humans could have enjoyed it or because it had been lost
when humans could have known it" (*On the Social Contract*, Geneva
manuscript, I, ii, p. 159). The vision of the world and of history that
Rousseau proposes is much more tragic than that of his primitivist
contemporaries: society corrupts man, but man is truly man only because he has entered into society; there is no way out of this paradox.

But this judgment itself is overly hasty. For between the (original)
state of nature and the (contemporary) state of society, there exists a
third, intermediate state in which man is no longer an animal and is
not yet the miserable creature he is to become. This is, as it were, the
savage state; it is in this state that humanity experienced its greatest
happiness. "This period in the development of human faculties, occupying a just mean between the indolence of the primitive state and the
petulant activity of our vanity, must have been the happiest and the
longest-lasting epoch. The more one reflects on it, the more one finds
that this state was the least subject to revolutions, the best for man, and
that he must have left it only by some fatal accident" (*First and Second
Discourses*, p. 177). Rousseau neither believes that the return to the state
of nature is possible nor recommends that man aspire to find himself
once again in that savage state; but when he himself is looking for
something with which to replace the deplorable state of society in
which we live, he thinks again of a compromise between the state of
nature and the state of society, a modest or mixed ideal that would best
suit his disciple: "Emile is not a savage to be relegated to the desert.
He is a savage made to inhabit cities" (*Emile*, III, p. 205). This is a fact
that is rarely stressed in commentaries on Rousseau: while he is capable
of exploring, as a hypothesis, the pure state of nature or the pure state
of society, Rousseau opts for the "happy medium" when he has to
declare his own ideal. This superior state (even if it does not amount
to a real Golden Age—not everything is perfect among savages, far
from it) cannot be identified with the state of nature; it simply incorporates certain elements of that state.

The idea that Rousseau subscribes to the myth of the noble savage
is thus clearly untenable. And yet the attribution of that doctrine to

Rousseau is more than a simple coincidence. We need to note, in the first place, that Rousseau places savage peoples at the top of his hierarchy (even if he is unwilling to make them an example for the future of humanity)—those very savages that provoked the admiration of Amerigo and Montaigne, Lahontan and Diderot. In the second place, Rousseau does not refrain from asserting on occasion that the state of nature is nevertheless to be considered a Golden Age (thus contradicting statements he makes elsewhere). Recalling his own beginnings, and particularly the *First Discourse*, he describes his revelation in the following terms: "An unfortunate question from an Academy . . . showed him another universe, a true golden age, societies of simple, wise, happy men" (*Dialogues*, II, p. 131).

In the third place, finally, even though he refuses to identify those savage populations with natural man, Rousseau nevertheless uses the descriptions of them he comes across in travel narratives as a reservoir of images from which he can draw freely, borrowing characteristics to apply to his fictional man of nature. No sooner has the notion been introduced than he begins to enrich it with features and notations that derive from the very same narratives he criticized in Note 10 of the *Second Discourse*: "The reports of travelers are full of examples of the strength and vigor of men from the barbarous and Savage Nations," he writes in Note 6 (p. 205), and, when he attempts to prove that savage man was not afraid of animals, he refers at once to Hottentots and Caribs (pp. 144, 201). Does it have to be proved that savage man has no concern for the future? "Such is still nowadays the extent of the Carib's foresight: he sells his Cotton bed in the morning and comes weeping to buy it back in the evening, having failed to foresee that he would need it for the coming night" (p. 151). The Caribs are the ones he uses most often for his demonstrations, for they "of all existing Peoples have so far departed least from the state of Nature" (p. 165); it is for this reason, too, that in Note 10 Rousseau recommends with particular insistence that they be studied: it is "the most important voyage of all and the one that should be undertaken with the greatest care" (p. 220). But intact vestiges of natural man can be found elsewhere as well: thus, the first languages must have been "approximately like those which various Savage Nations still have today" (p. 173). Natural man cannot be identified with today's savages, but it is from the latter that we work back to the former.

"Let us therefore beware of confusing Savage man with the men we have before our eyes," Rousseau said at the outset (p. 146). However, he does not obey his own injunction, and his philosophical fiction interferes with his portrait of men and women of today. The savages, it must be added, do not get their due in these rapid evocations. Not only because they receive no more than glancing attention, but also because Rousseau, in the interests of his argument, regularly identifies his savage man with animals. "Such is the animal state in general, and according to Travelers' reports, it is also the state of most Savage Peoples" (p. 147). "The savages of America track the Spaniards by smell just as well as the best Dogs might have done" (p. 147). By and large Rousseau consistently attributes to savage man the features that Buffon, in his *Dissertation on the Nature of Animals*, took as characteristic of animals—for example, their relation to time or their idea of happiness. A great defender of equality among men, Rousseau may not really believe that the Caribs are halfway between men and animals, but, carried away by the allegorical usage he makes of ethnographic data, he says they are.

Thus, we end up having to distinguish between Rousseau's project and the way he himself carried it out—and to prefer the former decisively over the latter.

Chateaubriand

Pilgrimages West and East

François-René de Chateaubriand was the first specifically modern writer-traveler; he might be called the inventor of the voyage as it has come to be practiced in the nineteenth and twentieth centuries. His travel narratives have given rise to countless imitations; directly or indirectly, they have influenced the genre itself and through it the overall European perception of "the others."

For Chateaubriand, the voyage is a well-defined object of reflection. We find references to it, he reminds us, as far back as we can go in human history. He himself felt a need to travel, and so he set forth. In one of his early works, however, he offers a warning: "It is frequently the case that all the stranger can do, in a foreign land, is to exchange recollections for illusions" (*Les Natchez*, in English *The Natchez*, I, p. 31). Voyages have become more common in the modern period; should we rejoice at this or deplore it? "Is it good that communications should be so easy? Would the nations not better preserve their own character if they remain unaware of each other, while maintaining a religious fidelity to the habits and traditions of their forefathers?" (*Voyages*, p. lvii). Unlike Gobineau or Lévi-Strauss, Chateaubriand replies in the negative. Better knowledge of others may make it possible to improve oneself. But one must not take the next step and begin to dream, like Condorcet or Cloots, of a universal state that would eradicate national differences: on the contrary, such differences are precious and must be preserved. "The folly of the moment is to arrive at the unity of peoples and to make just one man of the entire species—so be it; but by acquiring general faculties, will not a whole series of private feelings perish?" (*Mémoires d'outre-tombe*, [Memoirs from Beyond the Grave], II, p. 965). The privileged knowledge of some beings, of some practices, of some places, is a treasure. As in other areas, a certain blending, or moderation, is the most satisfactory solution: neither total rupture with the others nor total fusion.

Chateaubriand himself made two major voyages. In 1791 he went to America; his sojourn there led to a travel narrative (published in 1827), a description in *Mémoires d'outre-tombe*, and a fictional complex dating from the last years of the eighteenth century, from which Chateaubriand extracted *Atala* in 1801 and *René* in 1802, but which he did not publish as a whole, in revised form, until 1826, under the title *Les Natchez*. Then in 1806–1807 he traveled to Greece, Palestine, and Egypt; he published an account of that trip in 1811 under the title *Itinéraire de Paris à Jérusalem* (Itinerary from Pairs to Jerusalem). Chateaubriand himself sought a meaningful way of articulating those two displacements in opposite directions. The trip to America was the project of a naive young man; the trip to the Orient took place in his maturity. "At the time of my trip to the United States, I was filled with illusions"; during the trip to the East, "I was no longer nourishing fantasies" (*Mémoires*, I, p. 257). Of the two opposing modes, Chateaubriand preferred lucidity when he wrote the *Itinéraire:* "At a riper age, the mind returns to more solid tastes: it seeks especially to be nourished by memories and examples from history" (*Itinéraire*, p. 107). However, at a still riper age (the corresponding section of the *Mémoires* was written in 1822 and revised in 1846, when Chateaubriand was nearly eighty years old), the preference is reversed, and the American adventures "come to mind today with a charm quite lacking in my memories of the brilliant spectacle of the Bosphorus" (I, p. 257): old age rejoins youth in the taste for innocence and illusion.

But the two voyages are articulated in a second, more significant way.

The West (America) is nature; the East is culture. There are human beings in America, of course, but they are savages who live in a state of nature scarcely distinguishable from the global natural cycle, whereas on the other side of the ocean we encounter a fundamentally human world. "The planes of the Ocean and the Mediterranean open routes to nations, and their shores are or have been inhabited by numerous and powerful civilized peoples; the Canadian lakes present only the nakedness of their waters, which adjoin bare land: solitudes separating other solitudes" (I, p. 244). The Indians of America have no history, because they have no writing; they do not cultivate the earth; and their monuments rapidly disappear into the forest. For these reasons they are forever young, but they also risk disappearing without a trace. In contrast, the Greeks and the Hebrews, the Arabs and the Egyptians are people identified with history, with civilization, with the entire set of religions, arts, and sciences.

The American voyage is thus a voyage into nature, and to the extent that the traveler encounters men and women, he finds them living in the state of nature. Things are clear to Chateaubriand even before he sets out. In the preface to *Atala*, written in 1801, he describes his project as follows: "I . . . conceived the design of undertaking a work, *l'épopée de l'homme de la nature*—which should exhibit the manners of uncivilized life" (p. v). We can see from this, first of all, that at this point Chateaubriand is thinking in terms borrowed from Rousseau, although he commits the usual error of interpretation by identifying the man of nature with contemporary savages; and we can also see that he has decided to obey Rousseau's injunctions. The latter indeed expressed regret that the philosophers who were his contemporaries—the Buffons, the Montesquieus, the Diderots—had not undertaken voyages of exploration. Philosophers had not taken his advice, and Rousseau himself never went farther abroad than London. But forty years later, his young disciple Chateaubriand heeded the call and set out for America in search of "natural man."

What must the community of natural men look like? It will manifest the familiar features of noble savages. They do not know "yours" and "mine": "The savage nations, under the empire of primitive ideas, have an invincible aversion to private property, the foundation of social order" (*Voyages*, quoted from *Chateaubriand's Travels in America*, p. 161). Consequently they live as equals in complete freedom to do as they like. "Not a single beat of my heart will be constrained, not a single one of my thoughts will be enchained; I shall be as free as nature; I shall recognize as sovereign only Him who lit the flame of the suns" (p. 43). It seems to go without saying that this natural world is preferable to the world of society.

However, Chateaubriand has scarcely had time to proclaim his convictions in the forests near New York when he makes a surprising discovery. In the heart of the woods he notices a shelter; in the middle of the shelter, a score of savages, "the first I had seen in my life," decorated with feathers and paint as expected; and amid these savages a little Frenchman, M. Violet, whose profession is unexpected to say the least: he is a dancing master. His Iroquois disciples have already done a good job of learning French dances, and he calls them "these savage ladies and gentlemen." "Is it not a crushing blow for a disciple of Rousseau to be introduced to savage life through a ball that General Rochambeau's former kitchen boy was throwing for the Iroquois? I felt very much like laughing, but I was cruelly humiliated" (*Mémoires*, I, pp. 225–226).

During his first encounter with savages, Chateaubriand thus discovers that there is something unrealistic in the project he thinks he has taken over from Rousseau. The Indians do not really seem to be any better than the French, and in particular the radical opposition that he had imagined is nonexistent: there are dancing masters in the heart of the forest, and the Iroquois have learned to bow. In place of the hierarchical opposition between the man of nature and the man of society, Chateaubriand discovers a world of blendings.

This is not the only disappointment that awaits him along the way. By dint of observing nature around him, he discovers that it is far from perfect, a fact which, he believes, contradicts Rousseau's idea (in reality, for Rousseau, everything that could be observed in one's surroundings belonged to the state of society, not to nature; and Rousseau agreed that this state should be condemned). In the preface to *Atala*, Chateaubriand declares: "I am not, like M. Rousseau, by any means an enthusiastic admirer of the savage life; and . . . I cannot consider *pure nature* as the most lovely thing in the world. Wherever I have had an opportunity of contemplating it, I have invariably found it disgusting" (p. xi). What counts in man, Chateaubriand goes on to say, is not his nature—that is, his animality—but his mind. "Very far from being of opinion that the man who thinks is a *degenerated animal*, I believe that it is thought alone which constitutes the dignity of man" (p. xi). The misreading of Rousseau continues, but never mind; what matters is that Chateaubriand has given up primitive exoticism.

A political partisan of a historical movement known as the Restoration, Chateaubriand takes great care to make it clear that it is absurd to cherish the past simply because it is past. "The good old days doubtless have their merits; but we have to remember that a political state is not better because it is lapsed and routine; otherwise we would have to agree that the despotism of China or India, unchanged for three thousand years, is the most perfect thing in this world" (*Voyages*, p. lvii). There is a factual reason for this refusal to valorize the past as such: primitive mores are not always good, and in any event would not suit men of today. And there is also a moral reason: the person who remains conservative "tries not to see that the human spirit is perfectible" (p. lviii). Rather than breaking with Rousseau, Chateaubriand thus replaces a bad interpretation of Rousseau with another, better one, inserting himself in a straight line of descent from the Enlightenment agenda.

The very freedom he so cherished in the state of nature now appears to him as less desirable than another form of freedom that is proper to the social state; and when in 1827 he transcribes his inflamed tirades in favor of natural liberty (they date from 1791), he cannot keep himself from noting: "I leave as they are these expressions of youth: the reader will kindly excuse them" (*Chateaubriand's Travels in America*, p. 213, note 60). In this distinction, for which Chateaubriand seems to be inspired by Benjamin Constant (but also directly by Rousseau), the liberty of savages is opposed to that of civilized peoples: "In that period of my life [the voyage to America], I knew liberty in the style of the ancients, the liberty that is the daughter of the mores of a fledgling society; but I was unacquainted with the liberty that is the daughter of enlightenment and of an old civilization, the liberty of which the representative republic has proved the reality: God willing, may it prove lasting!" (*Mémoires*, I, p. 216).

It obviously follows that Chateaubriand's project will be modified. His unconditional and *a priori* praise for savage peoples is replaced by a more balanced judgment. He recognizes first of all that the contrast between civilized peoples and savages is far from being as clear-cut as he had believed. "From the examination of these languages alone, it is clear that the peoples named by us as *savages* were far advanced in that civilization which involved the combination of ideas" (*Travels in Amer-*

ica, p. 120). The same conclusion may be drawn about political regimes: "Among the savages there are to be found all the types of governments known to civilized peoples, from despotism to republic" (p. 155). This more nuanced version allows him to describe the meeting between Europeans and Indians in terms other than the ones bequeathed by Rousseau: "The Indian was not *savage;* the European civilization did not act on the *pure state of nature;* it acted on the *rising American civilization*" (p. 178; emphasis added). It follows that the "savages" constitute not a homogeneous entity but a series of populations with distinctive characteristics: one must avoid attributing "the same traits to all the savages of North America" (p. 81). The savages, like all other men, have vices *and* virtues.

Finally, the book Chateaubriand plans to write can no longer be described as an "epic of natural man." The work that is available to us—*The Natchez*, completed by *Atala* and *René*, an ambitious and incomplete work that Chateaubriand revised and abandoned and finally published—is rather the epic of the *encounter* between savages and civilized peoples, between the Natchez and the French, in which we find a representation of the conflict experienced by Chateaubriand himself between his earlier ideas and those that came after his departure for America.

Savagery and Civilization

The initial aim of *The Natchez* was to illustrate the opposition between the state of nature and the state of society, by choosing an extreme representative to incarnate each one: the tribe of the Natchez in America, the court of Louis XIV in France. The goal of this confrontation is explicit. "The things of society and of nature, exhibited in their extreme opposition, will furnish thee with the means of weighing, with the least possible error, the good and the evil of the two conditions" (I, pp. 185–186). Ethnographic exploration is thus subordinated to moral and political investigation.

In the book it is Chactas, a Natchez Indian, who embodies the shift in Chateaubriand's attitudes toward nature and society. At first, Chactas does not question the superiority of savage life (that is, his own), for familiar reasons: instead of private property, equality and freedom are the rule. "'Enter the huts of the Iroquois, and thou wilt find neither great nor small, neither rich nor poor, every where peace of mind and liberty for man'" (I, pp. 198–199). Savage life has two additional advantages. First of all, the savages are beautiful (Atala is "divine"); second, they live in close contact with nature, here understood as the nonhuman world—landscapes, vegetation, animals—which is also of exceptional beauty. Chateaubriand left us some exemplary instances of exotic description ideally suited for eliciting nostalgia in generations of readers. "It was a beauteous night. The Spirit of the Atmosphere was shaking out his blue tresses, pregnant with the scent of the pines, and we could breathe the tenuous odor of amber floating up from the crocodiles asleep beneath the tamarinds by the river. The moon shone down from the cloudless blue, and its pearl gray light drifted over the hazy summit of the forest. No sound could be heard, save some vague far-away harmony permeating the depths of the woods. It was as though the soul of solitude were sighing through the entire expanse of the wilderness" (*Atala*, p. 29). This eulogy of savage life is coupled with criticism of civilized life. Following a series of peripeties, the young Chactas lands in France, where he casts an astonished and disapproving gaze on the contemporary world, in the manner of Lahontan's Adario or Montesquieu's Persians. What he sees around him are self-interested, petty, intolerant people; the persecution of Protestants plunges him into a state of perplexity mingled with horror. What is more, these people are overburdened with cares and they live in poverty. "I saw man brutalized by indigence, amidst a famished family, not enjoying the advantages of society, and having lost those of nature" (*The Natchez*, I, p. 192): once again, we might think we were reading Rousseau's criticisms of contemporary society. The so-called scholars are in reality ignoramuses who see the Indians as halfway between man and monkey, and the arts are of no use at all. "'The arts then contribute nothing to the happiness of life, and yet that is the only point in which you appear to excel us'" (I, p. 198). This is why Chactas does not hesitate to conclude that the state of nature is preferable to the state of society, with virtue reigning in the former and vice in the latter; he yearns to be back in his forests, and cannot keep from harboring the same wish for the more appealing of his interlocutors: "I . . . finished, as usual, by inviting my host to turn savage" (I, p. 199).

Up to this point we might have thought we were reading Lahontan's *Dialogues*. Chactas' narrative seems to be no more than an amplified version of Adario's: Adario had also turned up in France, and at about the same time. But the coincidence of names functions precisely as a warning device here. In the text of *The Natchez* there is indeed an Indian character called Adario. However, Chateaubriand's Adario is anything but an incarnation of wisdom: he is violent, a patriot to the point of inhumanity, the very antithesis of the good Chactas. Far from imitating Lahontan, Chateaubriand turns the message of his precursor into just one of the voices within his own book, and it is a voice that can be seen, little by little, to be wrong.

Learning truth is a progressive process. Thus, in the *Atala* episode, Chactas becomes aware of his compatriots' cruelty during a torture session to which Father Aubry is subjected: "To prevent him from talking, the enraged Indians forced a red-hot iron down his throat" (p. 80). Now one cannot have it both ways: either everything observed among the savages is not necessarily natural, or else nature is not always good. Chactas even risks his own life in pursuing his anthropological apprenticeship: "Those very Indians whose customs are so moving . . . now were calling loudly for my execution" (pp. 35–36). In another context, an increased familiarity with French architecture, music, and tragedy makes him aware of their greatness. Finally, ignorance is not purely and simply a good thing: as proof, there is Atala's death, a suicide to which she was driven by prejudices. Father Aubry explains this to the dying woman: "My daughter, . . . all your sorrows are born of ignorance. It was your primitive education and the lack of necessary teaching which brought on this calamity" (p. 64). We might think we were hearing Condorcet speaking in praise of instruction: even religion needs enlightenment!

What Chactas learns in particular is that good and evil are not rigidly compartmentalized, the one belonging to savages and the other to civilized peoples. Just like Natchez society, the century of Louis XIV merits both criticism and praise. At the same time, if we look more closely we discover resemblances beneath the superficial differences. When he begins to grasp what the French are saying to one another, to his great surprise Chactas finds "the conversation as free [*des propos aussi fins*] as that of the Hurons" (*The Natchez*, I, p. 183). Thus, without giving up the possibility of judging good and evil, one must give up the hope of being able to classify entire peoples or cultures in those terms. On other occasions, judgment is the result only of custom or an optical illusion. Finally, it is not because one is sensitive to "the advantages of nature" that one must scorn "the superiority of art" (II, p. 28): it all depends upon what the circumstances require.

This learning process leads to the granting of equal dignity to all human beings—"Have the woes of an obscure inhabitant of the woods less claim to our tears than those of other men?" (I, p. 17)—and to the observation that they are equally destined for happiness and misery. "Happiness is common to all nations and to all climates. The wretched Esquimaux on his ice-rock, is as happy as the European monarch on his throne: it is the same instinct which causes the hearts of mothers and lovers to throb among the snows of Labrador, and on the down of the swans of the Seine" (I, pp. 234–235). That is why the black slave Glazirne will protect the child of the Indian woman Celuta: the differences in race or country pale before the features we share because we belong to the same species. Chateaubriand draws these universalist and egalitarian precepts from the Christian tradition.

The universalism professed by the characters of *The Natchez* is not incompatible with patriotism, provided that the patriotic sentiment is understood not as a preference for one's compatriots over all other men, but as an attachment to a place, a landscape, to common memories, to the language of one's forefathers. Upon returning to Natchez country, Chactas weeps and kisses the ground of his birth; which does not prevent him from responding to Adario, "I think I love my country as well as thou dost, but I love it less than virtue" (III, p. 208). Adario, on the other hand, is on the side of blind patriotism (Rousseau would have said that he sides with Brutus, not with Christ), and it is hard to sympathize with him when he kills his own grandson rather than let him live among the French. Artaguette and Mila, on the contrary, illustrate, for the French and the Indians respectively, the possibility of combining a certain patriotism (Artaguette "longed to spill his blood for France"—I, p. 39) with a preference for universal values: "'Country!' rejoined Mila; 'What is country to me, if it is unjust?'" (III, p. 29).

The virtues of individuals thus count for more than the countries to which they belong. One of the great lessons Chactas learns is precisely this relative independence of the behavior of an individual with respect to his culture. Indians and Frenchmen may meet the same fate; conversely, within each of the two communities the greatest diversity reigns. "Prelates differing as widely in talents as in principles, literary men remarkable for the contrast of their genius, clubs of wits at war with each other . . . " (I, p. 181). The French are no better than the Natchez, and vice versa; the proponent of exoticism, who believes that foreigners are preferable to natives, is just as mistaken as the nationalist who believes the opposite. What Chactas discovers is that freedom is part of the definition of man. The proper opposition is not between us and the others, but between vice and virtue.

The ethico-political debate reaches its culmination on the occasion of Chactas' meeting with "Fénelon," to whom Chateaubriand entrusts the formulation of the book's moral. "Fénelon" listens attentively to Chactas, and does not wholly reject the latter's defense of savage life. In his reply he nevertheless undertakes to support, against primitivism, the universalist thesis of the equality of peoples—a thesis that cannot simply be reduced, however, to the relativist refusal to pass judgment. "'The men of all countries, when their hearts are pure, resemble one another, for it is then God who speaks in them, God who is ever the same. Vice alone produces hideous differences between us: beauty is but one; there are a thousand deformities'" (I, p. 199). Characteristically, Chateaubriand uses the word "beauty" in place of "virtue": his Christianity has a strongly aesthetic tinge.

But "Fénelon" does not stop there. Precisely because of the oneness of humanity, value judgments are possible; thus, he compares the relative merits of the state of nature and the state of society, and he concludes that the latter is superior. His arguments are borrowed in part from Rousseau (whom he thinks he is refuting). First of all, the transition to social life is an inevitable consequence of the increase in human population, and it is thus pointless to rebel against it. In the second place, the man of nature is spontaneously good, but he is not thereby virtuous; the distinction between vice and virtue is specific to the social state. "Fénelon" adds that humanity's ideal must not be nature (what is) but perfection (what should be); for this reason, the practice of the arts is a proof of superiority. "The arts bring us nigh to the Deity; they enable us to discover a perfection above nature, and existing only in our understanding" (I, p. 201). In the state of nature the law of the strongest rules—and this cannot be considered a sufficient basis for justice.

Chateaubriand can thus declare that *Atala*'s goal was "to show the superiority of the social to the savage life" (p. xiv). Converted to this new wisdom, Chactas—who had already been strongly influenced by Father Aubry's message—recognizes that Christianity is a superior religion and philosophy, even if he does not adopt it right away (he is converted only on his deathbed); but this Christianity is limited to an affirmation of the unity of the human species and of the need to distinguish good from evil. It could thus be said that *The Natchez* is, above all, a critique of exotic and primitivist reveries, a critique carried out in the spirit of the Enlightenment (which shows that the myth of the "noble savage" is the inverse of the spirit of the Enlightenment rather than being a direct emanation of that spirit).

And yet Chactas' ideal, like Chateaubriand's, seems somewhat different: not to embrace the life of society (and its highest form, Christian life) without reservation, but rather to attempt a synthesis between nature and society, between savages and civilized peoples, keeping only the good aspects of each state. After listening to "Fénelon," Chactas returns nevertheless to "nature" (as "Fénelon" has advised him to do, moreover), and he spends his life defending the Indians to the French and the French to the Indians; he cherishes the dream of being able to "'combine the liberty of the polished man with the independence of the Savage'" (I, p. 207). And just as Rousseau judged that the happiest moment of history had been a mixed moment, equidistant from the state of nature and the state of society, Chactas passes a superlative judgment on a population that occupies just such an intermediate position: "Of all the nations I have visited, this appeared to me to be the happiest; neither miserable, like the fisherman of Labrador, nor cruel, like the hunter of Canada, nor enslaved as was formerly the Natchez, nor corrupted like the European, the Sioux combines all that is desirable in the savage and in the civilized man" (I, p. 251). The thing is thus possible!

The World of Blendings

Once he has landed in America, Chateaubriand discovers a mixed world instead of a simple opposition between nature and society. America, on the whole, strikes him as "a curious mixture of the state of nature and the civilized state." Crawling "on all fours out of an Iroquois hut," he hears voices singing Paisiello and Cimarosa. "The spire of a new bell-tower rose up from the heart of an ancient forest" (*Mémoires*, I, p. 232); it is obvious that Chateaubriand sometimes equates the notions of "civilization" and "Europe."

But the most visible results of this mixture are negative. The Europeans have chased away the Indians, and sooner or later the Indians "will be obliged to undergo exile or extermination" (*Travels in America*, p. 176). Those who remain lose more and more of their culture, knowledge, and traditions every day. European commerce brings almost as much evil as war does; the old religious forms wither away, and the ancestral political structures are not replaced by anything else. "Our presents, our vices, and our arms bought, corrupted, or killed the individuals who made up these several powers" (p. 181). And the people of mixed race resulting from the biological mixture of the two groups, far from being a happy synthesis, as Chateaubriand would have liked, embody the failure of the encounter. "Speaking the language of their [European] fathers and of their [Indian] mothers, they have the vices of both races. These bastards of civilized nature and savage nature . . ." (*Mémoires*, I, p. 241).

We cannot but recognize that the encounter between the two worlds, which Chateaubriand liked to imagine in idyllic colors (Western and Eastern peoples exchanging mutual greetings in the name of their common humanity!), has instead brought out the worst features of both groups. On the side of "civilization," we find only military conquest and acquisitiveness: all technological innovations are used in the service of these two passions. On the side of "nature," we encounter perfidy and cupidity, lying and dissolution. The civilized peoples hold the savages in contempt, and the savages repay them with hatred. We can no longer dream about what Indian civilization might have become had it been exposed to a better influence, or had it continued to develop along its own lines. "A civilization of a nature different from ours could have reproduced the men of antiquity or have spread new enlightenment from a still unknown source" (*Travels in America*, pp. 178–179).

The Natchez is situated halfway between dream and disillusionment. All the characters in the book are the products of blendings, but more successful ones than those Chateaubriand observed. The best representatives of the civilized world are those who have kept (or acquired) something savage: for example, in America, Father Aubry, who converts Indians to Christianity but who also goes partway to meet them; or, in the court of Louis XIV, "La Fontaine" or "Fénelon," the latter declaring, "I am somewhat of a savage myself" (*The Natchez*, I, p. 196). Moreover, Chateaubriand explains his fondness for America by the fact that it had given him an "unruly education [*une éducation sauvage*]" (*Travels in America*, p. 8).

It is not that, in *The Natchez*, all mixtures are successful. There are

first of all those people who, like Chepar, the commander of Fort
Rosalie, simply do not perceive cultural difference: "In his eyes savage
America had the same aspect as civilized Europe" (*The Natchez*, I,
p. 43). There are also those, more numerous, who take from the other
only the defects. Thus, on the Indian side, there is Ondouré, a power-
hungry military leader (jealous of René) who, even though he detests
the whites, wants to be like them, and who has contracted all of their
vices. On the European side, there is Febriano, already a monstrous
Christian-Musulman hybrid, who imitates in turn only Ondouré's bad
points. Chactas stigmatizes all those whites who "seek not to polish us
Savages; they find it easier to turn Savages like us" (I, p. 246).

But alongside these negative examples, there are others who
demonstrate the possibility of a beneficial mixture. These are first of
all the women: Atala, a convert to Christianity; Celuta, René's wife;
Mila, a young woman in love with him. All these women have preserved
their original strength of character, but they have added to it a spiritual
openness that has led them to love whites, or the Indian friends of the
whites. There is also Outougamiz, Celuta's brother, who declares himself René's brother as well, and who remains loyal to him against all
odds. But it is obviously Chactas himself who is intended to embody
the happy combination of the good qualities of both human groups.
The preface to *Atala* describes him as "a savage, supposed to be born
with some genius, and who is more than half civilized" (p. xii). And
from his very first appearance, in *The Natchez*, he shows that there is
no watertight separation between the two states: when he speaks, René
hears "the panegyric on civilized man, pronounced by a savage amidst
a wilderness" (I, p. 28). He admires France even while remaining
critical of its mores; he loves his own country without being blind to
its defects. When he leaves France, "Fénelon" entrusts him with a
special mission—"'Be among your countrymen a protector of the
French'" (I, p. 206)—and, as the whole episode of René's adoption
shows, Chactas devotes himself fully to this mission, to the point of
being reproached by his countrymen for having "too great a fondness
for the strangers" (I, p. 64); the explanation is that he sees in this role
the image of his own destiny as a product of the crossing of two worlds.

Finally, there is René. He too is a dual being, and he occupies a
position diametrically opposed to Chactas', as the latter tells him: "I
see in you the civilized man who has become a savage; you see in me
the savage whom the Great Spirit has (I know not for what purpose)
chosen to civilize. Having entered life's path from opposite ends, you

have now come to rest in my place while I have gone to sit in yours. And so, we must have had a totally different view of things" (*Atala*, p. 22). The conclusion of this speech is somewhat surprising: we might have expected that, each man having gone halfway, the two would have had on the contrary quite similar views on everything. But there is more than one form of encounter between the two worlds, even for people of good will: Chactas might be said to be at home in Europe and in America, while René is a foreigner everywhere.

A Frenchman who has chosen to live among Indians, René looks critically upon European society and wants to be adopted by the Indians, who accept him. "The brother of Amelia had fallen asleep a civilized man, he awoke a man of nature" (*The Natchez*, I, p. 50). In the struggles that bring the Natchez into conflict with the French later on, René remains loyal to his new country, and goes to plead its cause with the French governor of Louisiana. In so doing, to be sure, he is defending not the Indians in preference to the French, but universal values in preference to national values: "As a Frenchman, I may appear guilty; as a man I am innocent" (II, p. 210).

But it is not true that René woke up one day to find himself a man of nature. Not because, as we now know, the opposition is not nearly as clear-cut as it first appeared; or because, according to Chateaubriand, the state of society is finally preferable to the state of nature; but because René never really tries to bring off the transformation. We learn his story in his own retrospective account, which constitutes the novel *René*: it is not his condemnation of civilized life that led him to flee Europe, but the impossible passion that had bound him to his sister Amelia. The conflict of Europe versus America (or civilization versus savagery) turns out to be neutralized, as it were, by another conflict, the one between political and private life, or between extroversion and introversion, in which René is wholly situated on the side of the second term. "'In Europe and in America, both Society and Nature have fatigued me,'" he writes in his last letter to Celuta (III, p. 152). René's inner life is unhappy, and as he has chosen to focus exclusively on his inner life, he trails his unhappiness with him wherever he goes.

In the last analysis, the French reject him while the Indians never really manage to take him in, and in René's eyes they are right. He will never succeed in turning himself into a savage; he remains with the Indians on the strength of a rejection rather than by virtue of a positive choice. "Soon I found myself lonelier in my native land than I had been on foreign soil" (*René*, p. 94). But he does not recognize himself any better in his new fatherland, for that is not what he needs; he thus takes on the condition of foreigner on a permanent basis rather than a temporary one. "This man, a stranger on the earth, sought in vain a spot of ground on which he might rest his head: wherever he had shown his face, he had created misery" (*The Natchez*, II, p. 242). In fact, instead of bringing peace and serenity to others, like Chactas, he carries desolation and sorrow in his wake. This is because he no longer knows how to love: "The void formed at the bottom of his soul could no longer be filled" (II, p. 127).

In his own way, then, René rejects the choice between civilized society and savage society—not because, like Chactas, he sees the good sides of both, but because he refuses to belong to any society. His attitude with regard to society, any society, is a sort of worst-case politics: the more unjust a society is, the more it confirms his choice. At the conclusion of his trial, he is unjustly condemned; but this fact delights him, for it proves in his eyes that society is bad not only in its crimes but in its laws. "To feel conscious of his innocence, and to be condemned by the law, would be, according to Rene's ideas, a sort of triumph over social order" (II, p. 213). Chactas is interested in the French when he is in France, and he is interested in the Natchez when he is in Natchez country; as for René, in either place he is interested only in himself. "Rene, living within himself, and, as it were, out of the world by which he was surrounded, scarcely noticed what was passing about him" (II, p. 157).

René would thus be a descendent of the egocentric subject Rousseau described in the *Confessions* and the *Reveries;* but he is also distinct from his ancestor in that egocentrism leads him to an indifference toward the world to which Rousseau laid claim but could never illustrate. René is the first modern nihilist, and he derives no benefit whatsoever from his dual cultural identity. What brought him to this pass (forbidden love) hardly matters; what counts is that he has gone beyond good and evil. That is why Father Souël, having heard his confession, condemns him severely: "Presumptuous youth, you thought man sufficient unto himself. Know now that solitude is bad for the man who does not live with God" (*René*, p. 113); and the concluding sentences of *The Natchez* declare him guilty in the eyes of God. But does Chateaubriand share these harsh judgments? If he wants us to share them, why does he give his hero not only his own first name but also an attractiveness that nothing in the narrative justifies? Chateaubriand in fact speaks of his "immense" soul, and René wins the irrevocable attachment of all the "good" people in the story—Chactas, Celuta, Outougamiz, Mila: would this not be a way of letting us know that René deserves more sympathy than Father Souël is prepared to grant him?

Ethnocentrism and Egocentrism

We must not let Chateaubriand's universalist positions obscure the fact that they coexist, in his discourse, with a purely national agenda. One reason for his trip to America was his desire to discover, between America and the Polar ice cap, a northern passage connecting the Pacific and the Atlantic oceans; he would reap personal glory from the discovery, of course, but also benefits for his own country. "Had I succeeded, I would have had the honor of imposing French names on unknown regions and of endowing my country with a colony in the Pacific Ocean" (*Mémoires*, I, p. 222). Prefiguring Tocqueville's attitude in this regard, Chateaubriand does not see any incompatibility between his critique of the evils of colonization, as it has been practiced in the Americas, and the search for new colonies to benefit France; he has no problem affirming the equality of all peoples even while he is support- ing the subjugation of some people to others. He continues to regret the abandonment of France's overseas territories. He is content to observe that their possession was in the French interest, without ever wondering whether it was also in the interest of the people who lived in them; but then of course the French are "the most intelligent, the bravest, the most brilliant nation on earth" (p. 220). Undertaken in view of a purely French goal, Chateaubriand's trip will be broken off for an equally French reason: he learns one day that the king has fled. "I stopped in my tracks and told myself: 'Go back to France'" (p. 257).

But alongside this finally rather banal ethnocentrism, Chateaubriand also manifests another sort that characterizes him better; it has to do with his artistic project itself, the one that results in *The Natchez*, completed by *Atala* and *René*. We know now, in fact, that Chateaubri- and did not go to America solely in order to make a geographical discovery, but also because he had a literary purpose: to write the epic of natural man. As it happened, he lacked information on the topic: "I must, like Homer, visit the nation I meant to describe" (*Atala*, Preface, p. vi). We have seen that in America Chateaubriand did not exactly find men of nature, but he most assuredly did discover his own poetic vocation. The confrontation between Europe and America furthered a purely personal project, that of producing beautiful works of art.

In fact, if Chateaubriand observed the Indians around him, he did so almost in spite of himself, or at least unintentionally. "It wasn't the Americans that I had come to see but something entirely different from the men I knew, something more in harmony with the natural order of my ideas" (*Mémoires*, I, p. 221). What Chateaubriand wants to see is entirely determined by his identity as a Frenchman, not by what the Americans are—which interests him hardly at all. And in the last analysis the characters in his book are the product not of his observation but of his imagination—which his travels in America have simply awakened. "In the desert of my early existence, I was obliged to invent characters to embellish it: I drew my own substance from creatures that I did not find elsewhere, and that I carried within myself" (p. 236).

In the preface to *The Natchez*, Chateaubriand relates how he borrowed the description of the mores of the Natchez and the story of their uprising from Father Charlevoix's *Histoire de la Nouvelle France* (History of New France); he takes pride in remaining faithful to his source, and in having merely, as a poet, "added to truth" (I, p. 10). Thus, rather than relying on facts observed in America, he uses a book he had read in France as his principal source. As for his poetic additions and their relation to the American reality, a good example, reported in the *Mémoires d'outre-tombe*, concerns the prototypes of Atala and Celuta. Chateaubriand is traveling with a group of Indians, among whom he sees two young women of mixed blood. Communication with them does not go very far: "I did not understand a word they were saying to me, and they did not understand me" (p. 250). After the fact, Chateaubriand discovers that these two girls were probably prostitutes. "The guides came right out and called them *painted ladies*, which shocked my sense of the proprieties [*ma vanité*]" (p. 250). This is virtually all he ever learns about them: we can hardly avoid being impressed, then, by the metamorphosis they undergo in his epic! "I do not know whether I have restored to them the vividness of the impression they gave me; at least I made one of them a virgin and the other a chaste spouse, in penance" (p. 255). But this brutal sublimation means that the characters in question tell us a good deal more about Chateaubriand himself than about Indian women. Is it not a form of violence— reserved exclusively to creator-artists—to be able to shape at will and as needed the identity of persons one has encountered?

Chateaubriand himself recognizes and acknowledges this: during the return trip, he relates, "I had with me not Eskimos of the polar regions but two savages of an unknown species: Chactas and Atala" (p. 272). A species unknown in America, it is true, but not in Europe, where they belong to the tribe of Adario (Lahontan's) and Orou (Diderot's)—that is, the tribe of allegorical savages, more or less good, more or less wise, products of the ideological necessities of the moment, and lacking any particular relationship to real Indians or Tahitians. Chateaubriand's Chactas is the bearer of a nobler message than Lahontan's Adario, but the one is no more an Indian than the other: both of them come straight out of the Parisian salons. And the same is true of the plot in which Chateaubriand implicates his artificial characters: with its murky conspiracies and its crimes of passion, it owes more to the *roman noir* of Matthew Gregory Lewis and Ann Radcliffe than to the human relations Chateaubriand had observed in America.

The style of *The Natchez* deserves special mention in this inventory of Chateaubriand's "aesthetic" ethnocentrisms. The author tells us that he had first produced a single manuscript, including the story of the Natchez and what would later constitute the story of his own travels. He subsequently undertook a double task: that of separating the two narratives, true and fictional, and that of transposing the latter from the novelistic to the epic genre. However, the second part of the project came to a halt halfway through the volume. Chateaubriand borrows this epic form from Homer, his unique source of literary inspiration at the time, he claims, apart from the Bible. This is why René is repeatedly called "Amelia's brother," and Chactas sometimes "the Nestor of the Natchez"; this is also why the text is studded with comparisons, "some brief, others long, in Homeric fashion," as Chateaubriand himself points out. At the time the *Itinéraire* was written, he was still of the opinion that this was the way to proceed: "Woe to him who does not see nature with Fénelon's eyes, and Homer's!" (*Itinéraire*, p. 58).

To be like Homer, Chateaubriand imitates Homeric style—and the result, it must be said, falls far short of the original. Chateaubriand was more inspired when he decided, still in imitation of Homer, to go off and meet the people he was going to describe; but, as we have seen, his meeting contributed very little to the writing of *The Natchez*. Homer is an epic author not because of his stylistic features but because he gave his poem a collective subject; it is by dissolving the poet's "I" in the anonymous voice of the people that one writes "like Homer," not by imitating his comparisons or his antonomasias. Now Chateaubriand gives us just one voice, introduces us to only one subjectivity: his own. As an epic, *The Natchez* is a failure.

Chateaubriand depicted himself both in Chactas and in René. Chactas expresses his convictions, in a philosophy that synthesizes Christianity and the Enlightenment. René embodies his inner experience: everywhere a foreigner, tired of everything, indifferent to fellow creatures, in perpetual self-contemplation. Now *The Natchez* is a book authored by René rather than Chactas, by the introvert rather than the extrovert: that is why the epic project was doomed to fail, whereas the *Mémoires*, some time later, would offer Chateaubriand an appropriate form. The author of *The Natchez* is interested only in himself, has no curiosity at all about others: this does not augur well for the writing of an epic! The universalism professed by Chateaubriand-Chactas turns out to be blocked by the egocentrism of Chateaubriand-René.

From Traveler to Tourist

The Natchez is a complex text in which universalism grapples with ethnocentrism and description of the world contends with description of the self. Things are simpler, relatively speaking, in the *Itinéraire de Paris à Jérusalem:* Chactas has disappeared, and René enjoys undivided rule. The *Mémoires d'outretombe* presented the trip to the East as a plunge into history and culture, in contrast to the Western trip, which was devoted to nature. The *Itinéraire* sets up a somewhat different articulation, for it includes three terms and not just two. The Indians and the Arabs are both savages—but in different ways. "In a word, everything in the American points to the savage who has not yet attained the state of civilization; with the Arab, everything points to the civilized man who has fallen back into the savage state" (*Itinéraire*, p. 268). The missing third term is Chateaubriand himself, the Frenchman, the European, who is passing judgment—and who clearly embodies contemporary civilization. The *Itinéraire* is structured around the alternation of two modes that are equally disastrous for knowledge of others: Chateaubriand's ethnocentrism as a Frenchman and his egocentrism as a writer.

The countries he visits have been civilized, but they have fallen back into barbarity. This is true of the Greeks and the Egyptians, but even more so of the Arabs in Palestine. "Nothing about them would an-

nounce the savage if they always kept their mouths closed; but as soon
as they start to speak, you hear a noisy, strongly aspirate language; you
notice shiny white teeth like those of jackals and snow leopards"
(p. 265). This description identifies them clearly with animality, their
very language consists exclusively of noise and breathing. We are far
removed from the author's generous remarks about the intelligence of
the Indian languages; and the lesson of "La Bruyère," which forbade
reducing individuals to the culture they come from, seems to have been
forgotten.

But the most serious case is that of the Turks, Chateaubriand's real
whipping-boys *(tête de Turc)*, for, like the Indians, they have not known
civilization in the past, but also, like the Arabs, they seem to have little
hope for civilization in the future; furthermore, they have subjugated
peoples like the Greeks who at least were civilized once upon a time.
The Turks, it seems, have two distinctive features, one of which arouses
Chateaubriand's hatred and the other his scorn: they spend their time
"ravaging the world or else sleeping on carpets, amidst women and
perfumes" (p. 175). With regard to their penchant for sleep, they are
inept, lazy, and ignorant creatures concerned only with sensual pleasures. With regard to their ravaging tendencies, they are all conquerors
whose successes are facilitated by their own cruelty; they destroy everything in their path and create nothing. "They are tyrants consumed
by their lust for gold, and they shed innocent blood without remorse
to satisfy it" (p. 81). Neither do they occupy a very high place on the
scale of humanity, in Chateaubriand's eyes: "I know no brute beast that
I do not prefer to such a man" (p. 176).

The underlying reason for the regression on the one hand and the
incurable barbarity on the other is Islam, the dominant religion in this
part of the world. The Koran does not incite believers to advance in
civilization any more than it teaches them to cultivate freedom; in this
it is inferior to Christian doctrine (which Chateaubriand has a tendency
to assimilate rather excessively to modern progressivism and individualism). That is why the war of the Christians against the Muslims—the
Crusades—was justified. "It was a matter . . . of seeing who was to get
the upper hand on earth, a cult that was an enemy of civilization,
systematically favoring ignorance, despotism, and slavery, or a cult that
has revived among modern peoples the learning and genius of antiquity,
and has abolished servitude" (p. 301). Chateaubriand not only produces
a tendentious image of Islam, he also clearly overlooks a good many

chapters of the history of Christianity, and he fails to mention that even in his own day slavery was legal in almost all Christian countries—including the French territories!

As for civilization, it begins where the influence of Islam leaves off—that is, in Venice (since the Greeks were once, but are no longer, civilized). Everywhere he goes, Chateaubriand finds additional reasons to love and admire his country, so superior are its achievements in all areas. What is most beautiful in Egypt, aside from the pyramids, the vestiges of a vanished civilization, are the French structures dating back to the Napoleonic campaigns. That is why Chateaubriand always insists on remembering that he is French, and seeks to live as much as possible as if he were in France. Following a quarrel, he has to present himself to the local commander; he is asked to take off his shoes and lay down his arms. "I had the dragoman tell them that a Frenchman followed the customs of his own country everywhere" (p. 195). A soldier tries to stop him short; the traveler strikes back with his whip, and sits down next to the commander. "I spoke French to him." In his speech, he praises the French, adding that "the glory of their arms was widespread enough in the Orient for people to have learned to respect their hats" (p. 196). But why must the Frenchmen take pride in keeping to his own customs wherever he goes? Is this still a consequence of the universalist agenda? Or is it, as Chateaubriand says elsewhere, because "there are two things that are revived in the heart of man as he advances in life, his fatherland and his religion" (p. 112)?

The Natchez was a critique of the myth of the noble savage, in the name of a preference for society and for civilization. The *Itinéraire*, a much more intolerant text, displays contempt not only for savage ways but for everything that does not resemble the narrator's urban mores. Here Chateaubriand declares: "People no longer believe in those societies of shepherds that spend their days in innocence, wandering in gentle idleness through the heart of the forest. We know that those honest shepherds wage war on each other so they can eat their neighbors' sheep. Their caves are neither carpeted with vines nor perfumed with the fragrance of flowers; they are stifling with their smoke, and suffocating with dairy odors" (pp. 380–381). The last remnants of exoticism in Chateaubriand's writing turn out to be condemned here: no more odors, no more tastes, no more promiscuity. Is not the cave he is mocking the very one *Atala*'s author described some ten years earlier? "We went back into the grotto, where the hermit spread a bed of cypress moss for Atala . . . I went to pick a magnolia blossom and laid it, moist with the tears of morning, on the head of my sleeping Atala" (pp. 51–52).

Between Chateaubriand's position in *The Natchez* and the one he adopts in the *Itinéraire*, the difference is more than one of shading. The universalist vision is, as we have seen, always threatened with ethnocentrism: the path of least resistance for the uncritical universalist consists in declaring that his own customs are *normal*, and in taking *his own* culture for nature in general. But even though there were some ethnocentric elements in *The Natchez*, the difference between the two texts is striking, and the universalist agenda itself seems to have been shelved. What is the reason for this? We may wonder whether there is not a correlation between this mutation and another one involving the representation of the author himself in the narrative. In *The Natchez*, Chateaubriand split his own role between Chactas and René, as we saw, without intervening in first-person form. In the *Itinéraire*, on the contrary, Chateaubriand himself is in question; and the character with whom we become acquainted has much in common with René. "The fault lies with my organization: I am incapable of benefiting from any sort of luck; I am not interested in any of the things that interest others . . . Had I been a shepherd or a king, what would I have done with my scepter or my crook? I would have been equally weary of glory and genius, of work and idleness, of prosperity and misfortune. Everything wearies me: I drag my *ennui* painfully along from day to day, and I go everywhere yawning at life" (p. 254). Like René, Chateaubriand is indifferent to the world and is interested only in himself; Chactas has quite simply disappeared. Universalism has been quelled by egocentrism.

In this book, Chateaubriand declares at the outset, "I speak eternally about myself" (p. 42). He is conscious of the fact that this sort of travel narrative diverges markedly from the traditional variety, and he justifies himself from the very first page of his preface: in this book he will relate not what he has seen but what he has felt; he will describe not others but himself. "Therefore I pray the reader to regard this Itinerary less as a voyage than as the Memoirs of one year of my life. I do not walk in the steps of a Chardin, a Tavernier, a Chandler, a Mungo Park, a Humboldt: I make no claim to have known the people among whom I was merely a passerby" (p. 41). The result is faithful to the intent: throughout the book Chateaubriand describes a year of his own life, not the lives of the Greeks, the Palestinians, or the Egyptians. Such a narrative aims to be not true (with regard to the world of which it speaks) but sincere (with regard to the speaker): "I will have achieved the goal I set myself if a perfect sincerity is felt from one end of this work to the next" (p. 42). And, characteristically, rather than seeking to take souvenirs away with him, he hopes to leave some behind; he even instructs an acquaintance to inscribe his name on the pyramids. We can hardly be astonished, under the circumstances, that Chateaubriand does not get more out of his two voyages: "Disappointed in my two pilgrimages to the West and the East, I had not discovered the polar passage, I had not come away with glory from the shores of the Niagara where I had gone looking for glory, and I had left it [glory] seated on the ruins of Athens" (*Mémoires*, I, p. 258). But if glory alone is the goal, is travel the solution?

From a passage omitted from the *Mémoires d'outre-tombe* (but preserved by Sainte-Beuve), we know the real reason for Chateaubriand's oriental journey: he went in search of "glory in order to win love" (p. 18). He wanted his mistress to see him glorified by the story of the dangers he had confronted, the distances he had covered. The Other had no place in this project. In fact, Chateaubriand's journey to the Orient, like his American journey, had more than one purpose; still, all of the author's motives concerned himself alone. And just as in his youth he needed to see natural peoples in order to put them into his epic, he now wants to write a Christian work, *Les Martyrs*, and he needs to observe what he is planning to discuss. "I was going in search of images, that is all" (p. 41). Chateaubriand wants to bring verbal expressions back from his travels the way others bring back pretty stones. But the words can come only from within; thus, he listens exclusively to his own voice.

Chateaubriand invented a character: in place of the ancient traveler we encounter the modern tourist in his book. The traveler had a bias in favor of the people of remote lands, and he sought to describe them to his compatriots. "But all the years together are not long enough to study the mores of men" (p. 41); moreover, modern man is in a hurry. The tourist will thus make a different choice: things, and no longer human beings, will be his objects of predilection—landscapes, monuments, ruins that are "worth the detour," that justify the trip. In Athens, Chateaubriand profits from the advice of a M. Fauvel, who strikes him as the ideal guide. Why? "I had gotten clear ideas on the monuments, the sky, the sun, the vantage points, the earth, sea, rivers, woods, and mountains of Attica, I could now correct my images, and give local color to my depiction of these celebrated sites" (p. 160). Only one thing is lacking in this list, and that is a human being. But there is an explanation: Chateaubriand is looking for local color for his descriptions (just as later tourists will collect images on the film in their cameras), not intersubjective experiences. If human beings do unfortunately turn up, he flees: "Naturally rather savage, it is not what is called society that I had come seeking in the Orient: I was impatient to see camels, and to hear the cry of the mahout" (p. 189). What tourist would hesitate to abandon human beings in order to go look at camels?

In one significant episode that Chateaubriand relates, he makes the acquaintance of a Turk (you cannot avoid them all). "He wanted to know why I was traveling, since I was neither a merchant nor a doctor. I answered that I was traveling to see peoples, and especially the Greeks, who were dead." This reply is not without ambiguity. Are we really talking about *peoples*, if their best representatives are dead? And furthermore how does one go about *seeing* the dead? Chateaubriand does not notice the problem, though his interlocutor does. "That made him laugh: he replied that because I had come to Turkey, I ought to have learned Turkish." Are there Turks after all whose characteristics are not limited to stupidity and cruelty? But Chateaubriand has little use for suggestions of this sort. He had already received similar advice in America, when he had outlined his projects to a certain Mr. Smith. "He advised me to begin by getting acclimatized, invited me to learn Sioux, Iroquois, and Eskimo, to live among the trappers and agents of Hudson Bay . . . This advice, whose wisdom I recognized at bottom, annoyed me" (*Mémoires*, I, pp. 224–225). Now, he no longer even recognizes its wisdom. "I found a better reason to give him for my travels, saying that I was a pilgrim from Jerusalem . . . This Turk could not understand that I would leave my country out of simple curiosity" (*Itinéraire*, p. 87). What this Turk cannot understand—and after all, he may not be the only one—is that curiosity for objects alone, and not for human beings, could motivate such a voyage. What he does not understand is that the human individual can become a self-sufficient entity, that a subject can live alone, that he may need camels, in an extreme case, but not other people.

Having chosen to privilege objects over subjects (having chosen to set himself up as unique subject), Chateaubriand systematically valorizes images at the expense of language, and thus, in practice, valorizes sight over hearing (we have seen how little interest he takes in the other senses). If one cherishes hearing, one will listen to other people's words, and will thus be obliged to recognize them as people. Sight, on the contrary, does not imply that one be looked at in turn: one may be satisfied to contemplate rivers and mountains, castles and churches. Chateaubriand expends great effort to get better views, and he always builds his descriptions around a purely visual spectacle. "If you take your place with me on the hill by the citadel, here is what you will see around you" (p. 100).

Or else, if it is absolutely necessary to deal with human beings, let them at least be dead ones. The past holds many more attractions than the present; there is no danger that it will challenge you, like those insolent Turks. Every contemporary site evokes memories of the past for Chateaubriand. Having reached the Jordan, he sees not a river but a "famous antiquity" (p. 261), and he tries to recall passages from the Gospels relating to the place; out and about in Jerusalem, he sees not a living city but the site of a historical narrative. The Egypt he sees is nothing but more of the past: "cradle of the sciences, mother of religions" (p. 372). Such is Chateaubriand's explicit message: "One likes to distinguish in these customs some traces of the old ways of life, and to rediscover among the descendants of Ishmael the memories of Abraham and Jacob" (p. 265).

Obviously, living beings sometimes interpose themselves between the dead and the traveler and keep him from concentrating; they must be gotten out of the way as quickly as possible. "Before speaking of Carthage, which is the only interesting object here, we have to begin by dispensing with Tunis" (p. 400). But it is on the site of ancient Sparta that Chateaubriand experiences his most pathetic disappointment. "Not one poor little ancient ruin as consolation in the midst of all that" (p. 94). Depressed by the way the present has taken over the past, he flees: "I left the castle in haste, despite the cries of the guides who wanted to show me modern ruins and tell me stories of agas, pachas, cadis, vayvodes" (p. 95). Modern ruins: how can anyone think of showing such vulgarities? And how can anyone be interested in living Turks, knowing that there are dead Greeks? Unfortunately, the living Greeks aren't worth much more than Turks, and they end up spoiling his trip: "It is futile in Greece to try to give oneself up to one's illusions: the sad reality pursues you . . . Women and children in rags, fleeing at the approach of a foreigner and a janissary . . . : this is the spectacle that pulls you away from the charm of memories" (pp. 169–170). The charm of the past has trouble overcoming the hideousness of the present.

Putting the dead before the living, and objects before subjects: here is Chateaubriand's dual legacy to modern tourists. The perception of others is reduced to its caricature, when it is not simply annihilated. Chateaubriand's itinerary (his ideological, not his geographical, itinerary) is a kind of illustration of the ambiguity of the terms "individual" and "individualism." Chateaubriand's universalism, as displayed by "Fénelon" and Chactas, indeed implies a recognition of the individual, who is not reduced to the characteristics of the group to which he belongs: it is necessary to appreciate not the Indians or the French but virtue, which is the same in all climates and to which every individual has access, though the price may be to break with the customs of one's own country. In this sense, individualism is the basis for humanism, and Chateaubriand is a worthy disciple of Rousseau. But René is also an individualist in another sense of the term, one that was anticipated moreover by Rousseau in other writings (the autobiographical texts): René is interested only in himself, for he is finally the only subject that counts. The subject has thus taken a new step here toward autonomy, and individualism has degenerated into egocentrism: the individual is no longer merely a necessary entity but also a sufficient one. The others are not only distinct from myself; they have become superfluous. "Man does not need to travel to grow; he bears immensity within himself," Chateaubriand declares in the conclusion of the *Mémoires d'outre-tombe* (II, p. 966).

Chateaubriand's starting point lies in a humanism that he perceives as Christian rather than "philosophical" (but in this regard the Enlightenment project, as Tocqueville reminded us, does not break with the spirit of Christianity). His destination is an attitude in which the failure to recognize others vies with an *a priori* contempt for others; such a rejection of others is well suited to the imperialist politics that is coming into play in the same period. The path leading from the one to the other is an abusive interpretation of the individualist requirement. At the beginning of the nineteenth century, Chateaubriand participated in a process destined to last into our own day: the perversion of some generous principles inherited from the preceding century, and their subjection to goals that are rigorously opposed to those same principles.

To the figures of this perversion with which we are already acquainted, such as nationalism and scientism, we must add egocentrism.

Loti

A Collector of Impressions

At the end of the nineteenth century in France, exoticism went by the name of Pierre Loti. In the late 1870s, this naval officer and prolific writer published a great number of works that combined fiction with travel narrative and that established the model of evasion in remote lands for a vast readership. We can get a sense of his work by examining the series consisting of *Aziyadé*, his first book, *Rarahu* (later called *Le Mariage de Loti* [*The Marriage of Loti*]), and *Madame Chrysanthème* (Madame Chrysanthemum). These books resemble each other in many respects. Each one recounts the adventures experienced by a certain naval officer named Loti with a woman in a faraway land (Turkey, Tahiti, and Japan, respectively). All three take the form of a private journal interspersed with personal correspondence. The first two books were originally published anonymously, and Loti was simply the name of the chief protagonist; the writer, whose real name was Julien Viaud, adopted the name Loti as his pseudonym, however, and published his later books under that name.

As a traveler, Loti at first appears to be at the other extreme from Chateaubriand-René. The greatest difference lies in the much livelier interest Loti takes in foreign countries. Chateaubriand scornfully rejected the suggestion that he should learn the language of the people he was visiting (Iroquois or Turkish), whereas at the end of a few months' sojourn in the country, Loti speaks Turkish in *Aziyadé*, "Tahitian" in *Rarahu*, and even (though less well) Japanese in *Madame Chrysanthème*. Chateaubriand refused to take off his shoes or his hat, as local custom required, and he announced that he wanted to follow French customs everywhere; Loti does just the opposite. "In Turkish fashion, we remove our shoes," he notes in *Aziyadé* (p. 54), and in *Madame Chrysanthème:* "I had left my shoes below, according to custom" (English trans., p. 121). In each case he follows the customs of the country in which he finds himself. And just as Chateaubriand was a Turkophobe, Loti is as much a Turkophile; the writer even becomes one of the chief defenders of the Turkish cause in the political debates of the early twentieth century.

And yet, over and above this opposition, which reflects the two writers' differing tastes, there is also an important structural resemblance: Loti is René's great-grandson. Like Chateaubriand's character, Loti underwent an emotional "catastrophe" in his youth, and he came away wounded, having lost his "delicacy of conscience and . . . moral sense" (*Aziyadé*, English trans., p. 39). He no longer loves anyone, neither the women he meets nor the friends who care for him; his heart is empty, or else full of bitterness; he is alone and he travels, unable to keep others from loving him and from being unhappy himself as a result. The nature of this "catastrophe" (surely a disappointment in love) is obscure, but in any event it does not involve an impossible passion for his sister. He actually does have a sister, but she wears him out with her sententious affection; Loti writes her unsentimental letters and receives replies in which he is urged to be reasonable!

What is more, Loti does not believe in anything, except perhaps his own pleasure, and thus as a rule of conduct he has decided to act with only his own enjoyment in view. "I have come to the conclusion that I have a right to do as I please, and that this insipid banquet of life requires all the spice that one can lend it" (p. 13). "There is no God. There is no moral law. Nothing exists of all we were taught to reverence. We have but one short life, from which it is reasonable to extract all the pleasure we can" (p. 39). God is dead and everything is permitted: in those years, the connection seemed automatic. Loti thus embraces René's egocentrism as compensation for the absence of transcendence. He himself cites Musset as his predecessor, but his friend Plumkett, in identifying the origin of this attitude, goes further back in time: "The eighteenth century . . . accepted these materialistic notions. God was merely a superstition. Morality was only another name for expediency, and society had become one vast field of action lying at the mercy of any man with brains enough to exploit it" (p. 82). But what was for Diderot a source of joyous liberation has now become the refrain of a melancholy complaint. Plumkett himself, for a time, counters this approach to life with humanist convictions, but before long he resigns himself and espouses Loti's cynicism.

From this point on, Loti's life is oriented toward a single goal: to collect sensations, or, better yet, impressions, as "spicy" as possible; and

Pierre Loti's novels become the guided tour to his collection. This is where the foreign country comes in: it makes possible the renewal that is indispensable to sensation and provides the interest—the *exoticism*— of the impression. Loti is explicit about this, particularly in *Madame Chrysanthème*. He recalls childhood as a paradisiacal period, for in that phase every thing benefits from its freshness and the component of mystery it conceals. "It seems to me that then only did I truly experience sensations or impressions" (p. 171). But childhood cannot last forever, and as one matures the charm is lost. "Well, I have grown up, and have found nothing that answered to my indefinable expectations" (p. 172). Sensations are dulled, impressions no longer leave their mark: in order to revive them, one sets out on a journey, even though what one finds is often only a pale copy of one's dreams.

In the dedication of *Madame Chrysanthème*, Loti declares: "It is very certain that the three principal personages are myself, Japan, and the *effect* produced on me by that country" (p. 5). Let us note first of all that Loti makes no claim that his Japan is the real Japan: on the contrary, he takes great pains to distinguish between the country and the effect it has on him. This feature is common to all his works. The foreign country really exists, and it serves as catalyst for the book; but it does not figure in the work itself: there we find only effects, impressions, subjective reactions. Loti's books are not deceptive, for they do not claim to be telling the truth about the country in question; all they propose to do is describe with sincerity the *effect* produced by the country on the narrator's soul. From another standpoint it is striking to note that the only human subject Loti lists among the "three principal personages" is "myself," whereas each of the books in question has the name of another character as its title. Such is indeed the logic of the egocentric voyage, which grants the dignity of subject to a single person—that is, the narrator himself.

The search for impressions is an existential attitude that is translated, within the books themselves, by an "impressionist" style of writing. This style affects the plot first of all, by reducing it to a bare minimum. In the opening pages, Loti arrives in a new country and embarks without too much difficulty upon a life shared with the woman he has chosen; in the closing pages, a ship sails away and he is on it—without the woman (the plot of *Aziyadé* is somewhat different). The essence of the story takes place between these two moments, but it does not depend upon the plot. It consists of numerous fragments noting minute incidents of life—a meeting, a visit, a walk, a landscape, a custom; as Loti says, the characters are constantly chasing after "some vague dream" (*Aziyadé*, p. 77). "My memoirs,—composed of incongruous details, minute observations of colours, shapes, scents, and sounds" (*Madame Chrysanthème*, p. 214). Here it is: the collection of impressions.

But how can these impressions be translated into words? Loti has some difficulty with this. The strangeness of the experience would disappear if it were expressed in the familiar words of the French language. Here is the central paradox of exoticism. "How to find words [in French] that convey something of that Polynesian night, of those desolate sounds of nature . . . ?" (*The Marriage of Loti*, p. 157). "To give a faithful account of those evenings, would require a more affected style than our own" (*Madame Chrysanthème*, p. 103). One possible solution is to use foreign words: Loti resorts to them often, but he is aware that the device is a facile expedient. He then resigns himself to labeling sensations rather than describing them: in an "exotic land" characterized by an "exotic grace" he leads an "exotic life." Or, if he is in the Orient (that is, in Turkey), everything strikes him precisely as . . . oriental. *Aziyadé* evokes "the perfumes of the East" (p. 24), "Oriental languor" (ibid.), "Oriental luxury" (p. 41), "Oriental workmanship" (ibid.), "Oriental charm" (p. 62); Loti concludes that "the near East . . . has remained more essentially Oriental than one would have imagined" (p. 39), and he even wonders whether he may be dealing with "the fantastic hallucinations of an Oriental visionary" (p. 43). In *Madame Chrysanthème* alone, a contemporary journalist counted thirty-three occurrences of the word *étrange*, twenty-two uses of *bizarre*, eighteen uses of *drôle*, and numerous repetitions of words such as *original* (original), *saugrenu* (preposterous), *pittoresque* (picturesque), *fantastique* (fantastic), *inimaginable* (inconceivable), *indicible* (unspeakable).

Finally, when he does consent to describe nature or human beings, Loti focuses primarily on the most characteristic aspects of each locality; in other words, for him the cliché is what reveals the truth. We are far removed from Chateaubriand's inventions here, and yet the same vein is being exploited. In Turkey, one breathes "aromatic perfume" (p. 36) and one is surrounded with "brooding glances fraught with fanaticism and mystery" (p. 42). In Polynesia, one contemplates "the slender coconut palms" on beaches white with "coral strands" while listening to "the monotonous and eternal soughing of the waves" (p. 30).

Loti's attitude toward these foreign countries is ambiguous. On the one hand, he submits to their charm, and finds a term of comparison that allows him to criticize European artifice and duplicity. In Turkey he dreams of sharing the lives of ordinary people, of living from day to day liberated from the conventional duties and social obligations that characterize the West. In Tahiti, he thinks he has before his very eyes a primitive race that lives in "an absolute indolence and a perpetual revery" (*The Marriage of Loti*, p. 37), a race that practices the generous hospitality appropriate to the Golden Age. In this context Loti evokes Chactas; but Diderot's Orou and Lahontan's Adario are close at hand as well. At the same time, these primitivist reveries never really call into question the narrator's choice, which is to return, at the end of his sojourn, to the highly civilized countries he came from.

It is in *Aziyadé* that Loti goes furthest toward identifying with others. At first, to be sure, he has the impression that he is participating in a travesty, that under his fez and his caftan he remains the same naval officer he has always been. Little by little, however, the country arouses his sympathy, and he can write from England to an old Turkish friend: "Sometimes I feel that yours is my proper dress, and that it is only now that I am really in disguise" (p. 172). He settles down in Istanbul, adopts the Turkish way of life, and finds happiness; at this point he gives up his self-centeredness, at least in part. He believes he is in love with Aziyadé, and he ends up joining the Turkish army; at the end of the book he dies in battle.

He is reborn in *Rarahu (The Marriage of Loti)*, but this time he does not succumb to the country's charms. Moreover, the attraction is described in negative terms. "Gradually those thousand little inextricable threads made of all the charms of Oceania were being woven about me; threads which at length form dangerous webs, veils over one's past, one's country, and one's family" (p. 80). At one point he is tempted to settle down, but he manages to dismiss the temptation without too much trouble. Finally, in Japan, he gets off to a bad start and he has many reservations, cautioning himself against any excessive feelings of sympathy. Then, little by little, he gets used to it, recognizes his initial unfairness and begins to feel almost at home: "I am even losing my Western prejudices" (*Madame Chrysanthème*, p. 280). Nevertheless, the final balance sheet is negative, and he leaves the country with no regrets: "At the moment of departure, I can only find within myself a smile of careless mockery for the swarming crowd of this Liliputian curtseying people,—laborious, industrious, greedy of gain, tainted with a constitutional affectation, hereditary insignificance, and incurable monkeyishness" (p. 328).

It is not only that Loti's identification with the country he is visiting diminishes; the identification is also blocked in fact by his feeling that he is leading a second or third life, entirely different and entirely separate from his earlier ones. This is not surprising in *Madame Chrysanthème*, where Loti indicates quite clearly that nothing of his "Japanese" identity will leave Nagasaki Bay; but even in *Aziyadé* the oriental identity will not influence the occidental one. If Loti loves cities like Istanbul, it is because there he may "assume as many different characters as he pleases" (p. 62), and he has the impression not that he has become a Turk but that he has added a Turkish existence to the rest. That is why, when he decides in a first phase to return home, he can shift from one identity to another without much difficulty. "And that is the end of Arif [his Turkish name]. That personage has now ceased to exist. The Eastern dream is ended. This episode . . . is over, past recall" (p. 156).

Now a Japanese Loti, a Tahitian Loti, even a Turkish Loti is never a Japanese, a Tahitian, a Turk, just as the effect produced by the country cannot be mistaken for the country itself. True identification is impossible, for the differences between "races" are insurmountable. Thus with Loti and Rarahu: "Between us there were gulfs, terrible barriers, never to be surmounted . . . between us who had become one flesh remained the radical distinction of race, the divergence of elementary concepts about all things . . . We were children of two separate and very different natures, and the union of our souls could only be transient, incomplete, and tormented" (*The Marriage of Loti*, p. 112). Likewise, there is a profound difference between the Japanese race and Loti's race, for the Japanese have "a world of ideas absolutely closed to ourselves" (p. 252), "distorted imaginations [*cervelles tournées à l'envers des nôtres*]" (*Madame Chrysanthème*, p. 98). Loti's vision of interracial communication is similar to that of his contemporary Gustave Le Bon: there is as much distance between one race and another as there is between humans and animals (races are species); there is thus no unity in the human race. "I feel my thoughts to be as far removed from theirs, as from the flitting conceptions of a bird, or the dreams of a monkey" (pp. 290–291). Of course, the Japanese are the ones who resemble birds or monkeys, not ourselves.

But Loti feels no regret over these communication problems, for the lack of comprehension is precisely what accounts for the charm: exoticism is nothing other than this mixture of seduction and ignorance, this renewal of sensation owing to strangeness. "They captivated me like incomprehensible things that one had never seen before," Loti writes (p. 251); elsewhere he evokes in a single breath all that he will miss: "customs and local color, . . . charm, . . . quaintness" (*The Marriage of Loti*, p. 184, note). That is why Loti, like Le Bon and countless others, is deeply hostile to the mixing of cultures, since any blending diminishes their coefficient of exoticism. Loti has only scorn for the Japanese who imitate the West (the same attitude a Japanese nationalist would have), and he predicts that the Japanese people "will soon degenerate into hopeless and grotesque buffoonery, as it comes into contact with Western novelties" (*Madame Chrysanthème*, p. 328). Similarly, the Maori race is bound to die out through contact with our civilization, "our stupid colonial civilization": "the wild Muse is driven out with the customs and traditions of the past" (p. 11). In order to benefit from exotic experience, people need to remain as far apart as possible.

Exoticism and Eroticism

The three books *Aziyadé*, *Rarahu*, and *Madame Chrysanthème* all tell the same story, but the story consists of two elements: a European visits a non-European country, and a man has an erotic relation with a woman. Loti invented this novelistic formula in which the two strands are linked both by a relation of necessity (the woman must be foreign in order to arouse Loti's desire) and by a relation of resemblance (the visitor loves the foreign country as the man loves the woman, and vice versa). Loti's originality lies in the way he makes exoticism coincide with eroticism: the woman is exotic, the foreigner is erotic. All his books, and not just *Rarahu*, could be rechristened *The Marriage of Loti*. The difference between countries coincides with the difference between the sexes; thus, Loti characterizes a go-between, who supplies French naval officers with girls, as an "agent for the intercourse of races" (*Madame Chrysanthème*, p. 29). Moreover, we see very few Japanese or Tahitian or Turkish men: the country is reduced to its women, which makes it all the easier to reduce the encounter with a country to a strictly individual relationship.

This dual relation, of man to woman and European to foreigner, is by no means symmetrical, nor could it be: an experience devoted to the search for impressions implies, as we have seen, that the traveler is the only human being elevated to the dignity of subject: the woman is only the foremost among his objects of perception. The male traveler is active: one day he arrives, another day he leaves. Between those two events we learn about his experiences and sensations. The woman and the foreign country (the woman because she is a foreigner, the country because it is eroticized) both allow themselves to be desired, governed, and abandoned; at no moment do we see the world through their eyes. The relation is one of domination, not reciprocity. The Other is desirable because it is feminine; but if the Other is objectified, this is woman's destiny. The man, for his part, enjoys the same superiority with respect to women that the European enjoys with respect to other peoples.

The meeting of man with woman (of subject with object) is above all a sensual experience. "Never before have my senses known such intoxication," Loti declares in *Aziyadé* (p. 24), and in *The Marriage of Loti* he speaks of "the unbridled passions of savage children" (p. 161). Sensuality is not on the agenda in Japan, and that is why the whole story of *Madame Chrysanthème* is actually only a parody of the other two. The same insignificant events (mice in the attic) provoke such dissimilar reactions on Loti's part that he ends up telling himself: "It really seems to me as if all I do here is a bitter parody of all I did over there" (p. 298).

The primordial role attributed to sensual experience explains why verbal communication counts for so little. Loti does learn the foreign language, but only to facilitate sensual contact. His relation with Aziyadé begins at a point when the two are incapable of exchanging a single word. When Loti learns Turkish, Aziyadé seems to be happy: "I wish I could devour the speech of your lips," she exclaims (p. 61). But Loti himself finds this sort of exchange superfluous: "Aziyadé conveys her thoughts to me not so much with her lips as with her eyes . . . She is so expert in this language of the eyes, that she might use the spoken word less than she does or even dispense with it entirely" (p. 62). Is not the best woman a silent woman? Similarly, Loti's knowledge of the

Maori language does not make his communication with Rarahu more fruitful: "She understood vaguely that there must be some gulf between her intellectual world and that of Loti" (*The Marriage of Loti*, p. 51). As for Chrysanthème, Loti likes her best when she is sleeping: "What a pity this little Chrysanthème cannot always be asleep; she is really extremely decorative . . . and like this, at least, she does not bore me" (*Madame Chrysanthème*, p. 121). It is true that Loti's Japanese leaves something to be desired, but he deems it superfluous to pursue his linguistic efforts any further. "What thoughts can be running through that little brain? My knowledge of her language is still too restricted to enable me to find out. Moreover, it is a hundred to one that she has no thoughts whatever" (p. 74).

What Loti experiences is also very different from what his mistresses experience. In the first place, it is always Loti who breaks off the relationship (since his ship is about to leave), whereas the woman remains, desolate, at home. At first glance, *Aziyadé* seems to constitute an exception, since Loti comes back to Turkey (and even dies there), but his return has nothing to do with the love relationship. Aziyadé herself is already dead; she has been abandoned, as her later avatars will be. Loti seems to love Aziyadé more than the others, and yet he never respects her as a subject endowed with her own free will; she exists for him only to the extent that she comes within his field of vision. The episode with Seniha attests to this: Loti would like to spend the night with this other seductive woman, but he also would like Aziyadé to know about it and not to protest. He has no doubt that such a situation will make her suffer, but he continues nevertheless to act in view of what he calls "my pleasure" (*Aziyadé*, p. 114). Similarly, during the final separation, he knows that he must not appear in Aziyadé's quarters if he does not want to compromise her; but after all, what does it matter? Is he not going off the next day? He thus goes to see her; Aziyadé's husband learns about it and condemns her to the isolation that will lead to her death.

Rarahu supposes that she is for Loti only "an odd little creature, a transient plaything who would quickly be forgotten" (*The Marriage of Loti*, p. 52); subsequent events prove her right. With Chrysanthème, things are even clearer: she is explicitly designated as an object-woman, a doll, a toy. "A fantastic and charming plaything" (p. 46); "I have chosen her to amuse me" (p. 74); "my dolly" (p. 91); "I took you to amuse me" (p. 323). Chrysanthème appears scarcely human to Loti:

she has "almost an expression, almost a thought" (p. 59). In a page of his journal, he promises to call her by her Japanese name, Kikou-San, instead of using the somewhat ridiculous translation "Chrysanthème." Significantly, the promise is not kept: his mistress is an object of amusement rather than a person. There is not the slightest hint of love here, and Loti remains with Chrysanthème "for want of something better" (p. 112). In fact, the relationship is explicitly compared to prostitution (but Rarahu's position was not very different): once again at sea, Loti decides, out of boredom and loneliness, to "get married"— that is, to move into a house with a woman, during his sojourn in Japan; he knows where to turn, and thus he gets Chrysanthème, "a little creature . . . that the agency of M. Kangourou has supplied me with" (p. 236). At the moment of the transaction, he is almost shocked, but only by the lack of modesty among Chrysanthème's relatives: "I feel really almost sorry for them; the fact is, that for women who, not to put too fine a point upon it, have come to sell a child, they have an air . . . of good-natured simplicity" (p. 58). Loti himself, however, feels no pangs at finding himself in the process of buying a child.

If we put ourselves in the position of the mistress, on the other hand, the relationship looks entirely different. Loti is everything to her; without him, she dies. Aziyadé tells him: "You are my God, my brother, my friend, my lover. When you go, it will be the end of Aziyadé. She will close her eyes and die" (p. 67). And her prediction comes true: at the moment of separation, "she was cold as ice" (p. 155); she falls ill immediately afterward and dies a few days later. In this respect *Madame Chrysanthème* presents an almost comical contrast. Whereas Madame Butterfly (the libretto of Puccini's opera was indirectly inspired by Loti's novel) commits suicide, Chrysanthème for her part does not suffer at all when her client leaves: he catches her humming as she confirms that the coins he paid her with are genuine. Loti is at once disappointed (women no longer die of sorrow for him) and relieved: he will have nothing on his conscience. "The fear that I might be leaving her in some sadness had almost given me a pang, and I infinitely prefer that this marriage should end as it had begun, in a joke" (p. 321). But it is not as a joke that the marriage begins and ends; it is as a commercial transaction, in which a woman's body has been rented in exchange for currency.

The case of Rarahu is especially painful. Loti chooses a country girl for himself and sets up housekeeping with her in Papeete. He knows that he will leave and that, once abandoned, Rarahu will never be able to return to her village; but that does not influence his decision in the slightest. "It was thus that she joyfully took the fatal step. Poor little wild plant, raised in the forest, she had just fallen, like so many others, into an unwholesome and artificial atmosphere where she was going to languish and droop" (p. 79). Thus, Loti knows that Rarahu will become a professional prostitute after he leaves and that she will end up in misery, but this prospect only intensifies his sensation. "I understood . . . that she was lost, lost in body and soul. That was perhaps for me an additional charm, the charm of those who are going to die" (p. 116). In order to quiet his own conscience, he extracts promises from Rarahu that he knows she will be unable to keep. Loti goes off; Rarahu—who has no thought for anyone but him!—would have liked him to take her with him, but there is never any question of this. She thereupon becomes consumptive (half Traviata, half Madame Butterfly); but before dying she has time to "fall." "All the sailors of the *Sea-Mew* liked her very much even though she had become emaciated. As for her, she went for all of them, any that were at all good-looking" (p. 187). Rarahu becomes an alcoholic, sleeps in the streets and within a few months she is dead.

The two phases of this relationship—the infatuation with the incomprehensible foreigner and the final abandonment—translate perfectly the ambivalence of Loti's exoticism. The European male is attracted and seduced, but he invariably goes back where he came from. He thus gains on both fronts: he has the benefit of the exotic experience (a foreign woman and a foreign country) without ever really calling into question his own belonging or his own identity.

The Colonial Novel

Loti did not stop at exploiting the exotic formula; he also imagined the opposite situation, in which a protagonist finds himself abroad against his will and dreams of returning home. Under these circumstances, exoticism is inverted to become nationalism, and xenophilia becomes xenophobia. The colonial situation lends itself particularly well to this sort of plot structure, for it provides a motive for the character's sojourn abroad. Significantly, in experimenting with this genre, Loti abandoned the first-person singular: we no longer have a diary but a third-person novel, *Le Roman d'un Spahi (The Romance of a Spahi)*, a book that was a great success when it was published and spawned many imitations.

Jean Peyral, the novel's hero, has enlisted for a five-year stint as a spahi (cavalryman) in the colonial army in Senegal. At first, he experiences the exotic mirage, the attraction of the unknown, but the mirage dissipates rapidly, and Jean dreams of going back to his own people, to his village in the Cévennes; he suffers from "homesickness for his native mountains, his village, and the cottage of his old people" (p. 30)—a sentiment totally foreign to "Loti" in the other three books. This explains a basic contrast: where, for himself, Loti saw a privilege, he sees in Jean's case only an attenuating circumstance, an excuse for reprehensible conduct. We have to understand, after all, that under such unfavorable conditions men are capable of anything. But what is worse is that these men actually stop suffering, and end up liking their country of exile. This land has bewitched Jean, it "cradles him and lulls him into a heavy, dangerous sleep, haunted by sinister dreams" (*Le Roman d'un Spahi*, p. 88). The spell woven by the foreigner is no longer a delight, it is a malediction (but the same thing was already true to some extent for Tahiti, another French colony).

There is nevertheless a woman here too, or rather a very young girl (like Aziyadé, Rarahu, and even Chrysanthème—this is Loti's favorite type), Fatou, who has grown fond of Jean and who shares his bed. At first, Jean accepts her "in the absence of anyone else" (*The Romance of a Spahi*, p. 178), but with time she grows more beautiful, and he feels tenderness and attachment for her. However, as the woman and the foreigner still coincide, and the foreigner here is unworthy of esteem, the woman also gradually reveals her bad nature. Rather than leave her, Jean gets into the habit of whipping her, "not very hard at first, but afterwards more so" (p. 180). On one occasion he is particularly angry: he strikes until he draws blood. Loti then allows us to see the scene through Fatou's eyes (which was impossible in the case of Aziyadé, Rarahu or Chrysanthème). What does Fatou think? She finds her punishment warranted. "She knew very well that she was wicked" (p. 191). What is worse, "the idea of that supreme struggle, in which she was going to clasp and embrace him and die by his hand, thus ending everything, pleased her" (p. 192). In this way Fatou's masochistic pleasure exempts Jean's sadistic pleasure from all reproach ("his rage increased as he struck"—p. 184), and Loti can close the description of this scene with an idyllic image: "A painter would have selected him as a complete type of noble charm and virile perfection" (p. 201). Fatou is thus a bad woman, dishonest and perverse; however, like Loti's other heroines, she loves her man much more than he loves her, and she cannot survive their separation. When she discovers Jean's corpse she commits suicide (rather than wait for tuberculosis to set in).

But how can Fatou's hold over Jean be explained? Once again, the relation between the sexes is above all a meeting of the senses; but this time it is intensified in the extreme owing to the extraordinary sensuality attributed to blacks. "*Anamalis fobil!* was shouted out of their unbridled desire, of the strength, the virility of the black overheated at the sun; hysterical . . . Alleluia of negro love" (p. 89). Fatou has a sensual charm that draws Jean into unimagined states of ecstasy. Moreover, all the black women are animated by feverish desires, and they plunge voluptuously into prostitution (as if prostitution were a matter of sensuality); nothing restrains their passion, and even when they see corpses they give way to "obscene gestures, and burlesque words . . . ; they violated the dead with dismal buffoonery" (p. 272).

This unbridled sensuality is the direct consequence of the blacks' animal nature, which differentiates them from the other human races. It is true that Loti also uses animal metaphors to describe the Japanese: "You look like ouistitis, like little china ornaments" (*Madame Chrysanthème*, p. 37); "a gaily dressed-up old monkey" (p. 96); "monkeyish-looking old ladies" (p. 230); "the monkeyish faces" (p. 198). But the procedure is much more systematic with blacks. They have gorilla faces, monkey voices, they grimace like ouistitis and gesticulate like chimpanzees (*The Romance of a Spahi*, pp. 9, 83, 107, 126, 170, 180, 260, 272 . . .). Jean does not like to see the palms of Fatou's hand, pink instead of black: "They reminded him of monkey's paws!" (p. 116); he is disturbed by this animal quality, and he tells her so, adapting his language to hers: "Little Monkey Girl [*Toi tout à fait même chose comme singe*]!" (p. 117). When she is not a monkey, she becomes a cat (like Chrysanthème) or else a dog: Jean "looked upon her, moreover, as an inferior creature" roughly equal to his dog; indeed she manifests toward him "the devotion of a dog for its master" (p. 125). As a result, Jean (but also Loti) treats Fatou as an inferior being, a slave, a cur.

Generally speaking, Loti practices the vulgar racialism that was certainly widespread in his day but that could conceivably have been absent in an "exotic" writer. *The Marriage of Loti* presents the sight of "a repellent thing" (p. 39): "an old Chinese entirely naked, washing his ugly yellow body in our limpid stream!" (p. 40). Yellow is intrinsically dirty and ugly and when one has such a disgusting body one should at least have enough shame to keep from exposing it to view. But in Japan, too, Loti has the misfortune of seeing only ugly yellow people. Now skin color influences many other personal characteristics: the yellow race has its odor, and a Japanese person has a "yellow head [*cervelle*]" (p. 123). But blacks are once again the "race" par excellence: in them everything is determined by color, and they all behave in the same (black) way. They have "black sweat" (in profusion), "black music," a "black heart," a "black soul" (*The Romance of a Spahi*, pp. 120, 125, 190), and so on. Now blackness has negative associations: "Among the men the blood that boiled up was 'black blood'; among the plants the sap was poison; the flowers had dangerous perfumes, and even the beasts were venomous" (p. 90).

The plot of *The Romance of a Spahi* does indeed involve interracial contact. Jean Peyral is white: "He was of the pure white race" (p. 13). He should not have allowed himself to be seduced by a black woman. He realizes this when he has sexual relations with Fatou for the first time: "It seemed to him that he was about to step over a fatal threshold, to sign with that black race a sort of deathly compact" (p. 93); but he cannot turn back. And his worst fears are realized: this pact with the impure race, tantamount to a pact with the devil, will lead him into degradation. In the end he manages to break away: "He had recovered his 'white man's' dignity, which had been soiled by contact with that black flesh" (p. 199).

Along the way, Loti gives us some glimpses into colonial life as led by the spahis. Passing through a village, they "kiss little girls," Loti writes (*Le Roman d'un spahi*, p. 56). But Jean, who does not want to be like his comrades in this respect, translates the episode into clearer language: he does not want to "rape little black girls the way they do" (p. 60). What he wants is to fight, to accomplish military exploits (to massacre some Negro king): "from time to time he found himself dying of impatience" (p. 95). At the end of the book, his goal is accomplished: the spahis are summoned to attack the hostile populations, to "set fire to the village, which would burn in the moonlight like a bonfire of straw" (*The Romance of a Spahi*, p. 255). Unfortunately, they fall into an ambush along the way and, assailed by "thirty black demons" (p. 260), Jean finally dies.

The Romance of a Spahi is racist, imperialist, sexist, and sadistic, which did not prevent the Académie Française from honoring Loti, a few years after the book's publication, by electing him to membership in preference to Zola; he was the youngest Academician in its history (in 1891 he was forty-one years old). With this book, written at the time of the great colonial expansion, Loti established the distinguishing features of the colonial novel (right up to contemporary adventure novels like Gérard de Villiers' "SAS" series, with their characteristic blend of racism and sadism) for the next century. Does this mean that Loti himself was a conscious advocate of colonialism? We may doubt this, on the evidence of articles that he published in *Le Figaro* in 1883, in which he described massacres carried out by the French army in Indochina. Despite Loti's recognizable taste for morbid details and scenes of cruelty, reading these texts remains a shattering experience: they provide a detailed description of the premeditated extermination of thousands of men who were trying to protect themselves from French bullets with wicker mats. The articles caused a scandal at the time, and the naval officer Julien Viaud nearly found himself in serious trouble. In *The Romance of a Spahi* itself, Loti does not spare us the atrocities committed by the French during the colonial war.

If we look more closely, we find that Loti did not take up any cause: he was neither for nor against the colonies. If he was against anyone, it was not the French soldiers in Indochina and Senegal, but the Parisian politicians and functionaries who initiated those wars and sent others off to fight them, pretending to ignore the fact that every war is made of up cruelty and suffering. Loti wants to remind his readers of that fact, but he does not go so far as to pass judgment on French policies. If he does not subscribe to an imperialist philosophy, like Renan or Leroy-Beaulieu, he is quite clearly not an anticolonialist either. *The Romance of a Spahi* is a symptom rather than a manifesto. In this book, as in his other novels, Loti captures the atmosphere of the times: he succeeds in expressing the feelings of a large number of his contemporaries.

What is more revealing, perhaps, is that the exotic novel and the colonial novel can coexist so easily in the same author and during the same years, whereas their intentions seem so contradictory: the one

glorifies foreigners while the other denigrates them. But the contradiction is only apparent. Once the author has declared that he himself
is the only subject on board and that the others have been reduced to
the role of objects, it is after all of secondary concern whether these
objects are loved or despised. The essential point is that they are not
full-fledged human beings.

Segalen

Redefinition of Exoticism

At the beginning of the twentieth century, Victor Segalen gave more
intense thought to the experience of exoticism than anyone else in
France. He himself saw this theme as the axis around which all his work
was organized. In a press notice written in 1916, referring to himself
in the third person, he wrote: "Exoticism understood as such: an
aesthetics of diversity—is moreover the center, the essence, the
justification of all the books Victor Segalen has written and no doubt
of those he intends to write" (*Essai sur l'exotisme*, p. 71). It is also the
explicit subject of *Essai sur l'exotisme* (Essay on Exoticism), a book
Segalen left unfinished but to which he repeatedly returned between
1904 and 1918; the notes he took in preparation for that work were
not published in journals until 1955 and not in book form until 1978.
This text offers the core of Segalen's reflections on the theme of
exoticism.

Segalen decided to rethink the problem from top to bottom. In the
literal sense, what is exotic is everything that is external to the observing
subject. As it happens, the notion had undergone an incredible narrow-
ing, coming to be identified only with *certain* contents, external to
certain subjects. At the time, in France, under the influence of Loti and
all those who followed in his footsteps, exoticism was reduced to a kind
of "tropicalism," or else to the description of the French colonies (seen
from the perspective of metropolitan France). Thus, the starting point
has to be a prophylactic work of dissociation between the general
notion and these overly specific contents. "Above all, clear the ground.
Throw out all the abusive and rancid contents of the word 'exoticism.'
Strip it of all its cheap finery: the palm and the camel; the pith helmet;
black skin and yellow sun" (p. 22; see also pp. 13, 19, 23, 53, 55, 66,
83, and so on). Segalen so resolutely rejects everything that goes into

contemporary "exotic" literature not because what it describes is not "exotic" (for its authors) but because, by virtue of their association with exoticism, the clichés—camel and coconut palm—screen off the exotic experience in its full amplitude. The first step, a necessary one, thus consists in setting aside the automatic associations, the reductions of exoticism to a *single* type of country or culture: "I have to strip away from the word 'diverse' and especially from the word 'exotic' all the overly specific notions with which they have been encumbered up to now" (p. 61).

This initial negative task makes it possible to give the field of exoticism an unlimited extension. First of all in the sense of geography itself: the tropics are by no means alone in their foreignness; Segalen remarks ironically that at the moment there is "little polar exoticism" (p. 13). But this is still too obvious. To spatial exoticism, in fact, we must add temporal exoticism: every past era is exotic for us, and—why not?—every era to come (although Segalen is disappointed in contemporary novels that anticipate the future). "Exoticism in time. Behind us: history. Escape from the contemptible, mean-spirited present. Elsewhere and once upon a time. The not-yet" (p. 28). In another limitation of the notion, the subject group has been identified on the cultural and national levels with Europeans on one side and Tahitians or Indians or Chinese on the other. Now one can also constitute groups on the biological rather than the social level; men (always the ones who travel, observe, write) will then discover the exoticism of women, will extend it "to the other sex" (p. 19), where they will experience no less powerful a difference than if they were to go to the other side of the globe. On the other hand, one particular illusion has to be discarded—namely, the idea that exoticism is to be found by frequenting the insane: "We discover ourselves so well in them" (p. 26).

A further step leads us to consider the exoticism that we human beings experience in confronting nature all around us: the mineral, vegetable, and animal worlds. To this can be added a sensory exoticism: visual experiences are profoundly foreign to those of hearing, which remain impermeable to those of smell, and so forth; and Segalen reproaches himself for having advocated, in his youth, the synesthesias of which the Symbolists were fond. He now has a different requirement: "Disallow, for a time, any comparison between the various arts" (pp. 40–41). Finally, within a given art form itself, the use of an unaccustomed style can produce the same effect of exoticism and defamiliarization: this is "transference achieved by form" (p. 27).

By extending the notion in this way, Segalen ends up with what he calls "universal exoticism" (p. 29), on the basis of which he defines "essential exoticism": the new definition of exoticism involves not multiplying exotic experiences but rather grasping them in their generality. For me, whatever is different from me is exotic. "Exoticism is everything that is other" (*Equipée* [Escapade], p. 513). "The notion of difference, the perception of diversity, the knowledge that something is not oneself" (*Essai,* p. 23). At the moment when the perceiving subject in a given experience can be distinguished from the object perceived, exoticism is born. "Essential exoticism: that of the object for the subject" (p. 37). "Exoticism" is thus synonymous with "alterity."

In practice, however, we never face anything but particular exoticisms; and Segalen himself went off to visit lands already privileged by traditional exoticism, such as Tahiti and China. But the resemblance is only superficial; Segalen's analysis of the notion has not gone for naught. We must not be taken in by "geographical" exoticism and suppose that this form alone exemplifies the encounter with the other; but, having understood this, we are still obliged to choose one form of exoticism over others: experience is necessarily specific. Segalen explains what he means by this at the beginning of *Equipée:* "It was not necessary, in order to experience the shock [of exoticism] to fall back upon the outdated expedient of a voyage . . . To be sure. But the episode and the setting of the voyage, better than any other subterfuge, allow for this rapid, brutal, pitiless, direct contact, and better mark each blow" (p. 366). The voyage is only a subterfuge, but it is the most appropriate one of all; it is a good means, provided that we do not also see it as an end.

What is essential, in this experience, is that its terms allow only for a relative definition. Only their positions permit us to identify the subject on the one hand, the object on the other; but this difference must remain pure, empty of all content. Segalen put his ideal of exoticism in poetic form in a "stele" entitled "Advice to the Worthy Traveller": in six short stanzas, he evokes the alternation of the city and the road, the mountain and the plain, sound and silence, crowds and solitude, in order to exalt not one term over the other but precisely the possibility of passing from one to the other; he has given up believing in "the merit of a lasting merit" ("Advice," p. 91). An earlier version of the same text is even more explicit: "Never choose one extreme or another, this quality rather than that one, but always both, provided that they follow on each other's heels in an opposition that you control.

Then only can you rejoice in the sole quality that does not disappoint, alternation, and appreciate its sure possession" (*Briques et tuiles* [Bricks and Tiles], pp. 74–75).

We are indeed dealing with a precept. Segalen is not content to observe exotic experience (or to bring together a variety of experiences under this heading), he also thinks that it is the most precious experience we are granted in our lives. But why? In a first phase, his response is simple: it is because he himself, Segalen, is personally convinced of it. But he also seeks more general reasons that lead him to react this way and that might apply to others as well; it turns out that he can identify them with the help of contemporary philosophy. Difference must be valorized, he believes, for only difference ensures the intensity of sensation. Now feeling is living, or at least it is the essential part of life. "Exoticism . . . as the fundamental law of the intensity of sensation, of the exaltation of feeling; thus of living" (p. 75). That is also why exoticism engenders energy: "Diversity is the source of all energy" (p. 79).

We may wonder whether this explanation is as satisfying as it seems to Segalen. Is the increased intensity of sensation a function of the increased difference between subject and object alone? The Surrealists later formulated a similar rule to measure the quality of metaphors: according to Breton, a metaphor is successful to the extent that its two terms, literal meaning and figurative meaning, are far apart. But maximal distance results in incomprehension, not the apogee of meaning. And experience itself requires large doses of familiarity and surprise in order to achieve its greatest power: total strangeness prevents sensation just as decisively as familiarity congeals sensations into automatisms. Do not familiar landscapes often give rise to the most powerful experiences? The second part of Segalen's reasoning is just as problematic: can one make the connection "feeling, thus living" with no further precautions? (Segalen resembles Péguy rather closely here.) In this animal conception of humanity, there is no room for thought, any more than there is room for inner joy and suffering. We may question whether Segalen himself would have accepted all the implications of his own formulas.

The same philosophy that taught him that to live is to feel taught him another lesson as well: that life itself is the highest value in life. "I believe it useless to go back and explain all over again what others, precursors, have acquired: the value of life" (p. 76). Segalen's immediate precursor here is his philosophy professor Jules de Gaultier, who is above all a popularizer and advocate of Nietzschean thought in France; another, scarcely more remote precursor is Gobineau, with his vitalist philosophy. Now if life is the supreme value, and exoticism the condition necessary for life, the conclusion is self-evident: nothing must be allowed to challenge the supremacy of pure alterity, of difference as such. "An imperishable acquisition: an acquisition of pleasure in diversity that no table of values called human can diminish . . . Beyond everything—beyond happiness or satisfaction—beyond justice and order . . . there remains this one certainty: the justification of a posited law of exoticism—of what is other—as an aesthetics of diversity" (*Equipée*, pp. 512–513). The pleasure of diversity dominates all the values derived from the idea of humanity; exoticism is beyond all justice, beyond good and evil.

Segalen is right to speak here of an aesthetics (the term also figures in the subtitle of the work he planned to write) rather than of an ethics: not only because the category of intensity takes precedence over the category of the just and the unjust, but also because aesthetics is, etymologically, the science of perception. The aesthetics of diversity is even, in Segalen's perspective, a pleonasm: "I understand . . . by aesthetics the exercise of this same sentiment [of diversity]" (p. 67). Beauty can be a measure of the intensity of acts; it cannot measure their rightness.

No single theory, not even a theory of essential exoticism, can make a greater claim to truth than any other—because theories, according to the radical Nietzschean relativism transmitted by Jules de Gaultier, do not come close to grasping the facts of this world; rather, they express the will of their author. At first Segalen, a good student and a modest one, applies this principle to his own convictions. "It is an aptitude of my own sensibility, the aptitude to feel diversity, that I am setting up as an aesthetic basis of my knowledge of the world. I know where it comes from: from myself. I know that it is no more true than any other; but also that it is no less true" (p. 30).

Up to this point Segalen is content to note this merely as a personal characteristic. "When this book was conceived, I believed it to be simply a 'way of seeing,' my own; and I agreed simply to state the way in which the world appeared to me most tastefully: in its diversities" (p. 75). But with the passing years, modesty gives way to a growing certainty, and thus he attempts to exempt his own doctrine from the general law of relativity. Various reasons lead him to invest his "theory of exoticism" with "a greater generality"; he has become aware that "all men [are] subject to the law of exoticism" (p. 76). From this point on, the quality he claims for the theory of exoticism is neither maximal intensity nor maximal authenticity with respect to his own experience, but rather greater truth value: the generality of the phenomenon proves to him that he is dealing with an impersonal law governing human behavior. Segalen thus rediscovers the paradox of all relativists, who declare all truths relative except their own, and who renounce all values so long as they are talking about the values of others. It is at precisely this point that Segalen's exoticism ceases to be "pure."

The Exotic Experience

The exotic experience is directly available to everyone; at the same time, it eludes the grasp of most. A child's life begins with a progressive differentiation of subject and object; as a result, the whole world, in the beginning, seems exotic to the child. "For him, exoticism is born at the same time as the external world . . . Everything the child wants is exotic" (*Equipée*, p. 45). However, as the child grows up, the sensation of exoticism is dulled, and the adult takes the existence of the world around him as self-evident. Each new object can provoke an initial astonishment, but the adult has by this time gotten into the habit of assimilating the new to the familiar; the element of surprise is quickly absorbed "by the adaptation to the milieu" (p. 21). A specific deficiency even develops, the inability to perceive novelty: this is what we know as déjà-vu.

The automization of perception is a process that must be prevented and reversed (the genealogy of exoticism according to Segalen is thus not very different from the one we found in Loti). The point of departure for the exotic experience is the same as for any perception: the identification of the object. However, as a next step the habitual process of assimilation (of the Other) and of accommodation (of one-self) must be blocked, and that object must be maintained as different from the subject; the priceless alterity of the Other must be preserved. Such is Segalen's definition of exoticism: "The lively and curious reaction of a strong individuality against an objectivity whose difference it perceives and tastes" (p. 25). The person who is able to practice exoticism—that is, to enjoy the difference between herself and her object of perception—is called an *exote:* it is she who "perceives the full flavor of diversity" (p. 29); she is the insatiable traveler. The difference need not be objectively very great: the true exote, like a collector able to enjoy infinitesimal nuances among the objects of his collection, appreciates the transition from red to reddish more than the transition from red to green.

The common experience starts from strangeness and ends in familiarity. The exote's special experience starts where the other ends—in familiarity—and leads toward strangeness. Accurate perception in fact implies a certain familiarity (otherwise we would not see everything); but no sooner is this familiarity acquired than we have to begin moving in the other direction, in order to maintain the exteriority of the object with respect to the subject. Faced with others, I must "imbue myself with them first, then extract myself from them, in order to leave them in their full *objective* flavor" (pp. 36–37). The object remains an object, and the subject, a subject: the encounter does not deprive either one of its freedom or its identity. The one must not be very much more powerful than the other: if the subject is stronger, it will absorb the other without a trace; if the object is stronger, then the subject risks being swallowed up, by relinquishing its own being. "Only those who possess a strong individuality can feel the difference" (p. 24). A solid sense of self is an indispensable condition for the exotic experience. One somewhat surprising consequence of this rule is that it is always better to travel alone: with a companion, one has already relinquished a part of oneself, in order to share the common experience, and one thus risks getting too close to the object. "Conclusion from a voyage made by the two best friends on earth: 'Travel alone!'" (*Voyage au pays du réel* [Voyage to the Land of Reality], p. 73).

The exotic experience is thus to be carefully distinguished from the experience of immersion in a foreign culture. The person who shares the life of the Chinese in every detail forgets that he is living with the Chinese, and by the same token no longer perceives them as such. Segalen notes a parallel between an individual's relation to a foreign culture and her relation with nature. "There exists a curious opposition between the sentiment of nature and life in nature. One only sees, feels, tastes nature with a great aesthetic joy when one is somewhat separate from it" (*Essai*, p. 36). Only city dwellers enjoy nature; farmers live in osmosis with it. Similarly, only those who do not feel they are Chinese can take pleasure in contact with Chinese society.

The existence of two phases in the exotic experience (one must imbue oneself, then extract oneself) implies that from the subject's point of view every object consists of two segments: one that, during the first phase, proves identical to the subject (to the fraction of the subject that participates in the experience); and one whose irreducible difference the subject discovers, during the second phase. "The subject espouses and for a time identifies with one of the parts of the object, and diversity explodes between him and the other party. Otherwise there is no exoticism" (p. 59). The two movements—and this is a crucial point—are both indispensable: without identification, one does not know the other; without the bursting forth of difference, one loses oneself. The scholar, who analyzes the object without projecting herself into it, misses the first part of the process; the lover, who fuses with the other, misses the second; one must be an exote to reconcile the two.

These are the major outlines of the exotic experience, as Segalen analyzed it. But it is not enough to describe this experience from within, the way a phenomenologist would; the experience must also be situated in the world. Taking up this perspective, Segalen discovers two major threats to exotes. The first derives from the very structure of the experience, the need for initial identification with the object. One always runs the risk of getting stuck there and losing oneself; the subject, then, "finds himself face to face with himself" (p. 29). The second danger arises from the finite nature of objects in the universe. The tragedy of earthlings is that the Earth is round. "On a sphere, to leave some point is already to begin to *approach it!* The sphere is monotony" (p. 52). The first trip around the Earth is not a victory but the discovery of a terrible limitation. "Most fortunately, Magellan died before the return trip. As for his helmsman, he was simply doing his job without suspecting the terrifying truth: there was no such thing as the far distance" (p. 78). For Segalen, as we have seen, only difference intensifies sensation; as a result any return to sameness is stale, marked by the "repugnant flavor of the déjà-vu" (*Equipée*, p. 505).

To counter these threats that loom perennially over the happiness of exotes, Segalen finds a series of responses that allow him to keep open the possibility of exotic experience (even though his responses are not always mutually compatible). First of all, even if the possible displacements are limited in number and always proceed in the same directions, nothing guarantees that one can get to know the people encountered; on the contrary, Segalen believes in the ultimate impenetrability of individual beings as well as of peoples. "Lovers would be horrified if, at the height of their shared passion—just when their joy is spreading, when it is so unitary that the two beings proclaim their consubstantiality—if they were to measure the inviolable barrier that separates the two lovers in their feelings, and will always separate them despite the apparent harmony of their unique joy" (*Essai*, p. 90). If there is a kind of madness on the part of lovers who seek to fuse together as one, the same thing is true of human groups. "The impenetrability of the races. Which is nothing but the extension, to the races, of the impenetrability of individuals. The treachery of language, and languages" (p. 27). Languages betray each other, and universal language does not exist; the unity of the human race is an empty phrase. The perfect encounter is only an illusion, but we must rejoice in this rather than deplore it: the experience of the exote is thus preserved.

But Segalen is not always sure he is right about this, and so he falls back on a second response, asserting that difference is an indispensable condition for all life and that every difference abolished is made up for at once by the emergence of another; otherwise life would come to a halt. "We may believe that *fundamental* differences will never end up as a truly seamless cloth, with no piecing together; and that the growing fusion, the falling of barriers, the great spatial foreshortenings, must themselves be made up for somewhere by new separations, unanticipated gaps" (p. 67). These differences, as we have seen, do not need to be large: the minuteness of the separation is compensated for by an improvement in our perceptual apparatus.

Segalen offers several examples in support of this second response. One has to do with a trick played on us by the process of identification: the European who identifies with China loses one sort of exoticism, it is true; but since he himself has changed, what is now exotic for him is Europe. He is playing a zero-sum game. "The exote, from the bottom of his patriarchal plot of land, summons up, desires, sniffs out elsewheres. But, living in these elsewheres—enclosing them, embracing them, savoring them—the ancestral plot now becomes suddenly and powerfully different. From this double game, this seesaw, a ceaseless, bottomless diversity" (p. 49). Segalen, who had visited Gauguin's hut shortly after the artist's death, believed that the last painting Gauguin had produced in Tahiti was of a Breton peasant in the snow. He was wrong, as it happened (that painting had been done in France), but the example illustrates perfectly the inversion he is talking about: the artist rediscovers his homeland because he is far away from it.

A second example of recreated difference comes up in the law of bovarysm, so named after the book that Jules de Gaultier devoted to the topic *(Le Bovarysme)*. Emma Bovary dreams of herself as romantic, different from what she is. In this she is not an exception but an illustration of a truth about all human beings: we are all possessed by unrealizable dreams. "Jules de Gaultier's law of bovarysm: every being who conceives of himself necessarily conceives of himself as other than he is" (pp. 23–24). But by the same token otherness is introduced at the very heart of identity, and there is no reason to fear its diminution in the absolute: however much I try to reduce the differences between others and myself, these differences will be reborn within myself. This consolation pleased Segalen so much that he decided to make Gaultier's expression the sole citation in his book, as well as its concluding statement: "'And he rejoiced in diversity' (reconquered)" (p. 60).

Thus, the dangers that have been hovering over the happiness of the exote are conjured away. Segalen's responses might be construed as excessively theoretical. But Segalen does not settle for constructing a theory; he constantly interrogates his personal experience as an exote, since that experience is his starting point, and he notes that it can be preserved. In this regard he actually went through several stages. Initially, he was shocked to find that travelers failed to encounter the Other, and were content to speak about themselves, under the pretext that they were bringing back the *impressions* the world had left with them. Segalen attempts to reverse this tendency in his first book, *Les Immémoriaux*; he is thus in a way writing as an anti-Chateaubriand or an anti-Loti. "Reaction no longer of the milieu on the traveler but of the traveler on the living milieu; I have tried to express it for the Maori race" (p. 18). He comes back to the same problem in a different mode in his second book, *Stèles*, which seeks to restitute a world and not the impressions produced by that world on the traveler's soul (here we can see Segalen as an anti-Claudel). "The attitude . . . thus cannot be the *I* that feels . . . but on the contrary the apostrophe of the milieu to the traveler, of the exotic to the exote, penetrating him, assailing him, awakening him, and *disturbing* him. It is the *thou* that will dominate" (p. 21).

The reaction to the omnipresence of the *I* is thus a valorization of the *thou*. But by letting the other speak alone in this way, one is cutting oneself off anew, although for different reasons, from the experience of alterity. One must thus also move beyond this second form of interaction. Here is how Segalen describes the variety of relationships in the case of China: "The simplest is to scorn and hate the Chinese, 'under the skin.' Many crude individuals, military and colonial types, are at this point and have never gone any further. In reaction, other people have gone over to scrupulous admiration and affection for the Chinese and for the *Chinese type*. Neither one nor the other, but beyond . . ." (*Voyage au pays du réel*, p. 37). Or in *Equipée:* "Not to be taken in either by the voyage, or by the country, or by the picturesqueness of daily life, or by oneself" (p. 371).

How can one describe that "beyond" of relationships of assimilation of the other or of loss of self in the other? How can one express that lucidity toward the other as well as toward the self? Segalen sometimes borrows another phrase from Gaultier and speaks of restitution not of the world but of a world view—which is not to be confused, on the other hand, with an impression produced by that same world. However this may be, he himself seems to have brought off this encounter of the third kind: fascinated by China, according to his friends he remains at the same time indifferent to it. And he himself confirms this: "Despite my intense experience of China, I have never felt the desire to be Chinese. Despite my intense experience of the Vedic dawn, I have never really regretted not being born three thousand years earlier, and a herder. Start from a good reality, the one that is, the one you are. Fatherland. Epoch" (*Essai*, pp. 57–58). In order to experience otherness, it is not necessary to stop being oneself. And the theoretical difficulties notwithstanding, the exotic experience is a reality.

We can observe an almost anecdotal example of this in the role Segalen reserves for citation within his *Essai sur l'exotisme* itself. A citation is in fact a segment of an Other, and one's attitude toward citation is revealing of the way one experiences exoticism. Now although Segalen is by no means unaware of his predecessors' writings (he lists them frequently), he has decided not to use any citations in his final version (except for Jules de Gaultier's one consoling sentence). This is because even as a citation maintains the other's text in a state of externality relative to oneself, the quoted passage guarantees that that other text is powerfully present, too powerfully, even though the excerpt never does justice to the whole from which it is taken. What can be done, in such a case? The solution is to fall back on other devices, especially allusion, indirect presence. "Literary allusion is a rather delicate game of ideas, which cites in veiled form . . . I shall often resort to allusion" (p. 62). It hardly matters, under the circumstances, if Segalen is right in this charge and in his choice; we can easily see how the practice he chooses obeys the rule he professes.

Struggles for Exoticism

The exotic experience thus has a good chance of being brought to fruition, as Segalen's own testimony indicates. But he does not find this reassuring, especially because it seems to him that the era he lives in is particularly disadvantageous to exotes. Segalen thus calls for a vigorous struggle against the enemies of exoticism.

Who are these enemies? We can divide them up, roughly speaking, into two categories. In the first category are all those who are unaware of others, those who are concerned only with themselves under all circumstances. Within this vast group there are several types. A first type includes colonials, businessmen, entrepreneurs: these people have interests—that is to say, they are interested only in themselves. A person of this sort "arrives with a desire for the most commercial form of native commerce possible. For him, differences exist only insofar as they will serve his swindling practices" (p. 40). The "Other," here, is the person who allows herself to be most easily deceived, who is ignorant of the rules of exchange that prevail in our society. A second type is constituted by the exotic writers who preceded Segalen, those self-centered travelers who were content to report the "impressions" made on them by the countries they visited. Segalen has nothing but scorn for these "hasty and wordy travelers" (p. 22); he has in mind in particular Chateaubriand and Loti, especially Loti, that collector of impressions. "Writers like Loti are mystically drunk and unconscious of their object, which they confuse with themselves, and with which they merge themselves recklessly" (p. 39); Loti is thus classified among the "pseudo-exotes," the "panderers of the sensation of diversity" (p. 34). But Claudel in China hardly merits more esteem, even if he is a better poet: despite his lengthy stay, he did not even learn the Chinese language. The popularizers fall into the same category, the ones who want to facilitate the experience of others by publishing guides and manuals—"China in Hand" or "All China in Three Hundred Pages" (*Briques et tuiles*, p. 90).

Another type deserves separate mention, so omnipresent is he, and so characteristic of our period: the tourist. A veritable scourge, according to Segalen, who sees tourists as animals in "wandering herds" (*Essai*, p. 46). There are two things wrong with tourists. On the one hand, their interest in foreign countries remains purely superficial. They are in a hurry; they try to accumulate "impressions" rather than trying to understand the other. They are not descendants of the earlier explorers but just the opposite: their antecedents are the most diehard stay-at-home types. "Traveling at the highest speeds in the most remote places, they always find their woolen socks, their savings, their armchairs, and their siestas" (p. 47). On the other hand, they bring about deplorable alterations in the populations they visit, which start to resemble what they think tourists want; in other words, tourists unwittingly transform all regions into their own likeness. "The tourist truly diminishes the exoticism of other countries" (p. 48).

Enemies of exoticism of the second sort are different, even if they sometimes have similar effects. These people no longer refuse to perceive others; rather, having perceived them and judged them different from themselves, they want to transform them—in the name of an illusory universality that is in fact nothing but the projection of their own customs and habits (the figure of ethnocentrism is recognizable here). In this category we can mention missionaries, whom Segalen had learned to hate in Tahiti, and also colonial administrators, who want to impose French customs on the four corners of the earth. "The very notion of a centralized administration, of laws good for all that [the administrator] *must* apply, distorts all his judgments from the outset, makes him deaf to the *disharmonies* (or the harmonies of diversity)" (p. 40). Once again targeted are all the authors of facile syntheses, those who are too quick to find oneness: "Chateaubriand . . . , V. Hugo . . . and G. Sand . . . did no more than dull the object in a mixture that blots out marvelous diversity! Delicious diversity!" (p. 37). Included finally are all those who, motivated by the love of technological progress (and perhaps by the profit motive as well), make travel more rapid and more accessible to larger numbers, thus diminishing the specificity of each culture. "Of the perfecting of voyages and the threats that ensue for the persistence of the flavor of exoticism" (p. 27).

Now this last category of enemies of exoticism is the one that strikes

Segalen as especially dangerous, for it corresponds to a specifically modern, but universal, movement, of equalizing and homogenizing. It is by observing contemporary events, "Turkish revolution, Chinese revolution, Russian revolution, even the war," that Segalen sees "how diverse values tend to merge, to become unified and degraded"—in short, how "the exotic tension of the world decreases" (p. 76). In fact, several countries, heretofore very different from the West, are undergoing violent mutations that bring them closer to European ideals. What is worse, these ideals valorize equality at the expense of hierarchy, so that exoticism is decreasing as much within these countries as it is from one country to another. Segalen, who himself does not hesitate to reject the "so-called human" values in the name of intensity and life, cannot keep from accusing democracy of abolishing all hierarchies of values.

It is striking to note how much Segalen has in common here with Loti, whom he despised. Loti had precisely the same understanding of the changes that had taken place in Turkey: "A constitutional Sultan! Why, it upsets all my established notions . . . From the point of view of the picturesque, Turkey will lose much through the application of this new system . . . Parliamentary Government will be the ruin of Turkey. There is no doubt about it" (*Aziyadé*, pp. 72–73). Loti is thus resolutely hostile, at least during this period, to "the levelling blasts, which . . . are blowing from the West" (p. 125). In this he is an exote, and not a pseudo-exote, for difference appears to him as a value in itself; and he is no less pessimistic than Segalen: "Some day, when man shall have made all things alike, the earth will be a dull, tedious dwelling-place, and we shall have even to give up travelling and seeking for a change" (*Madame Chrysanthème*, p. 16).

The specifically modern threat is thus a two-pronged one: democracy (equalization) within countries, communication (unification) among countries. The result verges on catastrophe. Segalen has just read in some books about physics that universal energy is constantly dwindling, that the world is threatened by entropy, and he perceives the fading away of exoticism as the loss of another form of energy, the invasion of another entropy. "If the homogeneous prevails in the underlying reality, nothing keeps us from believing in its coming triumph in perceptible reality, the one that we touch, grasp, and devour with all the teeth and taste buds of our senses. Then the kingdom of the lukewarm can arrive; the time of viscous mush with no inequalities, no pitfalls, no recoveries, a time prefigured more or less by the degradation of ethnographic diversity" (*Essai*, p. 67). Of all the fates that await us, entropy is the worst. Segalen is conscious of how much he owes Gobineau for his apocalyptic images of the future of the world, for he notes, in these same pages: "The degradation of exoticism. Gobineau: *De l'inégalité*" (p. 88).

What can we do to fight entropy? Pray, perhaps? "Unnameable Lord of the world, give me the other!—Div . . . no, diversity" (p. 77). But Segalen is not a believer. It seems to him more opportune to warn human beings and incite them to combat the attenuation of exoticism. "Diversity is decreasing. Therein lies the great terrestrial danger. It is thus against this danger that we must struggle, fight—die perhaps with beauty . . . Remedy against the degradation of the level of exoticism: exalt the partial exotic values that remain" (p. 78). And that is what Segalen himself does throughout all his work, in the *Essai sur l'exotisme* as well as in the texts that grow out of his contacts with Tahiti or China.

This struggle has to be carried out on both internal and external fronts. Within each country, the enemy is the tendency to diminish inequalities, to bring the various classes of the population closer together. In the olden days, the distance between God and man, king and people, heroes and humble folk, was irreducible. In certain privileged countries these differences have been maintained even into the present day. "There were considerable [differences] between the Tzar and the muzhik—the Son of Heaven and the people (the paternal theory notwithstanding)—and the princely cities of Italy were fine tools of diversity." All this has lapsed into decadence since the advent of democracy. "The sovereign people brings with it everywhere the same habits, the same functions" (p. 77). Segalen is horrified by the Chinese revolution, which places the republic in the position of Son of Heaven; he dreams of a political regime dominated by a powerful leader. He reacts with the same disgust, moreover, to the egalitarian movements in the Western countries: "Absolute condemnation of feminism, a sort of monstrous social inversion" (p. 78).

On the external front, peoples must be prevented at all costs from coming closer together. Segalen shares a rejection of intermixings with Gobineau, Loti, and Lévi-Strauss; if people must be in contact, let them at least go to war: "Mechanical voyages confronting peoples and (horror) mixing them, blending them without making them fight each other" (p. 77). The first version of his "Advice to the Worthy Traveller" spelled this out as follows: "Thus it is that . . . you will attain—not, what a horror, peace and eternal beatitude—but war, shocks and turbulence full of intoxication, of infinite diversity" (*Briques et tuiles*, p. 75). Segalen is as bellicose as Péguy (who is mentioned on the same page of the *Essai*), and, like him, when the First World War breaks out, Segalen rushes to the front. But even war seems disappointing in the modern world: "Exoticism of war in full degradation" (p. 79).

Does there exist a necessary link between the admiring description of the exotic experience and vitalist philosophy on the one hand and the valorization of social inequality and war on the other? We may doubt this, if only because the latter elements of Segalen's thought are forcefully asserted only toward the end of his life (notably in a text entitled "Imago Mundi" and dated Shanghai, 1917). We may be fond of alterity without reducing our values to the praise of life, and life to sensations. From another standpoint, there is indeed a relationship between Segalen's exoticism and his call to battle. His evocation of the meeting with the Other is thorough and nuanced; it remains partial, nevertheless, for it registers the role of difference but underestimates that of identity. From that point on, having become a defender of pure difference, Segalen refuses to imagine that individuals may have the same rights without ceasing to be different, that peoples may remain different from each other without necessarily going to war. His extremism (which is also to his credit: he remains internally consistent, and stands behind his convictions in their ultimate consequences) paradoxically also draws him closer to Barrès, whose exclusive attachment to his native soil Segalen tends to deride. Barrès loves only himself, while Segalen loves only the Other, it is true; but they converge in a philosophy of difference, in a radical relativism where only the labels vary, and in horrified contemplation of the convergence of peoples.

Modern Travelers

Artaud in Mexico

What becomes of these figures of exoticism as we approach the present day? Let us look at them through the example of a poet as "revolutionary" as Antonin Artaud. Artaud went to Mexico in 1936 and spent several months there. He gave a number of lectures, wrote newspaper articles, and took special interest in the rites of the Tarahumara Indians; his Mexican writings were collected (after his death) in two brief volumes entitled *Messages révolutionnaires* (partially translated in *Selected Writings*) and *Les Tarahumaras* (published in English as *The Peyote Dance*).

In Artaud's mind, Mexico is the opposite of France. Their national cultures are not actually at issue: France is simply the most familiar part of western Europe, as Mexico is the most familiar part of the rest of the world. Each of these two entities strikes Artaud as internally homogeneous. To the objection that there is more than one Mexico (there is the Aztecs' Mexico, the Toltecs', the Mayans', the Totonacs', and so on), Artaud would reply that his interlocutor "does not know what culture is, he is confusing the multiplicity of forms with the synthesis of a single idea" (*Selected Writings*, p. 364). Not only are all these cultures one and the same, but furthermore the great Mexican culture is one with Muslim, Brahman, and Jewish esoterism: "Who does not see that all these esoterisms are the same, and mean spiritually the same thing?" (p. 364). This is because for Artaud culture does not in fact consist in observable forms (customs, usages, rites) but in an attitude toward life, nature, and man. Artaud finds only two such attitudes, one illustrated by the French and the other by the ancient Mexicans.

How does he characterize them? The word he uses most frequently to identify the first attitude is "rationalist": European culture is a culture of reason. In agreement with the ordinary racialists, Artaud speaks of "reason, a European faculty" (p. 358); only his value judgment differs. This fundamental rationalism has several corollaries: the separation of body and mind, belief in progress, and "democratic ideas" (*Messages révolutionnaires*, p. 106). The enemy (for it is an enemy) is thus a sort of amalgam of Descartes and Condorcet, but Artaud also inveighs against sixteenth-century humanism, in whose place he would like to see a very different "humanism." His critique somewhat resembles Lévi-Strauss's: European humanism is much too narrow, for it has placed man at the center of the universe and has thus deprived nature of the place it deserves. "The Humanism of the Renaissance was not an expansion but a diminution of man, since Man stopped raising himself to the level of nature and brought nature down to his own size, and an exclusive concern with the human brought about the loss of the Natural" (*The Peyote Dance*, p. 62).

European rationalist culture is contrasted, logically enough, with "a magical culture" characteristic of the Mexicans and the other non-Europeans (*Messages*, p. 23). Artaud's quite metaphoric evocation of this culture seems to imply several things: "the destruction of individual consciousness" (*Selected Writings*, p. 369), which has been supplanted by a collective consciousness; the interpenetration of body and soul; the establishment of continuity between human beings and the world around them—earth and stars; and the submission of the world to the laws of universal analogy. "By means of very precise astrological data, drawn from a transcendent algebra, one can predict events and act on them" (*Messages*, p. 108).

In the texts he published in Mexico, Artaud sometimes ironizes about the Parisian public, which, so far as Mexico is concerned, lives in "a state of phantasmagoria" (*Selected Writings*, p. 368); but his own picture of the country and its culture is not much more in touch with reality. His Mexican readers must have been somewhat astonished to learn that the "subtle political structure [of their country] . . . has not changed fundamentally since the age of Montezuma" (p. 371). How does Artaud know this? He does not need to observe contemporary Mexicans; he knew it even before he had seen them: "I have spent a long time looking at the Gods of Mexico in the Codex, and it has become clear to me that . . ." (*Messages*, p. 43). Thus, what we have here is an intuitive and imaginative effort, a poetic re-creation—but one for which Artaud nevertheless claims a cognitive role: he proceeds, he says, "as a scholar, in the true sense of the word" (p. 69).

Artaud's attitude is hardly surprising, for he himself continually warns his readers that he has not come to Mexico in order to discover an unknown world. He knows in advance what he is looking for: the negation of European civilization, the animist world of his dreams. He is quite straightforward: "The only reason I went to the mountains of Mexico was to rid myself of Jesus christ, just as I hope one day to go to Tibet to purge myself of god and of his holy spirit" (*Selected Writings*, p. 443). The various countries of the world are supposed to allow him—in this never-realized project—to come to terms with his own religion and his own culture: if Artaud travels, it is especially not in order to learn about the world.

He has come to Mexico in search of whatever is different from Europe; that is why he rejects contemporary Mexico, sullied by contacts with Europe, and aspires only to come across vestiges of ancient Mexico, which stand a better chance of resembling his dreams. "I came to look for the survival of these notions in modern Mexico, or to wait for their resurrecion" (*Messages*, p. 110). This chronological primitivism leads him toward whatever is old, ancient, indigenous and authentic, toward a Mexico that antedates intermixing (if such a thing has ever actually existed). "My research will only deal with the part of the Mexican soul that has remained free from any influence of the European mind" (p. 105). The true culture, in fact, is the culture that preceded the mixing, the one that "is based on race and blood" (p. 22), not on external influences. Unfortunately, this layer of the Mexican soul turns out to be shallower than Artaud had anticipated: "I was hoping to find a vital form of culture here, and I have found only the corpse of the culture of Europe" (p. 130).

Artaud's attitude toward others—in the case in point, toward Mexicans—is thus by no means original. On the formal level, his spiritual family is that of all "allegorists": all those who make a purely allegorical use of others, a use dictated not by the identity of those others and what may be known about them, but by an autonomous ideological project, conceived independently of any contact with the people called upon to serve solely as example and illustration. In this respect Artaud resembles the eighteenth-century primitivists, from Lahontan to Diderot, who in the last analysis took very little interest in real Hurons or real Tahitians, but needed them as arguments to use in the context of specifically European and French quarrels. Artaud is thus a primitivist, even if the content of his primitivism is somewhat peculiar. He misunderstands the Mexicans (ultimately they interest him very little); he has come in search of elements of his own theses. In this the allegorist-writer repeats the gesture of the impressionist-traveler, who sees others only in terms of his own needs, without ever elevating them to the position of subject.

As for Artaud's ideas, they are inscribed within the Romantic, antihumanitarian, and antidemocratic tradition. Barrès could have written his statement about race and blood; Gobineau could be the author of Artaud's passages about the undesirability of cultural mixing. Artaud believes that the differences among races are irreducible (reason is a European faculty), and he is opposed to the idea of human universality; he is thus against any change that tends toward unification. Antonin Artaud himself was undeniably a very unconventional character; still, in his attitude toward others, only his style is his own.

Portraits of Travelers

Up to this point, we have used our own intuitive knowledge of the world of travels and encounters to interpret the thinking of writer-travelers. We can now reverse the perspective and interrogate this knowledge itself with the help of categories brought to light by the exoticist writers. Can our experience of travel be better understood with the help of authors of the past? Each of us will have a personal response to that question; but we can also join in reviewing a portrait gallery, in which the portraits no longer represent individual travelers but depict, somewhat after Segalen's fashion, the main categories of traveler. A portrait gallery rather than a typology: a typology supposes in fact that the constitutive features of each portrait form a system, whereas the protagonists we shall be considering here are identified on the basis of characteristics that stem from different facets, different phases of the voyage. I have settled on ten. Why ten and not five or fifteen? Rather than being the product of a deductive system, these portraits of travelers grow out of empirical observation: it happens that these types recur more frequently than others in travel and escape literature as it has been produced for the last century or so. Of course, every real traveler may slip by turns into the shoes of one or another of these rather abstract voyagers.

Thus, we shall no longer be dealing with positive or negative judgments passed on others, judgments of condemnation or praise. In the present perspective, it does not much matter whether our travelers are relativists or universalists, racialists or nationalists, primitivists or exoticists. At issue rather are the forms of interaction in which they engage with others in the course of their voyage. We shall thus be dealing with a relation that is no longer of representation (how does one view the others?) but of contiguity and coexistence (how does one live with the others?). This obviously implies interaction: travelers who pass through a foreign country without stopping, or who visit it while avoiding all contact with its inhabitants, have no role to play in our scenario.

1. *The assimilator.* This species, inventoried by Rousseau and Segalen, seems relatively rare in our day. The reason is that this type of traveler presupposes a certain crusading or Messianic spirit, whereas the beliefs from which such a spirit is derived are no longer very widespread. The assimilator wants to modify others so they will resemble him; in principle he is a universalist (he believes in the unity of the human spirit), but he ordinarily interprets the difference of others in terms of lack with regard to his own ideal. The classic figure of the assimilator is the Christian missionary, who seeks to convert others to his own religion;

such a conversion is not necessarily followed by a transformation of the nonreligious mores of the converts (the Jesuits in China were particularly accommodating on this point).

Christian proselytism coincides with the first great wave of colonization, in the sixteenth century. During the second wave, in the nineteenth century, what was exported was the idea of European civilization rather than Christianity; we saw this as a goal with Condorcet and as a practice with Jules Ferry. Segalen, let us remember, was just as hostile to the missionary in Tahiti as to the colonial functionary in Indochina or elsewhere; he took them equally to task both for misunderstanding other peoples and for wanting to change them by making them resemble Europeans (the universalism of the assimilators is generally a thinly disguised ethnocentrism). Today we can point to a third wave of Messianism that has characterized the twentieth century, consisting in the effort to export world revolution and to convert the most disparate peoples to one version of Marxist ideology or another; thus, we have colonies of a new type. Alongside these great waves, to be sure, there have been many others, of more or less reduced dimensions, which have led to assimilation on the local level; this process implies the physical superiority of the assimilator, who is supported by the army or the police.

2. *The profiteer.* The typical profiteer is neither priest nor soldier nor ideologue: he is a businessman—for example, a merchant or an industrialist. His attitude toward others amounts to using them for his own benefit; he speculates on their otherness the better to "swindle" them, as Segalen put it. Unlike the assimilator, the profiteer adapts well to all contexts, and does not need to be backed up by any sort of ideology. Dealing with native populations unfamiliar with the value of foreign objects, he sells dear and buys cheap; he uses the "others" as a low-cost labor force, exploiting them on their own ground or importing them (sometimes clandestinely) to his home territory. Of the others he knows only what he absolutely has to know in order to use them: he learns how to talk to them and to persuade them. The Other is caught up in a pragmatic relation; he is never the goal of the relation. In our day, there are almost no old-style colonials left, but a new figure has emerged, that of the consultant *(coopérant)*. Instead of exploiting the others, the consultant exploits (not always, of course) his own exceptional position among them. He is interested in the others only to the extent that they allow him to enjoy certain privileges: a better salary, a

Exoticism

higher-level job, more consideration, inexpensive servants, all this in the sunny climate characteristic of poor countries.

3. *The tourist.* The tourist is a visitor in a hurry who prefers monuments to human beings. He is in a hurry not only because modern man is hurried in general, but also because the trip belongs to his vacation time and not to his working life; his displacements abroad are compartmentalized into his paid holidays. The rapid pace of the trip is an initial reason why he prefers the inanimate order to the animate: knowledge of human ways, as Chateaubriand pointed out, takes time. But there is another reason for his choice: the absence of encounters with different subjects is much more restful, since it never puts our own identity into question. It is less threatening to see camels than men. Monuments are natural or cultural: they include everything that is out of the ordinary in nature, from mountain peaks to hot geysers, and everything that is ancient or artistic among human productions. The tourist attempts to collect as many monuments as possible in his travels; that is why he privileges images over language, the camera being his emblematic instrument, the one that will allow him to make his monument collection objective and eternal.

The tourist is not very interested in a country's inhabitants; still, he unwittingly influences them, as Segalen observed. Since the tourist is prepared to spend money, the native will seek to offer him what he asks for (or what he is expected to ask for). Thus, although without intending to, the tourist incites the natives to valorize the "typical": the production of objects supposed to be found in the country, the outfitting of establishments, sites, or "native" festivals. Little by little, local activities are replaced by the sale of souvenirs (which are produced, moreover, for economic reasons, in third countries); thus, the frantic search for local color leads, paradoxically, to homogenization.

Segalen was highly contemptuous of tourists, whose "herding" aspect he derided; this is not surprising in such an elitist thinker, and since Segalen's day mass tourism has made great strides. But the weaknesses of tourism do not arise from its collective nature: it is just as possible to "be a tourist" on one's own. From another standpoint, the initial contact with a foreign country is necessarily superficial: the touristic visit, if it arouses interest, can be the first stage in a more thorough acquaintance. The practice of tourism is not contemptible in itself; it is simply that, from the perspective of a relationship with representatives of another culture, it produces rather impoverished results.

4. *The impressionist.* The impressionist is a highly perfected tourist. First, he has much more time than the vacationer; next, he broadens his horizons to include human beings; finally, he takes back home with him not just simple photographic slides or verbal clichés, but, let us say, painted or written sketches. Still, he has in common with the tourist the fact that he himself remains the sole subject of the experience. Why does he set out? Sometimes, like Loti, because he no longer succeeds in *feeling* life at home, and the foreign framework allows him to rediscover his taste for life: "This insipid banquet of life requires all the spice that one can lend it" (*Aziyadé*, p. 13). On other occasions, because, as Baudelaire suggests in "L'Invitation au Voyage" ("The Invitation to a Journey"), he hopes to find a framework that matches the experience he is already living, the being he has already encountered: "Wouldn't you be framed in your own analogy, wouldn't you see yourself reflected, to speak like the mystics, in your own *correspondence?*" (*The Prose Poems and La Fanfarlo*, p. 55). I can decide to go to Venice because I am feeling melancholic, or to Capri because I am joyful.

The experience sought may be of a thousand different varieties: perception of sounds, tastes, unusual images, subjective observations about the mores of others, or erotic encounters (like the sailor with a woman in every port, or in the manner of specialized travel agencies). One common thread relates these travelers, who may be adventurers or contemplative types: when it comes right down to it what really interests them are the impressions that countries or human beings leave with them, not the countries or the people themselves. Or as Henri Michaux says in one of his travel narratives: "Once for all this is it: anyone who does not contribute to my betterment—zero" (*Ecuador*, p. 72). In this way the impressionist attitude is in profound harmony with the individualism that dominates our era: without necessarily being contemptuous of others (everyone has the same rights), I am interested in them only to the extent that they play a role in a project that is my own.

The impressionist attitude was systematized for the first time by Loti, whose heirs are numerous: figures as diverse as Henri Michaux in Asia or Roland Barthes in Japan are also "impressionists" (Barthes recognized his own debt to Loti). But they have not been servile imitators: in their cases, the amorous intrigue is set aside or kept quiet, and in particular the traveler does not claim to be revealing the universe by recounting his own experiences; the self-directed irony of a Michaux or a Barthes is there to prevent impressionism from turning into narcissism, as happens with Loti. By the same token, we note that the impressionist attitude is not negative in itself: the individual certainly has the right to his own experiences, and there is something affecting in the modesty of the impressionist who recognizes that he is only bringing back images of the foreign country, compared to the arrogance of the scholar who claims to be revealing its eternal nature. A two-fold danger persists, nevertheless: the image of the others risks being superficial, if not frankly mistaken (a risk that Michaux does not always manage to avoid), and the experience ceases to be innocent if it requires the instrumentalization of the Other and thus authorizes his suffering.

5. *The assimilated.* This is most often a person making just a one-way trip: the immigrant. He wants to know the others because something has brought him to live among them; he wants to be like them, because he wants to be accepted by them. His behavior is thus exactly the opposite of the assimilator's: he reaches out toward the others not to make them like himself, but to make himself like them (he wants to participate, for example, in the "American dream"). In this he differs from the migrant worker, the counterpart of the profiteer, who goes to a foreign country for a limited time only and has no intention of giving up his own culture—quite the contrary. When the process of familiarization and identification is far enough along, the immigrant becomes assimilated: he is "like" the others.

This attitude has a special variant in which assimilation does not extend to the full range of life but concerns professional life alone: here we are dealing with the expert in a foreign country. The expert makes frequent sojourns, and at least in a first phase seeks to understand the foreigners as they understand themselves: just as thoroughly, and in just the same way. The risk that arises then, whether the specialist is an ethnologist or a historian, is that his knowledge may become a simple reproduction of the knowledge that the inhabitants of the country have of themselves; yet as Segalen suggests, one can aim higher than the replacement of the domination of the *I* by that of the *thou*, of ethnocentric deformation by the local stereotype.

6. *The exote.* This is why, as we have seen, Segalen calls for a new attitude: to identify it we may as well continue using the term he created. In our day-to-day existence, the automatisms of life blind us: we take as natural what is merely conventional, and habit exempts a

multitude of gestures from perception. The foreigner does not have
the same handicap: not sharing our habits, he perceives them instead
of submitting to them. To the foreigner we are not natural, for the
foreigner constantly proceeds by way of implicit comparisons with his
own country, which gives him the privilege of discovering our lacks—
that is, what we do not see. This particular form of lucidity has been
observed for a very long time (it is the lucidity of Montesquieu's
Persians in Paris, to whom we shall return). Here is Michaux's formulation: "How could one not write about a country that has met you
with an abundance of new things and in the joy of living afresh? And
how could one write about a country where one has lived, bound down
by boredom, by contradiction, by petty cares, by defeats, by the daily
humdrum, and about which one has ceased to know anything? . . .
Knowledge does not progress with time. Differences are overlooked.
You compromise. You come to an understanding. And you cease to
come to conclusions . . . A passerby, with his innocent eye, is able
sometimes to lay his finger on the center" (*Un Barbare en Asie*, in
English *A Barbarian in Asia*, pp. 67–69).

But it is not a matter of complete naiveté, of total ignorance; we have
noted this with regard to Lévi-Strauss. It is much more a matter of an
unstable equilibrium between surprise and familiarity, between distancing and identification. The happiness of the exote is fragile: if he does
not know the others well enough, he does not yet understand them; if
he knows them too well, he no longer sees them. The exote cannot
install himself in peace and quiet: no sooner does he attain that state
than his experience has already grown stale. No sooner does the exote
arrive than he has to get ready to leave again; as Segalen said, he must
cultivate nothing but alternation. That is perhaps why the rule of
exoticism has often been converted from a precept for living into an
artistic device: Chekhov's *ostranenie* or Brecht's *Verfremdung* (French
distanciation, English "defamiliarization").

7. *The exile.* This individual resembles the immigrant in some respects, the exote in others. Like the former, he settles down in a country
that is not his own; like the latter, he avoids assimilation. However,
unlike the exote, he is not seeking to renew his experience, to exacer-
bate strangeness; and, unlike the expert, he is not particularly interested
in the people among whom he lives. Who is the exile? He is someone
who interprets his life in a foreign country as an experience of non-

belonging to his milieu, and who cherishes it for that very reason. The exile is interested in his own life, even in his own people; but he has observed that in order to protect this interest it would be best to live abroad, in a place where he does not "belong"; the status of foreigner is for him no longer temporary but permanent. The same feeling, in a less developed form, is what impels some people to live in large cities where the condition of anonymity prevents full integration or absorption into the community.

It would seem that the first great exile of French literature was Descartes, who chose to live in Holland not, as is sometimes believed, so he could publish freely what would have been forbidden in France (Descartes did not have censorship problems), or because he was fascinated by Dutch culture (he had no particular interest in it), but because this choice best suited the accomplishment of the philosophical and scientific task he had set himself. Being a foreigner, for Descartes, amounted to being free—that is, not dependent. "Situated as I am, with one foot in one country and one in another, I find my condition most happy in that it is free" (*Oeuvres* [Works], p. 1305). The first well-known author to express himself this way, Descartes was not to be the last. Let us listen to the Prince de Ligne, another great traveler: "I love my state of being a foreigner everywhere: a Frenchman in Austria, an Austrian in France, both in Russia, it is the way to please everywhere and to be dependent nowhere" (*Lettres écrites de Russie* [Letters from Russia], p. 68). In the twentieth century, writers have often followed Descartes' example and chosen exile to produce their work: Joyce and Beckett fled Ireland, Rilke could write only outside of Germany, García Marquez and Günther Grass wrote their "national" novels (*One Hundred Years of Solitude, The Tin Drum*) in Paris, and so on.

The disadvantage in the exile's situation (in this particular sense of the word) lies in the fact that at the outset he rules out significant relationships with the others among whom he is living. Explaining why he prefers Amsterdam to any other place in the world, Descartes wrote (to Guez de Balzac): "I go out walking every day amid the confusion of a great people, with as much liberty and repose as you could have along your paths, and I do not give any more consideration to the men I see there than I would to the trees one encounters in your forests, or the animals that graze there" (*Oeuvres*, p. 942). Exile allows Rilke to write the *Duino Elegies;* but does it make him perceive the natives he meets more intensely than he perceives trees and animals? This sort of exile is perhaps a happy experience; it is certainly not a discovery of others.

8. *The allegorist.* Allegory says one thing while implying another; the allegorist speaks of a (foreign) people in order to discuss something else—a problem of concern to the allegorist himself and his own culture. Thus, Lahontan used Hurons to talk about the lack of freedom and equality in France, and was quite unconcerned with the Hurons' own destiny. Diderot did the same thing with Tahitians in order to denounce European forms of sexuality, and Artaud enlisted Mexicans to serve his own world view. It is clear that personal acquaintance does not fundamentally modify the allegorist's behavior: Diderot did not go to Tahiti, while Artaud did travel to Mexico, but the allegorical use they made of others was the same. As it happens, all these authors were also primitivists, and they praise the foreigners in question; but it is just as easy to find negative allegories in which foreigners serve as bogeymen. However, in the end it hardly matters whether the content of the judgment is negative or positive: what counts is that the others are subject to the author's needs. In this sense, the allegorist is a profiteer, with the one difference that he is operating on the symbolic and not the material level.

The image of the Other in the allegorist's case comes not from observation but from the inversion of features found at home. We saw this with the classical projection of the Golden Age onto foreign peoples, but the same thing also happens in the modern period. Nizan explains: "We had been taught to think of the East as the opposite of the West. So once it was established that the collapse and decay of Europe was a simple, inescapable fact, the renaissance and flowering of the Orient became a fact equally obvious" (*Aden, Arabie*, English trans., p. 73). Similarly, in our day, the unconditional Third-Worldists project their dreams onto little-known countries and invert the features of the societies they observe around them; in so doing, they are practicing an updated form of primitivist allegorism.

9. *The disenchanted.* The stay-at-home never leaves his own country or even his own house, and does not regret it. But there are also travelers who have gone around the world and who nevertheless end up joining the stay-at-home in his praise of the home front: after setting out for the ends of the earth, they have discovered that the trip was

not necessary, that one could learn as much and more by concentrating on the familiar. The reasons given for this disenchantment, as well as the approach adopted by the traveler once he has gotten back home, may be either individual or collective. In the West, arguments for giving up foreign travel and devoting oneself to the inner voyage are generally borrowed from the Stoic tradition; it is in this spirit that Chateaubriand declared, as we recall: "Man does not need to travel in order to grow; he bears immensity within himself." In the Orient, the same preference is based on Taoist or Buddhist philosophy; and Michaux, after declaring in *Ecuador:* "Traveling does not broaden you so much as make you sophisticated, 'up-to-date,' taken in by the superficial . . . You can just as easily find your truth staring for forty-eight hours at some old tapestry" (p. 86), relies upon Oriental wisdom to conclude his *Barbarian in Asia* as follows:

> And now, said Buddha to his disciples, when about to die:
> "In the future, be your own light, your own refuge.
> "Seek not another refuge.
> "Go not to seek refuge other than in Yourselves.
>
> . . . . .
>
> "Pay no attention to another's way of thinking.
> "Hold fast in your own island.
> "GLUED TO CONTEMPLATION."
>
> (p. 186)

As soon as the voyager decided that what he was looking for was, at bottom, "his own truth," his own way of thinking, the voyage as such seems to have become superfluous. Having noticed that in the Orient he was interested in himself more than in anything else, Chateaubriand decided to stop traveling. But can we trust the advice to do the same, when it is offered precisely by a great traveler? Must we not set forth ourselves in order to discover, on our own, the futility of travel? And must we not become familiar with the not-self in order to understand the self?

The second way of renouncing travel lies in preferring, in distant lands, not the inner quest but the company of one's own compatriots. Not because they are better than foreigners, as the nationalist thinks, but because interaction with others can go further when those others are known quantities. This is the lesson Nizan brings back from his trip to Arabia: "There is only one valid kind of travel, and that is the journey toward men . . . We can give joy only to someone we know, and love is the perfection of knowing" (*Aden, Arabie*, p. 136, p. 138). This is obviously a much less individualist project than Michaux's, even if Nizan's concluding equation is questionable.

10. *The philosopher.* It is not certain whether the philosophical voyage, which differs from the rest, has ever taken place (philosophers are human beings like any other, and they are subject to being impressionists, or allegorists, or exiles, like Descartes); but one can imagine it, as Rousseau had already done (although he himself never set sail). Rousseau's recipe for the philosopher's voyage was the following: you must observe differences in order to discover properties. The philosophical voyage would thus have two facets, humility and pride, and two movements, the lessons to be learned and the lessons to be given. Observe differences: this task requires an apprenticeship, the recognition of human diversity. Such is the virtue of travel according to Montaigne: "To rub and polish our brains by contact with those of others" ("Of the education of children," I, 26, p. 112). And even if, for Montaigne as for Michaux after him, the goal is self-knowledge, travel is nonetheless indispensable: it is by exploring the world that one goes deepest into oneself. "This great world . . . is the mirror in which we must look at ourselves to recognize ourselves from the proper angle" (p. 116). Whatever the outcome, there is in this movement toward others a forgetting of self that brings the philosopher close to the assimilated traveler, for a time.

But the observation of differences is not the final goal; it is only the means for discovering properties—of things or beings, situations or institutions. Owing to his contacts with foreigners, the philosopher has discovered universal horizons (even if they are never definitively universal) that allow him not only to learn but also to judge. Why would I stop denouncing injustice just because it occurs outside the borders of my own country? Chateaubriand, who is often wrong, is right to condemn tyranny in Turkey; and Michaux is right to be indignant about the humiliation of human beings spurred by the caste system in India, right to express his horror at "the spectacle of the accumulation of monstrous inequalities, injustices, cruelties, harsh treatments, corruptions swathed in learned hypocrisies that are explained and labeled differently, of course, by the ruses of those who monopolize religion and the goods of the earth" (*Un Barbare en Asie*, p. 103). The philosopher is a universalist—as was also the assimilator, except for one thing: owing to his attentive observation of differences, his universalism is not a simple ethnocentrism, and he is usually content to pass judgment and to leave to others the problem of acting, of righting wrongs and improving destinies.

But it is time to leave our portrait gallery.

5

Moderation

Persian Letters

Defamiliarization

I have saved the example of Montesquieu for last, because I believe it incorporates the most successful effort within the French tradition to conceptualize the diversity of peoples and the unity of the human race at one and the same time. In the pages that follow, there can be no question of presenting an overall interpretation of Montesquieu's thought, or an analysis of each of his works; we shall have to settle for examining his thinking about the subjects that have preoccupied us up to now. Montesquieu reflected on these problems throughout his life, and the final result of his reflection is conveyed in his magnum opus, *The Spirit of the Laws*. But before we plunge into that work, let us linger a moment in the antechamber constituted by his first important text, *Persian Letters*.

This book recounts the visit of two Persians to Paris. Their vision of the Western world might be expected to be superficial and biased. But what we find is just the opposite: they are much more lucid about the facts of French life than are the French themselves. Thanks to these Persians, Montesquieu's readers discover a reality so familiar to them that they have been incapable of perceiving it. The descriptions produced by the Persians achieve their effect by feigning ignorance of what things are called (since the name makes the thing itself imperceptible owing to its very automatism) and by replacing these names with metaphoric or metonymic equivalents: priests become "dervishes," the rosary becomes "little wooden beads" (p. 82). Montesquieu thus makes conscious and systematic use of the device of defamiliarization evoked in connection with the "exote."

Does this mean that the Persians are lucid as a people and the French blind? Not at all. Near the middle of the book, Rica, one of the two Persians, copies the letter of a Frenchman living in Spain (letter 78): the Frenchman proves capable of drawing a penetrating portrait of the Spanish character. Rica, who has caught on to the device, adds in his commentary: "I should not be sorry, Usbek, to see a letter written to Madrid by a Spaniard travelling in France; I am sure that he would be able to avenge his country" (letter 78, p. 157). That Spaniard would be as lucid as the Persians Rica and Usbek; this is because they have the epistemological privilege of being foreigners. The "total ignorance of the way in which these [= our] dogmas are linked with our other truths" ("Some Reflections on the Persian Letters," p. 284), which character- izes foreigners' perceptions, turns out to be an advantage: associations, explanations, and habits tend to trivialize things and thus exempt them from critical examination. The foreigner, on the contrary, is always astonished: "I spend my life in inquiry," Usbek says in describing his Parisian experience. "Everything interests me, everything surprises me," and he adds: "Being a foreigner, I had nothing better to do than to study the crowd of people who were ceaselessly arriving and pro- vided me with something new all the time" (letter 48, p. 104). One of Rica's interlocutors can thus describe him as follows: "You who, being a foreigner, want to know about things, and know about them as they are" (letter 134, p. 239).

Thus, the condition of successful knowledge is that one not belong to the society described; in other words, one cannot both live in a society, in the strong sense, and know that society. The passion for knowledge implies a certain renunciation of life, including its pleasures, and Usbek is conscious of this from the beginning of his adventure: leaving Persia means that he is choosing knowledge of the world over life experience. "Rica and I are perhaps the first Persians to have left our country for love of knowledge, to have abandoned the attractions of a quiet life in order to pursue the laborious search for wisdom" (letter 1, p. 41).

A necessary but not a sufficient condition: one can be a foreigner in a country and still not manage to know it. This demonstration is made at the expense of a Frenchman in *Persian Letters*: Rica meets someone who, without ever having been in Persia, can tell him everything about his own country: "I mentioned Persia to him, but I had hardly uttered four words when he contradicted me twice over, on the authority of books by Messrs Tavernier and Chardin" (letter 72, p. 149; it adds piquancy to know that these two authors of travel narratives are Montesquieu's own principal sources). Once again, this is not a national trait; another Frenchman, who has not been to Persia either, offers a judicious analysis of that country nevertheless (letter 34), whereas Rhédi, another Persian, sees in Venice only how hard it is to accomplish his ablutions (letter 31). The privilege of the foreigner is exercised only if it is accompanied by genuine "love of knowledge."

But why does Rica need to imagine a Spaniard to tell Frenchmen the truth about themselves? Why cannot a Frenchman do the job? The overall plot of *Persian Letters* serves to illustrate the impossibility of that solution. The same Usbek who understands the Western world so well is blind to the realities of his own life: his harem, his relationships with his wives. He imagines that Roxane is resisting him because of her extreme modesty (letter 26), whereas we learn at the end of the book that her resistance betrays her rejection of Usbek and her love for someone else: "You were surprised not to find me carried away by the ecstasy of love; if you had known me properly you would have found in me all the violence of hate" (letter 161, p. 280). How does it happen that Usbek succeeds so well in one of his quests for knowledge and fails so pathetically in the other? How is it that he can analyze and condemn despotism when he sees it outside himself, in France or in Persia, but remains an exemplary despot in his personal life where his wives are concerned?

Montesquieu seems to have transposed onto relations among societies what La Rochefoucauld had established concerning relations among individuals within a society: we are blind to ourselves, we can only know others. On the social level, self-love turns out to be paired with *prejudices*, defined by Montesquieu in the preface to *The Spirit of the Laws* as "what makes one unaware of oneself" (p. xliv). As a collective rather than an individual (though still not universal) unconscious, prejudice constitutes the unconscious portion of a society's ideology. The human apparatus for knowing cannot grasp the subject perfectly because it also constitutes part of it; the ideal separation between knowing and living is only possible in exceptional circumstances, for to know is also to live. Objective knowledge of things "as they are" may be accessible to the ideal and disinterested foreigner; in self-knowledge, both for individuals and for social groups, the instruments for knowing are contiguous to the object to be known, and perfect lucidity is impossible. The eye cannot see itself, as La Rochefoucauld also pointed out.

But is this really what Montesquieu means? To accept it, we would also have to believe that Rica and Usbek really existed, really wrote letters which Montesquieu merely translated and adapted. Since this is not the case, and since Montesquieu does not conceal the fact—"Something which has often surprised me is the realization that these Persians knew as much as I did about the customs and way of life of our nation" (introduction, p. 40)—his message must be a different one. It is not the foreigner Usbek but indeed the Frenchman Montesquieu who is endowed with penetration and lucidity where his own society is concerned. He did not acquire these attributes, however, without detaching himself from himself and making a detour by way of Persia. Just like his protagonist, but with an even greater "love of knowledge," he has read Chardin and Tavernier, and this plunge into otherness is what has enabled him to be lucid about himself. That is why *Persian Letters* teems with information not only about the Persians (and the French) but also about Russians, Tartars, Chinese, Turks, and Spaniards; in the series of letters about the causes of depopulation (letters 112–122) as in the series about the world of books (letters 133–137), all countries and continents are taken into account. As D'Alembert says in "An Eulogium on President Montesquieu," describing the preparatory work for *The Spirit of the Laws:* "He had first made himself in some respect a stranger in his own country, better to understand it at last" (in Montesquieu, *The Complete Works*, I, p. xvi).

Self-knowledge is possible, but it implies prior knowledge of others; the comparative method is the only route to that goal. La Bruyère aspired to universality while limiting his observation and analysis to his own milieu, court life in France. Montesquieu reverses the order: to know one's own community, one must first know the whole world. The universal becomes the means for knowing the particular; the particular does not, in and of itself, lead to the general. If we do not know others, in the last analysis, we do not know ourselves; this is the case with the Muscovites. "Separated from other nations by the law of the land, they have kept their traditional customs all the more faithfully because they did not think that it was possible to have any others" (letter 51, pp. 112–113). Or, in an even more affecting case, one risks proclaiming, like

Fatmé, Usbek's wife: "I cannot imagine anything more delightful than
the wonderful beauty of your body" (letter 7, p. 47), even as she
ingenuously reveals the reason for her choice: "When I married you,
my eyes had not yet seen a man's face; you are still the only one whom
I have been allowed to see" (letter 7, p. 46).

But this does not mean that Montesquieu is lucid in any absolute
sense about his own society; he is simply less blind than others, thanks
to this detour by way of the rest of the world, and he has the great
advantage of knowing the limits of his own knowledge. In *Persian
Letters* he indicates these limits indirectly. The edition of 1758, published posthumously but prepared by Montesquieu himself, has an
alphabetical table of contents that includes the following entry: "Montesquieu (M. de). Depicts himself in the person of Usbek." Yet Usbek
was the very example of the person who is lucid about others and blind
about himself! Is this a way of telling us that *Persian Letters* itself has
its own blind spot, the author being aware of its existence but not its
location? And that the reader of *Persian Letters* who might think himself
completely lucid ought to look into his own "prejudices" as well?
Montesquieu concludes his "Reflections" (added to *Persian Letters* in
1754, the year before his death) with this deceptively reassuring sentence: "Certainly the nature and intention of the *Persian Letters* are so
manifest that they will deceive only those who wish to deceive themselves" ("Some Reflections on the Persian Letters," p. 289). But we
now know that we all wish to deceive ourselves! Is that Montesquieu
we hear chortling in his coffin?

Relative and Absolute

The quality of the observation depends upon the position of the observer. Can we extend this dependency to values other than those of
knowledge? Might Montesquieu be a supporter of the relativist party,
as it was represented in Montaigne's statements of principle? We might
be tempted to believe this at times. In any case what Montesquieu
observed around him was a grounding of judgment in personal values,
a projection of the self onto the world: "There are three estates in
France: the Church, the nobles of the sword, and the nobles of the
robe. Each has supreme contempt for the other two" (letter 44, p. 98).
"A philosopher is supremely disdainful of a man whose head is full of
facts; and is considered a visionary, in his turn, by the man who has a

good memory" (letter 145, p. 268). The Spaniards consider all other
people contemptible (letter 78); the French are astonished that there
are men outside France (letter 48), and "they look down on anything
foreign" (letter 100, p. 185). The head eunuch can write to Usbek:
"Each of your wives considers herself superior to the others because of
her birth, her beauty, her intelligence, or your love" (letter 64, p. 130),
but Usbek himself is myopic enough to boast of the matrimonial mores
at home and condemn those of the Europeans (letter 26). In short, it
is "only other people whom we ever find ridiculous" (letter 52, p. 114).
After looking this closely at human egocentrism, must we not conclude
that one judges always and exclusively in one's own terms, and that
there is no such thing as a universal standard of good and evil?

If this is the case in the ethical realm, it is even easier to demonstrate
that in the realm of aesthetic judgments everyone sets up his or her
own propensities as the ideal. Rica observes in one of his letters: "It
seems to me, Usbek, that all our judgments are made with reference
covertly to ourselves. I do not find it surprising that the negroes paint
the devil sparkling white, and their gods black as coal . . . It has been
well said that if triangles had a god, they would give him three sides"
(letter 59, p. 124).

Finally, the political order varies from region to region, as a function
of cultural and natural conditions, and it is reasonable to require that
laws conform to a country's mores. The only universal principle is the
principle of local and relative adaptation, Usbek thinks: "I have often
tried to decide which government was most in conformity with reason.
I have come to think that the most perfect is one which attains its
purpose with the least trouble, so that the one which controls men in
the manner best adapted to their inclinations and desires is the most
perfect" (letter 80, p. 158). Conformity with reason turns out to be
conformity with mores. The universal only underwrites the relative,
and the philosopher does not try to find out whether one goal is
preferable to another, but only seeks the one which is the most direct
path leading toward a given goal.

The very form of Montesquieu's book seems to confirm this conviction that only particular points of view about truth exist, not truth as
such. The epistolary form, like the dialogue form in Renan or Diderot,
makes it possible to express the most divergent positions, each from
the letter-writer's personal perspective. The ironic tone that pervades
so many of the letters makes it possible to grasp what is rejected but

not what is endorsed, and the fictional form itself is a way of abstaining from taking a stand: all the opinions expressed belong to fictional characters, not to Montesquieu himself, even if certain opinions seem to arouse his sympathy more than others.

In order to decide whether or not Montesquieu is a pure relativist, we would have to examine in somewhat greater detail the judgment that can be derived from *Persian Letters* about some human institution; no institution lends itself better to this than religion. Throughout the entire book, Montesquieu takes advantage of the device of defamiliarization to mock one practice or another of the Catholic Church (as this institution is seen through the eyes of Muslim observers): the pope's wealth, the role of bishops, the Inquisition, priestly celibacy, the absence of divorce, the dullness of theological tomes. But alongside all this he also examines the problem posed by the plurality of religions, each of which believes it is the best in the world.

The position Usbek (and perhaps Montesquieu himself) defends is the position of tolerance. The believers in the various faiths unfortunately resemble all other human groups in this respect: Jews, Christians, Muslims all consider themselves superior to the others, and they view those others as heretics. For which reason they often end up persecuting them: this is illustrated by the long story of the calamities of the virtuous Parsee Apheridon, who worships Zoroaster and is pursued for this reason by the Muslims (letter 67). "In order to love and conform to one's religion it is not necessary to hate and persecute those who do not conform to it" (letter 60, p. 125). On the contrary, a State that accepted the plurality of religions would have everything to gain: "Since in every religion there are precepts which are useful to society, it is as well that they should be obeyed with enthusiasm, and what is more likely to encourage this enthusiasm than a multiplicity of religions?" (letter 85, p. 165). And let no one object that the simultaneous presence of diverse religions threatens to lead to religious wars. The cause does not lie there; it is rather the "spirit of intolerance" that is to blame for this regrettable reaction.

Not only must one not persecute representatives of other religions, but one must not attempt to convert them, either. Usbek thinks he can establish a rigorous distinction between those who adhere to their own religion and those who seek to spread it. "It has been realized that zeal for the advancement of a religion is different from the attachment that one should have for it" (letter 60, p. 125). He returns twice to this point: "We suffer constantly from a certain desire to make other people share our views; it is part of our calling, so to speak. [Usbek is quoting a clergyman here.] This is as ridiculous as it would be to see Europeans trying to turn the Africans' face white, for the sake of human nature" (letter 61, p. 127). In letter 85, the spirit of proselytism is viewed as "the total eclipse of human reason." "One would have to be out of one's mind to think of the idea. Someone who tries to make me change my religion does so only, I presume, because he would not change his own, even if attempts were made to compel him; so that he finds it strange that I will not do something that he would not do himself, perhaps not even to be ruler of the world" (letter 85, p. 166).

This profession of faith in tolerance is thus based on two arguments. The first does not hold up to examination: unlike the color of one's skin, one can change one's religion; and we may even ask how else a religion could be propagated if not by conversion? It is perhaps absurd to judge beauty in absolute terms, but the same cannot be said for the value of religions: what is true of aesthetics is not true of ethics. The second is the argument based on reciprocity: not to do to others what you do not wish them to do to you. It is on this basis, too, that La Rochefoucauld established society and justice. But this rule, taken literally, does not suffice to prevent injustice: the judge must not pardon the assassin on the grounds that that is how he would want to be treated himself, if by misfortune he found himself in the chair of the accused (as Rousseau noted). And then this consideration is not applicable if the forces involved are disproportionate in size: the majority could then persecute the minority with impunity. As Usbek remarks, this is indeed what happened to the Protestants in France, to the Jews in Spain, and to the Parsees in Persia.

However, alongside this attitude of relativist tolerance with respect to religions, Usbek adopts another one. Rather than forswearing all comparisons among religions, Usbek's approach involves trying to find what they have in common, in order to constitute an irreducible core; obviously this can consist only of a set of abstract principles, detached from the particular ceremonies that characterize the various cults. Usbek sets himself to this task on several occasions (letter 35, letter 93), and he formulates his conclusions as follows: "Whatever religion one may have, obedience to the laws, love of mankind, and respect for one's parents are always the principal acts of religion" (letter 46, p. 101). These principles are no longer relative; and if a given doctrine did not adhere to them, it would not deserve to be called a religion.

Conversely, one must obey these absolute principles even if they are not cloaked in the prestige of religion. "If there is a God . . . he must necessarily be just . . . Consequently, even if there were no God, we should nonetheless still love justice, that is to say, make an effort to resemble this being of whom we have so exalted a conception, and who if he existed would be just necessarily. Even if we were to be free of the constraints of religion, we ought not to be free of those imposed by equity" (letter 83, p. 162).

Religions may be relative, but equity—that is, true justice—is not. Here is what goes against the grain of ethical relativism and pure tolerance. Usbek's position (and *a fortiori* Montesquieu's) is not as simple as it first appears. People are ethnocentric: they judge everything in terms of their own habits. An initial, immediate remedy would consist in making them aware of the existence of others, teaching them elementary tolerance. But one would then need to go deeper into things, and look for universal principles of justice.

These two movements are not clearly articulated in *Persian Letters*, and yet we cannot fail to discern them. Throughout the book, alongside the appeal for tolerance, there is this other, more obscure reference to absolute values. Usbek believes in "a certain politeness that is common to every nation" (letter 48, p. 105), as in the universal equality of men (letter 75); an absolute justice existed at least in the past, since Usbek can say that contemporary causes "have corrupted all its principles" (letter 94, p. 176). He is particularly explicit in letter 83: "Justice is eternal, and does not depend on human conventions" (p. 162); and elsewhere he refers again to "natural equity" (letter 129, p. 229). One of Rica's interlocutors also understands barbarity in an ethical rather than a historical sense: "These peoples were not truly barbarous, since they were free, but they have become so now that most of them have submitted to dictatorship, and lost the sweetness of freedom, which is in such close concord with reason, humanity and nature" (letter 136, p. 241). And Roxane, standing up to Usbek, explains: "I have amended your laws according to the laws of nature" (letter 161, p. 280)—that is, according to the laws that postulate the right to be free.

Liberty and Despotism

Liberty is in fact the value most often called for in *Persian Letters*, and despotism the evil most often condemned. Montesquieu's analysis proceeds on two levels. On the one hand he takes as his target Eastern political despotism, the form that reigns in Persia, Turkey, or Russia. In the first place, despotism is inefficient, and it makes no one happy— neither the population, which moreover declines systematically, nor the tyrant, who constantly fears for his life. In fact the despotic situation provokes an unintended convergence of extremes: no one is more like a slave than his master. "There is nothing which does more to bring our rulers down to the level of their subjects than the immense power they have over them" (letter 102, p. 188).

But despotism is also condemnable in justice, precisely because it flouts human freedom, which is an inalienable human property. If individual freedom is a right, the power of one person over another can never be a right. What is the source of power? Might alone; yet might does not make right. Montesquieu evokes an anecdote attributed to the English: two princes are fighting over the succession to the throne; one of them, having won, wants to condemn the other for treason. "'It is only a moment ago,' said the unfortunate prince, 'that it was decided which of us is the traitor'" (letter 104, p. 191). The winner claims to have not only might but also right on his side; not satisfied with having won the war, he also condemns his adversary as a criminal. But if the source of all power is might alone, there is no such thing as legitimate power. The only thing that can legitimate an instance of power is, paradoxically, its partial abandonment: legitimacy can be acquired *a posteriori* by the fact that the holder of power has consented to share it with others, to impose limits on himself. "Unlimited authority can never be legitimate, because it can never have had a legitimate origin" (ibid.).

On the other hand, and at even greater length, Montesquieu describes family despotism—that is, the oppression of women. Again the Orient offers an illustration. The women of the harem are not only deprived of their freedom; they are also beaten, humiliated, treated like animals. Sometimes their very lives are at risk. What is more, all this suffering is entirely futile. Inflicting it does not make Usbek happy; he no longer feels desire but only jealousy, against which he is defenseless. All his efforts and those of the eunuchs fail, moreover, for nature always wins out in the end: the logical outcome of tyranny is death, and the entire harem will be exterminated.

It is the eunuch, an important figure in *Persian Letters*, who best embodies the absurdity of despotism. In him, the exercise of power is deprived of the benefits that usually accompany it: he is a being separated from himself (letter 9), who lives only in images and not in things (letter 63); from the man-woman relation, he has dispensed with sexuality, so that only the power relation remains. "It is as if I become a man again on the occasions when I now give them orders" (letter 9, p. 50). The eunuch lives only by virtue of the authority he exercises and the obedience he elicits; he receives from his master "unlimited powers" (letter 148, p. 271), though the master himself had said elsewhere that those powers would never be legitimate; and he spends his life learning "the difficult art of commanding" (letter 64, p. 132). Punishments are his unique means of action, and the principle of his government is "fear and terror" (letter 148, p. 271). Ideally, a profound silence should reign everywhere (letter 64); this would be the last stage before death. If the eunuch can know pleasure, it is the pleasure that is inherent in the exercise of power as such, without any transitivity. "The pleasure of making myself obeyed gives me a secret joy" (letter 9, p. 50), and Solim, who replaces him at the end, also speaks of the "secret joy" that fills him at the sight of the blood he sheds (letter 160, p. 280). However, his condition is hardly more enviable than that of the slaves, for the relation of servitude puts two people in bondage: the slave who has become a eunuch finds himself merely "leaving a state of slavery in which you would always have to obey and entering one in which you would issue commands" (letter 15, p. 61), while Usbek perceives himself in the last analysis as resembling a vile slave (letter 156).

The character of the eunuch tells the true story of the relation between master and slave, tyrant and subjugated people. Neither man nor woman, he is literally master and slave at the same time; the sadism inherent in the position of master is the only joy available to him, since every external justification of power has been removed. Tyranny is not only cruel; it is also sterile, and it degrades anyone who exercises it.

Montesquieu's condemnation of despotism is unreserved. It is less obvious, however, that Montesquieu believes in the possibility of overcoming it, that he subscribes, in other words, to an optimistic view of history.

Power emanates from might; justice, from reason. But what if might were more powerful than reason? One of Rica's letters cites the words of "a very chivalrous philosopher" (Fontenelle?) about the inequality between men and women: "Nature has laid down no such law. Our authority over women is absolutely tyrannical; they have allowed us to impose it only because they are more gentle than we are, and consequently more humane and reasonable. Their superiority in these respects, which would doubtless have given them the supremacy if we were reasonable beings, has caused them to lose it because we are not" (letter 38, pp. 92–93). And Montesquieu goes even further in *The Spirit of the Laws:* "More gentleness and moderation, which, rather than the harsh and ferocious virtues, can make for a good government" (V, 17, p. 111). This is a tragic paradox: the more reason and humanity we possess, the less we want to tyrannize others, thus the easier it is for them to tyrannize us. Our very superiority is the cause of our inferiority.

It may be unreasonable to seek to convert others to our own religion; but not everyone is reasonable. If we do not do this while others do, we turn out to be in a situation of weakness and end up being converted ourselves. Do we have the right to renounce the protection of force in order to safeguard a doctrine that we believe superior to all others? To give up force is sensible only if everyone agrees to do it; otherwise it simply means that, in the absence of police, criminals rule as masters, and that, externally, in the absence of an army, the aggressor, who may also be a tyrant, will have a free hand to subjugate us (this is the paradox of pacifism). Rousseau remarked: "The wicked man gets advantage from the just man's probity and his own injustice. He is delighted that everyone, with the exception of himself, be just" (*Emile*, IV, p. 235, note). Does being reasonable imply being weak?

Usbek imagines that relations among societies could be governed by the same principles of justice that are applied within a society among individuals. "As between citizens, judges have to administer justice; as between nations, each nation has to administer it itself. In the second of these processes of justice the principles employed cannot be different from those which apply in the first" (*Persian Letters*, letter 95, p. 176). And Montesquieu has the same conviction when he writes *The Spirit of the Laws:* "Nations, which are to the entire universe what individuals are to a state, govern themselves as do the latter by natural right and by laws they have made for themselves" (XXI, 21, p. 392). Usbek also imagines that if a supreme weapon were to be invented, "by the unanimous consent of every country the discovery would be buried" (*Persian Letters*, letter 106, p. 194). However, he himself has already noted the degree to which the parallelism between the two levels of justice is deceptive, since in international relations no one occupies the position of judge. If disputes between individuals are settled, within a society, by public law rather than by force, it is because these individuals have delegated their judiciary power to a higher agency whose decisions they accept: "It is necessary for a third party to elucidate matters which each side, in its cupidity, tries to conceal" (letter 95, p. 177). But what third party will play this role between two countries? What country would allow an international agency to decide its fate? No society has had to "accept" the fact that another society should exist elsewhere; and no society seems to want to give up its weapons, especially if these weapons can "exterminate whole countries and nations" (letter 105, p. 192): what international agency could compel it to do so, since it has superior weaponry, and since weapons are power? Once again it is Rousseau who seems to get it right, rather than Montesquieu, in this connection: "Man to man, we live in a civil state subject to laws; people to people, each enjoys natural liberty" ("Ecrits sur l'abbé de Saint-Pierre," p. 610).

Usbek says: "We are surrounded by men who are stronger than we are. They can do us harm in a thousand different ways, and threequarters of the time they can do it with impunity" (*Persian Letters*, letter 83, p. 162). Here is a terrible observation. What hope do we have? "What peace of mind it is for us to know that all these men have in their hearts an inner principle which is on our side, and protects us from any action that they might undertake against us!" (letter 83, pp. 162–163). We know that Usbek believes in natural equity, lodged in the heart of every human being. But is he really sure of it? If he were, why would he evoke so insistently the opposite possibility? "But for that, we should be perpetually afraid. We should walk about among men as if they were wild lions, and we should never be sure for a moment of our possessions, our happiness, or our lives" (letter 83, p. 163). In his *Pensées*, Montesquieu used the conditional, significantly, when he wrote: "Being obliged to live with men, I should have been very pleased if there were in their hearts an inner principle that reassured me against them" (615). Or are we to think that we should act *as if* we believed in the existence of a natural justice, one that is independent of human conventions and desires? "Even if it were to depend on them [human conventions], this truth would be a terrible one, and we should have to conceal it from ourselves" (letter 83, p. 162).

It is Montesquieu who thus brings to light the impotence of reason, the triumph of power. And stating the message loud and clear is perhaps not a good way to conceal it. Ever since Montesquieu's day, the terrible truth has spread throughout the world.

The Spirit of the Laws

The Spirit of Nations

The Spirit of the Laws, published in 1748, nearly thirty years after *Persian Letters,* is a long and complex work. Its subject is the laws of human societies—of all countries and all times! Montesquieu observes the infinite diversity of laws and wonders about its cause. Three forces act in the production of laws: natural law, the nature of the government, and "physical and moral causes" (such as climate, forms of commerce, and many others). *The Spirit of the Laws* seems thus at first glance to take into account two types of values: values that are universal, and values that are dependent upon local conditions and thus relative. But what precise role is played by each type? How do the variable data and constant principles interact?

The diversity of countries and of their characteristics results from physical and moral causes; that is a fact which Montesquieu is the first to take into consideration in such a thoroughgoing way. But he is not satisfied to collect and juxtapose these characteristics; he goes further and declares that they form a coherent structure, which he designates, in this text, as the "general spirit" of a nation. The spirit of a nation is also the reflection of this structure in the mentality of its inhabitants; in more modern terms, we might speak of national ideology. Its first property is precisely its internal consistency. "Everything is closely linked together" (XIX, 15, p. 316), and: "Omit one of these practices, and you shake the state" (XIX, 19, p. 320). "To the extent that, in each nation, one of these causes acts more forcefully, the others yield to it" (XIX, 4, p. 310). The examples of controlled interaction among the various ingredients of the general spirit are innumerable. In the second place, the general spirit of a nation is omnipresent; it leaves its trace on each particular phenomenon, and is influenced in its turn. Finally, this spirit is modified only slowly, and any attempt to change it by force may bring about disastrous results; still, it is not immutable.

Montesquieu's study of society prefigures not only structural analyses (by his hypothesis about the internal coherence of the whole) but also the science of sociology itself (by the way he takes all the aforementioned factors into consideration). In *Persian Letters*, Montesquieu had already demonstrated his attentiveness to a level of social life that his moralist predecessors had neglected: he was concerned neither with man in general nor with psychological types, but with social groups (judges, parliamentarians, churchmen, writers, scholars, men of the world); the French scene of *Persian Letters* does not include a single proper name. In *The Spirit of the Laws*, the exploration becomes systematic: Montesquieu does not limit himself, like Montaigne or Pascal, to remarking that customs are numerous and varied; he undertakes to study them, which means that he tries to understand both the causes and the limits of their diversity: typology is to replace chaos.

This particularly innovative aspect of his work is at the same time the aspect that has aged least well: Montesquieu's erudition, immense for his time, has been outstripped (although it has taken many successors to outdo what he did all by himself). However, it is plainly the constitution of the object as such that is crucial, and not the content of any given description of the individual societies.

The characteristics of a country determine its laws, but this does not imply a rigid determinism. Montesquieu must be thinking in terms of relations of probability, of diffuse interaction, of "appropriateness" *(convenance)*, as he says, rather than of mechanical implication. He uses terms like "more often," "freer," "more moderate"; it is a matter of more or less, not all or nothing. "Government by one alone appears more frequently in fertile countries" (XVIII, 1, p. 285). "Island peoples are more inclined to liberty than continental peoples" (XVIII, 5, p. 288). Despotism occurs more frequently in countries with a large land mass and in extreme climates; moderate governments prosper in temperate climates—there is nothing astonishing about this—and republics are favored by small territories, monarchies by medium-sized ones. But one must not count too heavily on this: "If . . . despotism became established at a certain time, neither mores nor climate would hold firm" (VIII, 8, p. 118). The characteristics of countries and their general spirit can supply favorable conditions but nothing more; in the final analysis, peoples must make their own laws and their lives. It is possible "to conquer the laziness that comes from the climate" (XIV, 7, p. 237) even if "the empire of the climate is the first of all empires" (XIX, 14, p. 316); and Montesquieu declares that "bad legislators are those who have favored the vices of the climate and good ones are those who have opposed them" (XIV, 5, p. 236). The determinism of "phys-

ical and moral causes" thus does not deprive men of their freedom of
action and does not discharge them from responsibility for their actions.

The reason for the margin of indeterminacy reserved by Montesquieu in his research lies in human diversity and in the very plurality
of determinisms: each cause has multiple effects; each effect may stem
from numerous causes. "Although each effect depends upon a general
cause, so many other particular causes are mingled with it that each
effect has, in a way, a separate cause," Montesquieu says in another text
("Essai sur le goût," p. 851); or, elsewhere: "Most effects . . . come
about by such singular routes, and depend on such imperceptible or
such remote reasons that they cannot be foreseen" (according to the
summary of his lost "Traité des devoirs" [Treatise on Duties], p. 182).
The world is not irrational, but it can be impenetrable; it is over-
determined rather than undetermined—but on the surface that
amounts to the same thing. Thus, there are apparent exceptions to the
laws. It is for this reason that Montesquieu takes his stand at the
opposite pole from scientistic utopianism: he does not believe that the
laws of society can become perfectly transparent, or that a politics can
be based on the science that makes us aware of these laws.

But there is another reason for the uncertainty of the laws, and this
lies in the possibility of acting *against* them: in rebellion, or simply in
a deliberate decision. "Particular intelligent beings are limited by their
nature and are consequently subject to error; furthermore, it is in their
nature to act by themselves . . . As an intelligent being, he [man]
constantly violates the laws god has established and changes those he
himself establishes" (I, 1, p. 5). It is important to observe that, even if
Montesquieu does not use these terms, human freedom (in the political
rather than the philosophical sense) is what is actually at issue here,
and that Montesquieu sees freedom as attaining its apogee in the
human species; in other words, as Rousseau will assert somewhat later,
freedom is the defining characteristic of humanity.

This margin of freedom, however, must not be mistaken for chaos,
and human behavior must not be declared inaccessible to knowledge.
"I began by examining men," Montesquieu writes in his preface, "and
I believed that, amidst the infinite diversity of laws and mores, they
were not led by their fancies alone" (xliii). It is simply that the complex
determinism that governs the social world renders it partially opaque
and means that, even with the best intentions in the world, the legis-

lator always risks remaining ignorant of certain aspects of things. The only way to protect oneself against the disastrous consequences of a bad choice is not to opt for extreme solutions, or for unique principles; one must acknowledge the regular existence of exceptions. It is as necessary to get away from fatalism (the thought that one can change nothing in human destiny, that it is therefore useless to act) as from frantic intervention (the belief that everything depends upon the legislator—or whoever holds power).

Natural Law

Thus, cultural, social, and physical diversity is taken seriously for the first time and opened up for study; it is for this reason that, in our day, some have elected to see Montesquieu as the precursor or even the founder of the modern social sciences—of sociology or anthropology. But in the overall schema of his work these empirical elements seem counterbalanced by other elements of different origin. In this sense, Montesquieu simultaneously produces a book of general and comparative anthropology and a work of political philosophy, while continuing to oppose the modern aspiration toward purely empirical research with no value judgments attached. From this perspective Montesquieu is more an "ancient" than a "modern." We must doubtless turn to natural law to locate his universal principles.

Natural law takes up much less space in Montesquieu's work than the two other factors that determine the spirit of the laws; for this reason, certain commentators attribute to it a secondary role, seeing in it the traces of a heritage that Montesquieu had not managed to shed. But natural law is, in Montesquieu's own eyes, an essential ingredient of his doctrine, and in his "Defense of the Spirit of the Laws" he describes his starting point as follows: "The Author was attempting to overthrow Hobbes's system; a system the most terrible, it making all the virtues and vices depend on human establishments: and by endeavouring to prove, that all mankind are born in a state of war, and that the first natural Law, is that all should make war against all, he, like Spinoza, overthrows both all religion, and all morality" (*The Complete Works of M. de Montesquieu*, IV, p. 222). What Montesquieu contests in Hobbes and Spinoza—with whom in other respects he shares certain analyses—is the exclusive recognition of positive laws; unlike them, he is seeking a universal basis for morality and justice. Let us also recall the formula from *Persian Letters:* "Justice is eternal, and does not depend on human conventions" (letter 82, p. 162).

In a first phase, Montesquieu gives the term "law" its fullest extension: it applies to all relationships among all beings. But he then takes care to distinguish among several groups of laws: there are artificial laws (made by men) and natural laws; and he further subdivides the latter into two groups that might be called "natural law" on the one hand and "laws of nature" on the other. This last distinction is important: it breaks with the tradition that confused the two groups and it challenges in advance the attempt made by Diderot (and all later scientists) to base justice on nature, politics and morality on facts. The "laws of nature," which are at bottom simply the defining characteristics of human beings, can be divided, in Montesquieu's enumeration, into three groups: all men and women have a religious instinct, a biological instinct for self-preservation, and a social instinct.

The universal characteristics of our species act on individuals just as forcefully as the other laws of nature act on the entire animate and inanimate world. Natural law is something else entirely: it is the basis for justice in human societies, a set of principles that make it possible to judge the laws themselves. These principles are identical with the natural light of reason (and no longer with human nature). "There is, then, a primitive reason," Montesquieu exclaims at the beginning of his text (I, 1, p. 3), and he likes to quote a sentence from Cicero: "The law is the reason of the great Jupiter" (*Mes Pensées*, 185). An example may illustrate the difference between these two groups of laws: the State is absent from the state of nature, and thus the existence of a state does not follow from a "law of nature"; but "anarchy is contrary to natural law" (*Mes Pensées*, 1848).

The principal passage Montesquieu devotes to natural law is found at the very beginning of the book, in a defense of the principle of natural law against those who, like Hobbes, recognize only positive laws. "To say that there is nothing just or unjust but what positive laws ordain or prohibit is to say that before a circle was drawn, all its radii were not equal." And Montesquieu continues:

"Therefore, one must admit that there are relations of fairness prior to the positive law that establishes them, so that, for example, assuming that there were societies of men, it would be just to conform to their laws; so that, if there were intelligent beings that had received some kindness from another being, they ought to be grateful for it; so that, if one intelligent being had created another intelligent being, the created one ought to remain in its original dependency; so that one intelligent being who has done harm to another intelligent being deserves the same harm in return, and so forth" (I, 1, p. 4).

Montesquieu presents this list simply as an illustration of his project: his use of expressions such as "for example," or "and so forth," cannot be fortuitous. Nevertheless, its strategic place in the text requires us not to take it lightly. This inaugural list, coming on the heels of the "supposition" that societies exist, cannot in fact contain just a random set of examples.

Of the four laws cited, the first is the metalegal law: laws must be obeyed. But only the form of this proposition is universal, since the content of laws can vary from one country to another. In fact, such a proposition is necessarily implied also by all who defend positive law alone (otherwise there would be no means for doing so). In this connection there is no difference between Hobbes and Montesquieu, and the requirement of legality cannot, in itself, constitute natural law.

The third law is a law of subordination and dependency: children must submit to their parents. This law has a corollary: parents are obliged to protect their children. "Natural law orders fathers to feed their children" (XXVI, p. 6). On another occasion, Montesquieu compares this relation with the one binding magistrates to citizens (*Mes Pensées*, 1935).

Finally, the second and fourth laws are variants on a single principle: good will respond to good, evil to evil. It is "natural light," Montesquieu says, "which wants us to do to others what we would want to have done to us" (X, 3, p. 139). This is the law of reciprocity, and it is this law, for example, that allows Montesquieu to condemn slavery: not because slavery is not useful, but because those who defend it would not want to submit to it themselves. "Do you want to know whether the desires of each are legitimate in these things? Examine the desires of all" (XV, 9, p. 253): this is how Montesquieu formulates Kant's moral imperative.

But if we insist on looking for the content of natural law, the juxtaposition of these two "examples" has a new disappointment in store for us, for, rather than a universal principle, what we have is finally a trivial observation: society is made up of relations of reciprocity as well as of subordination. From what is, Montesquieu draws conclusions about what should be: certain laws must consecrate equality and others hierarchy; the latter will be as legitimate as the former. In any event, if a thing is as legitimate as its contrary (equality as legitimate as inequality), taken together the two things encompass the totality of possible relationships; thus, this does not give us any criterion for discrimination. It is not enough to say that equality stems from natural law, for inequality is based on the same thing; all one can say is that society includes symmetrical and asymmetrical relationships of reciprocity and subordination. Now if this is the case, we can no longer speak of universal principles: in Montesquieu's natural law we find no absolute value whatsoever.

Principles of Government

All we have left to do, then, is turn to the third force that acts upon laws, the nature and basis of governments, and see whether this force may not mask universal norms or whether, on the contrary, we shall have to reckon yet again with historical and geographical diversity. According to Montesquieu, the principles of government are articulated as follows:

$$
\begin{cases}
moderation \begin{cases} virtue \text{ (in } democracy\text{)} \\ \\ honor \text{ (in } monarchy\text{)} \end{cases} \\
fear \text{ (in } despotism\text{)}
\end{cases}
$$

Let us look first at the opposition between democracy and monarchy. "Virtue," Montesquieu explains, is egalitarian and individualistic, whereas "honor" is hierarchical and social. This opposition could thus be juxtaposed with the one that obtains between relations of reciprocity (symmetrical, egalitarian) and subordination (asymmetrical, inegalitarian), inherent in what Montesquieu called the "natural law" of societies. Each of these forms of government is based on certain "natural" characteristics of man, and favors their development to the point of making them predominant; consequently, neither of them is superior to the other. It is in the very nature of society to include egalitarian and inegalitarian relations; individual societies favor first one group, then another. Even if Montesquieu as an individual may have preferences for one of these terms over the other, since he does not live outside of time and space, he does not pronounce an absolute value judgment.

Thus, we shall be unable to find here the absolute criterion making it possible to tell good regimes from bad ones: "virtue" and "honor" are both worthy of respect.

There is only one hope left: to see whether this criterion may not lie in the opposition between fear and despotism, on the one hand, and moderation, on the other. "It is not a drawback," says Montesquieu in fact, "when the state passes from moderate government to moderate government, as from republic to monarchy or from monarchy to republic, but rather when it falls and collapses from moderate government into despotism" (VIII, 8, p. 118). Moderation, generally considered up to then to be a virtue of the individual (it is a synonym for temperance), acquires with Montesquieu the status of a political principle. Contrary to what Rousseau later affirms (in the *Second Discourse*), or Diderot (in the "Supplement"), Montesquieu posits a radical break between legitimate and illegitimate regimes, between monarchy and tyranny. The condemnation of despotism is as strong here as it was in *Persian Letters*. "One cannot speak of these monstrous governments without shuddering" (III, 9, p. 28). "The principle of despotic government . . . is corrupt by its nature" (VIII, 10, p. 119). It is for this reason that the description of despotic states is much less faithful to the historical facts than that of other regimes: the examples have to illustrate the principle, and Montesquieu does not hesitate to eliminate everything that would contradict his thesis. This is because he is not looking for empirical faithfulness here, but is out to characterize an ideal type obtained by deduction, whose dangers it is important to demonstrate. The particular despotisms that can be observed in the world interest Montesquieu only as potential illustrations; the logic of despotism matters more to him than the concrete interferences between despotism and the other forms of government.

The main reason Montesquieu condemns despotism is that it is directly opposed to the first law that figures in the "natural law" of societies—namely, the requirement of respect for laws—since despotism is defined by the absence of laws and rules. "Despotic government has fear as its principle; and not many laws are needed for timid, ignorant, beaten-down people" (V, 14, p. 59). "In despotic states there is no law" (VI, 3, p. 76). Despots "have nothing to rule their people's hearts or their own" (V, 11, p. 58). On the contrary, moderation is the same thing as legality: "A moderate government . . . maintains itself by its laws" (III, 9, p. 28). "In moderate countries law is everywhere wise;

it is known everywhere, and the lowest of the magistrates can follow it" (V, 16, p. 66).

Despotism is an evil because it excludes legality. But since laws vary from country to country, the existence of legality is a universal that is devoid of content. The observation of legality guarantees nothing: and what if a law is frankly iniquitous (as were, for example, the racial laws in France under the Vichy government)? Nothing prevents a tyrannical government in fact from legalizing its injustice, and from applying the law strictly, while remaining free to change the law to suit itself. This is the objection formulated by Benjamin Constant, in Condorcet's wake: "The laws could forbid so many things that there would still not be any liberty" (*Principes de politique* [Principles of Politics], p. 27). Does the last place in which we hoped to find the key to political judgments prove empty in its turn? Could Montesquieu's ambition to articulate universal principles and variable data turn out to be unfounded?

The Meaning of Moderation

Let us go back to the starting point. Over and beyond his explicit definitions, Montesquieu seems to give the term "moderation" another meaning, one that is revealed in the way he actually uses it. "Moderation" would be equivalent to "legality" only because legality is opposed to other forces. A power in itself, it can constitute a limit to all other power. Only force stops force. Now legality is force available to all; thus, it introduces a breach in the unity of power. It is not a value in itself, but only inasmuch as it embodies this sharing of powers. This requirement can be justified by the fact that the "nation" is necessarily heterogeneous, made up of individuals and groups with divergent interests; because of this the unity of powers is always an evil (it contradicts the nature of things) and their plurality a good. Tyrannical laws, even though they are laws, have nothing moderate about them, for they do no more than reinforce a single unitary power; the only moderate laws are laws that limit the other powers—that is, those that translate the heterogeneity of society within institutions. Here is the unique absolute value for Montesquieu: that power never be absolute—that is, unified. "Moderation" thus takes on a new meaning, close to that of "blending" (we have already seen that, despite surface appearances, this ideal of blending was not absent from Rousseau's writings).

Any distribution or sharing of powers is a good thing, because it weakens monopoly. Such is the more general meaning of the words "moderation" and "despotism": despotism is a state in which power is unified; moderation implies the multiplicity of power, the copresence of several powers. "In despotic government, power passes *entirely* into the hands of the one to whom it is entrusted" (V, 16, p. 65; emphasis added): it is the refusal to share that is the root of evil. On the contrary, a monarchy, for example, requires the monarch to delegate a portion of his power while retaining another portion; what is more, the very principle of his government, honor, imposes a limit on his power (III, 10). The monarch and the despot are both alone at the top, within the state, but the resemblance does not go much further: power is in the one case shared and in the other monolithic.

Moderation-with-legality, the simple existence of laws, is the minimal protection against the arbitrariness of force. But from the perspective of the concrete operation of states, it is not a sufficient condition: the next step consists in establishing a true *balance* of powers. Political liberty "is present only when power is not abused . . . So that one cannot abuse power, power must check power by the arrangement of things" (XI, 4, p. 155). Moderation-with-equilibrium is moderation in the strong sense. "In order to form a moderate government, one must combine powers, regulate them, temper them, make them act; one must give one power a ballast, so to speak, to put it in a position to resist another" (V, 14, p. 63). Which leads Montesquieu to distinguish different types of power within a state: legislative, executive, and judiciary. The distribution of these powers among different bodies ensures the maintenance of liberty: when two forces are present, "the one will be chained to the other by their reciprocal faculty of vetoing" (XI, 6, p. 164), and the powers will thus be "counter-balanced" (XI, 18, p. 182). Legality ensures the right to liberty; the distribution of powers makes it possible to enjoy that right. In the modern period, this counterbalancing is ensured by the plurality of parties, the existence of a majority and an opposition—in states that are rightly termed "constitutional-pluralist," a term that corresponds exactly to the two meanings of the word "moderation" for Montesquieu.

We must note here that, if this interpretation of his thought is accurate, Montesquieu can be said to have discovered a universal principle of political life, in certain respects comparable to Kant's moral imperative (an action is good if it can be universalized)—an imperative that we have already encountered in Montesquieu's work (it is what makes him prefer the universal to the national) and that is also strongly affirmed by Rousseau. "The less the object of our care is immediately involved with us, the more it becomes equitable, and the love of mankind is nothing other than the love of justice" (*Emile*, IV, p. 252). Equity *is* generality. Just as this principle does not identify any particular actions as good, but proposes a logical rule that allows us, in any circumstance, to recognize good and evil, Montesquieu's principle does not declare that a given regime is good and another one bad (regimes are too varied; particular conditions play too great a role); instead, it proposes a general rule that is universally applicable, although its content may vary.

The efficacity of these principles—and their true universality—comes from the fact that they are formal and not substantive. Their universality does not depend on an identity existing in the world—in which case they would be fragile indeed—but on the oneness of man's capacity to think, and thus on the very definition of the human. But the resemblance between the two universals stops there. And this is hardly surprising, since Rousseau and Kant are talking about individuals and Montesquieu about societies. Whereas the first two complete the individual entity by reminding us of our common membership in the same species, Montesquieu stresses the necessarily heterogeneous character of the whole: it is made up by turns of groups and of individuals. Where Rousseau and Kant must posit unity, Montesquieu reminds us of diversity. The surprise, of course, comes from the fact that diversity itself is what provides politics with its universals.

The means at the disposal of moderation are powerful; still, despotism is powerful as well, and the outcome of the struggle cannot be determined in advance. Sometimes Montesquieu sounds optimistic: "The principle of despotic government is endlessly corrupted . . . Other governments are destroyed because particular accidents violate their principle: this one is destroyed by its internal vice" (VIII, 10, p. 119). But if the death of despotisms is inevitable, their birth seems no less so. Where does despotism come from? Whether from within or without, it is imposed "by a long abuse of power or by a great conquest" (VIII, 8, p. 118). But "it has eternally been observed that any man who has power is led to abuse it" (XI, 4, p. 155); and the strongest have always sought to conquer the weakest. What is an abuse of power? It is not necessarily the transgression of laws, the renunciation of legality (of the minimal form of moderation); it is simply the unshared exercise of power. Its very use constitutes abuse (we may recall the formula of *Persian Letters:* "Unlimited authority can never be legitimate" (letter 104, p. 191); not to abuse power means not to use it (singlehandedly, or always, or everywhere). The advent of despotism is no accident; it is the end result of what constitutes the defining characteristic of mankind according to Hobbes, with whom Montesquieu is in full agreement here: the impulse to power. Reflecting on this paradox—everyone respects freedom, and it is the rarest thing in the world—Montesquieu adds: "A despotic government leaps to view, so to speak; it is uniform throughout; as only passions are needed to establish it, everyone is good enough for that" (*The Spirit of the Laws,* V, 14, p. 63).

Despotism is a translation, on the social level, of features that characterize every human being: passion, the desire for power, the will to unify. It is as "natural" to man as society itself. That is why it is essential, without counting on the natural goodness of man, on the "inner principle" that Usbek invoked, to try to provide human beings with good institutions, which will prevent these seeds of despotism from flowering. The struggle for liberty must be endlessly begun anew.

Uniformity and Plurality

Let us now come back to the laws themselves. Of the three forces that act on them, the spirit of the nations is infinitely variable, and along multiple parameters: one cannot imagine two countries having the same geographical situation, the same history, the same mores. Natural law presents itself as universal, but in reality the universal requirement of submitting to laws changes content according to the nature of the laws of each country, and the requirement of equality is neutralized by the recognition of legitimate nonegalitarian relationships. That is why the ultimate results of this interaction, laws, necessarily differ from one country to another: "The government most in conformity with nature is the one whose particular arrangement best relates to the disposition of the people for whom it is established . . . Laws should be so appropriate to the people for whom they are made that it is very unlikely that the laws of one nation can suit another" (I, 3, p. 8). And yet this relativism, faithful to certain of Usbek's declarations, runs up against a limit, one that arises from the principles of government: tyranny is an evil in all climates, and moderation is a good.

The spirit of the laws is not simply universalist, or purely conventional. Unlike those who, like Montaigne, know only all or nothing and end up embracing a purely relativist credo (even as they contradict it with an absolutist practice), unlike those who decide that if everything is not subject to rigorous laws then nothing can be, Montesquieu accepts both positions from the outset and seeks to articulate them, to assess the respective strength of determinism and of freedom, the degree of equilibrium between the universal and the relative.

Thus, he warns repeatedly against confusing one point of view with another. It is not because political virtue and vice depend on the context in which they are produced that there is no longer any way to distinguish between vice and virtue (XIX, 11)! When he sets out to analyze torture, Montesquieu exclaims: "But I hear the voice of nature crying out against me" (VI, 17, p. 93); and, speaking about slavery, he asserts that it is "contrary to the fundamental principle of all societies" (XV, 2, p. 248), that "slavery is against nature" (XV, 7, p. 252). Reflecting on the fate of the American Indians exterminated by the Spaniards in the name of a goal deemed noble (conversion to the Christian religion), Montesquieu rejects this "Machiavellian" argument and adds: "Crime loses nothing of its blackness by its usefulness. It is true that actions are always judged by their success; but this judgment is itself a deplorable abuse within Morality" (*Mes Pensées*, 1573). However, when one is speaking about laws, one must first see in what framework they are inscribed. "Laws that appear the same do not always have the same effect" (XXIX, 6, p. 604); and, conversely: "Laws that seem contrary are sometimes derived from the same spirit" (XXIX, 10, p. 607). Among themselves, laws "form a well-linked, consistent system," and "in order to judge which of these laws is more in conformity with reason, they must not be compared one by one; they must be taken all together and compared together" (XXIX, 11, p. 608).

The new articulation between absolute values and particular facts remained incomprehensible to Montesquieu's contemporaries. Throughout the eighteenth century, and whatever the political convictions his critics held in other respects (the revolutionaries turned out to agree with the conservatives on this point), he was accused of having abandoned natural law and the moral ideal, and of having granted too important a role to the variations among peoples and to heterogeneity within the state itself (it was not until the twentieth century that Montesquieu was reproached for an *excess* of moralism). Helvétius attacked the book when it was still in manuscript form: its author does not pay enough attention to "just maxims," he does not demonstrate adequately "the idea of perfectibility" ("Letter . . . to Montesquieu," p. 286). Rousseau himself, usually so clairvoyant, misses the mark on the subject of Montesquieu who, he says, "was careful not to discuss the principles of political right. He was content to discuss the positive right of established governments, and nothing in the world is more different than these two studies" (*Emile*, V, p. 458). Condorcet remains blind to the absolute values Montesquieu is defending: "Why has not Montesquieu in the Spirit of Laws spoken of the justice or the injustice of the laws he quotes, and the motives which he attributes to the laws? Why has he not laid down some principles which would enable us to discriminate among the laws flowing from a legitimate power, those which are unjust, and those which are conformable to justice?" ("Observations on the Twenty-ninth Book of the Spirit of Laws," p. 263). Finally Bonald, although coming from the opposite political horizon, since he is the great theoretician of the counterrevolution, takes up the same criticism: I am combating *The Spirit of the Laws*, he says, "because its author is seeking only the motive or the *spirit* of what is, and not the principles of what ought to be" (*Théorie du pouvoir politique et religieux* [Theory of Political and Religious Power], I, Preface, p. 12).

Montesquieu recognizes the diversity of cultural and geographical environments, and sees them as a reason to maintain the diversity of laws: the mind of an individual is not a blank slate, it is informed by the culture to which the individual belongs, and peoples themselves order their behavior in relation to their history. Rousseau follows him on this point; but Helvétius has nothing but scorn for the traditions, for this "chaos of barbarian laws" ("Letter to M. Saurin," p. 291), and in another reproach to Montesquieu he says: "You compromise with prejudice" ("Letter of Helvetius to President Montesquieu," p. 285). Condorcet prefers to return to the separation that prevailed in juridical texts prior to Montesquieu—those between laws based on principles of justice (natural law) and arbitrary laws of no importance—rather than have to recognize that all people do not have the same laws. "Those laws which appear as if it were necessary they should be different in different countries, or exacted on objects which should not be regulated by general laws, consist for the most part of commercial regulations, or are founded on prejudices and habits which should be extinguished, and one of the best means of doing so, is to cease from giving them the countenance of the laws" ("Observations," p. 274). Laws must be based on reason alone. Now reason is universal; thus, laws will be universal as well. We have also seen that, from this postulate, Condorcet drew the obvious conclusion—namely, the need to set up a universal State.

Bonald likewise takes care to set aside civil laws, which have to take into account the diversity of regions and professions. But this is a way of stepping back, the better to leap ahead: for all the rest, the laws proceed rigorously from the structure of the world itself, which is a divine creation. "The fundamental laws, political laws, civil laws, internal or external, are relationships that derive *necessarily from the nature of things*" (*Théorie*, I, sect. VI, 3, p. 436). "The Mosaic laws are the commentary on this divine text, and the laws of all peoples must be their application" (II, sect. III, 2, p. 105). Moral laws in turn "are the same in all religious societies" (II, sect. IV, 1, p. 134).

Here we have to note that this absolutist position brings Bonald closer to Condorcet than to the other conservatives, like Burke in England or de Maistre in France, who for their part remain faithful to Montesquieu's teaching. Montesquieu in effect could have written de Maistre's famous passage criticizing the constitutions that came out of the Revolution (and in which, moreover, de Maistre mentions Montesquieu): "The 1795 constitution, like its predecessors, was made for *man*. But there is no such thing as *man* in the world. During my life, I have seen Frenchmen, Italians, Russians, and so on; thanks to Montesquieu, I even know that one can be *Persian*; but I must say, as for *man*, I have never come across him anywhere; if he exists, he is completely unknown to me . . . A constitution that is made for all nations is made for none: it is a pure abstraction, an academic exercise of the mind, according to some hypothetical ideal" (*Considérations sur la France*, published in English in *The Works of Joseph de Maistre*, p. 80). This passage, taken out of context, is often wrongly interpreted as a declaration of general relativism. But de Maistre is no less absolutist than Bonald on a whole series of subjects; it is simply that positive laws constitute an exception in this regard.

Montesquieu recognizes another form of diversity, within society this time: no nation is perfectly homogeneous; and it is because he takes this essential characteristic of societies into account that he advocates the separation and the balance of powers. In so doing, he refuses to think (thus breaking with the tradition extending from Aristotle to Rousseau) that particular interests are in themselves an evil for the State; he even sees in their defense a guarantee against the tendency of the State to invade everything. He will not be forgiven this position any more than his recognition of the diversity among nations. According to Helvétius, the "intermediate orders . . . are at variance with the natural rights of those whom they oppress" ("Letter . . . to President Montesquieu," pp. 286–287). Rousseau, who has been seen to appreciate intermediate states and blending, condemns all forms of special interest and of separation of powers as soon as he adopts the perspective of the State (in *On the Social Contract*). Sieyès does the same (in his speech of 2 Thermidor, Year III). Bonald is unreservedly opposed to anyone who, "straying from the simple and true idea of the *unity* and *indivisibility of power*, loses himself in the laborious combinations of division and balance of *powers*" (Preface, p. 8). There is and there must be only one power; truth lies in extremes, not in the middle.

It follows that the remedy Montesquieu has proposed, moderation, will be judged unsuitable. Condorcet exclaims: "It is not by the spirit of moderation, but by the spirit of justice, that criminal laws should be mild, that civil laws should tend to equality, and the laws of the municipal administration to liberty and prosperity" ("Observations," p. 261). Helvétius had already explained that, if the English constitution was praiseworthy, this was not because of the balance of powers, but because it included some truly good laws, and he concluded: "I believe . . . in the possibility of a good government, where . . . one may see the general good necessarily resulting, without your balances or particular interests. Such would be a simple machine, the springs of which being easily regulated, would render unnecessary the complicated appendages of wheels and balances" ("Letter . . . to President Montesquieu," p. 289). This "simple machine" will in fact be constructed some forty years later: it is the Jacobin State, whose emblem is another simple machine, the guillotine. Helvétius, Condorcet, and Bonald know where good lies, and think only about the best ways to subordinate the State to it. Montesquieu knows that good exists, but not where it is to be found; what he tries to do, then, is to put in place institutions that facilitate the search for good while ensuring that, even in the case of error as to the nature of the good, the losses will be minimized.

Compared to the utopians, Montesquieu often comes across as a conservative: his first reaction is always to want to leave things as they are. With the exception of tyranny, no injustice seems to trouble him unduly. "I do not write to censure that which is established in any country whatsoever. Each nation will find here the reasons for its maxims" (*The Spirit of the Laws*, Preface, p. xliv), and also, perhaps recalling Montaigne: "In all this I do not justify usages, but I give the reasons for them" (XVI, 4, p. 266). We may wonder whether Montesquieu is telling us what he really thinks, here; another formula, one from his book *Mes Pensées* describing *The Spirit of the Laws*, rings truer: "This book being made for no State, no State can complain about it. It is made for all men" (193). Impartiality does not mean neutrality. What the entire work suggests is that, at the very least, changes in laws are called for when the laws no longer correspond to the social conditions to which they were bound but which have changed over time. We may go even further: if he had not had an ideal in mind, Montesquieu would not have bothered to write *The Spirit of the Laws*: one must not take him too literally when he assures us that he is renouncing all "censorship." His book itself is the response to a situation that he judges threatening: the possible advent of despotism in France. But in order to remain faithful to the spirit of Montesquieu, we should add the following: one will react differently to injustice depending on whether one lives in a moderate State or in a despotic State. Moderate states also have unjust laws; but there people will fight them with means that are legal in themselves, since they are available to citizens. Only the absence of such means—that is, despotism—authorizes recourse to force (but Montesquieu prefers not to linger over this particular case).

The constant search for balance between the general and the particular justifies Montesquieu's ambition to consider himself a moderate, on the epistemological level as well as on the ethical level. He is convinced that the mixed, the plural, are best suited to human societies, for such is the very nature of these societies. "I shall continue to repeat: moderation governs men, not excesses" (XXII, 22, p. 426). Such is likewise the principle that ought to inspire the legislator: "I say it, and it seems to me that I have written this work only to prove it: the spirit of moderation should be that of the legislator; the political good, like the moral good, is always found between two limits" (XXIX, 1, p. 602). This is what the experience of life has taught him, and we may recall that Montesquieu also prefers a certain mediocrity to the extremism embodied by warriors and saints (VI, 9).

This is why he is prepared to admit that it may be necessary to modify the requirement of liberty itself, a requirement that is nevertheless his ideal. How could I require extreme liberty, he writes, "I who believe that the excess even of reason is not always desirable and that men almost always accommodate themselves better to middles than to extremities?" (XI, 6, p. 166). No, "there are cases where a veil has to be drawn for a moment, over liberty, as one hides the statues of the gods" (XII, 19, p. 204). He explains elsewhere: "Even liberty has appeared intolerable to peoples who were not accustomed to enjoying it. Thus is pure air sometimes harmful to those who have lived in swampy countries" (XIX, 2, pp. 308–309). Let us note that Montesquieu does *not* claim that there is no difference between tyranny and liberty, between pure air and swampy air. He only says that under certain circumstances we are not sensitive to the differences; the absolutes thus must be tempered. Otherwise, neutral or even good measures will be perceived as harmful or tyrannical, "when those who govern establish things that run counter to a nation's way of thinking" (XIX, 3, p. 309).

This position, which consists in rejecting the simplicity of monolithic systems, has elicited the greatest number of reservations, owing to its inherent difficulty. Montesquieu's contemporaries did not appreciate his book; ours have not read it. Moreover, he had no illusions as to his readers' judgment: "I had the fate of all moderate people," he writes in a letter to the Marquis of Stainville (May 27, 1750), "and I find myself to be like those in-between folk whom the great Cosmo de Médicis likened to people living on the second floor of a building who are bothered both by the noise from above and the smoke from below."

A Well-Tempered Humanism

At this point I shall stop reading others and speak for myself. Not that I have been silent up to now: throughout this book, I have sought to debate the questions raised by others, supporting or contesting their positions as the case may be. I have tried to find out not only what my authors were asserting but also whether their assertions were correct; thus, I have repeatedly had to take a stand. And yet my reader may have felt some annoyance (or weariness) at my reluctance to present my own opinions on the issues under discussion in a systematic way. I could not do this, first of all, because I did not know them all in advance—far from it. I have made discoveries about my own convictions while looking for truths, with and against my authors. To be sure, I "made" this book, but in another sense of the word, the book has made me. The second reason I have chosen not to state my own views systematically up to now is that I prefer the quest for truth to its possession, and I want my reader to share this preference; more than anything, I cherish opinions that are developed in the course of dialogue. This whole book is an effort to illustrate that idea. If I "take the floor" unilaterally at this point, it is not because I have changed my mind about dialogue; it is because I have come to the end of an itinerary (one that has lasted several years), and I feel a kind of obligation to tell the reader where I am now and what I make of the trip. Rather than offering definitive conclusions, I offer the provisional end point of my inquiry: a simple inventory. Others will be able to use this same itinerary, I hope, to reach conclusions that elude me at present.

Let us maintain a certain distance with respect to the history of thought and go back to the great questions debated in this book. "Us" and "them," I said: how can we, how must we behave with respect to those who do not belong to the same community as ourselves? The first lesson learned is that we have to stop basing our reasoning on a distinction like that one. It is true that human beings have done just this from time immemorial, merely shifting the object of their praise. Following the "rule of Herodotus," they have judged themselves the best in the world, and they have declared others bad or good according to the degree of their proximity. Or, conversely, using the "rule of Homer," they have found that the most distant peoples were the most fortunate and the most admirable, whereas they have seen only decadence in themselves. But both views are mirages, optical illusions. "We" are not necessarily good, and the "others" are not either; the only thing to be said on the subject is that openness toward others, a refusal to reject them out of hand, is a positive quality in any human being. The separation that counts, Chateaubriand would suggest, is the separation between good people and bad, not between ourselves and others; individual societies for their part blend good and evil (in unequal proportions, to be sure). In place of a facile judgment based on the purely relative distinction between those who belong to my group and those who do not, we must make judgments based on ethical principles.

This first conclusion raises two major problems in its turn. What is the significance of our belonging to a community? And how are we to legitimize our judgments?

I. Human beings are not only individuals belonging to the same species; they also belong to specific and various groups within which they are born and act. The most powerful group today is the one called a nation—that is, the more or less perfect (but never total) coincidence between a State and a culture. Belonging to humanity is not the same thing as belonging to a nation—the man is not the citizen, Rousseau said; there is even a latent conflict between the two that may come out into the open if we are obliged to choose between the two corresponding sets of values. Men and women, in this sense of the word, are judged on the basis of ethical principles; as for citizens, they behave according to a political perspective. Neither of these two aspects of human life can be eliminated, nor can one be reduced to the other: it is better to remain aware of this sometimes tragic duality. At the same time, their radical separation, their restriction to spheres that never communicate with each other can be equally disastrous: as witness we can take Tocqueville, who defended morality in his philosophical and scholarly work and advocated the extermination of indigenous populations in his political speeches. Ethics is not politics, but ethics can erect barriers that politics will not have the right to cross; belonging to humanity does not exempt us from belonging to a nation and cannot substitute for it, but human feelings must be able to restrain reasons of State.

The following argument is often heard, as well: I love my own children better than my neighbor's; this is a natural feeling that no one need be ashamed of. Is it not just as natural to prefer my compatriots to foreigners and to reserve special treatment for them? Is it not natural to subordinate the man to the citizen, and ethics to politics? Such reasoning is based on a two-fold confusion. The first is of the psychological order: it consists in transferring the properties of the family to the nation, by analogy. Now between these two entities there is no continuity. The family ensures immediate interaction with other human beings; its principle may be extended, in the extreme case, to all the people we know—but no further. The nation is an abstraction with which we have as little immediate experience as with humanity. The second confusion is of the ethical order: the fact that a thing *is* does not mean that it *should be*. Moreover, individuals make the correction perfectly well themselves, and do not confuse love with justice. We love our own child more than our neighbor's, but when both children are in the house, the pieces of cake we serve them are the same size. And after all, pity is no less natural than selfishness. It is a property of human beings to see beyond their own interests, and it is because of this that the ethical feeling exists; Christian ethics and republican ethics alike merely systematize and particularize this feeling. "National preference" is no more based on facts than it is on values.

But what is a nation? To this question there have been many answers, which can be sorted into two major categories. On the one hand, the idea of nation is constructed following the model of race: it is a community based on "blood"—that is, a biological entity over which the individual has no control at all. We are born French, German, or Russian; we retain that identity to the end of our days. From this perspective, the dead decide for the living, as Barrès and Le Bon put it, and the present of the individual is determined by the past of the group. Nations are impermeable blocks: thoughts, judgments, feelings—everything differs from one nation to the next. From another standpoint, belonging to a nation is conceived along the lines of a contract. Some individuals, as Sieyès said, decide one day to establish a nation; and the thing is done. More seriously, it has been declared that to belong to a nation is above all to accomplish an act of will, to make a commitment to live together by adopting common rules, thus by envisioning a common future.

These two concepts, the nation as race and the nation as contract, are opposed point for point. The one is physical and the other moral, the one is natural and the other is artificial, the one is determinism and the other freedom. Yet the choice between them is not simple: each of us can feel intuitively that both concepts include some truth and that both leave a good deal out. But can we reconcile two contraries? The best-known attempt to do this, Renan's, is a failure: it does not suffice simply to add up two "criteria" when the second annuls the first.

The antinomy of the two "nations" can nevertheless be overcome if we agree to think of nations as cultures. Just as "race" does, culture exists prior to the individual, and we cannot change our culture from one day to the next (as we can change citizenship, by an act of naturalization). But culture also has features in common with the contract model: it is not innate but acquired; and though acquisition may be a slow process, it depends in the final analysis on the will of the individual, and it may depend on education. How does one learn a culture? By mastery of the language, above all; by familiarization with the country's history, its landscapes, and the mores of its original population, governed by a thousand invisible codes (it would obviously be a mistake to identify the culture with what is found in books). Such an apprenticeship takes years and years, and the number of cultures one can know in depth is very limited, but we do not have to have been born into a culture to acquire it: blood has nothing to do with it, nor even genes. Furthermore, not all native-born citizens necessarily possess the culture of their country: one can be French by origin and still not participate in the cultural community.

The interpretation of nation as culture (which originates with Montesquieu) makes it possible to preserve the grains of truth present in the concept of nation as contract or as "race" (whereas these latter two concepts are posterior to Montesquieu). At the same time, this interpretation makes it possible to get around the antinomy of man and citizen: here, there is no path toward the universal except the path that traverses the particular, and whoever masters one specific culture has a chance of being heard throughout the world. Still, it must be specified that culture is not necessarily national (it is even only exceptionally so). It is first of all the property of a region, or of an even smaller geographical entity; it may also belong to a given layer of the population, excluding other groups from the same country; finally it may also include a group of countries. One thing is certain: mastery of at least one culture is indispensable to the full development of each individual. Acculturation is possible and often beneficial; deculturation is a threat. Just as one need not be ashamed to love one's own family members more than others, without being thereby driven to practice injustice, one need not be ashamed of one's attachment to a language, a landscape, a custom: this is what makes us human.

II. What is the status, then, of the legitimacy of our judgments, and how are we to resolve the conflict between the universal and the particular? It would be convenient to start off by considering an opinion, widely held today, that might be summarized as follows. The universalist pretention has turned out, over the centuries, to be nothing but a mask worn by ethnocentrism. Thus, the universalist ideology is responsible for events that number among the most unfortunate in recent European history—namely, the colonial conquests. Under the pretext of spreading "civilization" (a universal value if there is one), a few western European countries have helped themselves to the wealth of all the others and have exploited numerous faraway peoples to their own advantage. Universalism is imperialism. This is not, moreover, the only domain in which the harm done by the universalist ideology can be observed: even within states, heterogeneity has been stifled in the name of these same (pseudo)-universal ideals. That is why it is time to leave claims to universalism behind, and to recognize that all judgments are relative: relative to a time, to a place, to a context. This relativism need not be confused with nihilism or with cynicism (the rejection of all values); from this standpoint, values are recognized, but their extension is limited. Today's good is not yesterday's, and each of us is a barbarian in our neighbor's eyes: let us learn to draw the conclusions to which these self-evident facts lead.

This familiar discourse, of which there are more detailed variants, contains a series of approximations, simplifications, and imprecisions that may lead, with the best intentions in the world, to unacceptable conclusions. We must therefore, if we hope to arrive at a more satisfying overall picture (but without giving up the condemnation of colonialism), untangle these allegations one by one.

In the first place, it is unacceptable to assert that universalism is *necessarily* a form of ethnocentrism—just as it was unacceptable to represent human beings as never being capable of rising above personal interests. Such an ultra-determinist affirmation, implying the impossibility of distinguishing between what is and what should be, leads to absurdity. But it is equally false, on a historical and no longer a theoretical level, to assert that colonial imperialism is intrinsically connected with the universalist ideology. We have seen this in the foregoing pages: colonialist politics is prepared to use any means at hand, it makes undiscriminating use of all the ideologies that come its way, universalism as well as relativism, Christianity as well as anticlericalism, nationalism as well as racism. On this level, ideologies reveal not the motive for actions but rather justifications that have been added after the fact, discourses of self-legitimation that must not be taken literally. If the universalist ideology proved to turn up more frequently than others in colonialism, that would attest to just one thing—namely, that it had enjoyed greater prestige. Ideology as a motive (and no longer as a camouflage, an embellishment added after the fact) is, as we have seen, of a different order: here we are dealing with nationalism, which has been responsible moreover for the other wars fought, during this same period, among the European countries themselves.

In the second place, it is not true that the ethnocentric perversion is the only, or even the most dangerous, perversion of universalism. As we have seen, the universal project risks two sorts of distortion, the one "subjective," the other "objective." In ethnocentrism, the subject identifies her own values, naively or disingenuously, with values in general; she projects the characteristics proper to her own group onto an instrument designed for universality. In scientism, on the contrary, one finds values outside oneself, in the objective world—or rather, one entrusts the task of finding them to science. The scientistic approach does not necessarily produce ethnocentric results; quite the contrary, it is customarily used to restrain the movement of the very society that deploys it. Now scientism is more dangerous today than ethnocentrism, if only because no one, or almost no one, is proud to call himself ethnocentric (one can imagine *unmasking* an ethnocentrist), while the invocation of science amounts to reliance on one of the most solid values of our society. To see that this danger is not merely theoretical, it suffices to recall that the two deadliest regimes in recent history, Stalin's and Hitler's, both invoked a scientific ideology, both justified their practices by recourse to a science (history or biology).

In the third place, relativism, which is presented as a miraculous solution to our problems, is not really a solution at all. Why bother to avoid Charybdis only to leap into Scylla's arms? There is no need to get locked into the sterile alternative that opposes ethnocentrism to relativism. The latter doctrine is as indefensible at the level of logical consistency as it is at the level of contents. The relativist inevitably ends up contradicting himself, since he presents his doctrine as absolute truth, and thus by his very gesture undermines what he is in the process of asserting. Furthermore and more seriously, the consistent relativist writes off the unity of the human species. Now this is an even more dangerous position than the naive ethnocentrism of certain colonialists. The absence of unity allows exclusion, which can lead to extermination. What is more, a relativist, even a moderate one, cannot denounce any injustice, any violence, that may happen to be part of some tradition other than his own: clitoridectomy would not warrant condemnation, nor would even human sacrifice. Yet it might be argued that the concentration camps themselves belonged, at a given moment of Russian or German history, to the national tradition. The situation is hardly any better with the particular forms of relativism known as nationalism and exoticism.

The popular view of universal and relative judgments is thus not satisfactory. But with what can it be replaced? How can we simultaneously get rid of the dangers of perverted universalism (of ethnocentrism and scientism alike) and those of relativism? We can do so only if we succeed in giving a new meaning to the universalist requirement. It is possible to defend a new humanism, provided we are careful to avoid the traps into which the doctrine that goes by the same name has sometimes fallen over the centuries. In this connection, so as to make the difference quite clear, it may help to speak of a *critical humanism*.

The first point to stress is that this humanism is not presented as a new hypothesis about "human nature," still less as a project for unifying the human race within a single State. With reference to Lévi-Strauss, I ended up using the expression "universalism of itinerary" to refer not to the fixed content of a theory of man, but to the necessity of postulating a horizon common to the interlocutors in a debate, if this debate is to be of any use. Universal features derive in fact not from the empirical world, which is an object of observation, but from the workings of the human mind itself. That is why authors like Buffon, who set up features of a specific culture as a universal norm (certain people are savages because they paint their eyebrows blue), and those like Montaigne, who challenge any claim of universality by lining up contradictory examples, are both wrong. When Rousseau proposes to consider pity as the natural foundation for social virtue, he is not unaware of the existence of pitiless men. Universality is an instrument of analysis, a regulatory principle allowing the fruitful confrontation of differences, and its content cannot be fixed: it is always subject to revision.

What is properly human is obviously not one particular cultural feature or another. The context in which human beings come into the world subjects them to multiple influences, and this context varies in time and space. What every human being has in common with all others is the ability to *reject* these determinations; in more solemn terms, let us say that liberty is the distinctive feature of the human species. My milieu unquestionably induces me to reproduce the behaviors it valorizes; but the possibility of breaking free from these behaviors exists as well, and that is essential. And it will not do to argue that, in rejecting one determination (in refusing to conform to the tastes of my milieu, for example), I necessarily become subject to another (I submit to the received ideas of a different milieu): even if we were to suppose this to be true, the gesture of breaking away would still remain meaningful. That is what Montesquieu and Rousseau meant, Montesquieu who saw the specificity of the human race in the fact that people do not always obey their laws, and Rousseau for whom *perfectibility* was the primary characteristic of the human condition: not one quality or another, then, but the capacity to acquire any of them. The French language is not universal, *pace* Rivarol; the aptitude for learning a language is.

If we understand universality in this way, we rule out any shifting away from universalism toward ethnocentrism or scientism (since we refuse to set up any particular content as a norm), but we still avoid falling into the trap of relativism, which renounces judgment, or at least transcultural judgment. It is universality itself, in fact, that gives us access to absolute values. What is universal is our belonging to the same species: that is not very much, but it is enough to serve as a basis for our judgments. A desire is legitimate if it can become the desire of all, said Montesquieu. And for Rousseau, the more general the interest, the more equitable it is; justice is nothing but another name for taking the entire human race into account. This founding principle of ethics will be completed by the great political principle also noted by Montesquieu: the unity of the human race must be recognized, but also the heterogeneity of the social body. It then becomes possible to make value judgments that transcend the frontiers of the country where one was born: tyranny and totalitarianism are bad in all circumstances, as is the enslavement of men or women. This does not mean that one culture is declared *a priori* superior to others, a unique incarnation of the universal; but it does mean that existing cultures can be compared, and that more may be found to praise in one place, more to criticize in another.

III. We must finally confront another question, one that pertains more directly to the historical material examined in this book. This material involves the contributions of France, over the last two hundred fifty years and more, to the debates concerning *ourselves and the others*. Among the ideas we have examined, certain ones seem to have played a preponderant role. The idea of racialism, seconded by its older brother scientism; Ernest Renan can serve as emblematic figure here.

The idea of "republican" nationalism, as held by Michelet, Tocqueville, or Péguy. The idea of egocentrism, the major figure of modern exoticism, inaugurated by Chateaubriand and followed by Loti and the other "impressionists" (whereas the older exoticism consisted rather in making allegorical use of the others). Scientism, nationalism, egocentrism: I have given labels and abstract definitions to these phenomena, but they correspond to particular historical formations, and no deductive system would have allowed me to anticipate them in advance (which is not the case for ethnocentrism). What is the significance of these three attitudes (and of some others with which they have a great deal in common)?

In order to answer this question, I find myself obliged to go beyond my theme, broad as it is already, and ask myself two more questions. Do these great figures of the misrecognition of others—for that is indeed what is at stake here—have anything in common? And how do they relate to the ideologies that have dominated public life in France during the same period?

The most general ideological conflict, characteristic of the period in question, is the conflict between holism and individualism, to use Louis Dumont's terminology—that is, between *communities* in which the whole is in the dominant position with respect to its elements, and the *societies* in which individuals count for more than the whole to which they belong; or, to remain on a more concrete level, between the Old Regime and the Republic. But this conflict does not seem, at first glance, to be particularly relevant to our subject. Before the Revolution as well as afterward, there were universalists and "particularists," nationalists and "exoticists." The choice of an attitude toward others does not depend directly upon one's preference for holism over individualism or vice versa. Before the Revolution, colonization was vested in the Christian ideal (all people are equal, thus the best religion—Christianity—is equally suited to all); afterward, it continued embellished with a secular ideal (reason belongs to all climates, but we are its most advanced representatives; thus, we have not only the right but also the duty to spread it everywhere—and for this we must first occupy the territories). We may suppose that for the colonized populations the difference must not have been particularly noticeable. The respect for traditions, like the respect for hierarchies, is more closely related to the holistic spirit than to individualism; but both survive easily, as we have seen, in democratic countries.

Neither scientism nor nationalism nor exacerbated egocentrism is a direct emanation of the Old Regime. And the representatives of the holistic ideology take up little space in the foregoing analyses. We have noted in passing a few enemies of democracy—Gobineau and Taine, Le Bon and Maurras, Segalen and sometimes even Lévi-Strauss (Bonald and de Maistre, those great counterrevolutionary ideologues, have been evoked in other contexts); but on the one hand their thought is far from being purely holistic, and on the other hand, on the subjects that fall within our purview here, their thought converges with that of confirmed democrats. We must add that, just as they cannot be explained by the holistic ideology, scientism, nationalism, and egocentrism do not derive from a Romantic spirit either—that is, from a spirit that would be the simple negation of the Enlightenment or Revolutionary spirit. On certain points, Romanticism is directly opposed to Enlightenment rationalism and universalism; but as far as our topic is concerned, there is a clear affiliation between the "Romanticism" of Chateaubriand, Michelet, and Renan and their faithfulness to the major tenets of individualist philosophy as it was elaborated in the seventeenth and eighteenth centuries.

Others besides myself have already made similar observations; and they have concluded that the humanist ideology bore direct responsibility for the advent of the scientistic, nationalistic, and egocentric doctrines—doctrines which can be linked in turn, with a certain plausibility, to the great massacres (military, colonial, or totalitarian) that mark the history of the last two centuries. In this connection, some have spoken of a certain "dialectic of Enlightenment," which in their view has led to the revelation of the true face of an ideology that likes to present itself under nobler or more seductive banners. It is no longer a question of an enemy external to democracy, but of the inevitable—"tragic"—outcome of the democratic project itself. Does such a conclusion follow from the analyses that precede?

The answer is categorically no. Once again, the law of the excluded middle does not apply: if the choice that we are offered lies in the following question—"are our ills due to holism or individualism?"—we have to challenge the choice itself. Other responses are possible: the one I have reached amounts to saying that scientism, nationalism, egocentrism, although not foreign to the Enlightenment spirit, represent a deflection of that spirit rather than its logical consequence. The "bad guy" in this story is neither an external enemy nor the protagonist who had been taken up to now for the hero; the villains are the helpers, the acolytes, the companions of that hero, who have long been thought indispensable but who are not indispensable at all; on the contrary, they threaten to destroy the work of their presumed master.

Two facts in particular lead me to this conviction. The first is the observation of a logical incompatibility between humanist principles on the one hand and scientistic, or nationalistic, or egocentric practices on the other. Scientism seeks to be rational, but it ends up putting science in the place of religion, and by the same token negating science in its very essence: this is the case with Saint-Simon, Comte, and Renan. As for Tocqueville, Michelet, or Péguy, they are obliged to resort to contorted arguments in order to reconcile humanism and patriotism. Chateaubriand (like his successors) has to confront the paradox that follows from his simultaneous affirmations: I love the entire human race, but I am interested only in myself.

The second reason I do not believe that humanism leads inevitably to its own perversions lies in the very possibility (which I hope I have illustrated) of analyzing the scientistic, nationalistic, or egocentric distortions with the help of concepts and principles that derive from humanism itself. I did not know, when I began the research that led to this book, that Montesquieu and Rousseau were going to judge Chateaubriand and Michelet, Renan and Péguy; but that is exactly what happened. Montesquieu and Rousseau, in fact (to whom, if my inquiry had been international, I could have added Kant), embody, at their best, the humanist philosophy that allowed me to observe the distortion of its project during the nineteenth century. It is Rousseau who asserts that ethics must not be subject to science; that cosmopolitanism and patriotism are incompatible, and that the former is superior to the latter; that one cannot imagine an asocial individual. It is Montesquieu who finds, in moderation, a universal principle of political life, independent of the objective conditions proper to each country; who shows that attention to cultures (to "the spirit of the nation") does not necessarily imply blind patriotism; who highlights the role of the social group to which the individual belongs. Montesquieu and Rousseau are the ones who refuse to see human life as governed by a seamless determinism, and who recognize in liberty the distinctive feature of humanity. The ideals that they advance allow us to understand the "deviations" of the nineteenth century, and to condemn them. These deviations, far from constituting the apogee of humanism, are its down-fall.

Although they are enemies of the humanist philosophy, scientism, nationalism, and egocentrism present themselves not as such but rather as inevitable consequences, necessary complements, of that very philosophy. And it is true that, historically, they develop during the course of the same century of Enlightenment: scientism, in the materialism of Helvétius and Diderot, or in the utopianism of Condorcet; nationalism and egocentrism in certain passages of Rousseau himself, isolated from their context and from his work taken as a whole. Thus, these doctrines of deviation do not present themselves openly, as declared enemies; instead they appear fraudulently cloaked, as it were, in the ideals of humanism and the Revolution; witness Chateaubriand, Michelet, Renan, and countless others. This is what explains the interpretive errors of certain historians, who have taken at face value what was only a clever camouflage or a naive illusion, and who have condemned humanism for the misdeeds accomplished in the name of these ideologies of deviation. For this same reason, these latter ideologies appear to me to be a much greater threat to the maintenance of democratic principles than are the vestiges of the Old Regime, which amount to an anachronistic nostalgia for absolute monarchy. This is why I have dwelled at such length on the former and so little on the latter.

Does this mean that everything is perfect in Montesquieu's thought, and Rousseau's? Of course not. Moreover, on occasion they disagree (but less often, I think, than is commonly supposed); I have thus sometimes had to choose one over the other. At other times I have found myself obliged to contradict them both, even when they themselves were in agreement. But above all, it must be stressed that their practice often fails to measure up to their theory. We saw this in connection with their representations of distant peoples. Even though (in *Persian Letters*) Montesquieu had so skillfully analyzed the pitfalls of ethnocentrism and the advantages of defamiliarization, in *The Spirit of the Laws* he offers a purely conventional, and ultimately degrading, picture of Indians and Africans, Chinese and Japanese. Even though Rousseau had set forth the principles for getting to know others appropriately (you must observe differences in order to discover properties), he places "savages" midway between men and animals. We find the same disparity between the condemnations in principle Montesquieu and Rousseau proffered with regard to slavery, and their lack of zeal, to put it mildly, in the struggle to abolish slavery. There are other examples; there is no point in concealing the inconsistencies in the behavior of these two men.

The fact remains nevertheless that, if we are capable of judging Montesquieu and Rousseau today, and sometimes harshly, it is owing to an ideal that they themselves helped establish. It would be ridiculous to regret the fact that the ideal is superior to reality. It is much more interesting to profit from the elevated aspects of Montesquieu's thought, and Rousseau's, than to settle complacently for the mean-spirited observation that they did not always live up to their own principles. Let us keep in mind here, then, not so much their errors but their accomplishments: the possibility both writers glimpsed, each in his own way, of recognizing differences among human groups without renouncing the universal framework; the idea that, since individuals and societies are essentially heterogeneous entities, only mixed, or moderate, solutions can suit them in the long run (so far as Rousseau is concerned, we need to take his work as a whole into account, in order to reach this conclusion, and avoid looking at just one part of it, such as *On the Social Contract* or the *Confessions*, in isolation).

The confrontation of Montesquieu's and Rousseau's humanism with scientism, nationalism, and egocentrism, as these doctrines developed during the nineteenth century, leads me to yet another observation. Each of the last three doctrines is limited to a single aspect of human life, and eliminates or dismisses the others. For subscribers to scientism, universality is all that counts (everyone belongs to the same species); this primary identity implies that the same laws should be imposed everywhere, with the goal of setting up a single universal State. Cultural differences (or national differences, in the cultural sense) are viewed as negligible: Comte suggested that people would settle for adding a national ribbon to the universal flag. Individual differences are no more worthy of attention. Conversely, the nationalist challenges both the universal reference and the tendency of individuals to make themselves autonomous (witness Michelet, or Tocqueville at certain points, or Barrès). In its turn, egocentrism—exemplified by René and his countless descendants—is concerned only with itself; it neglects both the universal perspective and that of national cultures. The results are deplorable in each case.

Now the lesson of Montesquieu and Rousseau consists in affirming the necessity of all three aspects of the human being, of all three levels of organization of human life, and in cautioning against the elimination of one or two of them to the benefit of the third. Montesquieu is capable of recognizing the individual's right to autonomy, to personal security, to personal freedom; that does not keep him from being aware of the power of belonging to a culture (the spirit of nations). Finally, although his contemporaries did not always perceive this, he does not give up the universal either, the only ground on which value judgments can be based: tyranny is condemnable in all climates, and what is beneficial to humanity must be preferred to what is good for the fatherland. The same is true for Rousseau, who describes the various relations in which man finds himself involved as follows: "Now that Emile has considered himself in his physical relations with other beings and in his moral relations with other men, it remains for him to consider himself in his civil relations with his fellow citizens" (*Emile*, V, p. 455). Private life, social and cultural life, and moral life must be neither suppressed nor interchanged; human beings are multiple, and reduction to unicity amounts to mutilation.

But it is not enough to contrast humanism with its distortions, and to prefer the former to the latter; we still need to investigate the origins of the distortions. Things seem relatively clear where egocentrism is concerned. It is a simple hypertrophy of the principle of individual autonomy, an excess in a direction in which the first steps were taken by humanist philosophy itself: egocentrists have not been content to see the individual as a necessary entity; they have made her a self-sufficient whole. Now the same cannot be said of nationalism, scientism, racialism, or exoticism. If these doctrines have "taken" so effectively, it is because they have conveyed values that manifestly required expression yet found no other outlet. We can enumerate them: scientism puts science in the place of religion; nationalism valorizes membership in a social and cultural group; racialism affirms the necessary hierarchy of human beings; primitivist exoticism again valorizes community over dispersed and atomized individuals, and it privileges interpersonal relations over relations established between persons and things.

If we examine this list of the values that are implied or asserted by the distortions of humanism, we can draw two conclusions. The first is that all these values originate in the holistic ideology. It is the holistic society in fact that respects the religious consensus, the hierarchy of beings and positions, the group rather than the individual, the social rather than the economic. It is just as if the victory of the individualist ideology, which is at the root of the modern democracies, had been accompanied by repression of the holistic values—which, however, could not allow themselves to be treated this way, and so resurfaced in the more or less monstrous forms of nationalism, racism, and totalitarian utopianism.

The second conclusion follows from the first. Both the holistic ideology and the individualist ideology, in certain respects, are simply partial representations of the world. They declare specific characteristics of human life to be primordial, and to these they subordinate the others. This means that it is a mistake to see all the good on the one side and all the bad on the other. Our contemporary attachment to the values that have emerged from individualism (from humanism) cannot be called back into question. But it would be very much in our interest, as Louis Dumont has already suggested, to *temper* this humanism with values and principles from other horizons. This is possible whenever we are dealing not with radical incompatibilities but instead with rearticulations among dominant and subordinate elements. It is even the only hope we have of mastering the forces at work behind these holistic values: we need to try to tame them, if we do not want to see them reappear decked out in the grotesque but threatening masks of racism or totalitarianism.

Working toward this end means finding new expressions for the repressed holistic values. Scientism was able to prosper only because it came to fill the void left by the departure of religion as a guide to behavior. This place must indeed be filled, but not by the worship of science; the great ethical principles around which the democratic consensus is formed must come to exercise control over the applications of science as well as over the excesses of ideology. Racialism codifies the existence of hierarchies among beings. It is useless to deny the existence of these hierarchies, or our need for them, but we need to get rid of naive biologism, and openly assume our own hierarchies, which are spiritual, not physical: nothing obliges us to subscribe to a relativism according to which everything has the same worth. Nationalism valorizes belonging to a group. One must be blind to believe that this belonging is useless or negligible (even if pulling away from the group may have its own merits). What can be affirmed, on the other hand, is that a strong feeling of cultural belonging does not in any way imply civic patriotism, and that the groups to which one belongs are multiple in size and nature: family, neighborhood, city, region, country, group of countries, on the one hand; profession, age, sex, milieu, on the other. Primitive exoticism evokes with nostalgia the places and times in which individuals knew how to remain "human" with each other, or to communicate with nonhuman nature; one can in fact aspire to these values without adopting a macrobiotic diet.

A well-tempered humanism could insure us against taking yesterday's wrong roads, and today's. Let us break down simplistic associations: demanding equality as the right of all human beings does not in any way imply renouncing the hierarchy of values; cherishing the autonomy and freedom of individuals does not oblige us to repudiate all solidarity; the recognition of a public morality does not inevitably entail a regression to the time of religious intolerance and the Inquisition; nor does the search for contact with nature necessarily take us back to the Stone Age.

One final word. Montesquieu and Rousseau may have understood better than others the complexities of human life, and they may have formulated a nobler ideal; even so, they found no panacea, no solution to all our problems. For they knew that, even if a sense of fairness, the discrimination of good and evil, the ability to rise above oneself, are the defining qualities of mankind (contrary to what other thinkers, pessimists or cynics, maintain), so are self-centeredness, lust for power, and the taste for monolithic solutions. The "flaws" of individuals, like those of societies, are just as intrinsic as their greatest merits. It is thus up to each individual to try to make the best prevail over the worst. Certain social structures ("moderate" ones) facilitate this task; others ("tyrannical" ones) make it more complex. Everything possible must be done to enable the former to prevail over the latter; but no social structure exempts us from the work that is incumbent upon each individual person, because none leads automatically to the good. Wisdom is neither hereditary nor contagious: one attains it more or less, but always and only alone, not by virtue of one's membership in a group or a State. The best regime in the world is never anything but the least bad, and even if it is the one under which we live, everything still remains to be done. Learning to live with others is part of this wisdom.

Bibliography

Ageron, Charles-Robert. *France coloniale ou parti colonial?* Paris: Presses Universitaires de France, 1978.

Alembert, Jean d'. "Eloge de Montesquieu." In Montesquieu, *Oeuvres complètes.* Paris: Seuil, 1964. Pp. 21–32.

Arendt, Hannah. *The Origins of Totalitarianism.* New York: Harcourt, Brace, 1951.

Aristotle. *The Politics.* Trans. H. Rackham. London: W. Heinemann (Loeb Classical Library), 1944.

Aron, Raymond. *Main Currents in Sociological Thought.* 2 vols. Trans. Richard Howard and Helen Weaver. New York: Basic Books, 1965, 1967.

Artaud, Antonin. *Messages révolutionnaires* (1936). Paris: Gallimard, 1971.

—— *The Peyote Dance (Les Tarahumaras,* 1936). Trans. Helen Weaver. New York: Farrar, Straus and Giroux, 1976.

—— *Selected Writings.* Trans. Helen Weaver. New York: Farrar, Straus and Giroux, 1976.

Atkinson, Geoffrey. *The Extraordinary Voyage in French Literature.* New York: B. Franklin, 1967.

—— *The Sentimental Revolution: French Writers of 1890–1740.* Seattle: University of Washington Press, 1966.

Aulard, François-Alphonse. *Le Patriotisme français de la Renaissance à la Révolution.* Paris: E. Chiron, 1921.

Barrès, Maurice. "Une Enquête aux pays du Levant" (1923). In *L'Oeuvre de Maurice Barrès.* 20 vols. Paris: Club de l'Honnête Homme, 1965–1969. Vol. 11, pp. 104–503.

—— Intervention: "Chambre des députés; Séance du 12 juillet 1906." In *L'Oeuvre de Maurice Barrès.* Paris: Club de l'Honnête Homme, 1965–1969. Vol. 5, pp. 571–573.

—— "Lettre à Maurras" (1908). In Charles Maurras, *Enquête sur la monarchie.* Paris: Nouvelle Librairie Nationale, 1924. Vol. 2, pp. 2–6.

—— *Scènes et doctrines du nationalisme* (1902). 2 vols. Paris: Plon-Nourrit, 1925.

Barthes, Roland. *The Empire of Signs* (1970). Trans. Richard Howard. New York: Hill and Wang, 1982.

Barzun, Jacques. *Race: A Study in Superstition* (1937). New York: Harper and Row, 1965.

Baudelaire, Charles. "The Invitation to a Journey" (1857). In *The Prose Poems and La Fanfarlo*. Trans. Rosemary Lloyd. Oxford: Oxford University Press, 1991. Pp. 53–55.

Bénichou, Paul. *Le Temps des prophètes*. Paris: Gallimard, 1977.

Berlin, Isaiah. *Against the Current*. Harmondsworth: Penguin, 1979.

—— *Four Essays on Liberty*. Oxford: Oxford University Press, 1969.

Bonald, Louis de. *Théorie du pouvoir politique et religieux* (1796). 3 vols. Paris: A. Le Clère, 1843.

Bossuet, Jacques-Bénigne. *Politics Drawn from the Very Words of Holy Scripture* (1704). Trans. Patrick Riley. Cambridge: Cambridge University Press, 1990.

Bouillier, Henry. *Victor Segalen* (1961). Rev. ed. Paris: Mercure de France, 1986.

Buffon, Georges-Louis Leclerc de. *Buffon's Natural History*. 10 vols. London: H. D. Symonds, 1797–1807.

—— *The History of Man and Quadrupeds*. Vol. 3 of Buffon, *Natural History, General and Particular*. Trans. William Smellie. London: T. Cadell and W. Davies, 1812.

—— *A Natural History, General and Particular, Containing the History and Theory of the Earth, A General History of Man, The Brute Creation, Vegetables, Minerals, &c.* 2 vols. Trans. William Smellie. London: Richard Evans, 1817.

Bugeaud, Thomas-Robert. *Par l'Epée et par la charrue: Ecrits et discours de Bugeaud*. Paris: Presses Universitaires de France, 1948.

Cahm, Eric. *Péguy et le nationalisme français: De l'affaire Dreyfus à la Grande Guerre*. Paris: Cahiers de l'Amitié Charles Péguy, 1972.

Chateaubriand, François-René de. *Atala, René* (1801, 1802). Trans. Irving Putter. Berkeley: University of California Press, 1952.

—— *Chateaubriand's Travels in America* (1827). Trans. Richard Switzer. Lexington: University of Kentucky Press, 1969.

—— *Itinéraire de Paris à Jérusalem* (1811). Paris: Garnier-Flammarion, 1968.

—— *Mémoires d'outre-tombe* (1850). 2 vols. Paris: Ministère de l'Education Nationale, 1972.

—— *The Natchez: An Indian Tale* (1826). 2 vols. London: H. Colburn, 1827.

—— "Preface." In *Atala; or the Amours of Two Savages in the Desert*. Trans. from the French. London: Gale, Curtis, and Fenner, 1813. Pp. x–xv.

Chinard, Gilbert. *L'Amérique et le rêve exotique dans la littérature française aux XVIIe et XVIIIe siècles*. Paris: Hachette, 1913. Rpt. Geneva: Slatkine, 1970.

Cloots, Anacharsis. "Anacharsis à Paris, ou, Lettre de Jean Baptiste Cloots à un prince d'Allemagne." In *Adresse d'un Prussien à un Anglais*. Paris: Desenne, 1790.

———— "Discours prononcé à la barre de l'Assemblée nationale" (1790). In *Procès-verbal de l'Assemblée nationale*, vol. 22. Rpt. in Cloots, *Adresse d'un Prussien à un Anglais*. Paris: Desenne, 1790. Pp. 21–34.

———— *La République universelle, ou Adresse aux tyrannicides*. Paris: Chez les Marchands de Nouveautés, 1792.

Comte, Auguste. *Système de politique positive*. 4 vols. Paris: L. Mathias, 1851–1854.

Condorcet, Marie-Jean-Antoine-Nicolas de Caritat. "De l'influence de la révolution d'Amérique sur l'Europe" (1786). In *Oeuvres*. 12 vols. Paris: F. Didot Frères, 1847–1849. Vol. 8, pp. 3–113.

———— "Observations on the Twenty-ninth Book of the Spirit of Laws, by the Late M. Concorcet." In Destutt de Tracy, *Commentary*. Pp. 261–282.

———— "Reception Speech at the French Academy" (1782). In *Selected Writings*. Ed. Keith Michael Baker. Indianapolis: Bobbs-Merrill, 1976. Pp. 3–32.

———— [pseud. M. Schwartz, pasteur à Bienne]. *Réflexions sur l'esclavage des nègres* (1781). Neufchâtel: Société Typographique, 1781.

———— *Sketch for a Historical Picture of the Progress of the Human Mind* (1793). Trans. June Barraclough. London: Weidenfeld and Nicolson, 1955.

Constant, Benjamin. "De M. Dunoyer et de quelques-uns de ses ouvrages" (1826). In *De la Liberté chez les Modernes*. Paris: Hachette, 1980. Pp. 543–562.

———— *Principes de politique* (1806). Geneva: Droz, 1980.

Derathé, Robert. "Patriotisme et nationalisme au XVIIIe siècle." *Annales de philosophie politique* 8 (1969): 69–84.

Descartes, René. *Oeuvres et lettres*. Paris: Gallimard (Pléiade), 1953.

Destutt de Tracy, Antoine Louis Claude. *A Commentary and Review of Montesquieu's Spirit of Laws* (1798). Philadelphia: William Duane, 1811.

Diderot, Denis. "Supplement to Bougainville's 'Voyage.'" In *Rameau's Nephew and Other Works*. Trans. Jacques Barzun and Ralph H. Bowen. Garden City, N.Y.: Doubleday, 1956. Pp. 183–239.

———— *Tablettes*. In Grimm, Diderot, Raynal, Meister, et al., *Correspondance littéraire, philosophique et critique*. 22 vols. Paris: Garnier Frères, 1882. Vol. 16, pp. 218–228.

Duchet, Michèle. *Anthropologie et histoire au siècle des Lumières*. Paris: Flammarion, 1978.

Dumont, Louis. *Essays on Individualism: Modern Ideology in Anthropological Perspective* (1983). Chicago: University of Chicago Press, 1986.

Durand-Maillane, Pierre-Toussaint. *Histoire apologétique du Comité ecclésiastique de l'Assemblée nationale.* Paris: F. Buisson, 1791.

Ferlus, Dom François. *Le Patriotisme chrétien: Discours prêché aux Etats du Languedoc en 1787.* Montpellier: Impr. J.-F. Picot, 1787.

Ferry, Jules. "Discours du 28 juillet 1885, à la Chambre." In *Discours et opinions.* 7 vols. Paris: A. Colin, 1893–1898. Vol. 5, pp. 172–220.

———— "Préface, 'Tonkin et la mère-patrie'" (1890). In *Discours et opinions.* Paris: A. Colin, 1893–1898. Vol. 5. pp. 538–564.

Ferry, Luc, and Alain Renaut. *Heidegger and Modernity* (1988). Trans. Philip Franklin. Chicago: University of Chicago Press, 1990.

Galard, Jean. "Descartes en Nederland." In Paul Blom et al., eds., *La France aux Pays-Bas: Invloeden in het verleden.* Vianen: Kwadraat, 1985. Pp. 51–88.

Gaultier, Jules de. *Bovarysm* (1892). Trans. G. Spring. New York: Philosophical Library, 1970.

Gellner, Ernest. *Nations and Nationalism.* Ithaca, N.Y.: Cornell University Press, 1983.

Gérando, Joseph Marie de. *The Observation of Savage Peoples.* Trans. F. C. T. Moore. Berkeley: University of California Press, 1969.

Girardet, Raoul. *L'Idée coloniale en France: De 1871 à 1962* (1972). Paris: Hachette, 1986.

———— *Le Nationalisme français: Anthologie* (1966). Paris: Seuil, 1983.

Gobineau, Joseph-Arthur de. *Essai sur l'inégalité des races humaines* (1853–1855). Vol. 1 of *Oeuvres.* Paris: Gallimard (Pléiade), 1983.

Godechot, Jacques, ed. *Les Constitutions de la France depuis 1789.* Paris: Garnier-Flammarion, 1970. Rpt. Flammarion, 1988.

Goldschmidt, Victor. *Anthropologie et politique: Les principes du système de Rousseau.* Paris: Vrin, 1984.

———— "Introduction à Montesquieu." In *Ecrits.* 2 vols. Paris: Vrin, 1984. Vol. 2, *Etudes de philosophie moderne,* pp. 29–77.

Gouhier, Henri. *La Jeunesse d'Auguste Comte et la formation du positivisme.* 3 vols. Paris: J. Vrin, 1933–1941.

Gusdorf, Georges. *L'Avènement des sciences humaines au siècle des Lumières.* Vol. 6 of *Les Sciences humaines et la pensée occidentale.* Paris: Payot, 1973.

Helvétius, Claude Adrien. *De l'esprit, or, Essays on the Mind and Its Several Faculties* (1758). London: Dodsley, 1759.

———— "Letter of Helvetius to President Montesquieu" (1747). In Destutt de Tracy, *A Commentary and Review of Montesquieu's Spirit of Laws.* Philadelphia: William Duane, 1811. Pp. 285–289.

———— "Letter to M. Saurin" (1747). In Destutt de Tracy, *A Commentary and Review of Montesquieu's Spirit of Laws.* Philadelphia: William Duane, 1811. Pp. 290–292.

Herodotus. *Herodotus.* Trans. A. D. Godley. 4 vols. Cambridge, Mass.: Harvard University Press (Loeb Classical Library), 1920.

Hitler, Adolf. *Mein Kampf* (1925–1927). Trans. Ralph Manheim. Boston: Houghton Mifflin, 1971.

Homer. *The Iliad*. Trans. A. T. Murray. 2 vols. Cambridge, Mass.: Harvard University Press (Loeb Classical Library), 1947.

——— *The Odyssey*. Trans. A. T. Murray. 2 vols. Cambridge, Mass.: Harvard University Press (Loeb Classical Library), 1960.

Ives de Paris. *Morales chrétiennes* [*Les Morales chrestiennes*, by Père Yves de Paris]. 3rd ed. 4 vols. Paris: D. Thierry, 1643.

Kant, Immanuel. *Foundations of the Metaphysics of Morals, and What Is Enlightenment?* Trans. Lewis White Beck. Indianapolis: Bobbs-Merrill, 1979.

Kohn, Hans. *The Age of Nationalism: The First Era of Global History*. New York: Macmillan, 1962.

——— *The Idea of Nationalism*. New York: Harper, 1944.

La Bruyère, Jean de. *The Characters of Jean de la Bruyère* (1688). Trans. Henri van Laun. New York: Brentano's, 1929.

——— *The Characters or the Manners of the Age; with The Characters of Theophrastus, translated from the Greek, and a Prefatory Discourse to them by M. de la Bruyère*. London: John Bullard, 1699.

——— "Discours prononcé à l'Académie française" (1694). In *Oeuvres complètes*. Paris: Gallimard (Pléiade), 1951. Pp. 501–523.

Lahontan, Louis-Armand de Lom D'Arce. *Dialogues curieux entre l'auteur et un sauvage de bon sens qui a voyagé, et Mémoires de l'Amérique septentrionale*. Paris: A. Margraff, 1931. Rpt. of vols. 2 and 3 of *Nouveaux Voyages de Monsieur le baron de Lahontan dans l'Amérique Septentrionale*. 3 vols. The Hague: I. Delorme, 1707–1708.

——— *New Voyages to North America*. 2 vols. in one. London: Printed for H. Bonwicke et al., 1703.

Lanessan, Jean-Marie Antoine de. *L'Expansion coloniale de la France*. Paris: F. Alcan, 1886.

——— *L'Indo-Chine française*. Paris: F. Alcan, 1889.

——— *Principes de colonisation*. Paris: F. Alcan, 1897.

La Rochefoucauld, François de. *Maximes* (1665). Paris: Garnier, 1967.

Le Bon, Gustave. *The Psychology of Peoples* (1894). New York: G. E. Stechert, 1912.

Leroy-Beaulieu, Paul. *De la Colonisation chez les peuples modernes* (1874). 2 vols. Paris: F. Alcan, 1902.

Léry, Jean de. *History of a Voyage to the Land of Brazil Otherwise Called America*. Trans. Janet Whatley. Berkeley: University of California Press, 1990.

Lévi-Strauss, Claude. "Entretien de Claude Lévi-Strauss avec Jean-Marie Benoist." *Le Monde*, 21–22 January 1979, p. 14.

——— *L'Identité*. Seminar directed by Claude Lévi-Strauss (1977). Paris: Presses Universitaires de France, 1983.

—— *Introduction to the Work of Marcel Mauss* (1950). Trans. Felicity Baker. London: Routledge and Kegan Paul, 1987.

—— *The Naked Man* (1971). Trans. John Weightman and Doreen Weightman. New York: Harper and Row, 1981.

—— *The Raw and the Cooked* (1964). Trans. John Weightman and Doreen Weightman. New York: Harper and Row, 1969.

—— *The Savage Mind* (1962). Trans. from the French. London: Weidenfeld and Nicolson, 1966.

—— *Structural Anthropology* (1958). Trans. Claire Jacobson and Brooke Grundfest Schoepf. New York: Basic Books, 1963.

—— *Structural Anthropology*, vol. 2 (1973). Trans. Monique Layton. New York: Basic Books, 1976.

—— *Tristes Tropiques* (1965). Trans. John Weightman and Doreen Weightman. New York: Atheneum, 1974.

—— *The View from Afar* (1983). Trans. Joachim Neugroschel and Phoebe Hoss. New York: Basic Books, 1985.

Ligne, Charles-Joseph, Prince de. *Lettres écrites de Russie*. N.p., 1782.

Loti, Pierre [pseud. of Julien Viaud]. *Aziyadé* (1879). Trans. Marjorie Laurie. London: Kegan Paul International, 1989.

—— *Madame Chrysanthème* (1887). Trans. Laura Ensor. London: George Routledge and Sons, 1897.

—— *The Marriage of Loti* (1880). Trans. Wright and Eleanor Frierson. Honolulu: University Press of Hawaii, 1976.

—— *The Romance of a Spahi*. Trans. G. F. Monkshood. New York: Brentano's, 1930.

—— *Le Roman d'un spahi* (1881). Paris: Presses Pocket, 1987.

Lovejoy, Arthur Oncken. "The Supposed Primitivism of Rousseau's *Discourse on Inequality*" (1923). In *Essays in the History of Ideas*. Baltimore: Johns Hopkins University Press, 1948. Pp. 14–37.

Maistre, Joseph-Marie de. *The Works of Joseph de Maistre*. Trans. Jack Lively. New York: Macmillan, 1965.

Mathiez, Albert. *La Révolution et les étrangers*. Paris: Renaissance du Livre, 1918.

Maurras, Charles. "L'Avenir du nationalisme français" (1949). *Oeuvres capitales*. 4 vols. Paris: Flammarion, 1954. Vol. 2, pp. 523–532.

—— *Enquête sur la monarchie* (1909). Paris: Nouvelle Librairie Nationale, 1924.

—— "Mes Idées politiques" (1937). Excerpted in "La Patrie," *Oeuvres capitales*. Paris: Flammarion, 1954. Vol. 2, pp. 263–272.

Michaux, Henri. *Un Barbare en Asie* (1933). Paris: Gallimard, 1982.

—— *A Barbarian in Asia*. Trans. Sylvia Beach. New York: New Directions, 1949.

—— *Ecuador: A Travel Journal by Henri Michaux* (1929). Trans. Robin Magowan. Seattle: University of Washington Press, 1970.

Michelet, Jules. *France before Europe*. Boston: Roberts Brothers, 1871.

—— *La France devant l'Europe* (1871). In *Oeuvres complètes*. 21 vols. Paris: Flammarion, 1971–1982. Vol. 20, pp. 641–712.

—— *Histoire de France* (1833–1869). Vol. 4 of *Oeuvres complètes*. Paris: Flammarion, 1971–1982.

—— *History of France*. 2 vols. Trans. Walter K. Kelly. London: Chapman and Hall, 1844.

—— *Introduction à l'histoire universelle* (1831). In *Oeuvres complètes*. Paris: Flammarion, 1971–1982. Vol. 2, pp. 217–258.

—— *The People* (1846). Trans. John P. McKay. Urbana: University of Illinois Press, 1973.

Mill, John Stuart. *The Earlier Letters of John Stuart Mill*. Ed. Francis E. Minerka. Vols. 12–13 of *Collected Works*. Toronto: University of Toronto Press, Routledge and Kegan Paul, 1963.

Montaigne, Michel de. *The Complete Essays of Montaigne* (1580–1588). Trans. Donald M. Frame. Stanford: Stanford University Press, 1958.

Montesquieu, Charles de Secondat. "Analyse du Traité des devoirs" (1725). In *Oeuvres complètes*. Paris: Seuil, 1964. Pp. 181–182.

—— *The Complete Works of M. de Montesquieu*. 4 vols. Translated from the French. Dublin: W. Watson et al., 1777.

—— "Essai sur le goût" (1754). In *Oeuvres complètes*. Paris: Seuil, 1964. Pp. 845–852.

—— *Mes Pensées*. In *Oeuvres complètes*. Paris: Seuil, 1964. Pp. 853–1082.

—— "Montesquieu au Marquis de Stainville." In *Oeuvres complètes*. 3 vols. Paris: Nagel, 1955. Vol. 3, pp. 1306–1308.

—— *Persian Letters* (1821). Trans. C. J. Betts. Harmondsworth: Penguin, 1973.

—— "Some Reflections on the Persian Letters." In *Persian Letters*. Trans. C. J. Betts. Harmondsworth: Penguin, 1973. Pp. 283–284.

—— *The Spirit of the Laws* (1748). Trans. Anne M. Cohler, Basia Carolyn Miller, and Harold Samuel Stone. Cambridge: Cambridge University Press, 1989.

Nizan, Paul. *Aden, Arabie* (1932). Trans. Joan Pinkham. New York: Monthly Review Press, 1968.

Pascal, Blaise. *Pascal's Pensées* (1657–1662). Trans. Martin Turnell. London: Harvill Press, 1962.

Péguy, Charles. *L'Argent*. In *Cahiers de la quinzaine* 14.6 (1913).

—— *L'Argent suite*. In *Cahiers de la quinzaine* 14.9 (1913).

—— "Lettres à Millerand." In Auguste Martin, "Correspondance Péguy

Alexandre Millerand," *Feuillets de l'Amitié Charles Péguy.* 178 (15 June 1972), 1–48; 179 (15 July 1972), 1–32; 180 (25 August 1972), 1–10.

—— "Memories of Youth." In *Temporal and Eternal.* Trans. Alexander Dru. New York: Harper and Brothers, 1958. Pp. 17–87.

—— *Notre Jeunesse.* In *Cahiers de la quinzaine* 11.12 (1910).

—— *Notre Patrie.* In *Cahiers de la quinzaine* 6.3 (1905).

—— *Victor-Marie, comte Hugo.* In *Cahiers de la quinzaine* 12.1 (1910).

Poliakov, Léon. *Aryan Myth: A History of Racist and Nationalist Ideas in France* (1971). London: Chatto, Heinemann for Sussex University Press, 1974.

Popper, Karl. *Conjectures and Refutations: The Growth of Scientific Knowledge* (1963). New York: Harper and Row, 1968.

Quella-Villéger, Alain. *Pierre Loti l'incompris.* Paris: Presses de la Renaissance, 1986.

Renan, Ernest. *Caliban* (1878). Trans. Eleanor Grant Vickery. New York: Shakespeare Press, 1896.

—— "La Chaire d'Hébreu au Collège de France" (1862). In *Oeuvres complètes.* 10 vols. Paris: Calmann-Lévy, 1947–1961. Vol. 1, pp. 143–172.

—— "Conférence faite à l'Alliance pour la propagation de la langue française" (1888). In *Oeuvres complètes.* Paris: Calmann-Lévy, 1947–1961. Vol. 2, pp. 1087–1095.

—— *Constitutional Monarchy in France* (1869). Boston: Roberts Brothers, 1871.

—— *De l'Origine du langage* (1848–1858). In *Oeuvres complètes.* Paris: Calmann-Lévy, 1947–1961. Vol. 8, pp. 9–123.

—— "Le Désert et le Soudan" (1854). In *Oeuvres complètes.* Paris: Calmann-Lévy, 1947–1961. Vol. 2, pp. 540–549.

—— "Des Services rendus aux sciences historiques par la philologie" (1878). In *Oeuvres complètes.* Paris: Calmann-Lévy, 1947–1961. Vol. 8, pp. 1213–1232.

—— "Discours à la conférence 'Scientia'" (1885). In *Oeuvres complètes.* Paris: Calmann-Lévy, 1947–1961. Vol. 1, pp. 859–861.

—— "Discours de réception à l'Académie française" (1879). In *Oeuvres complètes.* Paris: Calmann-Lévy, 1947–1961. Vol. 1, pp. 723–748.

—— *Discours et conférences* (1887). In *Oeuvres complètes.* Paris: Calmann-Lévy, 1947–1961. Vol. 1, pp. 719–965.

—— "Discours prononcé au Collège de France" (1884). In *Oeuvres complètes.* Paris: Calmann-Lévy, 1947–1961. Vol. 1, pp. 873–878.

—— *Drames philosophiques* (1888). In *Oeuvres complètes.* Paris: Calmann-Lévy, 1947–1961. Vol. 3, pp. 369–710.

—— *L'Eau de jouvence* (1881). In *Oeuvres complètes.* Paris: Calmann-Lévy, 1947–1961. Vol. 3, pp. 437–521.

—— "Examen de conscience philosophique" (1888). In *Oeuvres complètes.* Paris: Calmann-Lévy, 1947–1961. Vol. 2, pp. 1162–1182.

—— "The Future of Religion in Modern Society" (1860). In *Studies of Religious History and Criticism*. Trans. O. B. Frothingham. New York: Carleton, 1864. Pp. 342–394.

—— *The Future of Science* (1848). Boston: Roberts Brothers, 1891.

—— "La Guerre entre la France et l'Allemagne" (1870). In *Oeuvres complètes*. Paris: Calmann-Lévy, 1947–1961. Vol. 1, pp. 409–435.

—— "Histoire de l'instruction publique en Chine" (1847). In *Oeuvres complètes*. Paris: Calmann-Lévy, 1947–1961. Vol. 2, pp. 576–602.

—— *Histoire du peuple d'Israël* (1887–1891). Vol. 6 of *Oeuvres complètes*. Paris: Calmann-Lévy, 1947–1961.

—— *Histoire générale et système comparé des langues sémitiques* (1855). In *Oeuvres complètes*. Paris: Calmann-Lévy, 1947–1961. Vol. 8, pp. 127–589.

—— "L'Instruction supérieure en France" (1864). In *Oeuvres complètes*. Paris: Calmann-Lévy, 1947–1961. Vol. 1, pp. 69–97.

—— "Islamism and Science" (1883). In *The Poetry of the Celtic Races and Other Studies*. Trans. William G. Hutchinson. Port Washington, N.Y.: Kennikat Press, 1896; rpt. 1970. Pp. 84–108.

—— "Le Judaïsme comme race et comme religion" (1883). In *Oeuvres complètes*. Paris: Calmann-Lévy, 1947–1961. Vol. 1, pp. 925–944.

—— "Lettre à Gobineau" (June 26, 1856). In *Oeuvres complètes*. Paris: Calmann-Lévy, 1947–1961. Vol. 10, pp. 203–205.

—— "Lettre à M. Adolphe Guéroult" (1862). In *Oeuvres complètes*. Paris: Calmann-Lévy, 1947–1961. Vol. 1, pp. 674–679.

—— "Lettre à M. Strauss" (1870). In *Oeuvres complètes*. Paris: Calmann-Lévy, 1947–1961. Vol. 1, pp. 437–448.

—— "M. Cousin" (1858). In *Oeuvres complètes*. Paris: Calmann-Lévy, 1947–1961. Vol. 2, pp. 55–85.

—— "M. de Sacy et l'école libérale" (1858). In *Oeuvres complètes*. Paris: Calmann-Lévy, 1947–1961. Vol. 2, pp. 24–54.

—— *Mélanges d'histoire et de voyages* (1878). In *Oeuvres complètes*. Paris: Calmann-Lévy, 1947–1961. Vol. 2, pp. 305–707.

—— "La Métaphysique et son avenir" (1860). In *Oeuvres complètes*. Paris: Calmann-Lévy, 1947–1961. Vol. 1, pp. 680–714.

—— "Nouvelle Lettre à M. Strauss" (1871). In *Oeuvres complètes*. Paris: Calmann-Lévy, 1947–1961. Vol. 1, pp. 449–462.

—— "La Part de la famille et de l'état dans l'éducation" (1869). In *Oeuvres complètes*. Paris: Calmann-Lévy, 1947–1961. Vol. 1, pp. 523–542.

—— *Philosophical Dialogues and Fragments* (1876). Trans. Râs Bihârî Mukharjî. London: Trübner, 1883.

—— "Philosophie de l'histoire contemporaine" (1859). In *Oeuvres complètes*. Paris: Calmann-Lévy, 1947–1961. Vol. 1, pp. 29–68.

—— *The Priest of Nemi* (1885). Trans. R. C. S. Whitling. London: Mathieson, 1885.

—— *Questions contemporaines* (1868). In *Oeuvres complètes*. Paris: Calmann-Lévy, 1947–1961. Vol. 1, pp. 9–319.

—— *Recollections of My Youth*. Intro. G. G. Coulton. Boston: Houghton Mifflin, 1929.

—— "La Réforme intellectuelle et morale de la France" (1871). In *Oeuvres complètes*. Paris: Calmann-Lévy, 1947–1961. Vol. 1, pp. 333–407.

—— "Les Sciences de la nature et les sciences historiques" (1863). In *Oeuvres complètes*. Paris: Calmann-Lévy, 1947–1961. Vol. 1, pp. 633–650.

—— "The Share of the Semitic People in the History of Civilization" (1862). In *Studies of Religious History and Criticism*. Trans. O. B. Frothingham. New York: Carleton, 1864. Pp. 109–167.

—— "La Société berbère" (1873). In *Oeuvres complètes*. Paris: Calmann-Lévy, 1947–1961. Vol. 2, pp. 550–575.

—— *Souvenirs d'enfance et de jeunesse* (1883). In *Oeuvres complètes*. Paris: Calmann-Lévy, 1947–1961. Vol. 2. pp. 711–931.

—— "What Is a Nation?" (1882). In *Poetry of the Celtic Races and Other Essays*. Intro. William G. Hutchinson. London: Walter Scott Publishing, 1896. Pp. 61–83.

Renaut, Alain. "Les Deux Logiques de l'idée de nation." *Cahiers de philosophie politique et juridique* 14 (1988): 7–21.

Richter, Melvin. "Tocqueville on Algeria." *Review of Politics* 25 (1963): 362–398.

Robespierre, Maximilien Marie Isidore de. *Discours, 1793–1794*. Vol. 10 of *Oeuvres*. 10 vols. Paris: Presses Universitaires de France, 1967.

Roger, Jacques. *Les Sciences de la vie dans la pensée française du XVIIIe siècle*. Paris: Armand Colin, 1963.

Ronsard, Pierre. "Discours contre Fortune" (1559). In *Oeuvres*. Paris: Didier, 1970. Vol. 7.

Rousseau, Jean-Jacques. *Confessions* (1770). 2 vols. Intro. R. Niklaus. London: Dent, 1971.

—— "Ecrits sur l'abbé de Saint-Pierre" (1756–1757). In *Oeuvres complètes*. 4 vols. Paris: Gallimard (Pléiade), 1959–1969. Vol. 3, pp. 563–682.

—— *Eloisa: A series of original letters* (1758). 3 vols. London: John Harding, 1810.

—— *Emile, or, On Education* (1761). Trans. Allan Bloom. New York: Basic Books, 1979.

—— *The First and Second Discourses* (1749, 1754). Trans. Victor Gourevitch. New York: Harper and Row, 1986.

—— "Fragments politiques" (1754–1760). In *Oeuvres complètes*. Paris: Gallimard (Pléiade), 1959–1969. Vol. 3, pp. 473–560.

—— *The Government of Poland* (1772). Trans. Willmoore Kendall. Indianapolis: Bobbs-Merrill, 1972.

——— "Lettre à Beaumont" (1762). In *Oeuvres complètes*. Paris: Gallimard (Pléiade), 1959–1969. Vol. 4, pp. 927–1030.

——— *Lettres écrites de la montagne* (1764). In *Oeuvres complètes*. Paris: Gallimard (Pléiade), 1959–1969. Vol. 3, pp. 685–897.

——— *On the Origin of Language* (1755). Trans. John H. Moran and Alexander Gode. New York: Frederick Ungar, 1966.

——— *On the Social Contract, with Geneva Manuscript and Political Economy* (1761). Trans. Judith R. Masters. New York: St. Martin's Press, 1978.

——— *Politics and the Arts; Letter to M. D'Alembert on the Theatre* (1758). Trans. Allan Bloom. Ithaca, N.Y.: Cornell University Press, 1960.

——— *Rousseau, Judge of Jean-Jacques: Dialogues* (1772–1776). Vol. 1 of *Collected Writings of Rousseau*. Trans. Judith R. Bush, Christopher Kelly, and Roger D. Masters. Hanover, N.H.: University Press of New England, 1989.

Sade, Donatien-Alphonse-François, Marquis de. *The Complete Justine, Philosophy in the Bedroom, and Other Writings* (1795). Trans. Richard Seaver and Austryn Wainhouse. New York: Grove Press, 1965.

Saint-Arnaud, Arnaud-Jacques-Leroy de. *Lettres du maréchal de Saint-Arnaud*. 2 vols. Paris: Michel-Lévy Frères, 1855.

Saint-Simon, Henri de. "The Reorganization of the European Community" (1814). In *Henri de Saint-Simon: Selected Writings*. Trans. F. M. H. Markham. Oxford: Basil Blackwell, 1952. Pp. 28–68.

Saussure, Léopold de. *Psychologie de la colonisation française*. Paris: F. Alcan, 1899.

Segalen, Victor. *Briques et tuiles* (1909). Montpellier: Fata Morgana, 1975.

——— *Equipée* (1915), *Stèles* (1912). In *Stèles, Peintures, Equipée*. Paris: Plon, 1970.

——— *Essai sur l'exotisme* (1904–1918). Montpellier: Fata Morgana, 1978.

——— *Steles*. Trans. Andrew Harvey and Iain Watson. London: Jonathan Cape, 1990.

——— *Voyage au pays du réel* (1914). Paris: Le Nouveau Commerce, 1980.

Seillière, Ernest. *Le Comte de Gobineau et l'aryanisme historique* (1908). Vol. 1 of *La Philosophie de l'impérialisme*. 4 vols. Paris: Plon-Nourrit, 1903–1908.

Shklar, Judith Nisse. *Men and Citizens: A Study of Rousseau's Social Theory*. Cambridge: Cambridge University Press, 1969.

——— *Montesquieu*. Oxford: Oxford University Press, 1987.

Sieyès, Emmanuel Joseph. "Opinion sur la constitution, présentée à la Convention nationale, le 2 thermidor, an 3 [20 July 1795]." Bound with "Opinion sur la jurie constitutionnaire." N.p., 1795.

——— *What Is the Third Estate?* (1789). Trans. M. Blondel. Ed. S. E. Finer. London: Pall Mall Press, 1963.

Sternhell, Zeev. *Maurice Barrès et le nationalisme français* (1972). Brussels: Complexe, 1985.

Strauss, Leo. *Natural Right and History*. Chicago: University of Chicago Press, 1965.

Taguieff, Pierre-André. *La Force du préjugé: Essai sur le racisme et ses doubles.* Paris: La Découverte, 1988. Rpt. Gallimard, 1990.

Taine, Hippolyte. *Derniers Essais de critique et d'histoire*. Paris: Hachette, 1894.

———— *Essais de critique et d'histoire* (1866). Paris: Hachette, 1923.

———— *Histoire de la littérature anglaise* (1864). 12th ed. 5 vols. Paris: Hachette, 1905–1906.

———— "Introduction." In *History of English Literature*. Trans. H. Van Laun. 4 vols. Philadelphia: Gebbie Publishing, 1897. Vol. 1, pp. 1–36.

———— *The Origins of Contemporary France* (1876–1896). Ed. Edward L. Gargan. Chicago: University of Chicago Press, 1978.

———— "The Philosophy of Art in the Netherlands" (1868). In *The Philosophy of Art*. Trans. John Durand. 2 vols. New York: Henry Holt, 1877, 1901. Vol. 2, pp. 157–346.

Thevet, André. *Singularitez de la France antarctique* (1557). Paris: La Découverte, 1983.

Tocqueville, Alexis de. *Correspondence and Conversations of Alexis de Tocqueville with Nassau William Senior.* 2nd ed. 2 vols. London: Henry S. King, 1872. Rpt. (2 vols. in one) New York: Augustus M. Kelley, 1968.

———— "Correspondance d'Alexis de Tocqueville avec Arthur de Gobineau." In *Oeuvres complètes*. 16 vols. Paris: Gallimard, 1951–1989. Tome 9, pp. 39–306.

———— *Democracy in America*. Trans. George Lawrence. New York: Harper and Row, 1966.

———— "Deux Lettres sur l'Algérie" (1837). In *Oeuvres complètes*. Paris: Gallimard, 1951–1989. Tome 3, vol. 1, pp. 129–153.

———— "L'Emancipation des esclaves" (1843). In *Oeuvres complètes*. Paris: Gallimard, 1951–1989. Tome 3, vol. 1, pp. 79–111.

———— *"The European Revolution" and Correspondence with Gobineau*. Trans. John Lukacs. Garden City, N.Y.: Doubleday, 1959.

———— "L'Inde, plan de la suite de l'ouvrage" ["Ebauches d'un ouvrage sur l'Inde"] (1843). In *Oeuvres complètes*. Paris: Gallimard, 1951–1989. Tome 3, vol. 1, pp. 476–482.

———— "Intervention dans la discussion de la loi sur le régime des esclaves dans les colonies" (1846). In *Oeuvres complètes*. Paris: Gallimard, 1951–1989. Tome 3, vol. 1, pp. 112–126.

———— *Journey to America*. Trans. George Laurence. New Haven: Yale University Press, 1962.

———— Letter to Lamoricière (April 5, 1846). Cited in part in André Jardin,

Alexis de Tocqueville, 1805–1859. Paris: Hachette, 1984. Chapter 13, "L'Algérie," pp. 302–327.

———— "Lettres à J. S. Mill." In *Oeuvres complètes.* Paris: Gallimard, 1951–1989. Tome 6, vol. 1, pp. 289–352.

———— "Notes du voyage en Algérie de 1841." In *Oeuvres complètes.* Paris: Gallimard, 1951–1989. Tome 5, vol. 2, pp. 191–218.

———— "Rapport fait au nom de la commission chargée d'examiner la proposition de Tracy relative aux esclaves des colonies" (1839). In *Oeuvres complètes.* Paris: Gallimard, 1951–1989. Tome 3, vol. 1, pp. 41–78.

———— "Rapports sur l'Algérie" (1847). In *Oeuvres complètes.* Paris: Gallimard, 1951–1989. Tome 3, vol. 1, pp. 308–418.

———— *Selected Letters on Politics and Society.* Trans. James Toupin and Roger Boesche. Berkeley: University of California Press, 1985.

———— "Travail sur l'Algérie" (1841). In *Oeuvres complètes.* Paris: Gallimard, 1951–1989. Tome 3, vol. 1, pp. 213–282.

Vespucci, Amerigo. *The Letters of Amerigo Vespucci and Other Documents Illustrative of His Career.* Trans. Clements R. Markham. London: Hakluyt Society, 1894.

Voltaire, François-Marie Arouet. *Annals of the Empire* (1753). Trans. William F. Fleming. New York: St. Hubert Guild, 1901.

———— "Essay on the Customs and the Spirit of Nations" (1756–1775). In *The Age of Louis XIV and Other Selected Writings.* Trans. and abridged by J. H. Brumfitt. New York: Washington Square Press, 1963. Pp. 240–311.

———— *Philosophical Dictionary* (1764). Trans. Peter Gay. 2 vols. New York: Basic Books, 1962.

———— "Thoughts on the Public Administration" (1752). In *The Works of Voltaire.* Ferney Edition. 42 vols. Paris: E. R. DuMont, 1901. Vol. 37, pp. 223–239.

———— *Traité de métaphysique* (1734). In *Oeuvres complètes.* 52 vols. Paris: Garnier Frères, 1877–1885. Vol. 22, pp. 189–230.

Weil, Simone. *The Need for Roots.* Trans. A. F. Wills. London: Routledge and Paul, 1952.

Index

Other books in the *Convergences* series:

Philip Catherine I remember you
Criss Cross records